The Problem of Evil as Described by Nietzsche

Friedrich Nietzsche

GRAPEVINE INDIA

Published by

GRAPEVINE INDIA PUBLISHERS PVT LTD

www.grapevineindia.com
Delhi | Mumbai
email: grapevineindiapublishers@gmail.com

Ordering Information:
Quantity sales: Special discounts are available on quantity
purchases by corporations, associations, and others.
For details, reach out to the publisher.

First published by Grapevine India 2023

Contents

Thus Spoke Zarathustra
Part One

Zarathustra's Prologue

1

When Zarathustra was thirty years old, he left his home and the lake by his home and went into the mountains. Here he enjoyed his spirit and his solitude, and did not tire of this for ten years. Finally, however, he had a change of heart — and one morning, rising with the dawn, he stood before the sun and spoke to it thus:

"You great star! What would your happiness be if you had not those for whom you shine!

For ten years you have come up here to my cave: you would already have been weary of your light and this journey were it not for me, my eagle, and my serpent.

But we waited for you each morning, relieved you of your overflow, and blessed you for it.

Behold! I am weary of my wisdom; like the bee that has gathered too much honey, I need the hands that stretch out for it.

I want to dispense and distribute, until the wise once more enjoy their folly and the poor once more enjoy their riches.

That is why I must descend to the deep, as you do in the evening when you pass beyond the sea and bring light even to the underworld, you over-rich star!

Like you I must go down, as people say; I want to go down to them.

So bless me then, you tranquil eye, that can look without envy upon even an all-too-great happiness!

Bless the cup which wants to overflow, so that the water flows golden out of it, carrying in every direction the reflection of your delight!

Behold! This cup wants to become empty again and Zarathustra wants to become a man again."

— Thus began Zarathustra's downgoing.

2

Zarathustra climbed down the mountain alone and he came across no one.

But when he came to the forest, an old man stood before him, one who had left his holy hut to search for roots in the forest. And thus spake the old man to Zarathustra:

"This wanderer is no stranger to me: many years ago he passed by here. Zarathustra he was called; but he has changed.

At that time you carried your ashes to the mountain: would you now carry your fire into the valleys? Do you not fear the arsonist's penalty?

Yes, I recognize Zarathustra. Pure is his eye, and no loathing lurks about his mouth. Does he not move along like a dancer?

Changed is Zarathustra, become a child is Zarathustra, an awakened one is Zarathustra: what do you want now with those who sleep?

As though in a sea you have lived in your solitude, and the sea has borne you up. Alas, you want to go ashore? Alas, you want to drag your body around again, yourself?

Zarathustra answered: "I love mankind."

"Why," said the holy man, "do you think I went into the forest and into solitude?

Was it not because I loved man all too much?

Now I love God: man, I do not love. Man is too imperfect a thing for me.

The love of mankind would kill me."

Zarathustra answered: "Did I speak of love? I am bringing mankind a gift."

"Give them nothing," said the holy man. "Take something from them rather and carry it with you — that would suit them best: if only it suits you!

And if you want to give them something, give no more than an alms, and let them beg for that!"

"No," answered Zarathustra, "I give no alms. I am not poor enough for that!"

The holy man laughed at Zarathustra and spoke thus: "Well, see to it that they accept your treasures! They are mistrustful of hermits and do not believe that we come in order to give.

Our steps ring too lonely through the streets. And what if at night in their beds they should hear a man walking, long before the sun comes up, then they probably ask themselves: where is that thief going?

Remain in the forest and do not go to man. Go rather to the animals, even!

Why not be like me — a bear among bears, a bird among birds?"

"And what does the holy man do in the forest?" asked Zarathustra.

The holy man answered: "I make songs and sing them, and when I make songs I laugh, cry, and hum: thus I praise God.

With singing, crying, laughing, and humming I praise the God that is my God. But what do you bring us as a gift?"

When Zarathustra heard these words, he saluted the holy man and said:

"What would I have to give you? But let me hurry away quickly, lest I take something instead!"— And so they parted from each other, the old man and Zarathustra, laughing like two boys.

But when Zarathustra was alone, he spoke thus to his heart: "Could it be possible, then? This old saint in his forest has heard nothing yet about God being dead."

3

When Zarathustra came to the next town which lay by the forest, he found many people gathered in the marketplace there: for it had been promised that a tightrope walker would be seen. And thus spake Zarathustra to the people:

"I teach you the Superman. Man is something that must be overcome. What have you done to overcome him?

All beings hitherto have created something beyond themselves. And you would be the ebb of this great flood, to return even to the beast rather than overcome the man?

What is the ape to man? A laughingstock or an object of shame. And that is just what man shall be for the Superman: a laughingstock or an object of shame.

You have made your way from worm to man, and much in you is still worm.

Once you were apes, and even now man is still more of an ape than any ape.

But he who is wisest among you is likewise only a hotbed and hybrid of plant and phantom. But do I command you to become plants or phantoms?

Behold, I teach you the Superman!

The Superman is the meaning of the earth. Let your will say: the Superman shall be the meaning of the earth!

I entreat you, my brothers, remain true to the earth and do not believe those who hold out supernatural hopes for you. They are poisoners, whether they know it or not.

They are despisers of life, dying ones and poisoned themselves; the earth is sick of them — let them leave it, then!

Once the sin against God was the greatest sin; but God died, and with that these sinners died, too. Now the worst sin is the sin against the earth, to regard the innards of the inscrutable more highly than the meaning of the earth.

Once the soul looked upon the body with contempt: and at that time this contempt was the highest thing: the soul wanted the body scrawny, scary, starved. Thus the soul thought to escape the body and the earth.

Oh, this soul was itself still scrawny, scary, and starved; and cruelty was the delight of this soul!

But you as well, my brothers, tell me: what does your body proclaim about your soul? Is your soul not dearth and dirt and a wretched comfort?

Verily, man is a filthy stream. One must be a veritable sea in order to absorb such a filthy stream and not become unclean.

Behold, I teach you the Superman: he is that sea, in him your great contempt can be submerged.

What is the greatest thing you can experience? It is the hour of great contempt, when even your happiness turns to disgust, and your reason and virtue too.

The hour when you say: 'What does my happiness matter? It is dearth and dirt and a wretched comfort. But my happiness should justify being itself!'

The hour when you say: 'What does my reason matter: Does it not crave knowledge the same way a lion craves food? It is dearth and dirt and a wretched comfort!'

The hour when you say: 'What does my virtue matter? It has not yet made me mad. How weary I am of my good and evil! That is all dearth and dirt and a wretched comfort!'

The hour when you say: 'What does my justice matter? I do not see that I am fire and coal. But the just are fire and coal.'

The hour when you say: 'What does my pity matter: Is pity not the cross upon which he who loves mankind is nailed? But my pity is no crucifixion.'

Have you ever spoken thus? Have you ever cried thus? Alas, if only I had ever heard you cry thus!

Not your sin but your complacency cries out against heaven, the very stinginess of your sin cries out against heaven!

Where is the lighting which licks you with its tongue? Where is the madness with which you should be injected?

Behold, I teach you the Superman: he is that lightning, he is that madness!"—

When Zarathustra had spoken thus, someone from the crowd cried out:

"We have heard enough from the tightrope walker; now let us see him, too!" And all the people laughed at Zarathustra. The tightrope walker, however, who thought these words applied to him, set about his task.

4

But Zarathustra looked at the people and wondered. Then he spoke thus:

"Man is a rope suspended between animal and Superman — a rope over an abyss.

A dangerous going-over, a dangerous on-the-way, a dangerous lookingback, a dangerous shuddering and standing still.

What is great about man is that he is a bridge, not an end: what can be loved about man is that he is a going-over and a going-under.

I love those who do not know how to live except as downgoers, for they are going over.

I love the great despisers, for they are the great reverers and arrows of longing for the opposite shore.

I love those who do not first seek a reason beyond the stars for going under and sacrificing themselves: but they sacrifice themselves for the earth, that the earth may one day be the Superman's.

I love him who lives in order to know and wants to know in order that the Superman may live. And thus he wills his own downgoing.

I love him who works and invents in order to build the Superman's house and to prepare plant, animal, and earth for him: for thus he wills his own downgoing.

I love him who retains not one drop of spirit for himself but wants it all to be virtue's spirit: thus he strides as spirit across the bridge.

I love him who makes out of his virtue his fancy and his fate: thus for the sake of his virtue he wants to live and no longer live.

I love him who does not want too many virtues. One virtue is more virtue than two, because it is more of a hook to hang ones' fate on.

I love him whose soul squanders itself, who wants no thanks and gives none in return: for he always bestows and wants no part of preserving himself.

I love him who feels ashamed when the dice turn up in his favor, and who then asks: "Am I a false player?" — for he wants to go under.

I love him whose golden words are cast before his deeds, and who does even more than he promises: for he wants his downgoing.

I love him who justifies the future and redeems the past: for he wants to perish in the present.

I love him who castigates his God because he loves Him: for by the wrath of his God he must perish.

I love him whose soul is deep even in the wounding, and whom a little thing can ruin: thus he gladly goes across the bridge.

I love him whose soul is overfull, so that he forgets himself, and in whom all things exist: thus all things become his downgoing.

I love him who is of a free spirit and a free heart: thus his head is only the innards of his heart; his heart, however, drives him to his downgoing.

I love all those who are like heavy raindrops falling individually from the dark cloud that hangs over man: they herald the coming of the lightning and perish as heralds.

Behold, I am a herald of the lightning and a heavy raindrop from the cloud:

this lightning, however, is called the Superman." ——

5

When Zarathustra had spoken these words, he looked at the people again and became silent. "There they stand," he said to his heart, "there they laugh:

they do not understand me, I am not the mouth for these ears.

Must one first batter their ears so they learn to hear with their eyes? Must one rattle like drums and penitential preachers? Or do they only believe stammerers?

They have something which they are proud of. But what do they call that which they are proud of? They call it culture; it distinguishes them from the goatherds.

That is why they are unwilling to hear the word 'contempt' applied to themselves. So I will appeal to their pride instead.

So I will speak to them of what is most contemptible: that, however, is the last man."

And thus spake Zarathustra to the people:

"It is time for man to set himself a goal. It is time for him to plant the seed of his highest hope.

His soul is still rich enough for that. But one day this soul will be poor and tame, and no higher tree will be able to grow on it anymore.

Alas! The day is coming when man will no longer loose the arrow of his longing beyond man, and the string of his bow will have forgotten how to sing.

I tell you: a man must still have chaos within himself in order to give birth to a dancing star. I tell you: you still have chaos within yourselves.

Alas! The day is coming when man will no longer give birth to a star. Alas! The day of the most despicable man is coming, of him who can no longer despise himself.

Behold! I present to you the last man.

'What is love? What is creation? What is longing? What is a star?' — thus asks the last man, and blinks.

The earth is then grown small, and on it hops the last man, who makes everything small. Like the flea, his kind cannot be exterminated; the last man lives the longest.

'We have discovered happiness' — the last men say, and blink.

They have left the regions where living was hard: for warmth is needed.

They still love their neighbor and rub up against him: for warmth is needed.

Becoming sick and harboring mistrust they consider sinful: one proceeds with caution. He is a fool who still stumbles over stones or men!

A little poison now and then: that makes for pleasant dreams. And a lot of poison in the end for a pleasant death.

One still works, for work is a form of entertainment. But one takes care not to get too caught up in it.

No one is rich or poor anymore: both are too much trouble. Who still wants to rule? Who still wants to obey? Both are too much trouble.

No shepherd and one herd! Everyone wants the same, everyone is the same:

he who feels otherwise goes freely to the madhouse.

'Formerly, all the world was mad' — the finest ones say, and blink.

They are clever and know all there is to know: so there is endless mockery.

They still quarrel, but they are soon reconciled — otherwise they might spoil their appetite.

They have their little pleasures for the day and their little pleasures for the night: but they revere their health.

'We have discovered happiness' — the last men say, and blink."

And here ended the first speech of Zarathustra, also known as "The Prologue":

for at this point the cries and mirth of the crowd interrupted him. "Give us this last man, O Zarathustra," — thus they cried — "make us into these last men! Then we will present you with the Superman!" And all the people rejoiced and clucked their tongues. Zarathustra, however, was sad and said to his heart:

"They do not understand me: I am not the mouth for these ears.

No doubt I have lived too long in the mountains; I have listened too much to the trees and the brooks: now I speak to them as though to goatherds.

Unmoved is my soul and clear, like the mountains in the morning. But they think me cold and a scoffer with awful jokes.

And now they look at me and laugh: and while they laugh, they hate me still. There is ice in their laughter."

6

Then something happened, however, that silenced every tongue and entranced every eye. For in the meantime the tightrope walker had begun his 13 performance: he had come out of a small door and was walking along the rope, which was stretched between two towers so that it hung over the people and the marketplace. When he was just halfway across, the small door opened once again, and out jumped a colorful, buffoonish fellow who quickly followed after him.

"Move it, lamefoot," he cried in a terrible voice, "get going, lazybones, chiseler, whey-face! So I don't tickle your heel with my foot! What do you think you're doing here between these towers? Back in the tower is where you belong, behind bars, you who bar the way of one who is your better!" — And with every word he came closer and closer to the tightrope walker: but when he was only one step behind him, that terrible thing happened which silenced every tongue and entranced every eye: — he yelled like the devil and sprang over the one who was in his way. This one, however, seeing his rival thus victorious, lost both his head and his toehold; he cast his pole away and shot quicker than it itself into the depths, a descending whirl of arms and legs. The marketplace and the people were like the sea when a storm comes on: they all flew apart from each other and on top of each other, especially where the body was about to fall.

Zarathustra remained standing there, however, and the body landed right next to him, badly bruised and battered but not yet dead. After a while, the shattered man regained consciousness and saw Zarathustra kneeling beside him.

"What are you doing here?" he said at last. "For a long time I knew that the devil would trip me up. Now he's about to drag me off to hell: do you want to prevent him?"

"On my honor, friend," answered Zarathustra, "all that of which you speak does not exist. There is no devil and there is no hell. Your soul will be dead even sooner than your body: fear nothing henceforth!"

The man looked up mistrustfully. "If you speak the truth," he said, "then I lose nothing when I lose my life. I am not much more than an animal, taught to dance by means of blows and meager fare."

"Not at all," said Zarathustra. "You have made danger your calling; there is nothing to be despised in that. Now, your calling calls you away for good: therefore, I will bury you with my own hands.

After Zarathustra had said this, the dying man answered no more; but he moved his hand as if to seek Zarathustra's hand in gratitude. —

7

Evening came on meanwhile, and the marketplace concealed itself in darkness:

then the crowd dispersed, for even curiosity and terror get tired. Zarathustra, however, remained sitting next to the dead man on the ground, engrossed in thought, oblivious of the time. Finally, though, it became night, and a cold wind blew over the solitary one. Then Zarathustra arose and said to his heart:

"Verily, a fine catch Zarathustra has made today! No men he caught but a corpse instead.

Uncanny is man's being and still without meaning: a buffoon can spell his doom.

I want to teach man the meaning of his being, which is the Superman, that lightning from the dark cloud of man.

But I am still far away from them, and my sense does not speak to their senses. To men I am still something midway between a fool and a corpse.

Dark is the night, and dark are the ways of Zarathustra. Come, you cold and stiff companion! I will carry you to where I can bury you with my own hands."

8

After Zarathustra had said this to his heart, he loaded the corpse on his back and proceeded on his way. And he had not gone a hundred paces when a man snuck up to him and whispered in his ear — and behold! It was the buffoon from the tower! "Go away from this town, O Zarathustra," he said. "Too many hate you here. The good and the just hate you and call you their enemy and despiser; the believers in the true belief hate you and call you a danger to the multitude. You were lucky they laughed at you; and truly, you spoke like a buffoon. You were lucky to have sided with that dead dog; when you degraded yourself that way, you saved yourself for the day. But go away from this town — or tomorrow I will jump over you, a living man over a dead one." And when he had said this, the man disappeared; Zarathustra, however, continued on down the dark streets.

At the town gate he met the gravediggers: they shone a torch in his face, recognized Zarathustra, and mocked him exceedingly. "Zarathustra's carrying the dead dog away: good thing he's become a gravedigger, because our hands are too clean for this mess. Perhaps Zarathustra wants to steal a morsel from the devil? Well then! Good luck at mealtime, too! If only the devil's not a better thief 15 than Zarathustra! — he'll steal both of them, he'll gobble both of them up!" And they laughed with each other and stuck their heads together.

Zarathustra said not a word to that and went on his way. After traveling a couple of hours, past forests and marshes, he heard too much of the hungry howling of wolves, and he himself felt hungry. So he stopped at a lonely house, in which a solitary light was burning.

"Hunger has ambushed me," said Zarathustra, "like a robber. In forests and marshes hunger has ambushed me, and in the deep of night.

My hunger has strange moods. Often it comes to me only after mealtimes, and today it didn't come all day: where could it have tarried?"

And with that Zarathustra knocked at the gate of the house. An old man appeared; he carried the light and asked: "Who comes to me and my bad sleep?"

"A living man and a dead one," said Zarathustra. "Give me something to eat and drink, I forgot it today. He who feeds the hungry refreshes his own soul: thus speaks wisdom."

The old man went away but came right back, offering Zarathustra bread and wine. "This is a bad area for those who hunger," he said; "therefore I live here.

Man and beast come to me, the hermit. But bid your companion eat and drink too; he is wearier than you." Zarathustra answered: "My companion is dead; I could hardly persuade him to join in."

"That doesn't concern me," said the old man morosely; "he who knocks on my door must also take what I offer him. Eat and fare thee well!"

After that Zarathustra went on again for two hours, trusting to the way and the light of the stars: for he was accustomed to night walking and loved to look into the face of all that was at rest.

But when the morning dawned, Zarathustra found himself in a deep wood, and no path showed itself to him anymore. Then he laid the dead man in a hollow tree at his head — for he wanted to protect him from the wolves — and laid himself down on the moss and earth. And immediately he fell asleep, fatigued in body but with an unmoved soul.

9 Zarathustra slept a long time, and not only the rosy dawn but also the morning passed over his face. At last, however, he opened his eyes: astonished, Zarathustra looked into the forest and the stillness; astonished, he looked into himself. Then he rose up quickly, like a sailor who has just spotted land, and shouted for joy: for he had perceived a new truth. And he spoke to his heart thus:

"A light has dawned upon me: I need companions, and live ones — not dead companions and corpses I can carry with me wheresoever I will.

But I need live companions, who follow me because they themselves want to — and there, wheresoever I will.

A light has dawned upon me: not to the people shall Zarathustra speak, but to companions! No shepherd of the herd and herd dog shall Zarathustra be!

To lure many away from the herd — that is why I have come. People and herd shall be angry with me: the shepherds shall call me a robber.

Shepherds I say, but they call themselves the good and the just. Shepherds I say: but they call themselves the believers in the true belief.

Behold the good and the just! Whom do they hate the most? The one who breaks their tables of values, the breaker, the lawbreaker: — that, however, is the creator.

Companions the creator seeks, and not corpses, and not herds and believers, either. Co-creators the creator seeks, those who write new values on new tables.

Companions the creator seeks, and co-harvesters: for to him all things stand ripe for the harvest. But he lacks the hundred sickles: so he plucks the ears of corn and is irritable.

Companions the creator seeks, and those who know how to whet their sickles. Annihilators they will be called, and despisers of good and evil. But they are harvesters and celebrators.

Co-creators Zarathustra seeks, co-harvesters and co-celebrators Zarathustra seeks: what does he have to do with herds and shepherds and corpses?

And you, my first companion, fare thee well! Well I buried you in your hollow tree, well I hid you from the wolves.

But now I part from you, the time is up. Between one dawn and the next a new truth has come to me.

Not a shepherd shall I be, not a gravedigger. Never again will I talk with the people: I have spoken to the dead for the last time.

I will join with the creators, the harvesters, the celebrators: I will show them the rainbow and all the steps to the Superman.

I will sing my song to the lonesome and the twosome; and to him who still has ears for the unheard-of, I will make his heart heavy with my happiness.

To my goal will I go, I will go it my way; over the dawdlers and delayers will I jump. Thus may my going be their downgoing!"

10

Zarathustra had said this to his heart as the sun stood at noontide: then he looked inquiringly on high — for he heard above him the sharp cry of a bird. And behold! An eagle described wide circles through the air, and on him there hung a serpent, not like its prey but like a lady-love: for it had curled itself around the eagle's neck.

"They are my animals!" said Zarathustra, and rejoiced in his heart.

"The proudest animal under the sun and the wisest animal under the sun — they have gone out scouting.

They want to find out whether Zarathustra still lives. Indeed, do I still live?

More dangerous have I found it among man than among beasts; dangerous ways goes Zarathustra. May my animals lead me!"

After Zarathustra had said this, he reflected on the words of the holy man in the forest, sighed, and spoke to his heart thus:

"Would that I were wiser! Would that I were wise through and through, like my serpent!

But that is asking the impossible: therefore I ask that my pride always accompany my wisdom!

And if one day my wisdom should leave me: alas, she loves to fly away! —

may my pride then fly off — with my folly!" —

— Thus began Zarathustra's downgoing.

Zarathustra's Speeches

On The Three Metamorphoses

I speak to you of three metamorphoses of the spirit: how the spirit becomes a camel, the camel a lion, and finally, the lion a child.

There are many hard things for the spirit, the strong load-bearing spirit in which reverence dwells: in its strength it longs for the hard and the hardest.

What is hard? Thus asks the load-bearing spirit; thus it kneels down like a camel and wants to be well-laden.

What is the hardest thing, you heroes? Thus asks the load-bearing spirit, that I may take it upon myself and rejoice in my strength.

Is it not this: to abase yourself in order to hurt your pride? To let your folly shine in order to mock your wisdom?

Or is it this: to part from your cause when it celebrates its victory? To climb high mountains in order to tempt the tempter?

Or is it this: to nourish your knowledge on acorns and grass, and to suffer the hunger of the soul for the sake of truth?

Or is it this: to be sick and send the consolers home, and to make friends with the deaf, who never hear what you want them to?

Or is it this: to wade in dirty water, when it is the water of truth, and not reject cold frogs and hot toads?

Or is it this: to love those who despise us, and to reach out our hand to the ghost that wants to frighten us?

All these hardest things the load-bearing spirit takes upon itself: like the well-laden camel that hurries into the desert; so the spirit hurries into its desert.

But in the loneliest desert the second metamorphosis takes place: here the spirit becomes a lion; freedom it wants to take as its prey, and to be master of its own desert.

Its last master it seeks here: to him and to its last god it wants to be an enemy; it wants to wrestle for victory with the great dragon.

What is the great dragon which the spirit no longer wants to call God and master? "Thou shalt," the great dragon is called. But the spirit of the lion says, "I will."

"Thou shalt" lies in wait for him, sparkling gold, a scaly beast upon whose every scale a golden "Thou shalt" shines.

Thousand-year-old values shine on these scales, and thus speaks the mightiest of all dragons: "All the values of things — they shine on me.

All value has already been created, and all created value — that is me. Verily, 'I will' shall not be anymore!" Thus speaks the dragon.

My brothers, why is the lion required in the spirit? Why is the resigned and reverent beast of burden not enough?

To create new values — that, even the lion cannot yet do. But to create for itself the freedom for new creation — that the lion's might might do.

To create freedom for itself and a holy 'Nay' even before duty: for that, my brothers, the lion is required.

To assume the right to new values — that is the most terrifying assumption for a load-bearing and reverent spirit. Verily, to it it is preying and the act of a beast of prey.

"Thou shalt" it once loved as its holiest thing: now it must find delusion and despotism in even the holiest thing, to take freedom from its love as its prey:

for this preying, the lion is required.

But tell me, my brothers, what can the child do that even the lion could not do? Why must the preying lion yet become a child?

The child is innocence and forgetting, a new beginning, a game, a self-rolling wheel, a first movement, a holy Yea-saying.

Yes, for the game of creation, my brothers, a holy Yea-saying is required: the spirit now wills its will, he who has lost the world gains his world.

I have spoken to you of three metamorphoses of the spirit: how the spirit becomes a camel, the camel a lion and finally, the lion a child. —

Thus spake Zarathustra. And at that time he resided in the town which is called: The Dappled Cow.

On The Academic Chairs Of Virtue

People praised a certain wise man to Zarathustra, one who knew how to speak well about sleep and virtue: he was greatly revered and rewarded for this, and all the youth would sit before his academic chair. Zarathustra went to him, and with all the youth he sat before his academic chair. And thus spake the wise man:

"Honor and modesty before sleep! That is the first thing! And avoid all who sleep badly and stay awake nightly!

Even the thief is modest before sleep: he always steals silently through the night. But the night watchman is shameless; shamelessly he carries his horn.

Sleeping is no mean feat: indeed, it takes staying awake the whole day.

Ten times a day you must overcome yourself: that makes for a good weariness and is opium for the soul.

Ten times a day you must be reconciled with yourself again; for overcoming is a bitterness, and he who is unreconciled sleeps badly.

Ten truths a day you must find; otherwise you will still seek truth at night, and your soul will remain hungry.

Ten times a day you must laugh and be cheerful; otherwise your stomach, that father of affliction, will disturb you in the night.

Few know this: but one must have all the virtues in order to sleep well.

Shall I bear false witness? Shall I commit adultery?

Shall I covet my neighbor's handmaid? All that would go badly with good sleep.

And even if one has all the virtues, one must still understand one thing:

how to send the virtues themselves to sleep at the right time.

So they don't quarrel amongst themselves, the nice little ladies! Or over you, you unfortunate soul!

Peace with God and with your neighbor: good sleep demands it so. And peace with your neighbor's devil as well! Or else he will haunt you at night.

Reverence and obedience for authority, even crooked authority! Good sleep demands it so. Can I help it that power likes to walk on crooked legs?

He who leads his sheep to the greenest pastures shall always be called the best shepherd: that goes well with good sleep.

I do not want many honors, nor great treasures: they inflame the spleen.

But one sleeps badly without a good name and a little treasure.

Small company is more welcome to me than bad: but they must come and go at the right time. That goes well with good sleep.

The poor in spirit please me very much, also: they promote sleep. Blessed are they, especially if you always give them their way.

Thus the day passes for the virtuous one. When night comes, then I take good care not to summon sleep! He, sleep, the lord of all the virtues, does not like to be summoned!

Instead I think about what I did and thought that day. Ruminating thus, I ask myself patiently, like a cow: All right, what were your ten overcomings?

And what were the ten reconciliations and the ten truths and the ten laughs with which your heart enjoyed itself?

Weighed and swayed this way by forty thoughts, sleep, the unsummoned one, the lord of all the virtues, steals upon me suddenly.

Sleep taps at my eyes: they grow heavy. Sleep touches my mouth: it stays open.

Verily, on soft soles he comes to me, this dearest of thieves, and steals from me my thoughts: dumb I stand there, like this academic chair.

But not for long do I stand there: soon, I lie there."

When Zarathustra heard the wise man speak thus, he laughed in his heart:

for with that a light had dawned upon him. And thus he spoke to his heart:

"To me this wise man here with his forty thoughts is a fool: but I believe he is well-versed in sleeping.

Happy indeed is he who lives nearby this wise man! Such sleep is contagious; even through a thick wall it is contagious.

A magic dwells in his very academic chair. And not in vain do the youth sit before this preacher of virtue.

His wisdom is: be awake in order to sleep well. And verily, if life had no sense and I had to choose nonsense, then for me too this would be the most choosable nonsense.

Now I clearly understand what was once sought above all when teachers of virtue were sought. Good sleep was being sought, and poppy-flower virtues along with it!

To all these celebrated wise men in their academic chairs, wisdom was sleep without dreams: they knew no better meaning of life.

Even today, to be sure, there are some like this preacher of virtue, and not always so honorable: but their time is up. And they will not be standing much longer: soon they will be lying.

Blessed are the sleepy: for they shall soon nod off.—

Thus spake Zarathustra.

On The Afterworlders

Once Zarathustra too cast his fancy beyond man, like all afterworlders. The work of a suffering and tormented God the world then seemed to me.

A dream the world then seemed to me, the fiction of a God, colored smoke before the eyes of a discontented deity.

Good and evil and joy and sorrow and I and you — colored smoke before creative eyes it seemed to me. The creator wanted to look away from himself, — so he created the world.

Drunken joy it is for the sufferer to look away from his suffering and lose himself. Drunken joy and losing-of-oneself the world once seemed to me.

This world, eternally imperfect, the image of an eternal contradiction and an imperfect image thereof — the drunken joy of an imperfect creator: — thus the world once seemed to me.

Thus I too once cast my fancy beyond man, like all afterworlders. But was it in fact beyond man?

Alas, brothers, this God I created was of man's making and madness, like all gods!

Man he was, and only a poor fragment of man and ego: out of my own ashes and embers he came to me, this phantom, and verily, he did not come to me from beyond!

What happened, my brothers? I overcame myself, the sufferer; I carried my own ashes to the mountain, I devised a brighter flame for myself. And behold!

The phantom retreated from me!

Now, it would be suffering for me and torment for one in recovery to believe in such phantoms: now it would be suffering for me and humiliation.

Thus I speak to afterworlders.

Suffering and impotence it was — that created all afterworlders; and that brief madness of happiness which only the greatest sufferer experiences.

Weariness, which wants the ultimate in one leap, one death leap. A poor ignorant weariness not even willing to will anymore: that created all gods and afterworlds.

Believe me, my brothers! It was the body that despaired of the body, — it groped with the fingers of the deluded spirit upon the ultimate walls.

Believe me, my brothers! It was the body that despaired of the earth, — it heard the belly of being speak to it.

And then it wanted to get through the ultimate walls with its head, and not only with its head, — across to the "other world."

But that "other world" is well-hidden from man, that inhuman, unhuman world which is a heavenly nothing; and the belly of being does not speak at all to man except as man.

Verily, all being is hard to prove and hard to move to speech. Tell me, you brothers, is not the strangest of all things still the best proved?

Yes, this ego and this ego's contradiction and confusion still speak most honestly about its being, this creating, willing, valuing ego, which is the measure and value of things.

And this most honest being, the ego — it speaks of the body and still wants the body, even when it poeticizes and romanticizes and flutters about with broken wings.

More and more honestly it learns to speak, this ego: and the more it learns, the more words and honors it finds for the body and the earth.

A new pride my ego taught me, which I now teach to man: no longer to hide his head in the sand of heavenly things, but to carry it freely, an earthly head that creates meaning for the earth.

A new will, I teach man: to want to follow the path that man has blindly followed and call it good and no longer slink aside from it, as the sick and the dying do!

It was the sick and the dying who despised the body and the earth and devised the heavenly and the redeeming blood-drops: but even these sweet and gloomy poisons they took from the body and the earth!

They wanted to escape their misery, and the stars were too far for them.

Then they sighed: "Oh that there were heavenly paths to sneak into another existence and into happiness!" Then they devised their bypaths and their bloody little draughts!

They fancied themselves transported from their bodies and this earth, these ingrates. But whom can they thank for the convulsions and delight of their transport? Their bodies and this earth.

Zarathustra is gentle with the sick. Verily, he is not angry at their kind of consolation and ingratitude. May they become convalescents and overcomers and create a higher body for themselves!

Nor is Zarathustra angry with the convalescent who looks tenderly upon his illusion and sneaks around the grave of his God in the middle of the night:

but to me his tears still speak of sickness and a sick body.

There have always been many sick people among those who write verse and "converse" with the Lord; furiously they hate those in the know and that youngest of virtues known as honesty.

They always look backward toward dark ages; then indeed delusion and belief were a different thing; reason's fury was likeness with God, and doubt was sin.

All too well I know these godlike ones: they insist upon being believed in and that doubt is sin. All too well I also know what they themselves believe in most.

Verily, it is not in afterworlds and redeeming blood-drops that they most believe: they also believe most in the body, and to them their own body is the thing-in-itself.

But to them it is a sickly thing, and they would gladly slough their skin.

Therefore they hearken to the preachers of death and preach afterworlds themselves.

Hearken rather, my brothers, to the voice of the healthy body: it is a purer and more honest voice.

The healthy body, perfect and foursquare, speaks more purely and honestly:

and it speaks of the meaning of the earth. —

Thus spake Zarathustra.

On The Despisers Of The Body

I want to say a word to the despisers of the body. Not that they should teach and learn differently, but only bid farewell to their own bodies — and thus become silent.

"Body am I and soul" — so speaks the child. And why should we not speak like children?

But the awakened one, the knowing one says: Body am I completely and nothing else; and soul is only a word for something in the body.

The body is a great reason, a multiplicity with one meaning, a war and a peace, a herd and a shepherd.

Your little reason, my brother, which you call "spirit," is also a tool of your body, a little tool and toy of your big reason.

"I," you say, and are proud of this word. But the greater thing — which you do not want to believe in — is your body and its big reason: it does not say "I," it does "I."

What sense feels, what spirit knows, these never are an end in themselves.

But sense and spirit want to persuade you that they are the end of all things: so vain are they.

Sense and spirit are tools and toys: behind them still lies the self. Even with the eyes of the senses the self seeks, even with the ears of the spirit it listens.

Continually the self listens and seeks: it compares, compels, conquers, destroys. It rules and is also the ego's ruler.

Behind your thoughts and feelings, my brother, there stands a mighty commander, an unknown wise man — he is called self. He lives in your body, he is your body.

There is more reason in your body than in your best wisdom. And who knows precisely what your body needs your best wisdom for?

Your self laughs at your ego and its proud leaps. "What are these leaps and flights of fancy to me?" it says to itself. "A detour to my end. I am the ego's leading strings and the prompter of its ideas."

The self says to the ego, "Feel pain here!" And the ego suffers and thinks on how it may suffer no more — and that is just how it should think.

The self says to the ego, "Feel pleasure here!" Then the ego rejoices and thinks on how often it may yet rejoice — and that is just how it should think.

I want to say a word to the despisers of the body. Their contempt makes for their respect. What is it that created respect and contempt and worth and will?

The creative self created for itself respect and contempt, it created for itself joy and sorrow. The creative self created spirit for itself as the hand of its will.

Even in your folly and contempt, you despisers of the body, you serve your self. I tell you: your self itself wants to die and turns away from life.

No longer can it do what it most wants to do: — create beyond itself. This is what it most wants, this is its entire burning desire.

But now it has become too late for that: — so your self wants to go under, you despisers of the body.

Your self wants to go under, and therefore you have become despisers of the body! For you can no longer create beyond yourselves.

And therefore you are angry now with life and with the earth. An unconscious envy is in the squint-eyed look of your contempt.

I do not go your way, you despisers of the body! You are no bridges to the Superman for me! —

Thus spake Zarathustra.

On Joys And Passions

My brother, if you have a virtue and it is your own virtue, then you have it in common with no one else.

Of course, you want to call it by name and caress it; you want to pull its ears and have some fun with it.

And behold! Now you have its name in common with the people and have become people and herd with your virtue.

You would have done better to say: "Inexpressible and nameless is this which is sweetness and agony to my soul and also the hunger of my innards."

Let your virtue be too lofty for the familiarity of names. And if you must speak of it, do not be ashamed to stammer.

Speak and stammer in this manner: "This is my good, this I love, thus it pleases me entirely, thus alone I want the good.

Not as a law of God do I want it, not as a human law and necessity do I want it: no signpost is it for me to super-earths and Edens.

It is an earthly virtue that I love: there is little cleverness in it, and reason least of all.

But this bird has built its nest by me: therefore I love it and embrace it, —

now it sits by me on its golden eggs."

In this manner you should stammer and praise your virtue.

Once you had passions and called them evil. But now you have only your virtues: they grew out of your passions.

You placed your highest goal in the heart of these passions: then they grew into your virtues and joys.

And whether you came from the race of the irascible or the sensual or the fanatical or the vengeful:

In the end all your passions became virtues and all your devils angels.

Once you had wild dogs in your cellar: but in the end they changed into birds and lovely songstresses.

Out of your poisons you brewed your balsam; your cow, affliction, you milked, — now you drink the sweet milk of her udder.

And nothing evil grows out of you anymore, unless it be the evil that grows out of the conflict of your virtues.

My brother, if you are lucky, then you have one virtue and no more: so you go more easily over the bridge.

Outstanding it is, to have a lot of virtues, but it is a hard lot; and many a man has gone into the desert and killed himself because he was weary of being the battle and battlefield of virtues.

My brother, is war and battle evil? But this evil is necessary: necessary is the envy and mistrust and backbiting amongst your virtues.

See how each of your virtues covets the highest place: it wants your whole spirit to be its herald, it wants your whole strength in wrath, love, and hate.

Each virtue is jealous of the other, and jealousy is a terrible thing. Even virtues can perish on account of jealousy.

He who is surrounded by the flame of jealousy turns at last, like the scorpion, the poisoned stinger against himself.

Alas, my brother, have you never seen a virtue slander and stab itself?

Man is something that must be overcome: and therefore you are to love your virtues —: for you will perish on account of them.—

Thus spake Zarathustra.

On The Pale Criminal

You are unwilling to kill, you judges and sacrificers, until the animal has nodded his head. Behold, the pale criminal has nodded his head: out of his eye speaks the great contempt.

"My ego is something that should be overcome: my ego is to me the great contempt of man." — Thus out of this eye it speaks.

That he judged himself, that was his highest moment: do not let the sublime one return again to his baseness!

There is no salvation for him who suffers from himself this way, unless it be a speedy death.

Your killing, you judges, should be an act of compassion, not of revenge.

And while you are killing, see to it that you yourselves justify life!

It is not enough that you make your peace with the man you kill. Let your sorrow be love for the Superman: so you justify your living — still!

"Enemy" you should say, but not "villain"; "invalid" you should say, but not "cad"; "fool" you should say, but not "sinner."

And you, red judge, were you to say aloud all you have already done in thought: then everyone would cry: "Away with this filth and poisonous worm!"

But the thought is one thing, the deed another, and the image of the deed yet another still. The wheel of causality rolls not between them.

An image made this pale man pale. He was equal to his deed when he did it, but after the deed was done he could not endure its image.

Then he saw himself ever after as the doer of one deed. Madness I call this:

the exception changed into the rule for him.

The chalk streak charms the hen; the stroke he struck charmed his poor reason — madness after the deed I call this.

Listen, you judges! There is yet another madness: it is that before the deed.

Alas, you have not crept deeply enough into this soul!

Thus speaks the red judge: "Why did this criminal commit murder? He wanted to rob." But I say to you: his soul wanted blood, not loot: he thirsted for the happiness of the knife.

But his poor reason did not grasp this madness and persuaded him: "What does blood matter! it said; "Don't you at least want to make some loot besides?

Take some revenge?

And he listened to his poor reason: like lead its words lay upon him, — so he robbed when he murdered. He did not want to be ashamed of his madness.

And now the lead of his guilt lies upon him again, and once again his poor reason is so stiff, so crippled, so heavy.

If only he could shake his head, then off would roll his burden: but who can shake this head?

What is this man? A heap of diseases which reach out into the world through the spirit: there they want to take their prey.

What is this man? A ball of wild snakes which seldom have peace together, — so they go forth alone and seek prey in the world.

Look at this poor body! What it suffered and longed for it interpreted for itself, — it interpreted it as blood lust and craving for the happiness of the knife.

Upon him who falls ill now falls that evil which is evil now: he wants to cause pain with that which causes him pain. But there have been other times and another evil and good.

Once doubt was evil and the will to self. At that time the sick became heretics and witches: as heretics and witches they suffered and wanted to cause suffering.

But your ears do not want to hear this: it hurts good people, you tell me.

What do I care about your good people!

Much about your good people disgusts me, and verily, it is not their evil.

Oh, how I wish they had a madness in which to perish like this pale criminal!

Verily, I wish their madness had the name of truth or faithfulness or justice:

but they have their virtue in order to live long and in wretched comfort.

I am a railing by the raging stream: clutch me if you can! Your crutch, however, I am not. —

Thus spake Zarathustra.

On Reading And Writing

Of all that is written I love only what a person has written with his blood.

Write with blood: and you will come to find that blood is spirit.

It does not come easy, making out alien blood; I hate the reading idlers.

He who knows the reader does nothing more for the reader. Another century of readers — and the spirit itself will stink.

That everyone is allowed to learn to read spoils in the long run not only writing but also thinking.

Once the spirit was God, then it became man, now it has even become riffraff.

He who writes in blood and aphorisms does not want to be read but to be learned by heart.

In the mountains the shortest path is from peak to peak: but for that you have to have long legs. Aphorisms should be peaks: and those to whom they speak, tall and lofty.

The air thin and pure, with danger near, and the spirit full of joyful malice:

that makes for a good match.

I want to have kobolds around me, for I am bold. Boldness, which scares ghosts away, creates kobolds for itself, — boldness wants to laugh.

I no longer feel as you do: this cloud I see beneath me, this blackness and heaviness over which I laugh, — precisely this is your thundercloud.

You look up when you crave elevation. And I look down because I am elevated.

Who among you can laugh and be elevated at the same time?

He who climbs the highest mountains laughs at all tragic plays and tragic realities.

Valiant, unconcerned, mocking, violent — thus wisdom wants us. She is a woman and always loves only a warrior.

You tell me: "Life is hard to bear." But why would you have your pride in the morning and your resignation in the evening?

Life is hard to bear: but do not pretend to be so tender! We are altogether fine load bearing asses and she-asses.

What do we have in common with the rosebud, which trembles because a drop of dew lies upon its body?

It is true: we love life not because we are used to living but because we are used to loving.

There is always some madness in love. But there is also always some reason in madness.

And even to me, well-disposed to life as I am, the butterflies and soap-bubbles and those of their kind among mankind seem to know the most about happiness.

To see these light, foolish, delicate, movable little souls flutter — that seduces Zarathustra to tears and song.

I would only believe in a God who knew how to dance.

And when I saw my devil, I found him serious, thorough, profound, solemn:

he was the spirit of gravity, — through him all things fall.

Not through wrath but through laughter does one kill. Come, let us kill the spirit of gravity!

I have learned to walk: since then I have let myself run. I have learned to fly:

since then I don't want a push first in order to get going.

Now I am light, now I fly, now I see myself under me, now a God dances through me.

Thus spake Zarathustra.

On The Tree On The Mountainside

Zarathustra's eye had perceived that a certain youth avoided him. And one evening as he walked alone through the mountains surrounding the town which is called "The Dappled Cow", behold: in his walking there he found the youth, who sat leaning on a tree, casting weary looks into the valley. Zarathustra took hold of the tree by which the youth was sitting and spoke thus:

"If I wanted to shake this tree here with my hands, I would be unable to do so.

But the wind, which we do not see, bends and torments it howsoever it will. We are bent and tormented the worst by invisible hands."

The youth arose dismayed and said: "I hear Zarathustra and I was just now thinking of him." Zarathustra replied:

"Why are you alarmed at that? — But it is the same with man as it is with the tree.

The more it wants to be up in the height and the light, the stronger its roots strive earthward, downward, into the dark, the deep, — into evil."

"Yes, into evil!" cried the youth. "How is it possible that you have discovered my soul?"

Zarathustra smiled and said: "Many a soul will never be discovered unless it is first invented."

"Yes, into evil!" cried the youth once more.

"You have told the truth, Zarathustra. I no longer trust myself ever since I wanted to be up high, and no one trusts me any longer, — how does that happen?

I am changing too fast: my today refutes my yesterday. I often skip steps when I climb, — no step forgives me for that.

When I am up high I always find myself alone. No one speaks to me, the frost of solitude makes me shiver. What do I want up high?

My contempt and my longing increase together; the higher I climb, the more I despise the one who climbs. What does he want up high?

How ashamed I am of my climbing and stumbling! How I hate the fleeing one! How weary I am, up high!"

At this point the youth fell silent. And Zarathustra contemplated the tree beside which they stood and spoke thus:

"This tree stands lonely here in the mountains; high above man and beast it has grown.

And if it wanted to speak, it would have no one who could understand it:

so high has it grown.

Now it waits and waits, — but what is it waiting for? It dwells too near the seat of the clouds: perhaps it waits for the first lightning?"

When Zarathustra had said this, the youth cried, with furious gestures, "Yes, Zarathustra, you speak the truth. I longed for my downgoing when I wanted the height, and you are the lightning I have been waiting for! Behold, what is left of me since you came among us? It is envy of you which has destroyed me!" — Thus spoke the youth and wept bitterly. But Zarathustra put his arm around him and led the lad away with him.

And when they had walked together for a while, Zarathustra began to speak thus:

"It breaks my heart. Better than your words can say, your eyes tell me of all your danger. You are not yet free, you are still in quest of freedom. Under-rested your quest has made you, and overwakeful.

You want to be at a free height, your soul thirsts for the stars. But your bad instincts also thirst for freedom.

Your wild dogs want to be at liberty; they bark with pleasure in their cellar when your spirit strives to unmake all prisons.

To me you are still a prisoner who imagines freedom: alas, clever become the souls of such prisoners, but also cunning and wicked.

Even the one who is liberated in spirit must purify himself. Much prison and putrefaction still remains in him: his eye must still become pure.

Yes, I know your danger. But by my love and hope I implore you: do not throw your love and hope away!

You still feel noble, and the others also still feel you are noble, though they hold a grudge against you and give you dirty looks. Know that the noble man stands in everyone's way.

The noble man also stands in the way of the good: and even when they call him good, they do so in order to do him in.

The new the noble man wants to create, and a new virtue. The old the good man wants, and that the old be preserved.

But that is not the danger of the noble man, that he will become one of the good, but that he will become a smart-aleck, a cynic, an annihilator.

Alas, I have known noble men who lost their highest hope. And then they slandered all high hopes.

Then they passed their lives shamelessly, engaged in brief pleasures, barely setting their goals beyond the day.

"Spirit is also sensuality" — so they said. Then the wings of their spirit broke in pieces: now it crawls around and soils what it gnaws on.

Once they thought of becoming heroes: now they are lechers. The hero is a horror and a source of remorse to them.

But by my love and hope I implore you: do not throw away the hero in your soul! Keep holy your highest hope! —

Thus spake Zarathustra.

On The Preachers Of Death

There are preachers of death: and the earth is full of those to whom turning away from life must be preached.

The earth is full of the superfluous, life is spoiled by the many-too-many.

May they be enticed by "eternal life" out of this life!

"Yellow ones": so the preachers of death are called, or "black ones." But I want to show them to you in still other colors.

There are the terrible ones who carry the beast of prey around in themselves and have no choice except lust or self-laceration. And even their lust is still self-laceration.

They have not yet become men, these terrible ones: may they preach turning away from life and pass away themselves!

There are the consumptives of the soul: hardly are they born and already they begin to die, longing for the teachings of weariness and resignation.

They would gladly be dead, and we should approve their wish! Let us beware of waking the dead and damaging these living coffins!

They meet a sick man or an old man or a corpse; and right away they say:

"Life is refuted!"

But only they are refuted, and their eye, which sees only this one facet of existence.

Wrapped in thick melancholy and eager for the little accidents that bring death: thus they wait and clench their teeth.

Or else: they reach for sweets and mock their childishness the while; they cling to their shoestring existence, and mock their still living on a shoestring.

Their wisdom runs: "A fool is he who stays alive, but such fools are we, and how! And this is surely the most foolish thing about life!" —

"Life is only suffering" — so others say, and they do not lie. So see to it that you cease! So see to it that the life which is only suffering ceases!

And let the teaching of your virtue run thus: "Thou shalt do away with thyself!

Thou shalt steal away from thyself!" —

"Sensuality is sin," — so say the ones who preach death, — "let us go aside and beget no more children!"

"Giving birth is laborsome," — say the others — "why still give birth? Only unfortunates are born!" And these, too, are preachers of death.

"Pity is necessary," — so says a third group. "Take what I have! Take what I am! Life will bind me that much less!"—

If they were truly full of compassion, they would destroy their neighbor's passion for life. To be evil — that would be their true goodness.

But they want to be released from life: what is it to them if with their chains and gifts they bind others ever more tightly! —

And you too, to whom life is fierce labor and unrest: are you not very weary of life? Are you not very ripe for the preaching of death?

All you to whom fierce labor is dear, and the fast, the new, the unfamiliar, — you are poor at enduring yourselves, your industriousness is a flight and a will to forget yourselves.

If you believed more in life, you would throw yourselves less into the moment. But in you you do not have enough of what it takes to wait — not even to vegetate!

Everywhere resounds the voice of those who preach death: and the earth is full of those to whom death must be preached.

Or "eternal life": it's all the same to me, — if only they pass away quickly!

Thus spake Zarathustra.

On War And Warlike People

We do not wish to be spared by our enemies, nor by those whom we love from the heart. So let me tell you the truth, then!

My brothers in war! I love you from the heart; I am and have been your like.

And I am also your best enemy. So let me tell you the truth, then!

I know the hatred and envy of your hearts. You are not great enough not to know hatred and envy. So be great enough then not to be ashamed of them!

And if you cannot be saints of knowledge, then at least be its warriors.

They are the companions and forerunners of such sanctity.

I see many soldiers: would that I saw many warriors! "Uniform" one calls what they wear: would that it were not uniform what they hide thereby!

You should be one of those whose eye always seeks an enemy — your enemy. And with some of you it is hate at first sight.

Your enemy you shall seek, your war you shall wage, and for your thoughts!

And if your thought should be defeated, then your honesty shall still cry victory meanwhile!

You shall love peace as a means to new wars. And the short peace more than the long.

You I advise not to work but to fight. You I advise not to peace but to victory.

May your work be a fight, may your peace be a victory!

One can only be quiet and sit still when one has bow and arrow: otherwise one squawks and squabbles. May your peace be a victory!

You say it is the good cause that hallows even war? I say to you: it is the good war that hallows every cause.

War and courage have done more great things than love of your neighbor.

Not your pity but your bravery has saved the unfortunate thus far.

"What is good?" you ask. To be brave is good. Let the little girls say: "Good is what is pretty and at the same time touching."

They call you heartless: but your heart is true, and I love the modesty of your cordiality. You are ashamed of your flow, and others are ashamed of their ebb.

You are ugly? Well then, my brothers! Put on the sublime, the mantle of the ugly!

And when your soul becomes large, it becomes high-spirited, and in your sublimity there is malice. I know you.

In malice the princeling and the weakling meet. But they misunderstand each other. I know you.

You may only have enemies to hate, not enemies to despise. You must be proud of your enemy: then your enemy's successes will also be your successes.

Rebellion — that is the distinction of a slave. May your distinction be obedience!

May your commanding itself be an obeying!

"Thou shalt" sounds sweeter to a good soldier than "I will." And all that is dear to you shall be that which has first been commanded to you.

May your love of life be love for your highest hope: and may your highest hope be the highest thought of life!

Your highest thought, however, shall be commanded to you by me — and it runs: man is something that shall be overcome.

So live your life of obedience and war! Who cares about long life! What warrior wants to be spared!

I do not spare you, I love you from the heart, my brothers in war! —

Thus spake Zarathustra.

On The New Idol

Somewhere there are still peoples and herds, but not by us: here there are states.

State? What is that? Well then! Open your ears, for now I will say a word to you about the death of peoples.

State is the name of the coldest of all cold monsters. It lies coldly, too; and this lie crawls out of its mouth: "I, the state, am the people."

It is a lie! It was creators who created peoples and hung a belief and a love above them: thus they served life.

It is destroyers who set up pitfalls for many people and call them "state":

they hang a sword and a hundred inordinate desires above them.

Where there is still a people, they do not know the state, and they hate it as the evil eye and a sin against customs and rights.

This sign I give to you: each people speaks its own tongue of good and evil; its neighbor does not understand it. Its language it has devised for itself in customs and rights.

But the state lies in all tongues of good and evil; and whatever it says, it lies — and whatever it has, it has stolen.

Everything about it is false; with stolen teeth it bites, the snaphappy one.

Even its innards are false.

Speech confusion of good and evil: this sign I give to you as a sign of the state. Verily, the will to death this sign signifies! Verily, it beckons the preachers of death!

Many-too-many are born: the state was devised for the superfluous ones!

Just look how it entices them, the many-too-many! How it gobbles and chews and re-chews them!

"There is nothing greater on earth than I: I am the regulating finger of God"

— thus the monster roars. And not only the long-eared and the short-sighted sink to their knees!

Alas, to you as well, you great souls, it whispers its gloomy lies! Alas, it divines the rich hearts which gladly squander themselves.

Yes, you too it divines, you conquerors of the old God! You have become weary of battle, and now even your weariness serves the new idol!

Heroes and men of honor it wants to set up around itself, the new idol!

Gladly it basks in the sunshine of good consciences, — this cold monster!

It will give you all when you worship it, the new idol: thus it buys the glimmer of your virtue and the glance of your proud eye.

By using you it wants to entice the many-too-many! Yes, a hellish piece of art has been devised here, a horse of death jingling in the trappings of divine honors.

Yes, a dying for many has been devised here which praises itself as life: verily, a heartsend to all preachers of death!

State I call it, where all are poison drinkers, good and bad: state, where all lose themselves, good and bad: state, where the slow suicide of all — is called "life."

Just look at these superfluous ones! They steal for themselves the works of inventors and the treasures of the wise — education they call their theft — and all becomes sickness and distress to them!

Just look at these superfluous ones! They are always sick; they vomit their gall and call it a newspaper. They devour each other and cannot even stomach themselves.

Just look at these superfluous ones! They acquire riches, by the which they become poorer. Power they desire, and first of all that lever of power, lots of money, — these impotent ones!

See them clamber, these quick monkeys! They clamber away, one atop the other, and so drag themselves into the mud and the abyss.

There to the throne they all want to go: it is their madness — as if happiness sat on the throne! Mud often sits on the throne — and oftentimes, too, the throne on mud.

Madmen they are all to me and clambering monkeys and overheated ones.

Their idol, the cold monster, smells evil to me: all together they smell evil to me, these idolaters.

My brother, would you smother in the fumes of their maws and lawless desires? Better to smash the window and jump outside.

Get away from the bad smell! Go away from the idolatry of the superfluous!

Get away from the bad smell! Go away from these human sacrifices!

The earth is still open for great souls. Many seats still stand empty for the lonesome and the twosome, around whom the smell of silent seas blows.

A free life still stands open for great souls. Verily, he who possesses little is so much the less possessed: praised be the little poverty!

There, where the state ends, only there begins the man who is not superfluous:

there begins the song of the necessary one, the unique and irreplaceable melody.

There, where the state ends, just look there my brothers! Do you not see it, the rainbow and the bridges of the Superman? —

Thus spake Zarathustra.

On The Flies Of The Marketplace

Flee, my friend, into your solitude! I see you deafened by the noise of the great men and stung all over by the stings of the little men.

Wood and rock know how to keep a worthy silence with you. Be again like the tree you love, the broad-branching one: silent and attentive it hangs over the sea.

Where solitude ends, there the marketplace begins; and where the marketplace begins, there begins also the noise of the great actors and the buzzing of the poisonous flies.

The best things in the world still amount to nothing without the one who first shows them: great men the people call these showmen.

The people have little grasp of greatness, that is: creativeness. But they have a taste for all showers and actors of great things.

Around the inventors of new values the world revolves — invisibly it revolves. But around the actors the people and the glory revolve: that is how "the world turns."

Spirit the actor has, but little conscience of the spirit. He always believes in that with which he makes the strongest belief, — the belief in himself!

Tomorrow he has a new belief, and the day after tomorrow a newer one.

Quick senses he has, like the people, and fickle moods.

To overthrow — to him that means: to prove. To drive crazy — to him that means: to convince. And blood strikes him as the best of all arguments.

A truth which slips only into fine ears he calls a lie and a nothing. Verily, he only believes in gods that make a great noise in the world!

The marketplace is full of solemn buffoons — and people boast of their great men: to them they are the men of the hour.

But the hour presses them: so they press you. And they also want from you a Yes or a No. Woe, would you set your chair between For and Against?

Do not be jealous on account of these pushy and absolute ones, you lover of the truth! Never yet has truth clung to the arm of an absolutist.

Return to your safety on account of these hasty ones: only in the marketplace is one assaulted with Yes? or No?

Slow is the experience of all deep wells: long must they wait before knowing what fell into their depths.

Apart from fame and marketplace all great things take place: apart from fame and marketplace the inventors of new values have always kept a place.

Flee, my friend, into your solitude: I see you stung all over by poisonous flies. Flee there, to where a rough, strong breeze blows!

Flee into your solitude! You have dwelt too near the small and the pitiful.

Flee from their invisible vengeance! Towards you they have nothing but vengeance.

Raise not a hand against them any longer! Countless are they, and it is not your lot to be a flyswatter.

Countless are these small and pitiful ones; and many a proud building has already been brought down by raindrops and weeds.

You are no stone, but already you have become hollow from many drops.

From many drops you will yet break and burst asunder.

I see you worn out by poisonous flies, I see you scratched bloody in a hundred places, and your pride refuses to get angry even once.

Blood they want from you in all innocence, blood their bloodless souls crave — and so they go on stinging in all innocence.

But you, deep one, you suffer too deeply even from small wounds; and before you have even healed, the same poison worm crawls over your hand.

You are too proud to kill these sweet-tooths. Beware, however, lest it become your fate to bear all their poisonous injustice!

They buzz around you with their praise, too: their praise is pushiness. They want to be close to your skin and blood.

They fawn upon you as upon a god or devil: they whine before you as before a god or devil. So what! Fawners and whiners they are and nothing more.

They often try as well to pass themselves off to you as charming. But that was ever the cleverness of the cowardly. Yes, the cowardly are clever!

They think about you a lot with their narrow souls, — you are always unthinkable to them! Whatever is thought about a lot becomes unthinkable.

They punish you for all your virtues. Deep down they only forgive you —

your mistakes.

Because you are gentle and fair-minded you say: "Guiltless are they in their small existence." But narrow souls think: "Guilt makes up all great existence."

Even when you are gentle to them, they still feel despised by you; and your good deed they repay with hidden bad deeds.

Your wordless pride always goes against their taste; they rejoice if for once you are modest enough to be vain.

That which we recognize in a man we also inflame in him. So beware of the small people!

Before you they feel small, and their lowness glimmers and glows in invisible vengeance toward you.

Have you not noticed how often they became silent when you walked up to them, and how their strength deserted them like smoke from a dying fire?

Yes, my friend, you are the bad conscience of your neighbors; for they are unworthy of you. Therefore they hate you and would gladly love to suck your blood.

Your neighbors will always be poisonous flies; that which is great in you, — that very thing must make them more poisonous and ever more fly-like.

Flee, my friend, into your solitude and to there where a rough, strong breeze blows! It is not your lot to be a fly-swatter. —

Thus spake Zarathustra.

On Chastity

I love the forest. In the cities it is bad to live; there are too many in heat there.

Is it not better to fall into the hands of a murderer than into the dreams of a woman in heat?

And just look at these men: their eyes say it — they know nothing better on earth than to lie with a woman.

Slime is at the bottom of their souls; and woe if on top of it this slime has spirit!

Would that you were as perfect as animals at least! But to animals belongs innocence.

Do I advise you to kill your senses? I advise you to have innocence of the senses.

Do I advise you to chastity? Chastity is a virtue with some, but with many it is nearly a vice.

They may well abstain: but the bitch Sensuality looks enviously out of all that they do.

Even unto the heights of their virtue and right into the cold spirit this creature and her discord follow them.

And how politely the bitch Sensuality knows how to beg for a piece of spirit when a piece of meat is denied her.

You love tragedies and everything that breaks your heart to smithereens?

But I am suspicious of your bitch.

Your eyes are too cruel for me and you look lustfully for sufferers. Has not your lechery merely disguised and described itself as pity?

And this parable too I offer you: Not a few who wanted to cast out their devils entered themselves into the swine thereby.

Chastity is not to be advised for those who find it hard, lest it become the way to hell — that is to slime and soul-lust.

Do I speak of filthy things? That is not the worst thing.

Not when the truth is filthy, but when it is shallow: that is when the knowing one is reluctant to go into its waters.

Verily, there are thoroughly chaste ones: they are gentler of heart; they laugh more readily and richly than you.

They laugh at chastity too and ask: "What is chastity?"

"Is chastity not folly? But this folly came to us, not we to it.

We offered this guest harbor and heart: now he dwells with us — let him stay as long as he wants!"

Thus spake Zarathustra.

On The Friend

"One is always too many around me" — so thinks the hermit. "Always one times one — in the long run that makes two!"

I and me are always too wrapped up in conversation: how could that be endured unless there were a friend?

For the hermit the friend is always the third person: the third person is the cork that prevents the conversation of the other two from sinking into the depths.

Alas, there are too many depths for all hermits. Therefore they long so for a friend and his height.

Our faith in others betrays wherein we would dearly love to have faith in ourselves. Our longing for a friend is our betrayer.

And often with our love we only want to overleap envy. And often we attack and make an enemy only in order to hide our vulnerability.

"At least be my enemy!" — thus speaks true reverence, which dares not ask for friendship.

If one wants to have a friend, then one must also be willing to wage war for him: and in order to wage war, one must be capable of being an enemy.

One should still honor the enemy in one's friend. Can you go near your friend without going over to him?

In his friend one should have his best enemy. You should be closest to him in your heart when you resist him.

You want to wear no clothes before your friend? It should be an honor to your friend that you show yourself to him as you are? But he wishes you to the devil for it!

He who makes no secret of himself makes others see red: all the more reason to fear nakedness! Of course, if you were gods, then you could be ashamed of your clothes!

You cannot dress finely enough for your friend: for you are to be an arrow and a longing for the Superman to him.

Have you ever seen your friend asleep, — to find out how he looked? What else is your friend's face, though? It is your own face in a rough and imperfect mirror.

Have you ever seen your friend asleep? Were you not frightened that your friend looked like that? Oh, my friend, man is something that must be overcome.

In divining and keeping silent the friend should be a master: you must not want to see all. Your dream should reveal to you what your friend does when he is awake.

Let your pitying be a divining: that you may first see whether your friend wants pity. Perhaps he loves in you the unbroken eye and the look of eternity.

Pity for a friend should hide itself under a hard shell: you should break a tooth biting on it. Thus it will have fineness and sweetness.

Are you pure air and solitude and bread and medicine for your friend? Many a man cannot loosen his own chains, and yet he is a savior to his friend.

Are you a slave? Then you cannot be a friend. Are you a tyrant? Then you cannot have friends.

All-too-long have a slave and a tyrant been concealed in woman. Therefore woman is not yet capable of friendship: she only knows love.

In woman's love there is injustice and blindness towards all that she does not love. And even in the knowing love of woman there is still sneak attack and lightning and night alongside the light.

Woman is not yet capable of friendship: women are still cats and birds. Or at best, cows.

Woman is not yet capable of friendship. But tell me, you men, who among you is capable of friendship?

O your poverty, you men, and your avarice of soul! As much as you give your friend I will yet give my foe, and I will be none the poorer for it also.

There is comradeship: may there be friendship!

Thus spake Zarathustra.

On The Thousand And One Goals

Many lands did Zarathustra see, and many peoples: thus he discovered the good and evil of many peoples. No greater power on earth did Zarathustra find than good and evil.

No people could live without first valuing; if they want to keep their standing, however, they must not value as their neighbor values.

Much that was good to this people was a mockery and a disgrace to another: thus did I find. Much did I find called evil here and adorned with purple honors there.

Never did one neighbor understand the other: ever did his soul marvel at his neighbor's madness and malice.

A table of the good hangs over every people. Behold, it is the table of their overcomings; behold, it is the voice of their will to power.

Whatever is hard they call praiseworthy; whatever is hard and indispensable is called good; and whatever relieves in even the direst need, the rare, the hardest,— that they praise as holy.

Whatever makes them rule and conquer and shine to the horror and envy of their neighbor: that they consider the height, the foremost, the measure, the meaning of all things.

Verily, my brother, if you only knew a people's need and land and sky and neighbor, then you could surely divine the law of their overcomings and why they climb this ladder to their hope.

"You shall always be first and stand apart from the others: your jealous soul shall love none other than a friend" — that made the soul of a Greek tremble:

with that he traveled the path of his greatness.

"To speak the truth and do well with bow and arrow" — that seemed both dear and hard to the people from whom my name comes — the name which is both dear and hard to me.

"To honor mother and father and do their will to the very roots of your soul" — this table of overcoming another people hung over themselves and grew powerful and eternal thereby.

"To practice loyalty, and for the sake of loyalty to risk honor and blood, even on evil and dangerous things": teaching themselves thus, another people mastered themselves, and thus mastering themselves, they became pregnant and heavy with great hopes.

Verily, men have given themselves all their good and evil. Verily, they did not take it, they did not find it, it did not come to them as a voice from heaven.

Man first implanted values in things in order to maintain his standing, —

he first created meaning in things, a human meaning! That is why he calls himself "Man," that is: the evaluator.

Valuing is creating: hear this, you creators! Valuing itself is of all valued things the treasure and jewel.

Only through valuing is there value: and without valuing the nut of existence would be hollow. Hear this, you creators!

A change in values, — that is a change in creators. He who must be a creator is always destroying.

Creators were peoples first, and only later, individuals; verily, the individual himself is but the latest creation.

Once peoples hung a table of values over themselves. A love which wants to rule and a love which wants to obey have together created for themselves such tables.

The pleasure in the herd is older than the pleasure in the I: and as long as the good conscience is called herd, the bad conscience only says: I.

Verily, the sly I, the loveless one that seeks its advantage in the advantage of many: that is not the beginning of the herd but its downgoing.

It was ever lovers and creators that created good and evil. The fire of love glows in all the names of the virtues, and the fire of anger.

Many lands did Zarathustra see, and many peoples: no greater power on earth did Zarathustra find than the works of the lovers: their names are "good" and "evil."

Verily, the power of this praising and blaming is a monster. Tell me brothers, who will subdue it for me? Tell me, who will throw a chain over the thousand necks of this beast?

Thus far there have been a thousand goals, for there have been a thousand peoples. Only the chain for these thousand necks is still lacking, the one goal is lacking. Mankind still has no goal.

But tell me though, my brothers: if the goal of mankind is still lacking, is not also — mankind itself still lacking? —

Thus spake Zarathustra.

On Neighborly Love

You crowd around your neighbor and have fine words for it. But I tell you:

your neighborly love is your bad love of yourselves.

You flee from yourselves to your neighbor and would like to make a virtue of it: but I see through your "selflessness."

The "you" is older than the "I"; the "you" has been canonized, but not yet the "I"; thus man crowds towards his neighbor.

Do I advise you to neighborly love? Rather I advise you to neighborly flight and love for the furthest!

Higher than love for the nearest is love for the furthest and future one; higher still than the love of man I consider the love of things and phantoms.

This phantom which runs here before you, my brother, is fairer than you; why not give him your flesh and bones? But you are afraid and go running off to your neighbor.

You cannot stand to be alone with yourselves and do not love yourselves enough: now you want to mislead your neighbor into love and gild yourselves with his mistake.

I wish that you could not stand any kind of nearest ones and their neighbors; then out of yourselves you would have to create your friend and his overflowing heart.

You call in a witness when you want to speak well of yourselves; and when you have misled him into thinking well of you, he himself thinks well of you.

Not only does he lie who speaks contrary to what he does know, but all the more so he who speaks contrary to what he does not know. And so you speak of yourselves in your dealings and deceive your neighbor with yourselves.

Thus speaks the fool: "Contact with men ruins character, especially if one has none."

The one goes to his neighbor because he seeks himself and the other because he wants to lose himself. Your bad love of yourselves makes solitude a prison for you.

It is those further away who must pay for your love of neighbor; and as soon as there are five of you together, a sixth one must always die.

I do not love your feast-days either: too many actors I found there, and often the spectators acted like actors, too.

Not the neighbor do I teach you, but the friend. May the friend be the feast of the earth for you and an anticipation of the Superman.

I teach you the friend and his overfull heart. But one must be a sponge if one would be loved by hearts that are overfull.

I teach you the friend, in whom the world stands complete, a bowl of the good, — the creative friend, who always has a complete world to bestow.

47 And as the world once rolled apart for him, so it rolls back together again for him in circles, like the development of good through evil, like the development of purpose from chance.

May the future and the furthest be the reason for your today: in your friend you shall love the Superman as your reason.

My brothers, I do not advise you to neighborly love: I advise you to love for the furthest.

Thus spake Zarathustra.

On The Way Of The Creator

Would you go into isolation, my brother? Would you seek the way to yourself?

Stay yet a while and hear me.

"He who seeks easily gets lost himself. All isolation is guilt": thus speaks the herd. And you have long belonged to the herd.

The voice of the herd will still resound in you, too. And when you say: "You and I are no longer of one conscience," it will be a pain and a plaint.

Behold, this pain itself is still brought forth by the one conscience: and the last glimmer of that conscience still gleams on your misery.

But would you go the way of your misery, which is the way to yourself?

Then show me your right and might to it!

Are you a new might and a new right? A first movement? A self-rolling wheel? Can you force even the stars to revolve around you?

Alas, there is so much lustfulness for the heights! There are so many convulsions of the ambitious! Show me that you are not one of the lustful and the ambitious!

Alas, there are so many great thoughts that do no more than a bellows: they inflate and make emptier.

You call yourselves free? Your ruling thought I want to hear and not that you have escaped from a yoke.

Are you one of those allowed to escape from a yoke? There are many who threw away their last value when they threw away their servitude.

Free from what? What is that to Zarathustra? But your eye should clearly announce to me: free for what?

Can you provide yourself with your own good and evil and hang your will up over yourself like a law? Can you be the judge of yourself and the avenger of your own law?

It is terrible being alone with the judge and avenger of your own law. Thus a star is thrown into empty space and into the icy breath of aloneness.

Today you still suffer from the many, you lone one: today you still have all your courage and your hopes.

But one day loneliness will make you weary, one day your pride will cringe and your courage will gnash its teeth. One day you will cry "I am alone!"

One day you will see your high no more and your low all too near; your very loftiness will frighten you like a ghost. One day you will cry: "All is false!"

There are feelings that would kill the loner; should they not succeed, well then, they themselves must die! But are you capable of being a murderer?

My brother, do you know the word "contempt" yet? And the agony of your justice, being just to those who despise you?

You force many to learn anew about you; they charge you harshly for that.

You went near them and passed right over them: that they will never forgive you.

You go above and beyond them: but the higher you climb, the smaller the eye of envy perceives you. The flier, however, is hated most of all.

"How could you be just to me!" — you must say — "I chose your injustice as my allotted part."

Injustice and filth they throw at the loner: but, my brother, if you would be a star, then you must shine for them none the less!

And beware of the good and the just! They like to crucify those who invent their own virtue — they hate the loners.

Beware also of holy simplicity! Everything that is not simple is unholy to them; they also like to play with fire — the stake.

And beware, too, of the attacks of your love! Too quickly the loner extends his hand toward anyone he happens to meet.

To many a man you may not give a hand, only a paw: and I want your paw to have claws, too.

But the worst enemy you can meet will always be yourself; you lie in wait for yourself in caves and forests.

Loner, you go the way to yourself! And your way leads past you yourself and your seven devils!

Heretic you will be to yourself and skeptic and witch and soothsayer and fool and sinner and scoundrel.

You must be willing to burn in your own flame: how could you become new unless you had first become ashes?

Loner, you go the way of the lover: you love yourself and therefore you despise yourself, as only lovers despise.

The lover wants to create because he despises! What does he know of love who has not had to despise precisely that which he loved?

With your love and with your creation go into your isolation, my brother, and only later will justice limp after you.

With my tears go into your isolation, my brother. I love him who wants to create beyond himself and thus go to ruin.—

Thus spake Zarathustra.

On Little Old And Young Ladies

"Why do you steal so shyly through the twilight, Zarathustra? And what do you hide so carefully under your mantle?

Is it a treasure that was given to you? Or a child that was born to you? Or are you yourself now going the way of thieves, you friend of the wicked?" —

Verily, my brother, said Zarathustra, it is a treasure that was given to me: it is a little truth that I carry.

But it is unruly like a young child, and if I do not hold its mouth it will cry too loudly.

As I went my way alone today, at the hour when the sun is sinking, a little old lady met me and spoke to my soul thus:

"Many things has Zarathustra also said to us women, but never has he spoken to us about woman."

And I replied to her: "About woman one should speak only to men."

"Speak also to me about woman," she said; "I am old enough to forget it immediately again."

And I complied with the little old lady and spoke to her thus:

"Everything about woman is a riddle, and everything about woman has one solution: it is called pregnancy.

Man is for woman a means: the end is always the child. But what is woman for man?

Two different things the true man wants: danger and play. Therefore he wants woman as the most dangerous plaything.

Man should be trained for war and women for the recreation of the warrior:

all else is folly.

All-too-sweet fruits — these the warrior dislikes. Therefore he likes woman; even the sweetest woman is bitter.

Woman understands children better than man, but man is more childlike than woman.

In the true man a child is hidden: it wants to play. Come on, you women, discover the child in man!

Let women be a plaything, pure and fine, like a precious stone illuminated by the virtues of a world yet to come.

Let the radiance of a star sparkle in your love! Let your hope be: "May I give birth to the Superman!"

Let there be bravery in your love! With your love you should head for him who fills you with dread.

Let your honor be in your love! Woman understands little else of honor. But let this be your honor: always to love more than you are loved, and never to be second.

Let man fear woman when she loves: then she makes any sacrifice, and everything else she considers worthless.

Let man fear woman when she hates: for at the bottom of his soul man is merely angry; woman, however, is downright mean.

Whom does woman hate the most? — Thus said the iron to the magnet: "I hate you the most, because you attract me but are not strong enough to draw me to you."

The happiness of man is: I will. The happiness of woman is: he wills.

"Behold, just now the world has become perfect!" — thus thinks every woman when she obeys out of complete love.

And woman must obey and find a depth for her surface. Surface is woman's nature, a mobile, stormy film on shallow water.

Man's nature, however, is deep: his torrent roars in subterranean caves; woman senses his strength but can make no sense of it. —

Then the little old lady replied to me: "Many charming things Zarathustra has said, especially for those who are young enough for them.

It is strange: Zarathustra knows little about women, and yet he is right about them! Is that because nothing is impossible with woman?

And now accept a little truth by way of thanks! I am old enough for it, anyway!

Bundle it up and keep its mouth shut: otherwise it will cry loudly, this little truth."

"Give me, woman, your little truth!" I said. And thus spake the little old lady:

"You go to women? Do not forget the whip!"—

Thus spake Zarathustra.

On The Adder's Bite

One day, because of the heat, Zarathustra had fallen asleep under a fig tree and had placed his arms across his face. Then an adder came and bit him on the neck, so that he cried out in pain. When he had taken an arm from his face, he took a look at the snake: it recognized Zarathustra by his eyes, wriggled awkwardly, and wanted to get away. "Not so fast," said Zarathustra, "you have not yet accepted my thanks! You have awakened me in time, my way is yet long."

"Your way is yet short," said the adder sadly; "my poison kills." Zarathustra smiled: "When did a dragon ever die from the poison of a snake?" — he said. "But take your poison back! You are not rich enough to give it to me." Then the adder fell upon his neck again and licked his wound.

As Zarathustra related this once to his disciples, they asked him: "And what, O Zarathustra, is the moral of your story?" Then Zarathustra answered them thus:

"The annihilator of morals the good and the just call me: my story is immoral.

But if you have an enemy, do not requite him good for evil: for that would put him to shame. Prove rather that he did you some good.

And better to be angry than to put to shame! And when you are cursed, it pleases me not that you then want to bless. Rather curse a little in return!

And if a great wrong has been done you, then quickly do five small ones in addition! Horrible to behold is he who alone a wrong oppresses.

Were you aware of this already? A shared wrong is half right. And only he who can take it should take a wrong upon himself!

A little revenge is more human than no revenge at all. And if the punishment is not also a right and an honor for the transgressor, I do not care for your punishments either.

It is nobler to admit being wrong than to insist on being right, especially if one is in the right. Only one must be rich enough for that.

I do not care for your cold justice; and out of the eye of your judges there always gazes the executioner and his cold steel.

Tell me, where is the justice which is love with seeing eyes to be found?

So devise for me the love which bears not only all punishment but also all guilt!

So devise for me the justice which acquits everyone except the one who judges!

Would you hear this, too? With him who would be thoroughly just, even the lie becomes mankindliness.

But how could I be thoroughly just? How can I give each his own? Let this be enough for me: I give each my own.

Finally, my brothers, beware of doing the hermit any harm! How could a hermit forget? How could he requite?

A hermit is like a deep well. It is easy to throw a stone in; but once it has sunk to the bottom, tell me, who will bring it out again?

Beware of offending the hermit! But if you have done so, well then, do him in as well!

Thus spake Zarathustra.

On The Child And Marriage

I have a question for you alone, my brother: like a plumb line I cast this question into your soul to see how deep it is.

You are young and wish for a child and marriage. But I ask you: are you a man who is allowed to wish for a child?

Are you the triumphant one, the self-conqueror, the master of the senses, the lord of your virtues? Thus I ask you.

Or does the beast and the utmost necessity speak out of your wish? Or isolation?

Or unrest within yourself?

I wish that your triumph and freedom would yearn for a child. Living monuments you should build to your victory and delivery.

Out beyond yourselves you should build. But first you yourself must be built, foursquare in body and soul.

Not only onward shall your seed be planted but upward! May the garden of marriage help you with that!

A higher body you should create, a first movement, a self-rolling wheel, — a creator you should create.

Marriage: thus I call the will of two to create the one who is more than those who created it. I call marriage the reverence for each other of those who will with such a will.

Let this be the meaning and truth of your marriage. But that which the many-too-many call marriage, these superfluous ones, — alas, what shall I call that?

Alas, this poverty of the soul in twos! Alas, this filth of the soul in twos!

Alas, this wretched comfort in twos!

All this they call marriage; and they say that marriages are made in heaven.

Well, I don't like it, this heaven of the superfluous! No, I don't like it, these animals entangled in the heavenly net!

And may the God who limps this way to bless what he has never joined together stay far away from me!

Do not laugh at such marriages! What child has not had reason to weep over his parents?

Worthy this man seemed to me and ripe for the meaning of the earth: but when I saw his wife, the earth seemed to me a house for the inane.

Yes, I wish that the earth would shake with convulsions when a saint mates with a goose.

This one set out like a hero in quest of truths, and at last he captured a little dressed-up lie. His marriage, he calls it.

That one was reserved in conversation and chose choosily. But in no time he spoiled his company for all time: his marriage, he calls it.

Another one sought a maid with the virtues of an angel. But in no time he became the maid of a woman, and now he even needs to be an angel, too.

Cautious have I now found all buyers, and they all have crafty eyes. But even the craftiest still buys his wife in a poke.

Many short follies — that is called love, by you. And your marriage makes an end of many short follies with one long stupidity.

Your love of woman and woman's love of man: ah, would that it were a fellow-suffering with suffering and veiled deities! But generally two animals hit upon each other.

But even your best love is only an ecstatic allegory and a painful flame. It is a torch to light you to higher ways.

Beyond yourselves you shall love one day! So first learn to love! And you must have had to drink the bitter cup of your love for that.

Bitterness is in the cup of even the best love: thus it produces longing for the Superman, thus it produces thirst in you, the creator.

Thirst in the creator, an arrow and longing for the Superman: speak, my brother, is this your will to marriage?

Holy I call such a will and such a marriage.—

Thus spake Zarathustra.

On Free Death

Many die too late, and some die too early. The teaching still sounds strange: "Die at the right time"

Die at the right time; thus Zarathustra teaches.

Of course, how could he who never lived at the right time ever die at the right time? Would that he had never been born! — Thus I advise the superfluous.

But even the superfluous still make a big to-do about their dying, and even the hollowest nut still wants cracking.

All take dying to be important: but death is not yet a feast. The finest feasts men have not yet learned to consecrate.

The consummating death I present to you, one which proves to be a prick and a promise to the living.

The consummator dies his death triumphantly, ringed round by hoping and promising ones.

Thus one should learn to die; and there should be no feast at which such a dying one does not consecrate the oaths of the living!

To die thus is best; second best, however, is: to die in battle and squander a great soul.

But equally hated by the fighter and the victor is your grinning death, which creeps up like a thief — and yet comes as master.

My death I commend to you, the free death which comes to me because I want it.

And when will I want it? — He who has a goal and a heir wants death at the right time for his goal and his heir.

And out of reverence for his goal and his heir he will hang up no more withered wreaths in the sanctuary of life.

Verily, I will not do as the rope-twisters do: they spin out their thread and as a result continually walk backwards.

Many a one becomes too old for his truths and triumphs, too; a toothless mouth no longer has the right to every truth.

And everyone who desires fame must take leave of honor in good time and practice the difficult art of — leaving at the right time.

When he tastes the sweetest, a person must stop letting himself be eaten:

this is known by those who want to be long-loved.

There are sour apples, of course, whose fate demands that they wait until the last day of fall: and they become ripe, yellow, and wrinkled all at the same time.

With some the heart ages first, and with others, the spirit. And some are old in youth: but late youth preserves long youth.

For many a man life is a failure: a poison maggot eats away at his heart. So let him see to it that his death is that much more of a success.

Many a man never becomes sweet; already in summer he rots. It is cowardice that keeps him attached to his branch.

Many-too-many live and much too long they hang on their branches.

Would that a storm came to shake all this rottenness and worm-eaten mess from the tree!

Would that there came preachers of speedy death! They would be the right storms and shakers of the trees of life! But I hear only the slow death preached and patience with all things "earthly."

Alas, you preach patience with earthly things? It is these earthly things which have too much patience with you, you blasphemers!

Verily, too early died that Hebrew whom the preachers of death honor: and it has been the doom of many ever since that he died too early.

As yet he had known only tears and the melancholy of the Hebrew, along with the hatred of the good and the just, — the Hebrew Jesus: then the longing for death came over him.

If only he had stayed in the desert and far away from the good and the just!

Perhaps he would have learned to live and learned to love the earth — and laughter as well.

Believe me, my brothers! He died too early: he himself would have recanted his teaching had he reached my age! He was noble enough to recant!

But he was still immature. Immaturely the youth loves, and immaturely he hates man and earth. Bound and heavy yet are his temperament and the wings of his spirit.

In the man, however, there is more child than in the youth, and less melancholy:

he has a better grasp of life and death.

Free for death and free in death, a holy naysayer when it is no longer time for yea: thus he grasps life and death.

That your dying be no blasphemy against man and earth: this I ask of the honey of your soul.

In your dying your spirit and your virtue should still glow, like a sunset sky over the earth: otherwise your dying has turned out badly.

So will I myself die, that you friends may love the earth more for my sake; and to the earth will I return, that I may rest in her who bore me.

Verily, Zarathustra had a goal; he threw his ball: now you, my friends, are the heirs of my goal; to you I throw my golden ball.

More than anything else I love to see you throw the golden ball, my friends!

And so I tarry a little longer on earth: forgive me for that!

Thus spake Zarathustra.

On The Bestowing Virtue

1

When Zarathustra had taken leave of the town to which his heart was attached and whose name is "The Dappled Cow," many followed him who called themselves his disciples and gave him escort. Thus they came to a crossroads:

then Zarathustra told them that from thenceforth he wanted to go it alone: for he was a friend of going it alone. But in parting, his disciples gave him a staff, upon whose golden handle a serpent had coiled itself around the sun. Zarathustra was pleased with the staff and leaned upon it; then he spoke thus to his disciples:

Tell me now: how did gold come to have the highest value? Because it is uncommon and useless and luminous and gentle in its brilliance; it always bestows itself.

Only as an image of the highest virtue did gold come to have the highest value. Gold-like gleams the glance of the bestower. Golden brilliance makes peace between moon and sun.

Uncommon is the highest virtue and useless, luminous it is and gentle in its brilliance: a bestowing virtue is the highest virtue.

Verily, I divine you well, my disciples; you strive, like I do, for the bestowing virtue. What would you have in common with cats and wolves?

This is your thirst, to become gifts and offerings yourselves: and therefore you have a thirst to heap up all riches in your soul.

Insatiably your soul strives for treasures and jewels, because your virtue is insatiable in its desire to bestow.

You force all things to you and into you, so that they flow back out of your fountain as gifts of your love.

Verily, a robber of all values such bestowing love must become; but whole and holy I call this selfishness. —

There is another selfishness, an all-too-poor, hungry kind that always wants to steal, — that selfishness of the sick, the sick selfishness.

With the eyes of a thief it looks upon all things brilliant; with hunger's greed it measures him who has plenty to eat; and always it crawls around the table of those who bestow.

Sickness speaks out of such craving, and invisible degeneracy; out of a sick body the thievish greed of this selfishness speaks.

Tell me, my brothers: what do we regard as a bad thing and the worst thing? Is it not degeneracy? — And we always suspect degeneracy when the bestowing soul is lacking.

Our way goes upward, from species to super-species. But we dread the degenerate sense which says: "Everything for me."

Our sense flies upward: thus it is a parable of our body, a parable of enhancement. Such parables of enhancement go by the names of the virtues.

Thus the body goes through history, a becomer and a battler. And the spirit — what is that to the body? The herald of its battles and victories, its comrade and echo.

All the names of good and evil are parables: they do not speak out, they only wink. A fool is he who seeks knowledge from them.

Heed every hour, my brothers, in which your spirit seeks to speak in parables:

there is the source of your virtue.

There your body is raised and resurrected; with its delight it enchants the spirit, so that it becomes the creator and evaluator and lover and benefactor of all things.

When your heart flows broad and full like a river, a blessing and a danger to those who border it: there is the source of your virtue.

When you are above praise and blame, and your will wants to command all things, as a lover's will: there is the source of your virtue.

When you despise the pleasant, and the soft bed, and you cannot bed down far enough away from the soft ones: there is the source of your virtue.

When you willers are of one will, and this turnaround in need you treat as necessity: there is the source of your virtue.

Verily, a new good and evil it is! Verily, a new deep roaring and the voice of a new wellspring!

Power it is, this new virtue; a commanding thought it is, and around it, a wise soul: a golden sun, and around it, the serpent of knowledge.

2

Here Zarathustra paused for a while and looked lovingly upon his disciples.

Then he continued to speak thus — and his voice had changed.

Remain true to the earth, my brothers, with the power of your virtue! Let your bestowing love and your knowledge serve the meaning of the earth! Thus I beg and beseech you.

Do not let them fly away from earthly things and beat against eternal walls with their wings! Alas, there has always been so much flown-away virtue!

Lead the flown-away virtue back to earth, as I do — yes, back to life and limb: that it may give the earth its meaning, a human meaning!

A hundred times hitherto has spirit as well as virtue flown away and blundered.

Alas, all this false thinking and blundering dwells in our body to this day:

body and will it has become there.

A hundred times hitherto has spirit as well as virtue tried and erred. Yes, man has been an experiment. Alas, much ignorance and error has become flesh in us!

Not only the reason of millennia — the madness as well breaks out in us.

Dangerous it is to be an heir.

Still we fight step by step with the giant Chance; and nonsense, no-sense, has ruled over the whole of mankind even to this day.

Let your spirit and your virtue serve the meaning of the earth, my brothers:

and let the value of all things be set anew by you! Therefore you shall be fighters!

Therefore you shall be creators!

Through knowing, the body purifies itself; by experimenting with knowledge, the body elevates itself; to those who are in the know all drives sanctify themselves; to those who are elevated the soul becomes elated.

Physician, heal thyself: thus you help your patient, too. Let this be his best help, to see with his own eyes the one who heals himself.

There are a thousand paths that have never yet been trodden, a thousand kinds of health and secret islands of life. Man and man's world is still unexhausted and undiscovered.

Wake up and listen, you loners! From the future come wings with secret wing-beats; and good tidings are proclaimed to fine ears.

You loners of today, you separatists, you shall one day be a people: out of you who have chosen yourselves, a chosen people shall arise: — and out of them, the Superman.

Verily, the earth shall yet come to be a place of recovery! And already there is a new odor around it, one bringing health, — and a new hope!

3

When Zarathustra had said these words, he paused, like one who has not said his last word; for a long while he weighed the staff doubtfully in his hand. At last he spoke thus: and his voice had changed.

Now I go alone, my disciples! You too go away now, and alone! So I will it.

Verily, I advise you: go away from me and protect yourselves against Zarathustra.

And better yet: be ashamed of him! Perhaps he has deceived you.

The man of knowledge must not only love his enemies, he must also be able to hate his friends.

One repays a teacher badly if one always remains only a pupil. And why do you refuse to pluck at my wreath?

You revere me; but what if one day your reverence comes tumbling down?

Beware lest a statue slay you!

You say you believe in Zarathustra? But what does Zarathustra matter?

You are my believers: but what do all believers matter?

You had not yet sought yourselves: then you found me. Thus do all believers; therefore all belief means so little.

Now I bid you lose me and find yourselves; and only when you have all denied me will I return to you.

Verily, with different eyes, my brothers, will I then seek my lost ones; with a different love will I then love you.

And once again you shall be my friends and the children of one hope: then for the third time will I be with you, to celebrate the noontide with you.

And that is the great noontide when man stands in the middle of his path between animal and Superman and celebrates his passage to evening as his highest hope: for it is the way to a new morning.

That is when the one going under will bless himself for being one who is going across; and the sun of his knowledge will stand at noontide.

"Dead are all gods: now we want the Superman to live" — let this be our last will and testament one day, at the great noontide! —

Thus spake Zarathustra.

Part Two

"— and only when you have all denied me will I return to you.

Verily, with different eyes, my brothers, will I then seek my lost ones; with a different love will I then love you."

Zarathustra, On The Bestowing Virtue (Part One)

The Child With The Mirror

Then Zarathustra went back again into the mountains and to the solitude of his cave and avoided men, waiting like a sower who has sown his seed. But his soul became full of impatience and desire for those whom he loved: for he still had much to give them. This, you know, is the hardest thing: to close the open hand out of love, and to preserve one's modesty as a giver.

Thus months and years passed for the solitary one; his wisdom grew, however, and through its plenty caused him pain.

But one morning he awoke even before the rosy dawn, reflected long upon his bed, and said at last to his heart:

"But what frightened me so in my dream that I awoke? Did not a child appear before me, carrying a mirror?

'O Zarathustra' — the child said to me — 'look at yourself in the mirror!'

But when I looked in the mirror, I screamed and my heart was shaken: for I did not see myself there, but a devil's grimace and scornful laughter.

Verily, all too well I understand the dream's sign and warning: my teaching is in danger, tares want to be called wheat!

My enemies have become powerful and have distorted the image of my teaching, so that my dearest ones must blush for shame at the gifts I have given them.

My friends have been lost to me; the hour has come for me to seek my lost ones!" —

With these words Zarathustra sprang up, not like an anguished man seeking air, but rather like a seer and singer whom the spirit moves. His eagle and his serpent looked upon him in astonishment: for like the rosy dawn an approaching happiness had spread over his countenance.

But what has happened to me, my animals? — said Zarathustra. Am I not transformed? Has blissfulness not come to me like a storm wind?

Foolish is my happiness, and foolishness will it speak: it is still too young — so have patience with it!

I am wounded by my happiness: all who suffer shall be my physicians!

To my friends I can go down again, and to my enemies too! Zarathustra can speak and bestow again, and show love to the dearest again!

My impatient love overflows in torrents, downwards, towards the rising and setting sun. From silent mountains and thunderstorms of pain my soul rushes into the valleys.

Too long have I longed and looked into the distance. Too long have I belonged to solitude: so I have unlearned silence.

Out-and-out mouth have I become, and the surging of a brook out of high rocks: down into the valleys will I plunge my speech.

And may my stream of love plunge into the impassable! How could a stream not find its way to the sea eventually?

Surely there is a lake in me, a solitary, self-contained one; but my stream of love carries it down with it — to the sea!

New ways I go, a new speech comes to me; weary have I become, like all creators, of the old tongues. No longer will my spirit wander on worn-out soles.

Too slowly runs all speech for me: — storm, into your chariot I leap! And even you will I whip with my malice!

Like a cry and a shout for joy will I cross over wide seas, until I find The Blessed Isles, where my friends reside: —

And my enemies among them! How I now love anyone to whom I may simply speak! Even my enemies belong to my blissfulness.

And when I want to mount my wildest horse, it is always my spear that helps me up best: it is my foot's ever-ready servant: —

The spear which I hurl against my enemies! How thankful I am to my enemies for letting me hurl it at last!

The tension of my cloud has been too great: between the lightning's laughter I want to hurl hail showers into the deep.

Violently my breast will heave then, violently will it sound its fury over the mountains: so will its relief come.

Verily, like a storm my happiness comes, and my freedom! But my enemies shall believe that the foul fiend rages over their heads.

Yes, you too will be frightened, my friends, by my wild wisdom; and perhaps you will flee from it, together with my enemies.

Ah, if only I knew how to entice you back with pipes of Pan! Ah, if only my lioness Wisdom would learn to roar tenderly! And many things we have already learned together!

My wild Wisdom became pregnant on lonely mountains; on rough rock she brought forth her young, her youngest.

Now she runs foolishly through the harsh desert and searches and searches for soft turf — my old wild Wisdom!

On your hearts' soft turf, my friends! — on your love she would love to make her beloved's bed! —

Thus spake Zarathustra.

On The Blessed Isles

The figs fall from the trees, they are ripe and sweet; and as they fall their red skin splits open. A north wind am I to ripe figs.

Thus like figs, my friends, these teachings fall to you: now drink in their juice and their sweet flesh! Fall is all around and clear skies and afternoon.

Behold, what fullness is around us! And from out of plenty it is lovely to look out upon distant seas.

Once people said God, when they looked upon distant seas; now, however, I have taught you to say: Superman.

God is a conjecture; but I want your conjectures to reach no further than your creative will.

Could you create a God? — So be quiet then about all gods! But I daresay you could create the Superman.

Perhaps not you yourselves, my brothers! But into fathers and forefathers of the Superman you could re-create yourselves: and may this be your best creation!

—

God is a conjecture: but I want your conjectures to be confined to the conceivable.

Could you conceive a God? — But this the will to truth should mean to you, that all things will be transformed into the humanly conceivable, the humanly perceivable, and the humanly perceptible! Your own senses you shall consider to that end!

And that which you have called world shall be re-created by you alone:

your reason, your image, your will, your love it shall itself become! And verily, for your bliss, you knowing ones!

And how would you endure life without this hope, you knowing ones? Neither into the unconceivable nor into the unreasonable could you have been born.

But that I may open my heart entirely to you, my friends: if there were gods, how could

I endure it, not to be a god! Therefore there are no Gods.

Well did I draw the conclusion; but now it draws me. —

God is a conjecture: but who could drink in all the agony of this conjecture without dying? Should belief be taken from the creator and soaring at eagle-distances from the eagle?

God is a thought that makes everything straight crooked and everything that stands whirl. What? Should time be gone and all things transitory be but a lie?

To think this is giddiness and dizziness for human limbs, as well as an upchuck for the stomach: verily, the giddy sickness I call it, to conjecture like this.

Evil I call it and misanthropic: all this teaching about the one and the complete and the unmoved and the sufficient and the intransitory!

All the intransitory — that is only a parable! And the poets lie too much! —

But of time and becoming the best parables should speak: they should be a praise and a justification of all transitoriness!

Creation — that is the great salvation from suffering and the lightener of life. But that the creator may come to life, suffering itself is required, and much transformation.

Yes, much bitter dying must be in you life, you creators! Thus you are advocates and justifiers of all transitoriness.

For the creator himself to be the new-born child, he must also be willing to be the mother and the mother's pain.

Verily, through a hundred souls I have gone my way, and through a hundred cradles and birth pangs. Many a farewell I have already taken; I know the heartbreaking last hours.

But my creative will, my fate, wills it so. Or, to say it to you more frankly:

just such a fate — my will wills.

All feeling in me suffers and is in prison: but my willing always comes to me as my emancipator and messenger of joy.

Willing sets free: that is the true teaching of will and freedom — thus Zarathustra teaches it to you.

No more willing and no more valuing and no more creating! Oh, may that great weariness always remain far away from me!

In knowing as well I feel only my will's pleasure in begetting and becoming; and if there is innocence in my knowledge, then it is because the will to beget is in it.

Away from God and gods this will has enticed me; what would there be to create then, if gods — were there?

But always it drives me back again to men, my fervent creative will; thus the hammer is driven to the stone.

Alas, you men, an image sleeps in the stone for me, the image of my image!

Alas, that it must sleep in the hardest, homeliest stone!

Now my hammer rages cruelly against its prison. From the stone pieces scatter; what does that matter to me?

I want to complete it; for a shadow came to me — the stillest and lightest of all things once came to me!

The beauty of the Superman came to me as a shadow. Alas, my brothers! Of what regard to me now are — the gods? —

Thus spake Zarathustra.

On The Pitying Ones

My friends, a sarcastic remark has reached your friend: "Just look at Zarathustra!

Does he not wander among us as if among animals?"

But it is better said this way: "The knowing one wanders among men as among animals."

To the knowing one, though, man himself is: the animal that has red cheeks.

How did that happen to man? Is it not because he has had to be ashamed of himself too often?

O my friends! Thus speaks the knowing one: shame, shame, shame — that is the history of man!

And that is why the noble-minded man commands himself not to put to shame: shame he demands of himself before all who suffer.

Verily, I care not for the merciful, who are blessed in their pitying: they are too lacking in shame.

If I must be filled with pity, then I do not want to be called pity-full; and if I am filled with pity it is preferably at a distance.

Preferably too I cover my head and run away before I am recognized: and so I bid you do, my friends!

May my fate always lead those untouched by suffering, like you, across my path, and those with whom I may have hope and meal and honey in common.

Verily, I may have done this and that for those who suffer; but I always seemed to do better when I learned to enjoy myself better.

As long as there have been men, man has enjoyed himself too little: that alone, my brothers, is our original sin!

And when we learn to enjoy ourselves better, then we unlearn best how to cause others pain and contrive pain.

Therefore I wash the hand that has helped the sufferer; therefore I wipe clean my soul, also.

For to have seen the sufferer suffering made me ashamed on account of his shame; and when I helped him, I came down hard on his pride.

Great obligations do not make us grateful but vengeful; and if a small favor is not forgotten it gets to be a gnawing worm.

"Be reserved in accepting! Distinguish by accepting!" — Thus I advise those who have nothing to give away.

I, however, am a giver: gladly I give, as a friend to friends. Strangers and paupers, however, may pluck the fruit themselves from my tree: there is less shame that way.

But beggars should be abolished entirely! Verily, it is annoying to give to them and annoying not to give to them.

And the same goes for sinners and bad consciences! Believe me, my friends:

the bite of conscience teaches biting.

Small thoughts, however, are the worst thing. Verily, better even to have wrought evil than to have thought small!

True you say: "The delight in little acts of spite spares us from many a big bad deed." But here one should not want to be spared.

Like a boil is the evil deed: it itches and scratches and breaks out, — it speaks honestly.

"Behold, I am sickness" — thus speaks the evil deed; that is its honesty.

But the small thought is like a fungus: it crawls and cowers and wants to be nowhere at all — until the whole body is rotten and withered with little fungi.

But to him who is possessed by a devil, I whisper this word in his ear: "Better for you still to rear your devil! Even for you there is still a way to greatness!"

—

Alas, my brothers! One knows a little too much about everyone! And many a man becomes transparent to us, but we are still far from being able to penetrate him through and through.

It is hard to live with men because keeping silent is so hard. And not towards him who is contrary to us are we most unjust, but towards him who means nothing at all to us.

But if you have a suffering friend, then be a resting place for his suffering, but a hard bed as it were, a field bed: thus you will serve him best.

And if a friend does you ill, then say: "I forgive you for what you did to me; but that you did it to yourself, — how could I forgive that?"

Thus speaks all great love: it overcomes even forgiveness and pity.

A person should hold fast to his heart; for once he lets it go, how soon he loses his head!

Alas, where in the world have there been greater follies than among the pitying ones? And what in the world has caused more suffering than the follies of the pitying ones?

Woe unto all lovers who do not yet have a height that is above their pity!

Thus spoke the devil to me once: "Even God has his hell: it is his love for man."

And lately I heard him say this word: "God is dead; God has died of his pity for man." —

So be warned against pity: from there a heavy cloud shall yet come to man!

Verily, I understand weather signs.

But mark this word as well: all great love is above pity, for the beloved it still wants to — create!

"Myself I offer up to my love, and my neighbor as myself" — the speech of all creators runs thus.

All creators, however, are hard. —

Thus spake Zarathustra.

On Priests

And one day Zarathustra gave his disciples a sign and said these words to them:

"Here are priests: and although they are my enemies, pass by them quietly and with sleeping swords!

Even among them there are heroes; many of them have suffered too much:

so they want to make others suffer.

They are bad enemies: nothing is more vengeful than their humility. And he who touches them is easily defiled.

But my blood is related to theirs: and I want to know that my blood is honored even in theirs." —

And when they had passed by, Zarathustra was seized with pain; and not long had he wrestled with his pain when he began to speak thus:

I pity these priests. They offend my taste, too; but that is the least thing to me, since I am among men.

But I suffer and have suffered with them; to me they are prisoners and marked men. He whom they call Savior has put them in fetters. —

In fetters of false values and fanciful words! Ah, if only someone could save them from their Savior!

Once as the sea tossed them about they thought they had landed on an island; but behold, it was a sleeping monster!

False values and fanciful words: they are the worst monsters for mortals, —

fate sleeps long in them and waits.

But at last it comes and watches and gulps and engulfs what has built huts upon it.

O, just look at the huts these priests have built! Churches they call their sweetly-scented dens!

O, that falsified light, that mustified air! Here, where up to its height the soul — cannot fly!

But thus their belief commands: "Up the stairs on your knees, ye sinners!"

Verily, even the shameless I would rather see than the distorted eyes of their shame and devotion!

Who created for themselves such dens and penitence-stairs? Was it not those who wanted to hide themselves and were ashamed before the clear sky?

And only when the clear sky looks again through shattered roofs and down again upon grass and red poppies by shattered walls, — will I again turn my heart toward the dwellings of this God.

That which contradicted them and caused them pain they called God: and verily, there was much heroic character in their worship!

And they knew no other way to love their God than to nail men to the cross!

As corpses they thought to live, in black they draped their corpses; even in their speech I still smell the foul odor of burial chambers.

And he who lives near them lives near black pools out of which the toad, that prophet of evil, sings his song of sweet melancholy.

Better songs they would have to sing for me to learn to believe in their Redeemer: more redeemed his disciples would have to look for me!

Naked I would like to see them: for beauty alone should preach penitence.

But whom could this muffled misery persuade?

Verily, their redeemers themselves did not come from freedom and freedom's seventh heaven! Verily, they themselves never trod upon the carpets of knowledge!

The spirit of these redeemers consisted of gaps; but into each gap they had placed their false idea, their stopgap, which they called God.

Their spirit was drowned in their pity, and when they were swollen and over-swollen with pity, a great folly always swam on top.

Eagerly and with great noise they drove their herd over their footbridge; as if there were but one footbridge to the future! Verily, these shepherds themselves still belonged to the sheep!

Small spirits and spacious souls these shepherds had: but, my brothers, what small countries even the most spacious souls have been so far!

Signs of blood they wrote on the path they took, and their folly taught that truth is proved by blood.

But blood is the worst witness of truth; blood poisons even the purest teaching and turns it into delusion and hatred of the heart.

And if someone goes through fire for his teaching, — what does that prove?

Verily, it means more when out of your own fire your own teaching comes!

Sultry heart and cold head: where these two meet there arises the hothead, the "Savior."

Greater ones there have been, verily, and higher-born ones, than those whom the people call Saviors, those enchanted hotheads!

And by ones greater yet than all Saviors have been must you, my brothers, be saved, if you would find the way to freedom!

Never yet has there been a Superman. Naked have I seen them both, the greatest and the smallest man:

They are still all-too-similar to each other. Verily, even the greatest man I found — all-too-human! —

Thus spake Zarathustra.

On The Virtuous

With thunder and heavenly fireworks must one speak to slack and sleeping senses.

But the voice of beauty speaks softly: it steals only into the most awakened souls.

Softly my shield trembled and laughed today; that is the holy laughter and trembling of beauty.

At you, you virtuous ones, my beauty laughed today. And her voice came to me in this way: "They want as well — to be paid!"

You want to be paid as well, you virtuous ones! You want a reward for virtue and heaven for earth and evermore for your today?

And now you are angry with me because I teach that there is no rewarder and paymaster? And verily, I do not even teach that virtue is its own reward.

Alas, that is my sorrow: reward and penalty have been laid into the ground of things — and now even into the ground of your souls, you virtuous ones!

But like a boar's snout my word shall tear up the ground of your soul; a plowshare I shall be called by you.

All the secrets of your soil shall come to light; and when you lie uprooted and split asunder in the sun, your falsehood will be separated from your truth.

For this is your truth: you are too pure for the filth of the words: revenge, penalty, reward, recompense.

You love your virtue as a mother does her child; but when have you ever heard of a mother who wanted to be paid for her love?

It is the dearest thing itself to you, your virtue. The thirst of the ring is in you: to attain itself again, that is why every ring struggles and gyrates.

And like the dying star is every work of your virtue: its light is still ever on the way and traveling — and when will it no longer be on the way?

Thus the light of your virtue is still on the way, even when the work is done. Though it now be dead and forgotten: its ray of light still lives and travels.

That your virtue is your very self and not a foreign thing, a skin, a covering:

that is the truth from the bottom of your souls, you virtuous ones! —

But certainly there are those to whom virtue is the spasm under the lash:

and you have hearkened too much to their cries!

And there are others who call virtue the idle-izing of their vices; and if for once their hatred and jealousy stretch out their limbs for a rest, their "justice"

becomes lively and rubs its sleepy eyes.

And there are others who are drawn downwards: their demons draw them down. But the more they sink, the more glowingly gleams their eye and the desire for their God.

Alas, their cries have pierced your ears, too, you virtuous ones: "That which is not me, that to me is God and virtue!"

And there are others who come along, heavy and creaking, like carts carrying rocks downhill: they speak much of dignity and virtue, — their brakeshoe they call virtue!

And there are others who are like workaday clocks that have been wound up; they tick and they tock and want their ticktock to be called — virtue!

Verily, with these I have my fun: whenever I find such clocks, I wind them up with my mockery; and thereby they must purr for me!

And others are proud of their handful of justice and desecrate all things for its sake: thus the world is drowned in their injustice.

Alas, how amiss the word "virtue" issues from their mouths! And when they say: "I am just," it always sounds like: "I am just — revenged!"

With their virtue they want to scratch out the eyes of their enemies; and they elevate themselves only in order to denigrate others.

And again there are those who sit in their swamp and speak out from among the reeds: "Virtue — that is sitting still in the swamp.

We bite no one and avoid him who wants to bite; and in all things we have the opinion that is given us."

And again there are those who love gestures and think: virtue is a sort of gesture.

Their knees perpetually adore and their hands are eulogies to virtue, but their hearts know nothing about it.

And again there are those who hold it a virtue to say: "Virtue is necessary"; but deep down they only believe that the police are necessary.

And many a man who cannot see the sublime in man calls it virtue to see his baseness all-too-closely: thus he calls his evil eye virtue.

And some want to be built up and straightened up and call it virtue; and others want to be thrown down — and that too they call virtue.

And so nearly everyone believes he has his share of virtue; and at the very least each one expects to be an expert on good and evil.

But Zarathustra did not come to say all these liars and fools: "What do you know of virtue? What could you know of virtue?" —

But that you, my friends, might become weary of the old words you have learned from the fools and the liars:

Become weary of the words "reward," "recompense," "penalty," "just revenge" —

Become weary of saying: "That an action is good is because it is selfless."

Alas, my friends! That your self may be in your action, as the mother is in the child:

let that be your word of virtue!

Verily, I daresay I have taken away from you a hundred sayings and your virtues' dearest playthings; and now you are angry with me, the way children get angry.

They were playing by the sea, — then a wave came and swept their playthings into the deep: now they weep.

But the same wave shall bring them new playthings and pour out new colorful shells before them!

So they will be consoled; and like them, my friends, you too shall have your consolation — and new colorful shells! —

Thus spake Zarathustra.

On The Rabble

Life is a fountain of delight, but where the rabble also drinks all wells are poisoned.

To all things clean I am well-disposed; but I do not care to see the grinning mouths and the thirst of the unclean.

They cast their eye down into the well: now their nasty smile gleams out of the well upon me.

They have poisoned the holy water with their lechery; and when they called their filthy dreams pleasure, they also poisoned the words.

The flame is put off when they put their damp hearts to the fire; the spirit itself seethes and smokes when the rabble approaches the fire.

Sickly sweet and overmellow the fruit grows in their hand: their glance makes the fruit tree withered at the top and about to topple in the wind.

And many a man who turned away from life only turned way from the rabble:

he refused to share fruit and flame and fountain with the rabble.

And many a man who went into the desert and suffered thirst with beasts of prey only refused to sit around the cistern with filthy camel drivers.

And many a man who came along like an annihilator and like a hailstorm to all fruited plains wanted plain and simple to jam his foot down the rabble's throat and stuff its mouth.

And that is not the mouthful which stuck in my throat the most, to know that life itself requires enmity and dying and torture-crosses: —

But I once asked and almost choked on the question: what? does life also find rabble necessary?

Are poisoned wells necessary and stinking fires and sullied dreams and maggots in the bread of life?

Not my hatred but my nausea gnawed hungrily at my life! Alas, I grew weary in spirit when I found even the rabble spirited!

And I turned my back on the ruling class when I saw what they call ruling:

bartering and bargaining for power — with the rabble!

Among men of a foreign tongue I lived, with stopped-up ears: that their bartering tongue might remain foreign to me and their bargaining for power.

And holding my nose, I walked morosely through all yesterday and today:

verily, all yesterday and today reeks from the writing rabble!

Like a cripple who has gone deaf and dumb and blind: thus I lived a long time, so as not to live with power- and pleasure- and writing rabble.

Laboriously my spirit climbed the stairs, and warily; alms of delight were its refreshment; life crawled along on a walking stick for the blind.

But what happened to me? How did I free myself from nausea? Who rejuvenated my sight? How did I fly to the height where rabble no longer sit at the well? Did my nausea itself create wings for me and spring-divining powers? Verily, to the summit I had to fly to find again the fountain of delight!

Oh, I found it, my brothers! Here at the summit the fountain of delight gushes forth for me! And it is a life in which no rabble can join in and drink!

Almost too furiously you flow for me, spring of delight! And often in wanting to fill it you empty the cup again!

And I must still learn to approach you more demurely: all-too-furiously my heart still flows toward you: —

My heart, upon which my summer burns, short, hot, melancholy, overhappy:

how my summer heart yearns for your coolness!

Gone; the lingering misery of my spring! Gone, the malice of my snowflakes in June! Summer have I become entirely, and summer-noon!

A summer at the summit with cold springs and blissful stillness: O come, my friends, that the stillness may be more blissful still!

For this is our height and our home: here we live too high and steep for the unclean and their thirst!

You friends, just cast your pure eyes into the fountain of my delight! How could it be troubled over that? It shall laugh back at you with its purity.

On the tree Future we build our nest; eagles shall bring us loners food in their beaks!

Verily, no food which the unclean could join in and eat! They would think they were feeding on fire and would burn their mouths!

Verily, no homesteads do we keep ready here for the unclean! An ice-lair our happiness would be to their bodies and to their spirits!

And like strong winds we want to live above them, neighbors to eagles, neighbors to snow, neighbors to the sun: thus do strong winds live.

And like a wind I will one day yet blow among them and take away the breath of their spirit with my spirit: thus my future wills it.

Verily, a strong wind is Zarathustra to all the lower ranks; and with such counsel he counsels his foes and all those who spit and spew: "Beware of spitting against the wind!" —

Thus spake Zarathustra.

On The Tarantulas

Behold, it is the tarantula hole! Do you want to see the tarantula itself? Here hangs its web: touch it, so that it begins to tremble.

Here it comes willingly: welcome, tarantula! Black on your back sits your triangle and token; and I know also what sits in your soul.

Vengeance sits in your soul: wherever you bite, a black scab grows; your venom makes the soul giddy with vengeance!

Thus I speak to you in parable, you who make souls giddy, you preachers of equality! Tarantulas you are to me and hidden seekers of vengeance!

But I will yet bring your hideaways to light: that is why I laugh my laughter of the heights in your face.

That is why I tear at your web, that your fury may lure you out of your hole of lies and your vengeance may jump out from behind your word "justice."

For that man be redeemed from revenge: that to me is the bridge to the highest hope and a rainbow after long storms.

But the tarantulas would have it otherwise, of course. "Precisely this we call justice, that the world be fraught with the storms of our vengeance" — thus they speak to one another.

"Vengeance and insult we shall wreak on all who are not our equals" —

thus the tarantula-hearts pledge to themselves.

"And 'will to equality' — henceforth that itself shall be the name for virtue; and against all things with power we will set up a howl!"

You preachers of equality, the tyrant-frenzy of impotence cries out of you thus for "equality": your most secret tyrant-desires disguise themselves thus in words of virtue!

Careworn arrogance, pent-up envy — your father's arrogance and envy perhaps:

that breaks out in you as the flame and frenzy of revenge.

What was mute in the father comes to speech in the son; and often I found the son to be the father's secret laid bare.

Inspired ones they resemble: and yet it is not the heart which inspires them, — but revenge. And when they become subtle and cold, it is not spirit but envy which makes them subtle and cold.

Their envy leads them also down the thinker's path; and this is the mark of their envy — they always go too far: so that at last their weariness has to lay down to sleep on the snow.

Vengeance sounds in their every complaint, there is painmaking in all their praisemaking; and to be judge they judge to be bliss.

But thus I advise you, my friends: mistrust all in whom the impulse to punish is powerful!

They are people of poor kind and breed; out of their faces peer the hangman and the bloodhound.

Mistrust all those who talk much of their justice! Verily, their souls lack not only honey.

And when they call themselves "the good and the just," do not forget that for them to be Pharisees nothing is lacking except — power!

My friends, I will not be confounded and confused with anyone else.

There are those who preach my doctrine: and at the same time they are preachers of equality and tarantulas.

That they speak in favor of life, although they sit in their holes turned away from life, these venomous spiders: this is because they want to cause pain.

They want to cause pain to those now in power: for it is with these that the preaching of death is still most at home.

If it were otherwise, the tarantulas would teach otherwise; and precisely they were formerly the best world-slanderers and heretic-burners.

With these preachers of equality I will not be confounded and confused.

For thus justice speaks to me: "Men are not equal."

And they shall not become so either! What would my love for the Superman be if I spoke otherwise?

On a thousand bridges and foot-paths they shall push towards the future, and more and more war and inequality shall be set amongst them: thus my great love makes me speak!

In their hostilities they shall become inventors of figures and phantoms, and with their figures and phantoms they shall yet fight the highest fight against each other!

Good and evil and rich and poor and high and low and all the names of values:

arms they shall be, and clashing signs, that life must overcome itself time after time!

Upward it wants to build itself with pillars and stairs, this very life: into vast distances it wants to look and out toward blissful areas of beauty, — that is why it requires height!

And because it requires height, it requires stairs and variance amongst climbers and stairs! Life wants to climb and in climbing to overcome itself!

And just look, my friends! Here where the tarantula's hole is, the ruins of an old temple rise upward, — just look with enlightened eyes!

Verily, like the wisest of men, he who once piled his thoughts upward in stone here knew the secret of all life.

That in beauty too there is struggle and inequality, and a war for power and superiority: that he teaches us here in the clearest allegory.

How divinely vault and arch are refracted here in a wrestling match: how with light and shade they strive against each other, the strivers divine —

Let us also be enemies so sure and fine, my friends! Divinely we will strive against each other! —

Woe! Then my old enemy, the tarantula, bit me! Divinely sure and fine it bit me on the finger!

"Punishment and justice there must be" — thus it thinks: "not for nothing shall he sing songs here in honor of hostility!"

Indeed, it has revenged itself! And woe! now it will make my soul giddy with vengeance also!

But so I do not whirl, my friends, bind me fast here to this pillar! I would still rather be a pillar-saint than a whirl of vengefulness!

Verily, no twirl- and whirlwind is Zarathustra; and if he is a dancer, certainly never a tarantella dancer! —

Thus spake Zarathustra.

On The Famous Wise Men

The people you have served and the people's superstition, all you famous wise men! — and not the truth! And that is precisely why they paid you reverence.

And that is also why they put up with your impiety, because to the people it was a joke and a by-way. Thus the master indulges his slaves and even takes delight in their high jinks.

But he who is hated by the people is as a wolf to the dogs: that is the free spirit, the foe of fetters, the non-adorer, the forest dweller.

To chase him from his lair — the people always called that "a sense of propriety":

against him they always set their sharpest-toothed dogs.

For "the truth is there: so there the people are! Woe, woe to those who seek!": thus it has resounded down the ages. You wanted to do right by the people in their veneration: you called that: "Will to truth," you famous wise men!

And your heart always said to itself: "I have come from the people: from there as well the voice of God has come to me."

Stiff-necked and clever, like the ass, were you ever as the people's advocate.

And many a mighty one who wanted to fare well with the people also harnessed in front of his charger — a little ass, a famous wise man.

And now I wish that you, you famous wise men, would finally throw off entirely your lion's skin!

The skin of the beast of prey, the mottled one, and the shaggy locks of the searching, researching, conquering one!

Alas, for me to learn to believe in your "truthfulness" you would first have to shatter your revering will.

Truthful — thus I call him who goes into godless deserts and has his revering heart shattered.

In the yellow sands and burned by the sun, he squints thirstily indeed for spring-abounding islands, where living things rest under dark trees.

But his thirst does not persuade him to become like these which are at ease; for where there are oases, there are also idols.

Hungry, violent, solitary, godless: thus the lion-will wills itself.

Free from the happiness of slaves, freed from gods and adoration, fearless and fearsome, great and solitary: such is the will of the truthful.

From time immemorial the truthful, the free spirits, have dwelt in the desert, as lords of the desert; in the cities, however, dwell the well-fed famous wise men, — the draft animals.

For they always draw, as asses — the people's cart!

Not that I am angry with them over that: but to me they remain in service and in harness, even when they glitter with golden trappings.

And they have often been good servants and praiseworthy. For thus speaks virtue: "If you must be a servant, then seek him whom your service best serves!

The spirit and the virtue of your master shall grow by virtue of your being his servant: so you yourself shall grow with his spirit and virtue!"

And verily, you famous wise men, you servants of the people! You yourselves have grown with the people's spirit and virtue — and the people through you! In your honor I say that!

But people you remain to me, even in your virtues, people with feeble eyes, — people who cannot shake a spear at spirit!

Spirit is the life which itself cuts into life: with its own agony it increases its own knowledge, — did you know that already?

And the spirit's happiness is this: to be anointed and consecrated with tears as a sacrificial animal, — did you know that already?

And the blind man's blindness and his searching and groping shall yet testify to the power of the sun into which he has looked, — did you know that already?

And with mountains the knowing one shall learn to build! That the spirit moves mountains means little, — did you know that already?

You know only the spirit's sparks: but you do not see the anvil that it is and the cruelty of its hammer!

Verily, you know not the pride of the spirit! But still less could you endure the modesty of the spirit if ever it wanted to speak!

And never yet have you dared to cast your spirit into a pit of snow: you are not hot enough for that! So you also do not know the delights of its cold.

But in all things you are too familiar with the spirit; and you have often made a poorhouse and a hospital for bad poets out of wisdom.

You are not eagles: so you have also never experienced the happiness of the terror of the spirit. And he who is not a bird should not nest above abysses.

Lukewarm ones you seem to me: but all deep knowledge flows cold. Icecold are the innermost springs of the spirit: a refreshment for hot hands and handlers.

Stiff and honorable you stand there, and with backs straight, you famous wise men! —

no strong wind and will drives you.

Have you never seen a sail going across the sea, rounded and distended and trembling from the violence of the wind?

Like a sail, trembling from the violence of the wind, my Wisdom goes across the sea — my wild Wisdom!

But you servants of the people, you famous wise men, — how could you go with me? —

Thus spake Zarathustra.

The Night Song

It is night: now all gushing fountains speak louder. And my soul too is a gushing fountain.

It is night: only now do all lovers' songs awake. And my soul too is the song of a lover.

Something unappeased, unappeasable is within me; it wants to be heard. A craving for love is within me which itself speaks the language of love.

Light am I: ah, to be night! But this is my loneliness, to be girded with light.

Ah, to be dark and nightly! How I would suck on the breasts of the light!

And even you would I bless, you twinkling little stars and glowworms up above! — and be blessed by your gifts of light.

But I live in my own light, I take back into me the flames that break out of me.

I know not the happiness of the receiver; and often have I dreamed that stealing must be even more blessed than receiving.

This is my poverty, that my hand never rests from giving; this is my envy, that I see waiting eyes and the illuminated nights of longing.

O, the unhappiness of all givers! O, eclipse of my sun! O, craving to crave! O, ravenous appetite in satiety!

They take from me: but do I ever touch their souls? There is a cleft between giving and receiving; and the smallest cleft is the last to be spanned.

A hunger grows out of my beauty: I would like to hurt those for whom I shine, I would like to rob those whose gifts were mine: thus I hunger after malice.

Drawing back the hand when a hand is already stretched out for it; hesitating like the waterfall, which hesitates even in its sudden plunge: thus I hunger after malice.

Such vengeance my abundance thinks up: such maliciousness wells up out of my loneliness.

My happiness in giving died in giving, my virtue grew weary of itself by virtue of its excess!

The danger for him who always gives is that he will lose his shame; the hand and heart of him who always dispenses has calluses from nothing but dispensing.

My eye no longer overflows over the shame of the supplicant; my hand has grown too hard for the trembling of filled hands.

Where have the tears in my eyes gone, and the bloom in my heart? O, the loneliness of all givers! O, the quietness of all light-givers!

Many suns revolve in desolate space: to all that is dark they speak with their light, — to me they are silent.

O, this is the light's enmity toward the giver of light: mercilessly it travels its course.

Unjust toward the giver of light in its heart of hearts, cold toward other suns — thus every sun travels.

Like a storm the suns fly along their course, that is their travel. Their inexorable will they follow, that is their coldness.

Oh, it is only you, you dark ones, you nocturnal ones, who create your warmth from the giver of light! Oh, only you drink milk and comfort from the udders of the light!

Alas, ice is around me, my hand burns itself on the icy! Alas, a thirst is in me that yearns for your thirst!

It is night: alas that I must be light! And have a thirst for the nightly! And loneliness!

It is night: now my longing bursts out of me like a fountain, — for speech I long.

It is night: now all gushing fountains speak louder. And my soul too is a gushing fountain.

It is night: only now do all lovers' songs awake. And my soul too is the song of a lover. —

Thus sang Zarathustra.

The Dance Song

One evening Zarathustra went with his disciples through the forest; and as he searched for a well, behold, he came upon a green meadow, quietly surrounded by trees and herbs: upon it maidens were dancing with each other. As soon as the maidens recognized Zarathustra, they stopped dancing; but Zarathustra stepped up to them with a friendly air and said these words:

"Don't stop dancing, you lovely maidens! No killjoy has come to give you the evil eye, no maiden-foe.

God's advocate am I before the devil; he, however, is the spirit of gravity.

How could I, you light things, be a foe of divine dancing? Or of maiden feet with beautiful ankles?

To be sure I am a forest and a night of dark trees: but he who is not afraid of my darkness will also find slopes of roses under my cypresses.

And he will also probably find the little god who is dearest to the maidens:

near the spring he lies, quietly, with closed eyes.

Verily, in broad daylight he fell asleep, the lazybones! Maybe he chased too long after butterflies?

Do not be angry with me, you beautiful dancers, if I scold the little god a little!

He will cry out, no doubt, and weep, — but he is a scream even when he weeps!

And with tears in his eyes he shall ask you for a dance; and I myself will sing a song to accompany his dance:

A dancing and mocking song on the spirit of gravity, my all-supreme most high and mighty devil, who is said to be "the master of the world." – And this is the song that Zarathustra sang when Cupid and the maidens danced together:

Into your eyes I looked lately, O Life! And into the unfathomable I then seemed to sink.

But you pulled me out with a golden fishing rod; scornfully you laughed when I called you unfathomable.

"Such is the speech of all fish," you said; "what they cannot fathom is unfathomable.

But I am only fickle and wild and in all things a woman, and not a virtuous one either:

Although you men call me 'the deep one' or 'the true one,' 'the eternal one,'

'the mysterious one'!

But you men always present us with your own virtues — ah, you virtuous men!"

Thus she laughed, the unbelievable one; but I never believe her and her laughter when she speaks ill of herself.

And as I talked confidentially with my wild Wisdom, she said to me angrily: "You want, you crave, you love, that alone is why you praise Life!"

Then I almost answered maliciously and told the angry one the truth; and you cannot answer more maliciously than to "tell the truth" to your Wisdom.

So that is how it stands amongst the three of us. Deep down I love only Life — and most of all, verily, when I hate her!

But that I am well-disposed towards Wisdom and often too well: that is because she reminds me so very much of Life!

She has her eyes, her laugh, and her little golden fishing rod: what can I do if they are both so alike?

And when Life asked me once: "Who then is this Wisdom?" — I said warmly, "Ah, yes! Wisdom!

One thirsts for her and is never satisfied, one looks through veils, one snatches through nets.

Is she beautiful? How should I know? But the oldest carp are still lured by her.

Fickle is she and defiant; often have I seen her bite her lip and comb her hair against the grain.

Perhaps she is wicked and false and in all things a female; but when she speaks badly of herself, precisely then she is most alluring."

When I said this to Life, she laughed spitefully and closed her eyes. "Of whom do you speak?" she said, "Of me, I presume?

And granted that you were right, — to say it to my face like that! But now at least speak of your Wisdom too!"

Ah, and now you have opened your eyes again, O beloved Life! And into the unfathomable have I again seemed to sink. – Thus sang Zarathustra. But when the dance was over and the maidens had gone away, he became sad.

"The sun has long since set," he said at last. "The meadow is damp, a coolness comes this way from the woods.

An unknown presence is around me and looks on pensively. What! You still live, Zarathustra?

Why? Wherefore? Whereby? Whereto? Where? How?

Is it not folly to still live?

Alas, my friends, it is the evening which inquires of me so. Forgive me my sadness!

Evening has come: forgive me that evening has come!"

Thus spake Zarathustra.

The Grave Song

"There is the grave-isle, the silent isle; there too are the graves of my youth.

I will carry an evergreen wreath of life there."

Resolving thus in my heart, I sailed across the sea. —

O, you sights and visions of my youth! O, all you glimpses of love, you divine moments! How did you die so quickly on me? I think of you today as my dead.

From you, my dearest departed, a sweet scent comes to me, heart-loosening and tear-inducing. Verily, it shakes and loosens the heart of the lonely seafarer.

Still I am the one who is richest and most to be envied — I the loneliest one!

For I have had you and you still have me: tell me, to whom, like me, have such rose-apples fallen from the tree?

I am still the earth and heir of your love, flourishing in your memory with many-hued, wild-growing virtues, O you most-beloved ones!

O, we were made to remain close to each other, you sweet strange wonders; and not like shy birds did you come to me and my desire — no, as trusting ones to the trusting one!

Yes, made for fidelity, like me, and for tender eternities: now I must call you out on your infidelity, your divine winks and blinks: no other names have I learned yet.

Verily, too quickly you died on me, you refugees. But you did not flee from me, nor did I flee from you: innocent are we in our infidelity to each other.

To kill me they strangled you, you songbirds of my hopes! Yes, at you, you dearest ones, malice has always shot its arrows — to hit my heart!

And they hit home! But you were always dearest to me, my possession and my being-possessed: therefore you had to die young and all-too-early!

They shot their shafts at the most vulnerable spot I had: that was you, whose skin is like down and even more like the smile that perishes at a glance!

But this word I want to say to my enemies: what is all man-slaughtering compared with what you did to me?

What you did to me is worse than all manslaughter; the irretrievable you took from me: — thus I speak to you, my enemies!

Why, you slew the sights and dearest wonders of my youth! My playmates you took from me, the blessed spirits! In their memory I lay down this wreath and this curse.

This curse upon you, my enemies! For surely you cut short my eternity, like a sound that breaks off on a cold night! It hardly came to me, like the blink of a divine eye, — like a wink!

Once upon a pleasant hour my purity spoke thus: "All living things shall be divine to me."

Then you attacked me with filthy phantoms; alas, where has that pleasant hour now flown?

"All days shall be holy to me " — thus the wisdom of my youth spoke once upon a time: verily, a speech of joyful wisdom!

But then you enemies stole my nights from me and sold them into sleepless agony: alas, where has that joyful wisdom now flown?

Once I longed for happy bird-signs; then you led an owl-monster across my path, an adverse sign. Alas, where did my tender longing fly then?

Once I vowed to renounce all disgust: then you changed my near and nearest into abscessed pus. Alas, where did my noblest vow fly then?

As a blind man I once walked blessed paths: then you threw filth on the blind man's path: and now the old blind-footpath disgusts him.

And when I did the hardest thing and celebrated the victory of my overcomings:

then you made those who loved me cry that I had caused them the most woe.

Verily, that was always your doing: you embittered for me my best honey and the industry of my best bees.

To my generosity you always sent the freshest beggars; around my pity you always pressed the incurably shameless. Thus you wounded my virtue in its faith.

And when I laid down even my holiest of offerings: at once your "piety"

placed its fatter gifts beside it: so that in the fumes of your fat even my holiest offering suffocated.

And once I wanted to dance as I had never yet danced; way up above all the heavens I wanted to dance. Then you won over my favorite minstrel.

And then he struck up a dreadful, dull tune; alas, like a gloomy horn he tooted in my ears.

Murderous minstrel, instrument of malice, most innocent man! There I stood, ready for the best dance: then you murdered my rapture with your rat-atat- tat!

Only in the dance do I know how to speak the parable of the highest things:

— and now my highest parable has remained unspoken in my limbs!

My highest hope has remained unspoken and unredeemed! And it has killed for me all the visions and consolations of my youth!

But just how did I endure it? How did I recover from and overcome such wounds? How did my soul rise again from these graves?

Well, an invulnerable, unburiable thing is in me, a rockblaster: it is called my will. Silently it strides and unaltered through the years.

Its walk it wants to walk, upon my feet, my old will; hard of heart its mentality is and invulnerable.

Invulnerable am I only in the heel. Ever have you dwelt there, the same as ever, most patient one! Ever have you broken through all graves!

In you still dwells the unredeemed what-not of my youth; and as life and youth you sit here hoping on yellow grave-ruins.

Yes, to me you are still the one who lays all graves to ruin: Hail to you, my will! And only where there are graves are there resurrections. —

Thus sang Zarathustra.

On Self-Overcoming

"Will to truth" you call it, you wisest ones, that which drives you and makes you feel alive?

Will to the conceivability of all beings: thus I call your will!

All being you want to first make conceivable: for you doubt with a healthy mistrust whether it is even conceivable.

But it shall bow and bend itself to you! Thus your will wills it. Smooth it shall become and subject to the spirit as its mirror and reflection.

That is your whole will, you wisest ones, as a will to power; and likewise when you speak of good and evil and evaluations.

You still want to create a world before which you can kneel: thus it is your ultimate hope and intoxication.

The unwise, I admit, the people, — they are like a river upon which a boat floats along: and on the boat sit the evaluations, solemn and disguised.

Your will and your values you have placed on the river of becoming; to me it betrays an ancient will to power which was believed by the people to be good and evil.

It was you, you wisest ones, who placed such guests on this boat and lent them pomp and proud names, — you and your ruling will!

Further the river now carries your boat; it must carry it. It matters little whether the broken wave foams and angrily opposes the keel!

The river is not your danger nor the end of your good and evil, you wisest ones: but that will itself, the will to power, — the unexhausted, teeming lifewill.

But in order that you may understand my word about good and evil, I also want to say a word about life and the nature of all things living.

After the living thing I went, down the greatest and the least of paths I went in order to discern its nature.

With a hundredfold mirror I even caught its glance when its mouth was closed: that its eye might speak to me. And its eye spoke to me.

But wherever I found living things, there I also heard the speech on obedience.

Every living thing is obedient.

And this is the second thing: whatever cannot obey itself will be commanded.

Such is the nature of living things.

But this is the third thing I heard: that commanding is harder than obeying.

And not only because whatever commands bears the burden of all that obeys and that this burden can easily crush it: —

Trial and risk there seemed to me to be in all commanding; and whenever it commands, the living thing runs a risk.

Yes, even when it commands itself: even then it must make amends for its commands. Judge and avenger and victim of its own law it must become.

But how does this come to pass? — thus I asked myself. What persuades the living thing to obey and command and even in commanding to practice obedience?

Now hear my word, you wisest ones! Test seriously whether I have stolen into the heart of life itself and right down to the roots of its heart!

Wherever I found a living thing, there I found the will to power; and even in the will of the servant I found the will to be master.

Persuaded by his will that the weaker should serve the stronger, he wants to be master over those weaker still; this pleasure alone he will not forego.

And as the lesser surrenders itself to the greater, to have pleasure and power over the least: so too the greatest surrenders itself and for the sake of power stakes — life thereon.

This is the surrender of the greatest, to be risk and danger and a roll of the dice with regard to death.

And where sacrifice and service and amorous looks exist: there too the will to be master exists. On secret paths the weaker steals into the stronghold of the stronger and right into the heart of the more powerful — and there steals power.

And this secret life itself told me: "Behold," it said, "I am that which must always overcome itself.

Of course you call it will to procreation or impetus toward a goal, toward the higher, the further, the more manifold: but all that is one and one secret.

I would rather go to my downfall than to renounce this one thing; and verily, where there is downfall and leaves falling down, behold, there life sacrifices itself — for power!

That I must be struggle and becoming and goal and going against goals:

alas, whoever divines my will can also divine well on what crooked paths it must travel.

Whatever I create and however I love it, — soon I must be an adversary to it and to my love: thus my will wills it.

And even you, knowing one, are only a path and footstep of my will: verily, my will to power wanders even on the feet of your will to truth!

He certainly did not hit the truth, he who shot at it with the term "will to existence": that will — does not exist!

For what does not exist cannot will; what is in existence, however, how could that still have a will into existence?

Only where there is life is there also will: not will to life, however; but — so I teach you — will to power!

Many things are valued more highly by the living than life itself; out of the valuing itself, however, speaks — the will to power!"

Thus life taught me once: and out of this I shall yet solve the riddle of your hearts, you wisest ones.

Verily, I say unto you: a good and evil that would be everlasting — that does not exist! Of itself it must overcome itself again and again.

With your values and words of good and evil you exercise your power, you evaluators; and this is your secret love and the glistening, trembling, and overflowing of your souls.

But a stronger power springs up out of your values, and a new overcoming:

egg and eggshell is shattered on it.

And he who must be a creator in good and evil: verily, he must first be a destroyer and shatter values.

Thus the highest evil belongs to the highest good: that, however, is the creative.

—

Let's just talk about this, you wisest ones, although it is bad. Silence is worse; all suppressed truths become poisonous.

And may all be shattered by our truths which — can be! There is still many a house to build!

Thus spake Zarathustra.

On The Sublime Ones

Calm is the bottom of my sea: who would ever guess that it holds droll monsters?

Immovable is my depth: but it sparkles with swimming riddles and laughter.

A sublime one I saw today, a solemn one, a penitent of the spirit: O, how my soul laughed at his ugliness!

With upraised breast and like those who suck in their breath: thus he stood there, and silent, the sublime one:

Draped with ugly truths, the spoils of his chase, and rich in torn raiment; many thorns adorned him as well — but no rose as yet did I see.

Not yet has he learned laughter and beauty. Gloomy has this hunter returned from the forest of knowledge.

He returned home from the struggle with wild beasts; but out of his seriousness a wild beast still peers — an unvanquished one!

Like a tiger he still stands there, ready to spring; but I do not care for these high-strung souls; to all who are drawn back taut my taste is ill-disposed.

And you say to me, friends, that there is no disputing taste and tasting? But all life is a dispute over taste and tasting!

Taste: that is weight and scale and weigher at the same time; and woe to all the living that would live without dispute and weight and scale and weighers!

If he would grow weary of his sublimity, this sublime one: only then would his beauty begin, — and only then will I taste him and find him tasty.

And only when he turns away from himself will he leap over his own shadow — and verily! into his sun.

All-too-long he sat in the shade, the cheeks of this penitent of the spirit turned pale; he almost starved on his expectations.

Contempt is still in his eye; and disgust lurks in his mouth. It is true that he rests now, but his rest has not yet lain out in the sun.

He should be like a bull; and his happiness should smell of the earth and not of contempt for the earth.

Like a white bull I want to see him, walking before the plowshare, snorting and bellowing; and his bellowing too should praise all things earthly!

His visage is still dark; the shadow of a hand plays upon it. His sense of vision is still overshadowed.

His deed itself is the shadow that is still upon him: the hand darkens the handler. He still has not overcome his deed.

Indeed I love the bull's neck on him: but now I still want to see the eyes of an angel.

He must still as well forget his heroic will: a lifted one he shall be, and not just a lofty one: — the ether itself shall lift him up, the will-forsaken one!

He vanquished monsters, he solved riddles; but still he should redeem his monsters and riddles, still he should change them into heavenly children.

Not yet has his knowledge learned to smile and to exist without jealousy; not yet has his streaming passion grown calm in beauty!

Verily, not in satiety shall his longing plunge and become silent, but in beauty! Grace belongs to the greatness of mind of the high-minded!

With his arm laid across his head: so the hero should rest, so he should also overcome his rest.

But precisely for the hero the beautiful is the hardest thing of all. The beautiful is unattainable by all violent wills.

A little more, a little less: that precisely is much here, that is the most here.

To stand with relaxed muscles and unharnessed will: that is the hardest thing for all of you, you sublime ones!

When power becomes gracious and descends to the visible: such descent I call beauty.

And from no one do I want beauty so precisely as I do from you, you man of power: may your goodness be your final self-conquest.

I believe you capable of any evil: therefore I demand goodness from you.

Verily, I have laughed often at the weaklings who believe themselves good because they have lame paws!

You should strive for the virtue of the pillar: the higher it rises, the ever finer and fairer, but internally harder and sturdier it becomes.

Yes, you sublime one, one day yet you shall be beautiful and hold your own beauty up to the mirror.

Then your soul will shudder with godly desires; and there will be worship even in your vanity!

For this is the secret of the soul: only when the hero has forsaken it is it approached in a dream, — by the superhero. —

Thus spake Zarathustra.

On The Land Of Culture

I flew too far into the future: horror seized me.

And when I looked around me, behold! time was my sole contemporary.

Then I flew backwards, homewards — and ever more hurriedly: thus I came to you, you present-day men, and into the land of culture.

For once I came with an eye for you and a goodly desire: verily, with longing in my heart I came.

But what happened to me? Even though I was so afraid, — I had to laugh!

Never had my eye beheld anything so mottled.

I laughed and laughed, while my foot still trembled and my heart as well:

"Here is certainly the home of all paintpots!" — I said.

With fifty blotches painted on your face and limbs: thus you sat there to my astonishment, you present-day men!

And with fifty mirrors around you which flattered and imitated the play of your colors!

Verily, there is absolutely no better mask you could wear, you present-day men, than your own faces! Who could — recognize you?

Written all over with the characters of the past, and these characters painted over with new characters as well: thus you have hidden yourselves well from all character interpreters.

And even if one were a tester of the reins: who would ever believe you had reins? Out of hues you seem to be baked and out of glued pieces of paper.

All ages and peoples look motley on account of your veils; all customs and beliefs speak motley on account of your gestures.

He who stripped you of veils and wrappings and hues and gestures: he would have just enough left over to scare the birds with.

Verily, I myself am the scared bird who once saw you naked and unpainted; and I flew away when the skeleton beckoned to me lovingly.

Rather would I be a day-laborer in Hades and among the shades of old!

Even the shades of Hades are fatter and fuller than you!

This indeed, is bitterness to my bowels, that neither naked nor clothed can I stand you, you present-day men!

Everything sinister in the future and whatever makes stray birds shudder is truly still more comfy and cosy than your "reality."

For so you speak: "Real are we completely, without beliefs and superstitions":

thus you plume yourselves — ah, still without plumes!

Indeed, how could you know how to believe, you mottled ones! — you who are walking refutations of belief itself and a discombobulation of all thought.

Unworthy of belief: that is what I call you, you real-ists!

All ages prate against each other in your spirits: and the dreams and pratings of all ages were still more real than your waking state is!

Unfruitful you are: therefore you lack belief. But he who must create has also always had his vatic dreams and astral signs — and has believed in belief!

Half-open gates you are, at which gravediggers wait. And this is your reality:

"Everything deserves to perish."

Alas, how you stand there before me, you unfruitful ones, how lean in the ribs! And many of you have undoubtedly made allowances for this.

And you have said: "No doubt a god stole something from me on the sly while I was sleeping. Enough, verily, to form himself a little female out of it!

"Marvelous is the poverty of my ribs!" — thus many of you present-day men have already said.

Yes, you make me laugh, you present-day men! And especially when you marvel over yourselves!

And woe unto me if I could not laugh at your marvelling and had to drink down everything adverse in your cups!

So I will make lighter of you, since I have something heavy to carry; and what is it to me if beetles and winged mites also alight on my bundle!

Verily, it shall not be heavier on me! And not from you, you present-day men, shall the great weariness come upon me. —

Alas, where shall I climb now with my longing? From every mountain I look out for father- and mother-lands.

But nowhere have I found a home; restless I feel in every city and ready to leave by every gate.

Alien to me and a mockery are the present-day men, to whom my heart was recently impelled; and expelled am I from father- and mother-lands.

So now I love only my children's land, the undiscovered land, in the most distant sea: towards it I command my sails to seek and seek.

In my children will I make amends for having been the child of my fathers:

and in all the future — for this present! —

Thus spake Zarathustra.

On Immaculate Perception

Yesterday as the moon arose, I fancied she was ready to give birth to a sun:

so broad and pregnant she lay on the horizon.

But she was a liar to me with her pregnancy; and I would sooner believe in the man in the moon than in the woman.

Certainly, he is not much of a man either, this timid night-wanderer. Verily, with a bad conscience he wanders over roofs.

For he is covetous and envious, the monk in the moon, covetous of the earth and of all lovers' delights.

No, I do not like him, this tomcat on the roofs! All who creep around halfclosed windows are loathsome to me!

Piously and quietly he wanders along on starry carpets:— but I dislike all lightly-treading men's feet upon which not even a spur jingles.

The step of everything honest speaks; but the cat sneaks away along the ground. Behold, along comes the moon, catlike and dishonest. —

This parable I offer to you sentimental dissemblers, you "pure perceivers"!

You I call — lechers!

You too love the earth and the earthly: I divine you well! — but there is shame in your love, as well as a bad conscience, — you resemble the moon!

To contempt for the earthly your spirit has been persuaded but not your innards: these, however, are the strongest thing about you!

And now your spirit is ashamed that it has given in to your innards, and in its shame it pursues crooked and lying ways.

"That would be the utmost thing for me" — thus your lying spirit tells itself: to look upon life without longing, and not like a dog with its tongue hanging out:

To be happy in looking on with a deadened will, without the grip and greed of self-seeking — cold and ashen all over but with drunken moon-eyes!

"That would be the dearest thing for me," — thus the seducee seduces himself — "to love the earth as the moon loves her and to touch her beauty with the eye alone.

And that is what I call the immaculate perception of all things, to want nothing from things: other than being allowed to lie before them like a mirror with a hundred eyes." —

O, you sentimental dissemblers, you lechers! You lack innocence in your desire: and so now you slander desire!

Verily, not as creators, procreators, and would-be merrymakers do you love the earth!

Where is innocence? Where the will to procreate is. And he who wants to create beyond himself has the purest will.

Where is beauty? Where I must will with all my will; where I want to cherish and perish, that an image may remain not only an image.

Cherishing and perishing: these have rhymed together for eternities. Will to love: that is also to be willing to die. Thus I talk to you cowards!

But now your emasculated leering wants to be called "contemplation"! And whatever is groped by cowardly eyes is to be baptized as "beautiful"! O, you besmirchers of noble names!

But this shall be your curse, you immaculate ones, you pure-perceivers, that you shall never give birth: even if you lie broad and pregnant on the horizon!

Verily, you stuff your mouths full with noble words: and we are to believe that your hearts runneth over, you liars?

But my words are low, despised, crooked words: I gladly pick up what falls under the table at your meals.

With them I can still — tell dissemblers the truth! Yes, my fishbones, mussel shells, and prickly leaves shall — tickle the noses of dissemblers!

Bad air is always around you and your meals: your lewd thoughts, lies, and secrecies are certain to be in the air!

First try believing in yourselves — in yourselves and your innards! He who does not believe in himself always lies.

A god's mask you hung up in front of yourselves, you "pure ones": into a god's mask your awful ringed-worm crawled.

Verily, you deceive, you "contemplative ones"! Zarathustra too was once the dupe of your godly exterior; he did not divine the serpents' coils with which it was stuffed.

Once I fancied I saw a god's soul at play in your play, you pure-perceivers!

Once I fancied no better art than your arts!

Snake-filth and foul odor the distance concealed from me: and that a lizard's cunning was crawling around lasciviously here.

But I came near to you: then day came to me — and now it comes to you, —

the moon's love affair has come to an end!

Just look there! Unprepared and pale he stands there — before the rosy dawn!

For here she comes already, the glowing one, — her love for the earth is coming! All solar love is innocence and creative desire!

Just look there, how impatiently she comes over the sea! Do you not feel the thirst and the hot breath of her love?

She wants to suck at the sea and drink its depth up to her height: now the sea's desire rises with a thousand breasts.

Kissed and sucked by the sun's thirst it would be; air it would be and height and a footpath of light and light itself!

Verily, like the sun I love life and all deep seas.

And this is what perception means to me: all things deep shall come up —

to my height! —

Thus spake Zarathustra.

On The Scholars

While I lay asleep, a sheep ate at the ivy-wreath upon my head, — ate it and said: "Zarathustra is no longer a scholar."

Said it and walked away awkwardly and proudly. A child told it to me.

I like to lie here where the children play, by the broken wall, amid thistles and red poppies.

To the children I am still a scholar, and to the thistles and red poppies too.

Innocent are they, even in their malice.

But to the sheep I am not anymore: thus my lot wills it — may it be blest!

For this is the truth: I have quit the house of the scholars and even slammed the door behind me.

Too long my soul sat hungry at their table; not, like them, am I trained in knowing as though it were nutcracking.

Freedom I love and the air over fresh earth; rather would I sleep on ox-hides than on their honors and respectability.

I am too hot and burned by my own thoughts: often they are ready to take my breath away. Then I must get out in the open and away from all dustencrusted rooms.

But they sit cool in the cool shade: in everything they just want to be spectators and to take care not to sit where the sun burns on the stairs.

Like those who stand on the street and gape at the people who pass by: so too they wait and gape at thoughts that others have thought.

If you grasp them with your hands, then they raise a cloud of dust around themselves like sacks of flour, and involuntarily; but who would ever guess that their dust came from grain and from the yellow delight of summer fields?

When they pretend to be wise, their small sayings and truths make my flesh creep: often there is an odor about their wisdom, as if it came from the swamp: and verily, I have even heard the frog croaking out of it!

Adept are they, they have clever fingers: what can my simplicity do next to their multiplicity? All threading and knitting and weaving their fingers understand:

thus they weave the stockings of the spirit!

Good clockworks are they: just be careful to wind them up properly! Then they indicate the hour without fail and make a modest noise besides.

Like millworks they work and like stampers: just throw them your seedcorn!

— they know indeed how to grind grain small and make white dust out of it.

They keep a strict eye on each other and do not trust themselves very well.

Inventive in sly little tricks, they wait for those whose knowledge goes on lame feet — like spiders they wait.

I always saw them prepare their poison with caution: and they always wore glass gloves on their fingers the while.

They also know how to play with loaded dice; and I have found them to play so eagerly that they sweat thereby.

We are alien to each other, and their virtues are even more opposed to my taste than their falsehoods and their loaded dice.

And when I lived with them I lived above them. They were livid with me over that.

They wanted to hear nothing about someone wandering over their heads; and so they placed wood and earth and filth between me and their heads.

Thus they muffled the sound of my step: and thus far I have been worst heard by the most learned.

All men's faults and weaknesses they placed between themselves and me:

— "false ceiling" they call it in their houses.

But in spite of that I wander over their heads with my thoughts; and even if I should wander on my own errors, I would still be over them and their heads.

For men are not equal: thus speaks justice. And what I will they would not dare to will!

Thus spake Zarathustra.

On The Poets

"Since I have come to know the body better," — said Zarathustra to one of his disciples — "the spirit is but quasi-spirit to me; and all the 'imperishable' is but a parable as well."

"So I heard you say once before," answered the disciple; "and at that time you added: 'But the poets lie too much.' But why did you say that the poets lie too much?"

"Why?" said Zarathustra. "I am not one of those whose why one may inquire about.

Is my experience but of yesterday? It was long ago that I experienced the reasons for my opinions.

Would I not have to be a tun of memory if I wanted to have my reasons with me as well?

It is already too much for me, keeping my opinions themselves; and many a bird keeps flying away.

And at times too I find a creature that has flown to my dovecot, an unknown one, and it trembles when I lay my hand upon it.

But what was it that Zarathustra once said to you? That the poets lie too much? — But Zarathustra too is a poet.

Do you now believe that he spoke the truth here? Why do you believe this?

The disciple replied: "I believe in Zarathustra." But Zarathustra shook his head and smiled.

Belief does not make me blessed, he said, especially not belief in me.

But assuming someone said in all seriousness that the poets lie too much:

he would be right, — we do lie too much.

We also know too little and are poor learners: so naturally we have to lie.

And who among us poets has not doctored his wine? Many a poisonous mish-mash has been brewed in our cellars, many an indescribable thing has happened there.

And because we know so little, we are heartily pleased with the poor in spirit, especially if they are little young ladies.

And we have a craving even for the things that the little old ladies tell each other in the evening. We call that the eternal-feminine in ourselves.

And as if there were a special secret passageway to knowledge, covered over for those who learn something: thus we believe in the folk and their "wisdom."

This, however, all poets believe: that whoever pricks up his ears while lying in the grass or upon lonely slopes learns something of the things which lie between heaven and earth.

And should tender emotions come to them, then the poets always fancy that Nature herself has taken a fancy to them:

And that she sneaks up to their ear to whisper secrets therein and amorous flatteries: of this they boast and brag before all mortals!

Alas, there are so many things between heaven and earth of which only the poets have let themselves dream!

And especially above the heavens: for all gods are poetic symbol, poetic swindle!

Verily, we are always drawn up there — namely, to the realm of the clouds:

on these we place our colorful manikins and call them gods and Supermen: —

Are they not just light enough for these chairs after all! — all these gods and Supermen.

Alas, how weary I am of all the inadequate absolutely destined to become event! Alas, how weary I am of the poets!

When Zarathustra spoke thus, his disciple became angry with him but remained silent. And Zarathustra too remained silent; and his eye had turned inward, as if it were looking into far distances. At last he sighed and took a breath. —

I am of today and days past, he said then; but there is something in me that is of tomorrow and the day after and thereafter.

I have grown weary of the poets, the old and the new; superficial they all seem to me and shallow seas.

They have not thought with enough depth: therefore their feeling has not sunk to the bottom.

Some lust and some boredom: that has heretofore been their best reflection.

All their harp jingle-jangle passes for a whiff and whisk of ghost with me; what have they thus far known of the fervor of tones? —

They are also not clean enough for me; they all muddy their water to make it seem deep.

And with that they gladly pass themselves off as mediators; but to me they remain meddlers and middlemen and half-and-halves and ones unclean! —

Alas, well did I cast my net into their seas and wanted to catch good fish; but always I pulled up an old godhead.

Thus the sea gave the hungry one a stone. And they themselves may well have come from the sea.

Surely one finds pearls in them: all the more similar are they themselves to hard shellfish. And instead of a soul I often found salt slime in them.

Even their vanity they learned from the sea: is not the sea the peacock of peacocks?

Even before the ugliest of buffaloes it twirls its tail, never does it grow weary of its lacy fan of silk and silver.

Defiantly the buffalo looks at it, his soul close to the sand, closer still to the thicket, but closest of all to the swamp.

What is beauty and sea and peacock-finery to him? This parable I speak to the poets.

Verily, their spirit itself is the peacock of peacocks and a sea of vanity!

Spectators the spirit of the poet requites — even if they should be buffaloes!

But of this spirit I have grown weary: and I foresee this spirit growing weary of itself.

Transformed already I have seen the poets, and their sights were set against themselves.

Penitents of the spirit I saw coming: they grew out of the poets. —

Thus spake Zarathustra.

On Great Events

There is an island in the sea — not far from Zarathustra's Blessed Isles —

upon which a volcano smokes constantly; of it people say, and especially the little old ladies among the people say, that it is like a boulder placed before the gate to the underworld: and downward through the volcano itself leads the narrow path which guides the way to this gate to the underworld.

Now about the time that Zarathustra took his rest on the Isles of the Blest, it happened that a ship cast anchor on the island where the volcano stands; and her crew went ashore to shoot rabbits. Near the midday hour, however, when the captain and his men were back together again, they suddenly saw a man coming towards them through the air, and a voice distinctly said: "It is time! It is high time!" But when the figure was nearest to them — it flew by quickly, however, like a shadow, in the direction of the volcano — then with great dismay they recognized that it was Zarathustra; then except for the captain himself they had all seen him before, and they loved him as the people love: so that love and awe are together in equal parts.

"Look at that!" said the old helmsman, "there goes Zarathustra into hell!" —

Around the same time that these sailors landed on the fire-island, a rumor was afloat that Zarathustra had disappeared; and when his friends were asked, they reported that he had embarked at night without saying where he intended to travel.

Thus unrest arose; after three days, however, the sailors' story added to this unrest — and then all the people said that the devil had taken Zarathustra. His disciples laughed of course at this talk; and one of them even said: "I would sooner believe that Zarathustra has taken the devil." But in the depths of their souls they were all full of misgiving and longing; and so their joy was great when on the fifth day Zarathustra appeared among them.

And this is the account of Zarathustra's conversation with the firehound:

The earth, he said, has a skin; and this skin has diseases. One of these diseases, for example, is called "man."

And another of these diseases is called "firehound": about him men have told themselves and let themselves be told a whole pack of lies.

To fathom this mystery I went across the sea: and I have seen the truth naked, verily! from the neck down.

Now I know how it is with the firehound; and also with all the eruptionand upheaval-devils, of whom not only the little old ladies are afraid.

"Out with you, firehound, out of your depth!" I cried, "and confess how deep this depth is! Where does what you huff and puff up here come from?

Richly you drink from the sea: your oversalted eloquence proclaims that.

Truly, for a hound from the deep you take too much of your nourishment from the surface!

At best I take you for the earth's ventriloquist: and whenever I have heard eruption- and upheaval- devils speak, I found them like you: salted, false, and shallow.

You know how to bellow and blacken with ashes! You are the best blowhards and are sufficiently learned in the art of making mud boiling hot.

Wherever you are, mud must be nearby, and much that is spongy, hollow, compressed: it wants to go free.

'Freedom' you all love to bellow most of all: but I forget my belief in 'great events' as soon as there is a lot of bellowing and smoke around them.

And believe me, friend Pandemonium! The greatest events — they are not our loudest but our stillest hours.

Not around the inventors of new noise: around the inventors of new values the world revolves; inaudibly it revolves.

And just admit it! Once your noise and smoke have passed away, but little has ever come to pass. What does it matter that a city has become a mummy and a statue lies in the mud?

And this word yet I say to the overthrowers of statues. That is indeed the greatest folly, throwing salt into the sea and statues into the mud.

In the mud of your contempt the statue lay: but that is precisely its statute, that out of contempt its life and living beauty may rise again.

With diviner features it stands now and sufferingly seductive; and verily! it will thank you yet for overthrowing it, you overthrowers!

And with this counsel I counsel kings and churches and all that are weak with age and weak in virtue — just let yourselves be overthrown! That you may come back to life, and that back to you may come — virtue! — " Thus I talked before the firehound; then he interrupted me sullenly and asked: "Church? What is that?"

"Church?" I answered, "that is a kind of state, and what is more, the lyingest kind. But be quiet, you hypocritical hound! No doubt you know your own kind best!

Like you yourself the state is a hypocritical hound; like you it likes to speak with smoke and bellowing, — to make believe, like you, that it speaks from the belly of things.

For by all means it means to be the most important creature on earth, the state; and it is believed to be, too." —

When I said this, the firehound acted as if insane with envy. "What?" he cried, "the most important creature on earth? And it is believed to be, too?" And so much gas and ghastly voices escaped from his throat that I thought he would choke with indignation and envy.

At last he calmed down and his panting subsided; as soon as he was quiet, however, I said laughingly:

"You are offended, firehound: thus I am right about you! And that I may still be right in the end, hear then of a different firehound: he really speaks from the heart of the earth.

Gold his breath exhales and golden rain: his heart wills it so. What are ashes and smoke and even hot slime to him?

Laughter flutters out of him like a colorful cluster of clouds, averse is he to the gurgling and spewing and griping of your bowels!

The gold, however, and the laughter — that he takes from the heart of the earth: for just so you know, — the heart of the earth is of gold."

When the firehound heard this, he could not stand to listen to me any longer. Ashamed, he tucked in his tail, said bow-wow in a mealy-mouthed manner, and crawled down into his hole.

Thus recounted Zarathustra. His disciples, however, hardly listened to him: so great was their desire to tell him of the sailors, the rabbits, and the flying man.

"What should I make of it?" said Zarathustra. "Am I then a ghost?

But it must have been my shadow. Most certainly you have heard something of the wanderer and his shadow?

This, however, is for certain: I must keep a tighter rein on him, — otherwise he will spoil my reputation yet."

And once again Zarathustra shook his head and wondered. "What should I make of it?" he said once again.

"Why did the ghost cry: 'It is time! It is high time!'

For what then is it — high time?" —

Thus spake Zarathustra.

The Soothsayer

—and I saw a great sadness come over mankind. The best grew weary of their works.

A doctrine came out, a belief ran alongside it: 'All is empty, all is the same, all has been!'

And from all the hills it rang out again: 'All is empty, all is the same, all has been!'

Well have we reaped: but for what reason has all our fruit turned rotten and brown? What fell down from the evil moon last night?

All work has been in vain, into poison our wine has been changed, an evil eye has singed our fields and hearts yellow.

Dry we have all become; and if fire lights on us, then like ashes we raise dust: yes, the fire itself we have made tired.

All our wells have run dry, even the sea has receded. All the ground wants to split, but the abyss will not swallow it!

'Alas, where is there still a sea in which we could drown': thus our lament sounds — over shallow swamps.

Verily, we have become too weary even for dying; now we lie awake and go on living — in burial chambers!"

Thus Zarathustra heard a soothsayer speak; and his prophecy touched him to the core and transformed him. Sad and weary he went around; and he became like those of whom the soothsayer had spoken.

"Verily," so he said to his disciples, "a little while then comes this long twilight.

Alas, how shall I bring my light safely through?

Would that it not be snuffed out in this sadness! To remoter worlds it shall surely be a light, and even to remotest nights!"

Thus Zarathustra went around sick at heart; and for three days he took neither food nor drink, had no rest, and lost all speech. At last it happened that he fell into a deep sleep. His disciples, however, sat up in long night-vigils around him and waited anxiously to see whether he would wake and speak again and get over his affliction.

And this is the speech that Zarathustra spoke when he awoke; his voice, however, came to his disciples as though from a great distance:

Hear then the dream I dreamed, you friends, and help me divine its meaning!

It is still a riddle to me, this dream; its meaning is hidden in it and imprisoned and does not yet fly over it with wings free.

All life I had renounced, so I dreamed. Night- and grave-watchman I had become, there, in the lonely mountain-fortress of Death.

I guarded his coffins up there: the damp vaults stood full of such trophies.

Out of glass coffins vanquished life looked at me.

I inhaled the odor of dusty eternities: sultry and dusty lay my soul. And who could ever air out his soul there?

The brightness of midnight was ever around me, loneliness cowered beside her; and thirdly, death-rattling stillness, the worst of my girlfriends.

Keys I carried, the rustiest of all keys; and I knew how to open the creakiest of all gates with them.

Like a most angry croaking the sound ran down the long corridors when the wings of the gate rose: unkindly cried this bird, unwillingly was it awoken.

But it was more frightening yet and more heart-wringing when it became quiet again and still all around, and I sat alone in this malicious silence.

So it went for me, and time crawled along, if there was still time: what do I know about it? But at last that which awoke me came to pass.

Three times blows beat on the gate, three times the vaults resounded and howled: then I went up to the gate.

Alpa! I cried, who carries his ashes up the mountain? Alpa! Alpa! Who carries his ashes up the mountain?

And I pressed in the key and heaved and strained at the gate. But not even a finger's breadth did it stand open:

Then a raging wind tore the wings apart: whistling, screeching, and penetrating, it threw a black coffin at me:

And in the raging and whistling and screeching the coffin burst open and spat out thousand-fold laughter.

And out of a thousand wry faces of children, angels, owls, fools, and childsized butterflies, it laughed and roared and jeered at me.

I was terribly frightened by it: it cast me down. And I screamed with terror like I have never screamed.

But my own scream awoke me: — and I became myself again. —

Thus Zarathustra related his dream and then fell silent: for he did not yet know the meaning of his dream. But the disciple whom he loved the most arose quickly, seized Zarathustra's hand and said:

"Your life itself explains this dream to us, O Zarathustra!

Are you not yourself the wind which with shrill whistling tears open the gates to the fortress of Death?

Are you not yourself the coffin full of colorful acts of malice and life's angelic masks?

Verily, like the thousand-fold laughter of a child Zarathustra enters all death chambers, laughing over these night- and grave-watchmen, and whomever else comes rattling along with gloomy keys.

You will frighten and upset them with your laughter; their swooning and coming-to will prove your power over them.

And even when the long twilight comes and the deadly weariness, you will not set in our sky, you advocate of life!

105 New stars you have let us see and new nightly splendors; verily, laughter itself you have stretched like a many-colored canopy over us.

Now the laughter of children will well up ever after out of coffins; now a strong wind will come triumphantly ever after to all deadly weariness: of this you yourself are our surety and soothsayer.

Verily, they themselves you dreamed, your enemies: that was your worst dream!

But as you awoke from them and became yourself again, so they shall wake up from themselves — and come to you!" —

So spoke the disciple; and now all the others crowded around Zarathustra and seized him by the hand and wanted to talk him into leaving his bed and his sadness and returning to them. But Zarathustra sat upright on his bed, and with a look not his own. Like one who returns home after a long time abroad, he looked upon his disciples and examined their faces; and still he did not recognize them. But when they raised him and set him on his feet, behold, suddenly his eye changed; he grasped everything that had happened, stroked his beard and said in a strong voice:

"Well then! This now has its day; but see to it, my disciples, that we prepare a good meal and without delay! Thus I intend to do penance for bad dreams!

The soothsayer, though, shall eat and drink at my side; and verily, I will yet show him a sea in which he can drown!"

Thus spake Zarathustra. But then he looked long and hard into the face of his disciple, the one who had served as his dream-interpreter, and shook his head. —

On Redemption

One day when Zarathustra crossed over the great bridge, he was beset on all sides by the cripples and beggars, and a hunchback talked to him thus:

"Behold Zarathustra! The people also learn from you and acquire belief in your teaching: but for them to believe entirely in you one more thing is required — you must first still convince us cripples! Here you now have a fine selection and truly, an opportunity with more than one knock! You can heal the blind and make the lame walk; and from him who has too much behind him you can also perhaps take a little away: — that, I think, would be the right way to make the cripples believe in Zarathustra!"

But to him who spoke here Zarathustra replied thus: "When you take away the hump from the hunchback, you take away his spirit — thus the people teach.

And when you give the blind man his sight, then he sees too many bad things on earth: so that he curses the person who healed him. But he who makes the lame man walk does him the greatest harm; for no sooner can he walk than his vices run away with him — thus the people teach with regard to cripples. And why should Zarathustra not also learn from the people when the people learn from Zarathustra?

This is the least thing to me, however, since I have been among men, to see that: 'This one lacks an eye and that one an ear and a third one a leg, and that there are others who have lost their tongue or their nose or their head.'

I see and have seen worse things and all sorts of things so loathsome that of each one I would not speak and of some I would not once keep silent: namely, men who lack everything save for one thing, of which they have too much —

men who are nothing more than a huge eye or a huge belly or something else huge, — inverted cripples I call such men.

And when I came out of my solitude and crossed over this bridge for the first time: then I could not believe my eyes and looked and looked again and finally said: 'That is an ear! An ear as big as a man! I took an even closer look: and, actually, under the ear something else was stirring, something pitifully small and poor and slight. And, upon my honor, the monstrous ear sat upon a small thin stalk, — the stalk, however, was a man! Whoever put a magnifying glass up to his eye could probably even make out a small envious face; also, that a bloated little soul was dangling from the stalk. The people, however, told me that the huge ear was not only a man, but a great man, a genius. But I never believed the people when they spoke of great men — and have maintained my belief that it was an inverted cripple who had too little of everything and too much of one thing."

When Zarathustra had spoken thus to the hunchback and to those who had the hunchback as their mouthpiece and advocate, he turned to his disciples with profound discontent and said:

"Verily, my friends, I walk among men as among the fragments and limbs of men! This is the frightful thing to my eye, that I find men shattered and scattered as over a battle- and butcher-field.

And if my eye flees from the now to the formerly, it always finds the same thing: fragments and limbs and terrible accidents — but no men!

The now and the formerly on earth — alas! my friends — that is my most unbearable thing; and I would not know how to live if I were not yet a seer of what is to come.

A seer, a willer, a creator, a future itself and a bridge to the future — and alas, still as it were a cripple on this bridge: all this Zarathustra is.

And you too have often asked yourselves: "Who is Zarathustra to us? What shall we call him? And like I myself you gave yourselves questions as answers.

Is he a promiser? Or a fulfiller? A conqueror? Or an inheritor? A harvest? Or a plowshare? A healer? Or one restored to health?

Is he a poet? Or one who is truthful? A liberator? Or a subjugator? A good guy? Or a bad guy?

I walk among men as among the fragments of the future: that future into which I look.

And this is my every thought, to compose and collect into one what is fragment and riddle and terrible accident.

And how could I stand being a man if man were not also the composer, riddle- reader, and redeemer of chance?

To redeem what is past and remold every 'It was' into 'I willed it so!' — only that would I call redemption!

Will — that is what the liberator and bringer of joy is called: thus I taught you, my friends! But now learn this in addition: the will itself is still a prisoner.

Willing liberates: but what is the name of that which puts even the liberator in chains?

'It was': that is what the will's gnashing of teeth and loneliest tribulation is called. Helpless against what has been done — of all things past it is an angry witness.

Backwards the will cannot will: that it cannot break time and time's inordinate desire, — that is the will's loneliest tribulation.

Willing liberates: what does willing devise for itself to be free of its tribulation and jeer at its jail?

Alas, every prisoner becomes a fool! Foolishly as well the imprisoned will rescues itself.

That time does not run backwards, this is its anger; 'That Which Was' —

this is what the stone it cannot roll is called.

And so it rolls stones out of anger and discontent and takes revenge on that which does not feel anger and discontent as it does.

Thus the will, the liberator, has become a perpetrator of pain; and on all that is capable of suffering it takes revenge because it cannot go backwards.

This, yes this alone is revenge itself: the will's ill-will toward time and its 'It was.'

Verily, a great folly dwells in our will; and it has turned out to be a curse on all things human that this folly learned spirit!

The spirit of revenge: my friends, this has been man's best reflection hitherto; and where there was suffering there always had to be punishment.

'Punishment,' the name, namely, that revenge has taken for itself: with a lying word it simulates a good conscience.

And because in the willer himself there is the pain of not being able to will backwards, — therefore willing itself and all life — must be punishment!

And then cloud after cloud rolled over the spirit: until at last madness preached: 'Everything passes away; therefore, everything deserves to pass away!'

'And this is justice itself, that law of time that she must devour her own children': thus madness preached.

'Things are morally ordered according to justice and punishment. O, where is the redemption from the flux of things and the punishment called "being"?

Thus madness preached.

'Can there be redemption when there is eternal law? Alas, unrollable is the stone "It was": all punishment must be eternal too!' Thus madness preached.

'No deed can be annulled: how could it be undone through punishment?

This, this is what is eternal in the punishment called "being," that this being must also be deed and debt again, eternally!'

'Unless the will finally redeems itself and willing becomes non-willing—':

but you know, my brothers, this fabulous song of madness!

I led you away from these fabulous songs when I taught you: 'The will is a creator.'

All 'it was' is a fragment, a riddle, a terrible accident — until the creative will says to it: 'But thus I willed it!'

— Until the creative will says to it: 'But thus I will it! Thus I will will it!'

But has it already spoken thus? And when did this happen? Has the will already been unharnessed from its own folly?

Has the will already become its own redeemer and bringer of joy? Has it unlearned the spirit of revenge and all gnashing of teeth?

And who has taught it reconciliation with time, and that which is higher than all reconciliation?

That which is higher than all reconciliation must the will which is the will to power will: but how does this happen? Who taught it to will backwards as well?"

— But at this point in his speech it happened that Zarathustra stopped suddenly and looked exactly like someone who was extremely frightened. With terrified eyes he looked at his disciples; his eyes pierced as with arrows their thoughts and hinter-thoughts. But after a little while he laughed again and said, appeased:

"It is hard to live with men because it is so hard to keep silent. Especially for a talkaholic."

— Thus spake Zarathustra. The hunchback, however, had listened to the conversation and covered his face the while; when he heard Zarathustra laugh, however, he looked up curiously and said slowly:

"But why does Zarathustra speak differently to us than he does to his disciples?"

Zarathustra answered: "What is remarkable about that? With hunchbacks one may well speak hunchbacked!"

"Very well," said the hunchback; "and with pupils one may well tell tales out of school.

But why does Zarathustra speak differently to his pupils than he does — to himself?"
—

On Man-Craft

Not the height: the descent is what is terrible!

The descent, where the glance plunges down and the hand grasps up. There the heart grows dizzy because of its double will.

Alas, friends, do you guess as well my heart's double will?

This, this is my descent and my danger, that my glance plunges to the height and my hand wants to stick to and stay at — the depth!

My will clings to man, with chains I bind myself to man, because it draws me up to the Superman: for there my other will has a mind to be.

And therefore I live blindly among men: precisely as if I knew them not: lest my hand lose its faith entirely in a sure thing.

I do not know you men: this darkness and consolation is often spread out around me.

I sit at the gateway for the sake of every knave and ask: "Who wants to cheat me?"

This is my first piece of man-craft, to let myself be cheated so as to be off my guard with cheaters.

Alas, if I had to be on my guard with men: how could man be an anchor for my hot-air balloon? Too easily would it sweep me up and away!

This providence lies over my destiny, that I must be without precaution.

And he who would not die of thirst among men must learn to drink from all glasses; and he who would remain clean among men must know how to wash himself even with dirty water.

And thus I often consoled myself: "Well then! Cheer up, old heart! A mishap failed you: enjoy this as your — happiness!"

This, however, is my next piece of man-craft: I spare the vain more than the proud.

Is not wounded vanity the mother of all tragedies? Where pride is wounded, however, there something better than pride may yet grow.

That life may look good, its play must be well-played: but for that, good actors are required.

All the vain I found to be good actors: they act and want to be looked upon with pleasure, — all their spirit is in this will.

They represent themselves, they invent themselves; in their presence I love to look upon life, — it cures melancholy.

Therefore I spare the vain, because they are the physicians to my melancholy and keep me attached to man as to a spectacle.

And then: who has fathomed the full depth of the vain man's modesty? I side and sympathize with him on account of his modesty.

From you he wants to acquire his belief in himself; he lives on your looks, he gobbles up praise from your hands.

He even believes your lies when you lie well about him: for deep down his heart sighs: "What am I!"

And if true virtue be that virtue which has no knowledge of itself: well, then the vain man has no knowledge of his modesty! —

This, however, is my third piece of man-craft, that I do not let your timidity spoil my view of the wicked.

I am happy to see the wonders which the hot sun hatches: tigers and palm trees and rattlesnakes.

Among men too there is a hot sun's handsome brood and many things wonder- worthy with regard to the wicked.

It is true, like your wisest men who did not appear all that wise to me: so too I found man's wickedness to be less than its reputation.

And often I asked with a shake of the head: "Why do you still rattle, you rattlesnakes?"

Verily, there is still a future even for evil! And the hottest south is still undiscovered by man!

How many things now called the most wanton wickedness indeed are but only twelve feet wide and three months long! Someday, however, greater dragons will come into the world.

For that the Superman may not lack his dragon, the superdragon, of which he is worthy: for that much hot sun must still glow on moist primeval forest!

Out of your wildcats tigers must first arise, and out of your poisonous toads, crocodiles: for the good hunter shall have good hunting!

And verily, you good and just ones! In you there is much that is laughable, and above all your fear of that which has hitherto been called "devil"!

Such a stranger you are in your souls to what is great, that to you the Superman would be frightful in his goodness!

And you wise and knowing ones, you would run away from wisdom's broiling sun, in which the Superman bathes his nakedness with pleasure!

You highest of men my eye has met! this is what I doubt in you and secretly laugh about: I suspect that you would call my Superman — devil!

Alas, I grew weary of these highest and best ones: from their "height" I longed to be out, up, out, and away to the Superman!

A shudder came over me when I saw these best ones naked: then I grew myself wings to soar off into distant futures.

Into futures more distant, into souths more southerly than any artist has ever dreamed: there, where gods are ashamed of all clothing!

But disguised I want to see you, you neighbors and fellow men, welladorned and vain and dignified in the role of "the good and the just."

And disguised will I myself sit among you, — in order to mistake myself and you: this, you see, is my last piece of man-craft. —

Thus spake Zarathustra.

The Stillest Hour

What happened to me, my friends? You see me confused, driven away, reluctant-compliant, ready to go — alas, to go away from you!

Yes, once more must Zarathustra go into his solitude: but this time the bear goes back into his den morosely!

What happened to me? Who ordered this? — Alas, my angry mistress wishes it so, she spoke to me; have I never told you her name before?

Yesterday toward evening my stillest hour spoke to me: this is the name of my terrible mistress.

And so it happened — for I must tell you everything, lest your hearts harden toward the suddenly departing one!

Do you know the terror of the one who is falling asleep? —

Down to his very toes he is terrified, because the ground seems to give way beneath him and the dream begins.

I tell you this in the form of a parable. Yesterday, at the stillest hour, the ground gave way: the dream began.

The hour-hand moved, the clock of my life took a breath — never have I heard such stillness around me: so that my heart was terror-struck.

Then it spoke without a voice to me: "You know it, Zarathustra?" —

And I cried out with terror at this whispering, and the blood left my face:

but I was silent.

Then it spoke again without a voice to me: "You know it Zarathustra, but you do not say it!"

And at last I answered, like one who was defiant: "Yes, I know it, but I will not say it!"

Then it spoke again without a voice to me: "You will not, Zarathustra? Is that really true? Do not hide in your defiance!" —

And I wept and trembled like a child and said: "Alas, I would indeed but how can I? Let me off this once! It is beyond me!"

Then it spoke again without a voice to me: "What do you matter, Zarathustra!

Speak your word and shatter!" —

And I answered: "Alas, is it my word? Who am I? I await the worthier one; I am unworthy even to shatter upon him."

Then it spoke again without a voice to me. "What do you matter? You are not yet humble enough for me. Humility has the toughest skin." —

And I answered: "What has the skin of my humility not already endured?

At the foot of my height I dwell: how high are my peaks? No one has yet told me.

But I know my valleys well."

Then it spoke again without a voice to me: "O Zarathustra, he who has mountains to move moves valleys and lowlands as well." —

And I answered: "My word has moved no mountains yet, and what I have said has not yet reached men. Yes, I went to men, but I have not yet arrived at them."

Then it spoke again without a voice to me: "What do you know of that? The dew falls on the grass when the night is most reticent." —

And I answered: "They mocked me when I found and made my own way; and my feet were truly trembling in those days.

And so they said to me: 'You forgot the way, now you have also forgotten the way of going!"

Then it spoke again without a voice to me: "What does their mockery matter?

You are one who has forgotten how to obey: now you shall command!

Do you not know who is most needed by all? He who commands great things.

To complete great things is hard: but what is harder is to command great things.

That is what is most inexcusable in you: you have the power, and you refuse to rule." —

And I answered: "I lack the lion's voice for commanding."

Then it spoke again as if in a whisper to me: "It is the stillest words which bring on the storm. Thoughts that come on dove's feet rule the world.

O Zarathustra, you shall go as a shadow of that which is to come: thus you will command and in commanding go before." —

And I answered: "I am ashamed."

Then it spoke again without a voice to me: "You must still become a child and be without shame.

The pride of youth is still upon you, lately you have become young: but he who would become a child must still overcome his youth." —

And I reflected a long time and trembled. But at last I said what I had had said at first: "I will not."

Then there was laughter around me. Woe, how this laughter tore apart my innards and slit open my heart!

And it spoke for the last time to me: "O Zarathustra, your fruits are ripe, but you are not ripe for your fruits!

So you must go again into your solitude: for you have yet to become mellow."

—

And it laughed again and fled: then it grew still around me, as if with a twofold stillness. But I lay on the ground and the sweat poured from my body.

— Now you have heard everything and why I have to go back into my solitude.

Nothing have I held back from you, my friends.

But this too you have heard from me, who of all men is still the most reticent — and wants to be!

I still had something to say to you, I still had something to give to you! Why did I not give it? Am I stingy then? —

But when Zarathustra had spoken these words, he was overcome by the violence of his pain and the imminence of his departure from his friends, so that he wept openly; and no one knew how to console him. In the night, however, he went away alone and left his friends.

Part Three

"You look up when you crave elevation. And I look down because I am elevated.

Who among you can laugh and be elevated at the same time?

Whoever climbs the highest mountains laughs at all tragic plays and tragic realities."

Zarathustra, On Reading And Writing (Part One)

The Wanderer

It was around midnight when Zarathustra made his way across the ridge of the island in order to make the opposite shore by early morning: for he meant to embark there. There was a good roadstead there, you see, where even foreign ships liked to anchor; they took with them many from the Blessed Isles who wanted to cross the sea. So as Zarathustra climbed the mountain now, he thought on the way of the many solitary wanderings he had made since his youth and of how many mountains and ridges and peaks he had already climbed.

"I am a wanderer and a mountain climber," he said to his heart, "the plains I do not love, and it seems I cannot sit still for long.

And as for what may yet come to me in the way of fate and experience, — a wandering will be in it and a mountain climbing: in the end one still only experiences oneself.

The time is past when accidents might still happen to me: and what could still befall me now that is not already my own!

It only comes back, it comes home to me at last — my own self and that part of it which has long been in foreign parts and scattered amongst all things and happenings.

And yet one thing I know: I now stand before my last peak and before that which has been saved up longest for me. Alas, I have to go up my hardest path!

Alas, I have begun my loneliest wandering!

But he who is of my kind does not shun such an hour: the hour which says to him: 'Only now you make your way to greatness! Peak and abyss — this is now resolved into one!

You make your way to greatness: what was hitherto your ultimate danger has now become your ultimate refuge!

You make your way to greatness: your best courage must now consist in this, that behind you no way exists anymore!

You make your way to greatness: no one shall sneak after you here! Your foot itself has erased the path behind you, and above it is written: Impossibility.

And if henceforth all ladders are lacking, then you must still know how to climb upon your own head: how else would you climb upwards?

Upon your own head and above and beyond your own heart! Now must the mildest in you become the harshest.

He who has always been very sparing of himself sickens at last from his very sparingness. Praised be that which hardens! I praise not the land where butter and honey — flow!

Learning to look away from oneself is necessary in order to see much: — this harshness is necessary for every mountain climber.

But he who is too forward with his eyes, like the knowing one, how could he see more than the foreground of anything?

You, however, O Zarathustra, would look at the ground and background of all things: so already you must climb over yourself, — onward, upward, until even your stars are beneath you!

Yes! To look down upon myself and even upon my stars: this would I first call my peak, this would be left behind as my last peak! —

Thus spake Zarathustra to himself while climbing, comforting his heart with hard aphorisms: for he was sore at heart like never before. And when he reached the top of the mountain ridge, behold, there lay the other sea spread out 117 before him: and he stood still and silent a long while. But the night was cold at this height and clear and starry-bright.

"I know my lot," he said at last with sadness. "Well then! I am ready! My last solitude has just begun.

Alas, this black sad sea beneath me! Alas, this pregnant, nightly spleen!

Alas, destiny and sea! To you I must now climb down!

Before my highest mountain I stand and before my longest wandering:

therefore I must first descend deeper than I ever have:

— deeper down into pain than I have ever descended, down into its blackest flood! So my destiny wills it: Well then! I am ready.

"Whence come the highest mountains?" So I asked once. Then I learned that they come from the sea.

This testimony is written in their stone and in the walls of their peaks.

From the deepest place must the highest come to its height. —

Thus spake Zarathustra at the summit of the mountain, where it was cold:

but when he came near to the sea and stood at last alone under the cliffs, then he had become weary on the way and was more full of longing than ever before.

"Everything still sleeps," he said; "even the sea sleeps. Sleepy and strange looks its eye casts at me.

But it breathes warmly, I feel it. And I also feel that it dreams. It tosses and turns, dreaming upon hard pillows.

Hark! Hark! How it groans with wicked recollections! Or wicked expectations?

Alas, I am sad with you, you dark monster, and even mad at myself for your sake.

Alas, that my hand has not strength enough! Gladly indeed, would I deliver you from bad dreams! — "

And as Zarathustra spoke thus, he laughed with melancholy and bitterness over himself. "What, Zarathustra!" he said; "would you sing solace even to the sea?

Alas, you love-rich fool Zarathustra, you over-trustful, over-joyful one! But thus were you always: trustful you always came to all that was frightful.

Every monster you wanted to caress. A whiff of warm breath, a little soft tuft of fur on its paw — and immediately you were ready to love it and lure it.

Love is the danger of the loneliest one, love of anything, as long as it lives!

Truly laughable is my folly and my modesty in love! — "

Thus spake Zarathustra and laughed a second time: but then he thought of his abandoned friends — and as if had sinned against them in his thoughts, he became angry with himself at the thought of his thoughts. And thereupon it came to pass that the laughing one wept:— with ire and desire Zarathustra wept bitterly.

On The Vision And The Riddle

1

When it became known among the sailors that Zarathustra was on board the ship — for there was a man from the Blessed Isles who had gone on board with him — there arose a great curiosity and expectation. But Zarathustra kept silent for two days and was cold and deaf with sadness, so that he answered neither looks nor questions. On the evening of the second day, however, he opened his ears again, though he still remained silent: for there were many strange and dangerous things to have an ear to on this ship, which came from afar and would travel even farther. But Zarathustra was a friend to all those who make long journeys and take a dislike to living without danger. And behold! at last in listening his own tongue was loosened, and the ice of his heart broke:— then he began to speak thus:

To you, the daring searchers, researchers, and whoever has set sail with subtle sails on frightful seas, —

To you, the riddle-intoxicated, the twilight-delighted, whose souls are lured by flutes to every mis-abyss:

— For you refuse to grope along a thread with a cowardly hand; and where you can divine you hate to deduce —

To you alone I relate the riddle that I saw, — the vision of the loneliest one.

—

Gloomy I walked lately through the corpse-hued gloaming, — gloomy and hard, with lips compressed. Not only one sun had set for me.

A path that climbed defiantly through rubble, a spiteful, lonely one to which neither herb nor shrub spoke any longer: a mountain path crunched under the defiance of my foot.

Striding silently over the scornful clatter of pebbles, trampling underfoot the stone that let it slide: thus my foot forced itself upwards.

Upwards: — although he sat on me, half-dwarf, half-mole; lame, laming; dripping lead into my ear, leaden-drop thoughts into my brain.

“O Zarathustra,” he whispered tauntingly, syllable by syllable, “you stone of wisdom! You threw yourself high, but every stone that is thrown — must fall!

O Zarathustra, you stone of wisdom, you slingstone, you star-destroyer!

You threw yourself so high, — but every stone that is thrown — must fall!

Sentenced to you yourself and your own stoning: O Zarathustra, you sure threw the stone far, — but it will fall back on you!”

Then the dwarf was silent; and that lasted a long time. His silence oppressed me, however: such a pairing truly makes one lonelier than being alone!

I climbed, I climbed, I dreamed, I thought, — but everything oppressed me.

I was like a sick man whose bad torment makes him weary and whose worse dream wakes him up again from his falling asleep. —

But there is something in me that I call courage: all ill humor it has killed for me hitherto. This courage at last bade me stand still and say:

“Dwarf! You! Or I!” —

Because courage is the best killer, — courage which attacks; for in every attack there is music playing.

Man, however, is the most courageous animal: with that he has overcome every animal. With music playing he even overcame every pain; but human pain is the deepest pain.

Courage also kills giddiness at abysses: and where does man not stand at abysses? Is seeing not itself — seeing abysses?

Courage is the best killer; courage also kills pity. But pity is the deepest abyss: however deeply man looks into life, so deeply too he looks into suffering.

But courage is the best killer, courage which attacks: it even kills death dead, for it says: "Was that life? Well then! Once more!"

In such a saying, however, there is much music playing. He that has ears to hear, let him hear. —

2

"Halt! Dwarf" I said. " I! or you! I, however, am the stronger of us two: you are unaware of my abysmal thought! That — you could not bear!" —

Then happened that which made me lighter: for the dwarf sprang from my shoulder, the snoop! And he squatted on a stone in front of me. But just at the place where we halted there was a gateway.

"See this gateway! Dwarf!" I continued: "it has two faces. Two paths come together here: no one has yet gone to the end of them.

This long lane back here: it lasts an eternity. And that long lane out there, — that is another eternity.

They oppose each other, these paths; they bang their very heads: — and here at this gateway is where they come together. The name of the gateway stands written above: 'Moment.'

But he who went further down one of them — ever further and ever farther:

do you think, dwarf, that these paths would eternally oppose each other?" —

"Everything straight lies," the dwarf muttered contemptuously. "All truth is crooked, time itself is a circle."

"You spirit of gravity!" I said angrily, "don't take the easy way out! Or I will let you crouch where you crouch, lamefoot, and I have carried you high!

"Behold," I went on, "this moment! From this gateway Moment a long eternal lane runs backwards: behind us lies an eternity.

All things that can run, must they not have run along this lane once before?

All things that can happen, must they not have happened, been done, and been over and done with once before?

And if everything has existed before: what do you make of this moment, dwarf? Must not this gateway too — have existed before?

And are not all things knotted firmly together in such a way that this moment draws all things to come after it? Consequently — — itself too?

Then of all things that can run: even in that long lane out there — they must run once more! —

And this slow spider that crawls in the moonlight itself, and you and I in the gateway whispering together, whispering of eternal things — must we not have existed before?

— and must we not return and run in that lane out there before us, in that long eerie lane — must we not return eternally? —"

Thus I talked, and ever more softly: for I was afraid of my own thoughts and hinter-thoughts. Then suddenly I heard a dog howling nearby.

Had I ever heard a dog howl like this? My thoughts ran back. Yes! When I was a child, in my most distant childhood:

— then I had heard a dog growl like this. And saw him too, hair bristling, head up, trembling, in the stillest midnight, when even dogs believe in ghosts:

— so that it moved me to pity. For just then the full moon passed quietly as death over the house, just then it stood still, a round glow, perfectly still on the flat roof, exactly as if on foreign property: — on account of that the dog had been horror-stricken then: for dogs believe in thieves and ghosts. And when I again heard such howling, it moved me to pity once more.

Where had the dwarf gone to now? And the gateway? And the spider? And all the whispering? Was I dreaming then? Had I awoke? Amidst wild cliffs I stood all of a sudden, alone, desolate, in the most desolate moonlight.

But there lay a man! And there! The dog, jumping, bristling, whining, — now he saw me coming — then he howled again, then he yelped: — had I ever heard a dog yelp so for help?

And verily, what I saw, the like of it I had never seen. I saw a young shepherd, writhing, retching, twitching, face contorted, with a heavy black snake hanging out of his mouth.

Had I ever seen so much loathing and pale horror on one face? He had fallen asleep, perhaps? Then the snake had crawled down his throat — there it had bitten itself fast.

My hand yanked at the snake and yanked: — in vain! I could not yank the lizard from his gizzard. Then out of me it cried: "Bite! Bite!

The head off! Bite!" — thus it cried out of me, my horror, my hatred, my loathing, my pity, all my good and bad cried with one cry out of me. —

You daring ones around me! You searchers, researchers, and whoever has set sail with subtle sails on unexplored seas! You riddle-happy ones!

Go ahead, solve for me the riddle I beheld then, interpret for me the vision of the loneliest one!

For it was a vision and a foreseeing: — what did I see then in an allegory?

And who is it that is yet to come one day?

Who is the shepherd into whose throat the snake crawled thus? Who is the man into whose throat all the heaviest, blackest things will crawl thus?

— But the shepherd bit, as my cry advised; he bit off a good mouthful! Far away he spewed the head of the snake —: and sprang up. —

— No longer shepherd, no longer man — a transfigured, light-bathed being that laughed! Never yet on earth has a man laughed as he laughed!

O my brothers, I heard a laughter that was no human laughter, — — and now a thirst eats at me, a longing that never ceases.

My longing for this laughter eats at me: O, how can I stand to live! And how could I stand to die now! —

Thus spake Zarathustra.

On Involuntary Bliss

With such riddles and bitterness in his heart Zarathustra sailed across the sea. But when he was four days' journey from the Blessed Isles and from his friends, then he had overcome all his pain: — triumphant and with firm feet he stood upon his fate once again. And then Zarathustra spoke thus to his jubilant conscience:

I am alone again and want to be, alone with the pure sky and the open sea; and it is afternoon again around me.

It was afternoon one day when I found my friends for the first time, afternoon as well the second time: — at the hour when all light becomes stiller.

For whatever happiness is still on the way between heaven and earth now seeks a bright soul for shelter: through happiness all light has now become stiller.

O afternoon of my life! One day my happiness also descended to the valley to seek shelter; there it found these open, hospitable souls.

O afternoon of my life! What did I not give up in order to have one thing: this live planting of my thoughts and this morning light of my highest hope!

Companions the creator once sought, and children of his hope; and behold, it was found he could not find them unless he first created them himself.

Thus am I in the midst of my work, going to my children and returning from them: for the sake of his children must Zarathustra perfect himself.

For deep down we love only our child and work; and where there is great love for oneself, it is a sign of pregnancy: thus I found it.

My children are still green in their first spring, standing next to each other and jointly jostled by the winds, the trees of my garden and best soil.

And verily! Where such trees stand next to each other, there blessed islands are!

But one day I want to dig them up and place each one alone by itself: that it may learn solitude and defiance and foresight.

Gnarled and crooked and with supple hardness shall it then stand by the sea, a living lighthouse of invincible life.

There, where the storms rush down into the sea and the mountain's snout drinks water, there each one shall one day have his day- and night- watches, for his trial and sentencing.

Tried and sentenced he shall be, to see whether he is of my kin and kind, —

whether he is master of a lofty will, taciturn, even when he does speak, and giving in so much that in giving he takes: —

— that one day he may be my companion and Zarathustra's co-creator and co-celebrator —: one that writes my will on my tablets: to the fuller perfection of all things.

And for his sake and his like I must perfect myself: therefore I turn aside from my good fortune now and offer myself to all misfortune — for my last trial and sentencing.

And verily, it was time for me to be on my way; and the wanderer's shadow and the longest while and the stillest hour — all said to me: "It is high time!"

The wind blew through the keyhole at me and said "Come!" The door flew open cunningly for me and said "Go!"

But I lay enchained by the love for my children: desire set this snare for me, the desire for love, to be my children's prey and lose myself in them.

Desire — to me this only means: having lost myself. I have you, my children! In this having, everything shall be surety and nothing desire.

But the sun of my love lay brooding over me, in his own juices Zarathustra was stewing — then shadows and doubt flew past me.

After frost and winter I even lusted: "O that frost and winter would make me crackle and crunch again!" I sighed: — then icy mists arose out of me.

My past burst its graves, many a buried-alive pain awoke; it had only enjoyed a good night's sleep, tucked away in a winding sheet.

Thus everything called out to me in signs: "It is time!" But I — heard it not:

until finally my abyss stirred and my thought bit me.

Alas, abysmal thought that is my thought! When will I find the strength to hear you burrowing and no longer be trembling?

Right up to the throat my heart throbs when I hear you burrowing! Your silence as well wants to throttle me, you abysmally silent one!

Never yet have I dared to summon you up here: quite enough to have carried you around with me! Not yet have I been strong enough for my final lion-wantonness and willfulness.

Your weight was always terrible enough for me; but one day yet I shall find the strength and the lion's voice to summon you up here!

Only when I have overcome myself in that will I then also be ready to overcome myself in that which is greater; and the seal of my perfection shall be a victory!

—

Meanwhile I still drift upon uncertain seas; Chance, the smooth-tongued one, flatters me; forwards and backwards I look —, still no end do I see.

The hour of my final struggle has not yet come to me, — or has it come to me even now? Verily, with mischievous beauty sea and life look all around at me!

O afternoon of my life! O happiness before night! O haven on higher seas! O peace in uncertainty! How I mistrust you all!

Verily, I am mistrustful of your mischievous beauty! I am like the lover who mistrusts the all-too-velvety smile.

Just as he nudges his beloved before him, tender even in his hardness, the jealous one, — so I nudge this blissful hour before me.

Hence, you blissful hour! With you an involuntary bliss came to me! Here I stand ready for my deepest pain: untimely you came.

Hence, you blissful hour! Better to take shelter there — with my children!

Hurry! And bless them before evening with my happiness!

There evening draws near even now: the sun is sinking. There goes — my happiness!
—

Thus spake Zarathustra. And he waited for his unhappiness all night: but he waited in vain. The night remained bright and still, and happiness itself drew nearer and nearer to him. Towards morning, however, Zarathustra laughed in his heart and said mockingly: "Happiness runs after me. That comes from my not running after women. Happiness, however, is a woman."

Before Sunrise

O heaven above me, you pure one! deep one! You light-abyss! Seeing you I shudder with godly desires!

To project myself to your height — that is my depth! To protect myself in your purity — that is my innocence!

The deity shrouds his beauty: so you conceal your stars. You do not speak:

so you reveal your wisdom to me.

Mute over the raging sea you rose for me today, your love and your modesty speaking revelation to my raging soul.

That you came to me beautifully, shrouded in your beauty, that you speak to me mutely, manifest in your wisdom.

O how could I not divine all the modesty of your soul! Before the sun you came to me, the loneliest one!

We have been friends from the very beginning: dread and grief and ground we have in common: even the sun we have in common.

We do not speak to each other because we know too much — : we are silent towards each other, we smile our knowledge towards each other.

Are you not the light to my fire? Do you not have the sister-soul to my insight?

Together we learned to fly; together we learned to rise above ourselves to our very selves and to smile without a cloud: —

— to smile down without a cloud out of lucid eyes and from a distance of miles, while under us aim and blame and constraint dampen like rain.

And when I wandered alone: for whom did my soul hunger in the night and on errant paths? And when I climbed mountains, whom did I seek on the mountains every time if not you?

And all my wandering and mountain climbing: it was only a necessity and a helping hand for the heavy-handed: — my whole will wants only to fly, to fly up into you!

And whom did I hate more than passing clouds and whatever defiles you?

And even my own hate I hated because it defiled you!

I am angry at the passing clouds, these prowling cats of prey: they take from you and me what is ours in common, — the vast, boundless Yea- and Amensaying.

We are angry at these meddlers and mediators, the passing clouds: these half-and-halves that have learned neither to curse nor to bless thoroughly.

Rather would I sit in a Diogenes tub under a closed heaven, rather sit in the abyss with no heaven, than see you, light-heaven, defiled by passing clouds!

And often I have longed to wire them fast with the jagged golden wires of lightning, so that I, like the thunder, could beat the kettledrum on their kettlebellies:—

— an angry kettledrummer, because they rob me of your Yea! and Amen!, you heaven above me, you pure one! light one! You light-abyss! — because they rob you of my Yea! and Amen!

For rather would I have clamor and thunder and weather-curses than this careful, doubtful cat-calm: and among men too I hate most all pussyfooters and half-and-halves and doubting, dawdling passing-clouds.

And "he who cannot learn to bless shall learn to curse!" — this bright teaching fell to me from the bright sky, this star stands in my sky even on black nights.

But I am a blesser and a yea-sayer, if only you are around me, you pure one!

light one! You light-abyss! — even into all abysses I then carry my blessing yeasaying.

A blesser I have become and a yea-sayer: I wrestled long for that and was a wrestler so that one day I might free my hands for blessing.

This, however, is my blessing: to stand above everything as its own heaven, its round roof, its azure bell and eternal surety: and blessed is he who blesses thus!

For all things are baptized at the font of eternity and beyond good and evil; good and evil, however, are themselves only shadowy go-betweens and damp calamities and passing clouds.

Verily, a blessing it is and no blasphemy when I teach: "Above all things stand the heaven of Chance, the heaven of Innocence, the heaven of Coincidence, the heaven of Exuberance."

"Von Chance" — this is the oldest nobility in the world, this I gave back to all things; I released them from their captivity under Purpose.

This freedom and heaven-serenity I placed like an azure bell over all things when I taught that above them and through them no "eternal will" — wills.

This exuberance and this folly I placed in place of that will when I taught:

"In all things one thing is impossible — Reason!"

A little reason to be sure, a seed of wisdom strewn from star to star, — this leaven is mixed in with all things: for the sake of folly wisdom is mixed in with all things!

A little wisdom is quite possible; but this blessed surety I found in all things: that on the feet of Chance they would still rather — dance.

O heaven above me, you pure one, lofty one! This is now your purity for me, that there is no eternal reason-spider and spider web: —

— that to me you are a dance floor for divine chance, that to me you are a table of the gods for divine dice and dice players!

But you are blushing? Did I speak the unspeakable? Did I blaspheme while meaning to bless you?

Or is it the modesty of being two that makes you blush? — Do you bid me go and be silent because now — day comes?

The world is deep — : and deeper than the day has ever conceived. Not everything can be uttered in the presence of day. But day comes: so let us now part!

O heaven above me, you modest one! glowing one! O you, my happiness before sunrise! Day comes: so let us now part! —

Thus spake Zarathustra.

On The Bedwarfing Virtue

1

When Zarathustra was back on solid ground again, he did not set off directly for his mountains and his cave, but took up many paths and questions, inquiring after this and that, so that he said of himself in jest: "Behold a river that in many twists and turns returns to its source!" For he wanted to learn what had happened to man in the meantime: whether he had grown larger or smaller. And one day he saw a row of new houses; then he was amazed and said:

"What do these houses mean? Verily, no great soul placed them here in his own image!

Perhaps a dimwitted child took them out of his toy box? Would that another child might put them back in the box again!

And these rooms and chambers: can men go in and out here? They strike me as being made for silk dolls or sweet-tooths, who are quite sweet on letting themselves be nibbled, too."

And Zarathustra stood still and mused. Finally he said, saddened: "Everything has grown smaller!"

Everywhere I see lower gateways: he who is of my kind still finds a way through, but — he must stoop!

O when will I return to my homeland, where I will not have to stoop anymore — not have to stoop anymore before the small ones!" — And Zarathustra sighed and looked off into the distance. —

That same day, however, he made his speech on the bedwarfing virtue.

2

I pass through this people and keep my eyes open: they do not forgive me for not being envious of their virtues.

They snap at me because I say to them: for small people small virtues are necessary — and because it is hard for me to accept that small people are necessary!

Here I am still like the cock in a strange farmyard whom even the hens peck at; but I take no offense at the hens for that.

I am polite towards them, as towards all small offenses; to be prickly towards what is small strikes me as wisdom for hedgehogs.

They all speak of me when they sit around the fire at night, — they speak of me, but no one thinks — of me!

This is the new stillness I have learned: their clamor around me spreads a mantle over my thoughts.

They clamor amongst each other: "What does this dark cloud want with us? Let us see to it that it brings no plague upon us!"

And the other day a woman pulled her child back to her when it wanted to come to me: "Take the children away!" she cried; "such eyes singe children's souls."

They cough when I speak: they think coughing to be an objection to strong winds, — they guess nothing of the blustering of my happiness!

"We have no time yet for Zarathustra" — thus they object; but who cares about a time that "has no time" for Zarathustra?

And if they praise me at all: how could I possibly go to sleep on their praise?

Their praise is a belt of thorns to me; it scratches me even when I undo it.

And this too I learned among them: the one who praises acts as if he were giving back, but in fact he wants to be given more.

Ask my foot whether it likes their lauding and luring strains! Verily, to such tick-tock time it wants neither to dance nor to stand still.

To a small virtue they want to laud and lure me; to the tick-tock of a small happiness they want to persuade my foot.

I pass through this people and keep my eyes open; they have grown smaller and are growing ever smaller: — that, however, is due to their teaching on happiness and virtue.

Namely, they are modest also in their virtue — for they want comfort.

With comfort, however, only a modest virtue sits well.

I suppose in their way too they learn to step and to step forward: I call that their hobbling —. With that they become a hindrance to anyone who is in a hurry.

And many of them go forward and look backward at the same time, with stiffened necks: I like to smash into them.

Foot and eye shall not lie, nor give each other the lie. But there is much lying by the small people.

Some of them will, but most of them are only willed. Some of them are genuine, but most of them are bad actors.

There are unwitting actors among them and unwilling actors —, the genuine ones are always rare, especially the genuine actors.

Of man there is little here: therefore their women act mannish. For only he who is man enough will redeem the woman in woman.

And this hypocrisy I found to be the worst among them: That even those who are in command feign the virtues of those who serve.

"I serve, you serve, we serve" — thus even the ruling hypocrisy prays here; and woe if the first master is but the first servant!

Alas, I guess the curiosity of my eye flew too far into their hypocrisies too; and well I guessed all their fly-happiness and their buzzing around sunny windowpanes.

So much kindness, so much weakness I see. So much justice and pity, so much weakness.

Round, kind, and goodly they are with each other, just as grains of sand are round, kind, and goodly with each other.

To embrace modestly a small happiness — this they call "resignation"! and at the same time they are already modestly eyeing a new small happiness.

At bottom they simply want one thing most of all: that no one do them ill.

So they get the jump on everyone and do them well.

But this is cowardice, even though it be called virtue.

And if for once they speak harshly, these small people : I hear only their hoarseness in it, — for every draught of air makes them hoarse.

Clever they are, their virtues have clever fingers. But they lack fists, their fingers do not know how to huddle behind fists.

To them virtue is that which makes modest and tame: with that they have made the wolf into a dog and man himself into man's best domestic animal.

"We place our chair in the middle" — this their smirking says to me — "and just as far away from dying gladiators as from satisfied pigs."

But this is — mediocrity: even though it be called moderation. —

3

I pass through this people and let fall many a word: but they know neither how to take it nor how to retain it.

They marvel that I came not to rail against lusts and vice; and verily, I came not to warn against pickpockets either!

They marvel that I am not ready yet to whet and abet their wit: as if they did not already have enough smart-alecks whose voices grate on me like slate pencils!

And when I cry: "A curse on all the cowardly devils in you that like to whine and fold their hands and adore": then they cry: "Zarathustra is godless."

And especially their teachers of resignation cry this —; but precisely into their ears I love to shout: Yes, I am Zarathustra the godless!

These teachers of resignation! Anywhere there is something small and sick and scabby, there they crawl, like lice: and only my nausea prevents me from squashing them.

Well then! This is my sermon for their ears: I am Zarathustra the godless who says here "Who is more godless than I that I may rejoice in his instruction?"

I am Zarathustra the godless: where am I to find my equal? And all those are my equals who give themselves their own wills and give up all resignation.

I am Zarathustra the godless: I cook every chance in my pot regardless. And only when it is fully cooked do I welcome it as my food.

And verily, many a chance came arrogantly to me: but more arrogantly still my will spoke to it, — then it lay there just begging on its knees —

— begging to find hearth and heart with me, and egging me on fawningly:

"Just look, O Zarathustra, how only a friend comes to a friend!" —

But why do I speak when no one has my ears? And so I will shout it out to all the winds:

You are growing ever smaller, you small people! You are crumbling, you comfort-creatures! You will yet come to ruin —

— by your many small virtues, by your many small omissions, by your many small submissions!

Too tender, too yielding: such is your soil! But for a tree to become great, it must take hard root around hard rock!

Even what you fail to do is woven into the web of all human future; even your naught is a spider web which feeds on the blood of the future.

And when you take, then it is like stealing, you small-virtued ones; but even among thieves honor speaks: "Thou shalt only steal where thou canst not rob."

"It will pass" — that too is a teaching of resignation. But I tell you, you comfort-creatures: it will take a pass at you and take more and more from you!

Alas, if only you would renounce all half-willing and become resolved in idleness as well as in action.

Alas, if only you would understand my word: "Always do what you will, —

but first be those who can will!"

"Always love your neighbor as yourself, — but first be those who love themselves —

— loving with a great love, loving with a great contempt!" Thus speaks Zarathustra the godless. —

But why do I speak when no one has my ears? It is still too early an hour for me here.

My own precursor am I among these people, my own cock-crow down dark lanes.

But their hour is coming! And mine is coming too! Hourly they become smaller, poorer, more unfruitful, — poor plant! poor soil!

And soon they shall stand there for me like dry grass and prairie, and verily!

weary of themselves — and thirsting, more for fire than for water!

O blessed hour of lightning! O mystery before noontide! —

One day yet I will make running fires out of them and heralds with tongues of flame: —

— one day yet they shall herald it with tongues of flame: It is coming, it is nigh, the great noontide!

Thus spake Zarathustra.

On The Mount Of Olives

Winter, a bad guest, sits by me at home; my hands are blue from the handshake of his friendship.

I honor him, this bad guest, but gladly let him sit alone. Gladly I run away from him; and if one runs well, one can escape him!

With warm feet and warm thoughts I run there, where the wind stands still, to the sunny hideout of my mount of olives.

There I laugh at my severe guest and even think well of him for removing flies from my place and silencing many small noises.

For he will not suffer it if a gnat wants to sing, or perhaps two; even the lane he makes lonely, so that the moonlight is frightened there at night.

A hard guest is he, — but I honor him and do not pray, like the weaklings do, to the potbellied fire-idol.

Even a little teeth-chattering rather than idol-worshipping! — thus my kind wills it.

And I am especially hostile towards all fervent, stuffy, steamy fireidols.

Him whom I love I love better in winter than in summer; better do I mock my enemies and more valiantly, now that winter sits in my home.

Valiant indeed, even when I crawl into bed —: there my holed-up happiness laughs and even raises holy hell, there even my lie of a dream laughs.

Me — a crawler? Not once in my life have I crawled before the mighty; and if ever I lied, then I lied out of love. That is why I am happy even in a winter bed.

A humble bed warms me more than a rich one, for I am jealous of my poverty.

And in winter she is most faithful to me.

I begin each day with an act of malice; I mock winter with a cold bath: my severe friend of the family grumbles at that.

I also tickle him gladly with a little wax candle: that he may finally let the sky out of its ashy-gray twilight.

For I am especially malicious in the morning: at that early hour when the pail rattles at the well and the horses neigh warmly down gray lanes: —

Impatiently I wait then for the bright sun to finally rise, the snow-bearded winter sky, the ancient wight and white-head, —

— the winter sky, the quiet one who often keeps even his sun quietly in hiding!

Could it be that I learned the long bright silence from him? Or did he learn it from me? Or did each of us invent it himself?

The source of all good things is thousand-fold, — all good high-spirited things spring to life out of joy: how could they ever do that — only once?

The long silence is also a good high-spirited thing, and like the winter sky, to look out from a bright, round-eyed countenance: —

— like him, to hide his sun and his inflexible solar will, verily, this art and these winter high spirits I have learned well!

My favorite art and act of malice it is, that my silence has learned not to betray itself through silence.

With chit-chat and rattling dice I outwit the solemn ones-in-waiting; my will and purpose shall give all these strict watchdogs the slip.

That no one may see down to my foundation and final will, — that is why I invented the long bright silence.

Many a shrewd man I found: he veiled his face and roiled his water so that no one could see down and through him.

Precisely to him, however, came the shrewder mistrusters and nutcrackers:

precisely his most-hidden fish they fished out!

But the clear, the valiant, the transparent — to me these are the shrewdest of the silent: their foundation is so deep that not even the clearest water — reveals it. —

You snow-bearded silent winter sky, you round-eyed whitehead above me!

O you heavenly likeness of my soul and its high spirits!

And must I not hide myself like one who has swallowed gold, — lest they slit open my soul?

Must I not walk on stilts, that they may overlook my long legs, — all these envy-imps and injury-pimps around me?

These smoky, room-warm, worn-out, withered, woebegone souls — how could their envy endure my happiness?

So I show them only the ice and winter on my peaks — and not that my mountain winds all the solar zones around itself besides!

They hear only my winter storms whistling: and not that I also travel over warm seas, like longing, heavy, hot, south winds.

They still feel pity at my haps and mishaps: — but my word is: "Let haphazard come to me: it is innocent, like a little child!"

How could they endure my happiness unless I set mishaps and polar bear caps and winter hardships and snowy heavens' coverings around my happiness?

— unless I myself sighed before them and chattered with cold and patiently let them swathe me in their pity!

This is the wise high-spiritedness and kind-spiritedness of my soul, that it hides not its winter and its ice storms; it hides not its chilblains either.

To one person solitude is the flight of the sick; to another solitude is the flight from the sick.

Let them hear me sighing and chattering from the winter cold, all these poor jealous jokers around me! With such sighing and chattering I still flee their heated rooms.

Let them sigh and sympathize with me over my chilblains: "From the ice of knowledge he will yet freeze to death!" — thus they lament.

In the meantime I run with warm feet here, there, and everywhere on my mount of olives: in the sunny hideout of my mount of olives I sing and mock all pity. —

Thus sang Zarathustra.

On The Apostates

1

Alas, already all lies withered and gray which but lately stood green and gay in this meadow! And how much honey of hope I carried from here to my beehives!

All these young hearts have already become old, — and not even old! only weary, vulgar, comfortable: — as they put it, "We have become pious again."

Just recently I saw them run out in the morning on brave feet: but their feet of knowledge grew weary, and now they even slander their morning bravery.

Verily, many of them once lifted their legs like dancers, the laughter in my wisdom winked at them: — then they thought better of it. Just now I saw one of them bent over — crawling to the cross.

Around light and freedom they once fluttered like gnats and young poets. A little older, a little colder: and already they are muddlers, mumblers, and mama's boys.

Did their hearts perhaps despair because solitude had swallowed me up like a whale? Did their ears perhaps hark longingly-long but in vain for me and my trumpet- and herald-calls?

— Alas! there are always but few whose hearts are long on spirit and high spirits; and among these the spirit remains patient, too. The rest, however, are cowards.

The rest: that is always the most, the commonplace, the superfluous, the many-too-many — all these are cowardly! —

He who is of my kind will also run across the experiences of my kind along the way: so that his first companions must be corpses and buffoons.

But his second companions — they will call themselves his believers: a lively bunch, with much love, much folly, much beardless veneration.

On these believers he shall not set his heart, he who is of my kind among mankind; in these springtimes and gay meadows he shall not believe, he who knows flighty-faint human nature!

If they could do otherwise, then they would will otherwise, too. Half-and halves spoil everything whole. That leaves become withered, — what is there to cry about in that?

Let them go ahead and fall, O Zarathustra, and do not cry about it!

Better yet, blow with a rustling wind amongst them, —

— blow amongst these leaves, O Zarathustra: that everything withered may scurry away from you even faster! —

2

"We have become pious again" — so these apostates confess; and many of them are even too cowardly to confess thus.

I look them in the eye, — I say it to their faces and to the redness of their cheeks: you are those who pray again!

But it is a disgrace to pray! Not for everyone, but for you and me and whoever has a conscience in his head! For you it is a disgrace to pray!

You know it well: the cowardly devil in you who is fond of hand-folding and placing-hands-in-lap and wants to have it easier: — this cowardly devil exhorts you: "There is a God!"

But with that you belong to the light-shunning class, those whom the light never leaves in peace; now every day you must stick you head deeper into darkness and dampness!

And verily, you have chosen the hour well: for even now the night birds are flying out again. The hour has come for all the light-shunning folk, the eveningand leisure hour, when they are not — "at leisure."

I hear and smell it: their hour for hunting and ranging, not for a wild hunt of course, but for a tame, lame, prying, soft sashayers'- and prayers'-hunt —

— for a hunt after soulful sneaks: all the hearts' mousetraps have been set once again! And wherever I lift up a curtain, a little night-moth comes rushing out.

Did it perhaps cower there together with another little night-moth? For everywhere I smell little hidden communities; and wherever there are little chambers, there are new devotees within and a devotees' haze.

They spend long evenings sitting together and talking: "Let us become like little children again and say 'Dear God!'" — ruined in mouth and stomach by the pious confectioners.

Or they spend long evening watching a cunning, watchful cross-spider that preaches prudence to the other spiders and teaches thus: "Under crosses there is good spinning!"

Or they spend the day sitting by swamps with fishing rods, thereby thinking themselves profound; but he who fishes where there are no fish I do not even call superficial!

Or they learn to play the harp in a godly-gay way from a poet of song who would love to harp his way into the young girls' hearts: for he has grown weary of the old ladies and their praises.

Or they learn to shudder from a learned half-wit who waits in dark chambers for the spirit to come to him — and the spirit completely deserts him!

Or they listen to an old hobo moan- and groan-whistler who has picked up the sadness of tones from the sad winds; now he whistles like the wind and preaches sadness in sad tones.

And some of them have even become night watchmen: now they know how to blow into horns and go about at night and wake up old things that have long since gone to sleep.

Five remarks about old things I heard last night by the garden wall: they came from such old, sad, dried-up night watchmen as these.

"For a father he doesn't care enough about his children: human fathers do this better!"

"He's too old! In fact, he doesn't care about his children at all anymore" —

thus answered the other night watchman.

"Has he any children then? No one can prove it unless he proves it himself! I have long wanted him to thoroughly prove it for once."

"Prove? As if he had ever proven anything! He finds proving difficult; he thinks the world of people believing in him."

"Yes! Yes! Belief saves him, belief in him. That's just the way of old people!

And that goes for us, too!"—

— Thus the two old night watchmen and light-frightmen spoke to each other and tooted sadly on their horns: so it was last night by the garden wall.

My heart, however, squirmed with laughter and was about to shatter and knew not, whither? and sank into my midriff.

Verily, it will be the death of me yet, to choke with laughter when I see drunken asses and hear night watchmen doubting God thus.

Is not the time long since past for even having such doubts? Who can still awaken such old, sleeping, light-shunning things?

With the old gods after all, the end has long since come to pass: and verily, a gay, goodly, godly ending they had!

They did not "twilight" themselves to death, — that is surely a lie! On the contrary: one day they laughed themselves to death!

That happened when a god himself came out with the ungodliest saying, —

the saying: "There is one God! Thou shalt have no other gods before me!" —

— an old grimbeard of a god, a jealous one, forgot himself this way: —

And then all the gods laughed and rocked back in their chairs and cried out:

"Is this not honest-to-Godliness, that there are gods but no God!"

He that has ears to hear, let him hear. —

Thus talked Zarathustra in the town which he loved and which is also surnamed "The Dappled Cow." For from here he had only two days journey back to his cave and his animals; his soul rejoiced continually, however, at the imminence of his return home.

—

The Return Home

O Solitude! My homeland, Solitude! Too long have I lived abroad, savagely in savage remoteness, not to return to you with tears!

Now just threaten me with your finger, the way mothers threaten, now smile at me, the way mothers smile, now just say: "And who was it that once stormed away from me like a stormwind? —

— who cried out in parting: I have sat too long with Solitude, I have unlearned silence! That — you have learned now, I presume?

O Zarathustra, I know everything: and that you were more forsaken among the many, you lone one, than you ever were by me!

Forsakenness is one thing, loneliness another: That — you have learned now! And that among men you will always be savage and strange:

— savage and strange even when they love you: for before anything else they want to be spared!

Here, however, you are at house and home with yourself; here you can speak out about anything and pour out all the reasons, here nothing is ashamed of hidden, hardened feelings.

Here all things come caressingly to your speech and flatter you: for they want to ride upon your back. Here on every simile you ride to every truth.

Upright and uprightly you can speak to all things here: and verily, it sounds like praise to their ears, for someone to speak to all things — straightforwardly!

But being forsaken is another thing. Then, do you remember, O Zarathustra?

When your bird shrieked overhead, when you stood in the forest perplexed, not knowing which way?, next to a corpse: —

— when you said: May my animals lead me! More dangerous have I found it among men than among beasts: — That was forsakenness!

And do you remember, O Zarathustra? When you sat on your island, a well of wine among empty buckets, giving and giving out, bestowing and bestowing out among the thirsty:

— until at last you alone sat thirsty among the drunken ones and complained nightly 'Is taking not more blessed than giving? And stealing not more blessed yet than taking?' — That was forsakenness!

And do you remember, O Zarathustra? When your stillest hour came and drove you away from yourself, when it spoke to you in a wicked whisper: 'Chatter and shatter!'—

— when it made you regret all your waiting and silence and discouraged your humble courage: That was forsakenness!" —

O Solitude! My homeland, Solitude! How blessed and tender your voice speaks to me!

We do not question each other, we do not complain to each other, we go openly together through open doors.

For it is open by you and bright; and here the hours pass by on lighter feet, too. For in the darkness time weighs more heavily on us than in the light.

Here the words and word-coffers of all being spring open for me: here all being wants to become word, here all becoming wants to learn speech from me.

But down there — there all speech is in vain! There forgetting and passingby is the best wisdom: That — I have learned now!

He who would get a grasp on all things human must grasp all things human. But my hands are too clean for that.

Even their breath I do not care to breathe; alas, to have lived so long amidst their clamor and bad breath!

O blessed stillness around me! O pure scents around me! O how from a deep breast this stillness draws pure breath! O how it listens, this blessed stillness!

But down there — there everything speaks, there everything is misheard.

One may ring in one's wisdom with bells: the traders in the marketplace will outjingle it with pennies!

Everything speaks by them, now one knows how to understand any more.

Everything falls to the ground, nothing falls into deep wells any more.

Everything speaks by them, nothing prospers and comes to a proper end.

Everyone cackles, but who wants to sit still on the nest and hatch the eggs?

Everything speaks by them, everything gets talked to death. And that which yesterday was still too hard for time itself and its tooth: today it hangs, gnawed and pawed away, from the mouths of the men of today.

Everything speaks by them, everything is revealed. And what was once called the secret and the secrecy of profound souls now belongs to the streettrumpeters and other butterflies.

O human nature, you curious thing! You noise on dark streets! Now you lie behind me again: my greatest danger lies behind me!

In sparing and pitying my greatest danger always lay; and all human nature wants to be spared and suffered.

With pent-up truths, with a fool's hand and a smitten heart, and rich in pity's little lies: — thus have I always lived among men.

Disguised I sat among them, ready to mistake myself in order to endure them, and readily telling myself: "You fool, you do not understand man!"

One unlearns man when one lives among men: there is too much foreground in all men — what can far-seeing, far-seeking eyes do there?

And when they mistook me: I, fool, spared them more than myself on that account: accustomed as I am to hardness towards myself, and often even taking vengeance on myself for this forbearance.

Stung all over by poisonous flies and hollowed out like a stone by the many drops of spite — thus I sat among them and still tried to persuade myself:

"Everything small is innocent of its smallness!"

Especially those who call themselves "the good" I found to be the most poisonous flies: they sting in all innocence, they lie in all innocence; towards me how could they be — just?

He who lives among the good — pity teaches him to lie. Pity makes the air stuffy for all free souls. For the stupidity of the good is unfathomable.

To conceal myself and my riches — that I learned down there: for I found everyone still poor in spirit. This was the lie of my pity that I knew in everyone.

— that I saw and smelled in everyone what was just enough spirit for them and what was already too much spirit for them!

Their strait-laced sages: I called them sagacious, not strait-laced, — thus I learned to slur words. Their gravediggers: I called them researchers and testers, — thus I learned to change words.

The gravediggers dig themselves sick. Bad fumes rest under old rubbish.

One should not stir up the morass. One should live upon mountains.

With blissful nostrils I breathe mountain freedom again! My nose is freed at last from the smell of all things human in nature!

Tickled by the keen air as if by a sparkling wine, my soul sneezes — sneezes and rejoices to itself: Gesundheit!

Thus spake Zarathustra.

On The Three Evils

1

In a dream, in my last dream of the morning, I stood today on a promontory, — beyond the world: held a pair of scales and weighed the world.

Alas that the rosy dawn came too early to me: she glowed me awake, the jealous one!

She is always jealous of the glow of my morning dream.

Measurable by him who has the time, weighable by a good weigher, wingable by means of strong wings, crackable by divine nutcrackers: thus did my dream find the world: —

My dream, a bold sailor, half-ship, half-gale, silent as a butterfly, impatient as a falcon: but how did it have the patience and leisure for world-weighing today!

Did my wisdom secretly speak to it perhaps, my laughing, waking day-wisdom which scoffs at all "infinite worlds"? For it says: "Where there is force, there number will also be mistress: it has more force."

How securely my dream looked upon this finite world, not curiously, not spuriously, not knock-kneed, not pleading:

— as if a full apple offered itself to my hand, a ripe golden apple with coolsmooth, velvety skin: thus the world offered itself to me: —

— as if a tree beckoned to me, a broad-branched and strong-willed one, curved into an armrest and even a footrest for the way-weary: thus stood the world on my promontory:

— as if delicate hands carried a shrine towards me, — a shrine open for the delight of modest, adoring eyes: thus the world offered itself to me today: —

— not riddle enough to scare human love away, not solution enough to lull human wisdom to sleep: — a humanly good thing the world was for me today, of which people have such bad things to say!

How I thank my morning dream for allowing me thus to weigh the world early this morning! As a humanly good thing it came to me, this dream and heartcomforter!

And that I may do the like by day and learn by and after observing its best: I will now place the three worst things on the scale and weigh them in a humanly good way. —

He who taught to bless also taught to curse: what are the three best-cursed things in the world? These I will place on the scale.

Sensuality, lust for power, selfishness: these three have hitherto been the best cursed, worst slanted and slandered, — these three I will weigh in a humanly good way.

Well then! Here is my promontory and there the sea; it rolls itself hither to me, shaggily, fawningly, the faithful old hundred-headed dog-monster that I love.

Well then! Here will I hold the scales over the rolling sea: and a witness too I will choose, to oversee, — you, you recluse-tree, you strongly-scented, broadlyarched one which I love! —

By what bridge does the Now pass to the Hereafter? By what force does the high force its way to the low? And what bids even the highest thing to everupwards grow?

Now the scales are balanced and still; three heavy questions I throw in, three heavy answers the other scale holds.

2

Sensuality: to all hair-shirted despisers of the body, their thorn and stake, and cursed as "the world" by all afterworlders: for it mocks and dupes all confusion- and delusion-teachers.

Sensuality: to the rabble, the slow fire on which they are burned; to all worm-eaten wood, to all stinking rags, the ready lust- and must-oven.

Sensuality: for the free hearts, innocent and free, an earthly garden of delight, all the future's excess thanks to the present.

Sensuality: only for the wilted a sweet poison; for the lion-willed, however, the great cordial and reverently-considered wine of wines.

Sensuality: the great metaphorical happiness for a higher happiness and the highest hope. For to many is marriage promised, and more than marriage, —

— to many that are stranger to each other than man and woman: and who has fully grasped how strange man and woman are to each other?

Sensuality: but I want hedges around my thoughts and even around my words, lest swine and swooners break into my garden!

Lust for power: the red-hot scourge of the hardest of the hard-hearted; the gruesome torture reserved for the cruelest ones themselves; the gloomy flame of living funeral pyres.

Lust for power: the wicked gadfly which is set upon the vainest people; the scorner of all uncertain virtue; it rides on every horse and every sort of pride.

Lust for power: the earthquake that breaks and breaks open everything rotten and hollow; the rumbling, grumbling shatterer of whited sepulchres; the flashing question mark next to premature answers.

Lust for power: before whose glance man creeps and stoops and drudges and becomes lower than serpent and swine: until finally the great contempt cries out of him —, Lust for power: the terrible schoolmistress of the great contempt that preaches in the face of cities and kingdoms "Away with you!" — until out of themselves there cries out "Away with me!"

Lust for power: which, however, also rises alluringly to the pure and solitary ones and up to self-sufficient heights, glowing like a love which paints crimson joys alluringly on earthy skies.

Lust for power: but who would call it lustmania when the high lusts downward for power! Verily, there is nothing sick or manic in such lusting and descending! That the lonely height may not be eternally alone and self-sufficing; that the mountain may come to the valley and the winds of the height to the plains: —

O who could find the right baptismal and moral name for such longing!

"Bestowing virtue" — thus Zarathustra once named the unnameable.

And at that time it also happened — and verily, it happened for the first time! — that his word glorified selfishness, the sound, healthy selfishness which wells up out of a mighty soul: —

— out of a mighty soul, to which the lofty body belongs, the handsome, triumphant, uplifting body around which every thing becomes a mirror:

— the supple, persuasive body, the dancer whose likeness and epitome the self-delighting soul is. The self-delight of such bodies and souls calls itself: "virtue."

With its words about good and bad such self-delight shelters itself as if with sacred groves; with the names of its happiness it banishes everything contemptible from itself.

It banishes everything cowardly from itself; it says: "Bad — that is cowardly!"

It thinks contemptible the ever-sighing, the ever-crying, the worry-warts, and whoever gleans the least little advantage.

It despises as well all woe-happy wisdom: for verily, there is also a wisdom which blooms in the dark, a nightshade wisdom which always says "All is vain!"

Shy mistrust it thinks little of, and anyone who demands oaths instead of looks and hands: also all the all-too-mistrustful wisdom, for such is the nature of cowardly souls.

It thinks even less of the quick-to-please, the doglike, who lie on their backs immediately, the submissive; and there is also a wisdom which is submissive and doglike and pious and quick to please.

Utterly hateful and distasteful to it is he who will never defend himself, he who swallows down poisonous spittle and evil glances, the all-too-patient, allsuffering, all-satisfied one: for that is slavish in nature.

Whether one be slavish before gods and godly kicks, or before humans and stupid human opinions: all slavish nature it spits on, this blessed selfishness!

Bad: so it calls all that is crest-fallen and slavish-knavish, unfree blinkereyes, depressed hearts, and that falsely compliant nature which kisses with thick lily-livered lips.

And mock-wisdom: so it calls all the wit which slaves, grayheads, and weary-warts affect; and especially the whole sick, sophomoric, sophistical priestly-foolishness.

The would-be-wise, however, all the priests, the world-weary, and those whose souls are slavish and womanish in nature, — O how all along their game has been to play a nasty game on selfishness!

And precisely this was meant to pass for virtue and to be virtue, that one play a nasty game on selfishness! And "selfless" — thus with good reason all these world-weary cowards and cross-spiders wished this term upon themselves!

But for all of them the day is now at hand, the transformation, the executioner's sword, the great noontide: many things shall then come to light.

And he who pronounces the "I" wholesome and holy and selfishness blessed, verily, he, a foreteller, tells likewise what he knows: "Behold, it is coming, it is nigh, the great noontide!"

Thus spake Zarathustra.

On The Spirit Of Gravity

1

My glib tongue — is of the people: too coarsely and cordially do I speak for the Angora rabbits. And my word sounds even stranger to all ink-fishes and quill-foxes.

My hand — is a fool's hand: woe to all tables and walls and whatever has room for fool's scrolling, fool's scrawling!

My foot — is a horse's foot; with it I trot and trample over hill and dale, criss-crossing the fields, devilishly pleased with all fast running.

My stomach — is an eagle's stomach, perhaps? For it loves lamb's flesh the best. Certainly, however, it is a bird's stomach.

Nourished on innocent things and on hardly anything, ready and impatient to fly, to fly away — this is now my nature: how could there not be something of a bird-nature therein!

And chiefly, that I may be an enemy to the spirit of gravity — this is birdnature:

and indeed, a sworn enemy, an arch-enemy, the original enemy! O where has my enmity not yet flown and misflown!

Of that I could well sing a song — — and will sing it: even though I am alone in an empty house and must sing it to my own ears.

There are other singers, of course, for whom only a full house can make their throats soft, their hands talkative, their eyes expressive, their hearts awake:— I am not like them. —

2

He who one day teaches men to fly will have removed all boundary stones; all boundary stones will themselves fly in the air for him, the earth he will baptize anew — as "The Light One."

The ostrich runs faster than the fastest horse, but he still sticks his head heavily into the heavy earth: so it is with the man who cannot yet fly.

Earth and life are heavy for him; and thus the spirit of gravity wills it! But he who would be light and a bird must love himself: thus I teach.

Of course not with the love of the sick and the diseased: for with these even self-love stinks!

One must learn to love oneself — thus I teach — with a wholesome and healthy love: to stand by oneself and not go roaming around.

Such roaming around dubs itself "neighborly love": the best lying and dissembling yet has been with these words, and especially by those whom all the world has found to be burdensome.

And verily, it is no commandment for today and tomorrow, to learn to love oneself. On the contrary, of all the arts this is the subtlest, slipperiest, latest, and most patient.

Because for its owner all that is his own is well-hidden; and of all treasure troves our own is the last to be unearthed — thus the spirit of gravity manages it.

Almost as early as the cradle we are showered with grave words and values:

"good" and "evil" — thus this dowry calls itself. For its sake we are forgiven for living.

And therefore one suffers the little children to come unto one, in order to prevent them betimes from loving themselves: thus the spirit of gravity manages it.

And we — we faithfully carry the dowry we are given, on hard shoulders and over rugged mountains! And if we sweat, they say to us: "Yes, life is hard to bear!"

But man is only hard for himself to bear! That comes from carrying too many strange things on his shoulders. Like a camel he kneels down and allows himself to be well-laden.

Especially the strong, load-bearing man in which reverence dwells: too many strange, heavy words and values he loads upon himself, — then life seems to him a desert!

And verily! Many a thing that is our very own is also hard to bear! And much that is inside man is like an oyster, namely, loathsome and slippery and hard to grasp —, — so that a noble shell with noble embellishment must plead on its behalf.

But this art too one must learn: to have a shell and a fine shine and a prudent blindness!

Many things about man deceive repeatedly, because many a shell is low and sad and too much shell. Much hidden goodness and strength is never divined; the tastiest dainties find no tasters!

Women know that, the daintiest ones do: a little fatter, a little thinner — O how much destiny lies in so little!

Man is hard to discover, and hardest of all for himself; the spirit often lies about the soul. Thus the spirit of gravity manages it.

But he has discovered himself who says: This is my good and evil: with this he has silenced the mole and dwarf which says: "Good for all, evil for all."

Verily, I also do not care for those who call every thing good and this the best of all possible worlds. Those I call the all-satisfied.

Pan-satisfaction, which knows how to taste everything: that is not the best taste! I honor the unruly choosy tongues and stomachs which have learned to say "I" and "Yes" and "No."

But to chew and digest everything — that is truly swinish in nature!

Always to say Ye-haw (Yes and Hee-haw) — only the ass has learned that, and those of his frame of mind! —

Deep yellow and hot red: thus my taste wills it, — it mixes blood with all colors. But he who whitewashes his house betrays a whitewashed soul to me.

Some in love with mummies, the others with ghosts, and both alike foes to all that is flesh and blood — O how they both run contrary to my taste! For I love blood.

And I refuse to reside and abide where everyone spits and spews: that is now my taste, — rather would I live among perjurers and thieves. No one carries gold in his mouth.

Even more repulsive to me, however, are all lickspittles; and the most repulsive human animal I found I christened parasite: it would not love and yet wanted to live on love.

Unhappy I call all those who have but one choice: to become evil beasts or evil tamers of beasts: among such men I would build no tabernacles.

Unhappy I also call all those who must always wait, — that runs contrary to my taste: all the publicans and tradesmen and kings and other land- and storekeepers.

Verily, I also learned waiting, and thoroughly so, — but only waiting for myself. And above all else I learned standing and walking and running and jumping and dancing and climbing.

My teaching, however, is this: he who would one day learn to fly must first learn standing and walking and running and jumping and dancing and climbing:

you do not fly into flying!

With rope ladders I learned to climb up to many a window, with nimble legs I clambered up high masts: and to sit atop high masts of perception seemed to me no mean bliss, —

— like a small flame flickering atop high masts: a small light, of course, but a great consolation to sailors driven off-course and castaways! —

By many means and methods I came to my truth: not by one ladder did I climb to the height where my eye roams about in my distance.

And only reluctantly did I ever ask about the way, — that always went against my taste! Rather I asked and assayed the ways themselves!

All my going has been a testing and a questioning: and verily, one must also learn to answer such questioning! That, however — is my taste:

— not good, not bad, but my taste, for which I no longer make a secret nor feel any shame.

"This — is now my way, — where is yours?" thus I answered those who asked me "the way." For the way — it does not exist!

Thus spake Zarathustra.

On Old And New Tables

1

Here I sit and wait, old broken tables around me and also new half-written tables. When will my hour come?

— the hour of my going down, my downgoing: for yet once more will I go unto men.

For that I now wait: for first the signs must come to me that this is my hour, — namely, the laughing lion with the flight of doves.

In the meantime I talk to myself as one who has the time. No one tells me anything new: so I tell myself to myself. —

2

When I came to men, I found them sitting on an old conceit: they all thought that for a long time now they have known what is good and evil for man.

All talk of virtue they thought to be an old played-out thing; and he who wanted to sleep well always talked about "good" and "evil" before going to sleep!

I disturbed this slumber when I taught: no one yet knows what good and evil is: — unless he be the creator!

— That, however, is he who creates man's goal and gives to the earth its meaning and its future: he first makes something be good or evil.

And I told them to overturn their old academic chairs and wherever that old conceit was seated; I told them to laugh at their virtue-masters and saints and poets and world-saviors.

At their gloomy wise men I told them to laugh, and at whomever was seated in warning like a black scarecrow on the tree of life.

On the great grave-highway I sat down, and even among carrion and vultures — and I laughed at all their days of yore and their rotten decaying splendor.

Verily, like penitential preachers and fools I cried out in rage and shame at all their things great and small, — that their best is so very small! That their worst is so very small! — thus I laughed.

My wise longing, begotten in the mountains, laughed and cried out of me thus, a wild wisdom indeed! — my great wing-tingling longing.

And often it carried me off and up and away and in the midst of laughter:

then I flew shuddering, an arrow, through sun-drunken raptures:

— out into distant futures which no dream had yet seen, into souths hotter than any artist ever dreamed: there, where dancing gods are ashamed of all clothing:

—

— because I speak in parables and halt and stammer like the poets: and verily, I am ashamed that I must still be a poet! —

Where all becoming seemed to me gods' dancing and gods' exuberancing, and the world was let out and let loose and fleeing back to itself: —

— as an eternal self-fleeing and self-seeking-again of many gods, as the blessed gainsaying, again- hearing, again-adhering to each other of many gods: —

Where all time seemed to me a blessed mockery of moments, where necessity was freedom itself playing happily with the thorn of freedom: —

Where I also found again my old devil and arch-enemy, the spirit of gravity, and all that he has created: constraint, statute, need and result and purpose and will and good and evil: —

For must there not be that which is danced over, danced across? Must there not for the sake of the light, of the lightest — be moles and heavy dwarves?" —

3

It was there also, by the way, where I picked up the word "Superman," and that man is something that must be overcome.

— that man is a bridge and not a goal: counting himself blessed on account of his noontide and evening as the way to new rosy dawns: —

— the Zarathustra-word on the great noontide and whatever else I hung above man like another purple sunset sky.

Verily, new stars likewise I let them see, together with new nights; and above the clouds and day and night I even spread laughter like a gay canopy.

I taught them all my aims and schemes: to collect and condense into one what is fragment in man and riddle and terrible chance, —

— as the composer, riddle-reader, and redeemer of chance I taught them to work on the future and creatively redeem —, all that has been.

To redeem the past in man and re-create every "It was," until the will says:

"But so I willed it! So I will will it —"

— this I called their redemption, this alone I taught them to call redemption.

— —

Now I await my redemption —, that I may go to them for the last time.

For once more will I go to men: to my ruin will I go in going down to them, in dying will I give them my richest gift!

This I learned from the sun when it goes down, aboundingly rich: from inexhaustible riches it showers gold into the sea, —

— so that even the poorest fisherman rows with golden oars! For this did I once see and in the watching did not weary of my tears. — —

Like the sun Zarathustra too wants to go down: now he sits here and waits, old broken tables around him, and also new tables, — half-written.

4

Behold, here is a new table: but where are my brothers who will carry it with me down to the valley and into hearts of flesh?

My great love for the furthest ones demands it thus: do not spare your neighbor!

Man is something that must be overcome.

There are many means and methods of overcoming: watch what you do! But only a buffoon thinks: "Man can also be passed over."

Overcome yourself even in your neighbor: and a right you can seize for yourself you should not allow to be given to you!

What you do, no one can do to you in return. Behold, there is no retribution.

He who cannot command himself shall obey. And many a man can command himself, but much is still lacking before he can also obey himself!

5

Thus the nature of noble soul wills it: they want nothing for free, least of all life.

He who is of the masses wants to live for free; but we others, to whom life has given itself, we are always thinking about what we can best give in return!

And verily, that is a grand speech which says: "What life promises us, that promise we shall keep — to life!"

One should not wish to enjoy where one does not give enjoyment. And —

one should not wish to enjoy!

For enjoyment and innocence are the most modest things: neither would be sought after. One should have them — , but one should rather seek even guilt and pain! —

6

O my brothers, he who is a firstling is always sacrificed. Now, however, we are firstlings.

We all bleed on secret, sacrificial altars, we all burn and broil in honor of ancient idols.

The best in us is still young; that excites old palates. Our flesh is tender, our skin is only a lambskin: — how could we not excite old idol-priests!

In our very selves he still dwells, the old idol-priest who broils our best for his feast. Alas, my brothers, how could firstlings not be sacrifices!

But thus our nature wills it; and I love those who will not preserve themselves.

The downgoers I love with all my love: for they go across. —

7

To be true — few can do that! And those who can do not even want to! The good can do it least of all, however.

O these good men! Good men never tell the truth; for the spirit to be good in such a way is a sickness.

They give way, these good men, they give up; their heart mimics, their foundation obeys: but he who obeys turns a deaf ear to hearing himself!

All that the good call evil must come together in order for one truth to be born: O my brothers, are you also evil enough for this truth?

The bold venture, the long mistrust, the cruel Nay, the disgust, the cut to the quick — how seldom these come together! From such a seed, however —

truth is begotten!

All knowledge hitherto has grown up next to a bad conscience! Break, break for me, you knowing ones, the old tables!

8

When the water has been planked over, when walkways and railings leap over the river: verily, he is not believed who then says: "All is in flux."

But even the blockheads contradict him. "What?" the blockheads say, "All in flux? Surely there are walkways and railings over the river?"

"Over the river all is stable, all the values of things, the bridges, the ideas, all the 'good' and 'evil': all that is stable!" —

But comes the hard winter, the river's animal trainer: then even the wittiest learn mistrust; and verily, not only the blockheads then say, "Do not all things —

stand still?"

"Basically all things stand still" — , that is a true winter teaching, a good thing for an unfruitful time, a good consolation for hibernators and homebodies.

"Basically all things stand still" —; against that, however, the thawing wind preaches!

The thawing wind, a bull which is no plow-bull, — a raging bull, a destroyer that breaks the ice with angry horns! Ice, however — — breaks walkways!

O my brothers, is not all now in flux? Have not all walkways and railings fallen into the water? Who would still hold onto "good" and "evil"?

 "Woe to us! Hail to us! The thawing wind blows!" — Preach thus, my brothers, through all the streets!

9

There is an old delusion called good and evil. Around soothsayers and astrologers the wheel of this delusion has hitherto revolved.

Once upon a time people believed in soothsayers and astrologers: and therefore they believed "Fate is everything: you shall, for you must!"

Then again, they mistrusted all soothsayers and astrologers: and therefore they believed "Freedom is everything: you are able, for you are willing!"

O my brothers, with regard to the stars and the future there has hitherto only been delusion, not knowledge: and therefore with regard to good and evil there has hitherto only been delusion, not knowledge.

10

"Thou shalt not steal! Thou shalt not kill!" — such words were once called holy; before them knees and heads were bent and shoes removed.

But I ask you: where have there ever been better robbers and killers in the world than these holy words?

Is there not in all life itself — robbing and killing? And that such words were called holy, was not truth itself — killed therewith?

Or was it a sermon of death that was called holy, that denies and advises against life? O my brothers, break, break for me the old tables!

11

My pity for all that is past is this, that I see: it is abandoned, —

— abandoned to the mercy, the mind, the madness of every generation that comes along and re-interprets all that has been as its bridge!

A great tyrant might arise, a clever monster who by his favor and disfavor could force and enforce all the past: until it became for him a bridge and a herald and an omen and a cockcrow.

This, however, is the other danger and my other source of pity: whoever is of the masses, his thoughts go back to the grandfather, — with the grandfather, however, time comes to an end.

Thus is all the past abandoned: for it may come that one day the masses become master and drown all time in shallow waters.

Therefore, O my brothers, a new nobility is required, as an adversary to all the rabble and all that is tyrannical and to write anew on new tables the word "noble."

For many noble sorts are required, and many sorts of nobles, for there to be nobility! Or, as I once said in a parable: "Is this not honest-to-Godliness, that there are gods but no God?"

12

O my brothers, I hallow you and show you the way to a new nobility; you shall be breeders and begetters and sowers of the future, —

— verily, not to a nobility you can buy like the shopkeepers do, and with shopkeeper's gold: for whatever has its price has little value.

Not where you come from but where you are going to, make this your honor from now on! Your will and your foot, which has a will to go beyond you yourself, — make this your new honor!

Verily, not that you have served a prince — what do princes matter? — or that you have become a bulwark for whatever stands, so that it stands more solidly!

Not that your kind have become courtly at court and you have learned to stand colorfully, like a flamingo, for long hours in shallow ponds: — for standing ability stands the courtier in good stead; and all courtiers believe that among the blessings after death belongs — permission to sit! —

And not that a spirit which they call holy led your forefathers into promised lands, which I promise not to praise: for where the worst of all trees grew, the crucifix — in that land there is nothing to praise! - — and verily, wherever this "Holy Spirit" led his knights, always in these expeditions there went foremost — goats and geese and geeks and Jesus freaks! —

O my brothers, not backward shall your nobility look, but onward! Exiles you shall be from all father and forefather lands!

Your children's land you shall love: let this love be your new nobility, — the undiscovered land, in the remotest seas! For that I bid your sails seek and seek!

In your children you shall make amends for being your fathers' children; thus shall you redeem all the past! This new table I place over you!

13

"Why live? All is vain! Living — that is threshing straw; living — that is burning oneself and still not getting warm." —

Such antiquated babble still passes for "wisdom"; but because it is old and smells musty it therefore acquires more honor. Even mold ennobles. —

Children might speak thus: they shy away from the fire because it has burned them! There is much childishness in the old books of wisdom!

And he who always "threshes straw," why should he be allowed to slander threshing? Such fools must certainly be muzzled!

They sit down at the table and bring nothing with them, not even a good appetite — and then they backbite "All is vain!"

But to eat and drink well, O my brothers, is certainly no vain art! Break, break for me the tables of the never-happy!

14

"Unto the pure all things are pure" — so speak the people. But I say to you:

Unto the swine all things become swinish!

That is why the dreamers and head-droopers, whose hearts also droop, preach: "The world itself is a filthy monster."

For all these are unclean spirits; but especially those who enjoy neither rest nor repose unless they view the world from the backside, — the afterworlders!

I say it to their faces, though it may not sound nice: The world is like man in that it has a backside — so much is true!

In the world there is much filth: so much is true! But the world itself is not therefore a filthy monster!

In this there is wisdom, that many things in the world smell bad: loathing itself creates wings and spring-divining powers!

In the best there is still something loathsome; and the best is still something that must be overcome. —

O my brothers, in this there is much wisdom, that in the world there is much filth! —

15

Such sayings I heard pious afterworlders saying to their conscience, and verily, without wickedness or falsehood — although there is nothing more false in the world or more wicked.

"Just let the world be! Raise not even one finger against it! They will yet learn to renounce the world for that reason."

"And your own reason — you should stifle and strangle it yourself; for it is a reason of this world, — for that reason you yourself shall learn to renounce the world." —

— Break, break to pieces, O my brothers, these old tables of the pious.

Chatter to pieces the sayings of the world-slanderers!

16

"He who learns much unlearns all violent desire" — this is whispered in all the dark alleys today.

"Wisdom makes weary, it is worth — nothing; thou shalt not desire!" —

this new table I found hanging even in open marketplaces.

Break for me, O my brothers, break for me as well this new table! The worldweary hung it up there, and the preachers of death, and the jailors too; for lo, it is also a sermon to servitude: —

Because they learned badly and not the best things, and everything too early and everything too quickly: because they ate badly — for that reason they all got an upset stomach, —

— for their spirit is an upset stomach: it recommends death! Then verily, my brothers, the spirit is a stomach!

Life is a fountain of delight: but all wells are poisoned for him out of whom an upset stomach, the father of affliction, speaks.

To know: that is delight to the lion-willed! But he who has grown weary is himself only "willed"; every wave plays with him.

And thus is it ever with the weaker sort of men: they lose themselves along the way. And at last their weariness simply asks: "Why did we ever go any way at all? It is all the same!"

It is music to their ears to hear this preached: "Nothing is worthwhile! Thou shalt not will" But this is a sermon to servitude.

O my brothers, like a fresh bluster-wind comes Zarathustra to all the wayweary; many noses will he yet get to sneeze!

Even through walls my free breath blows, and into prisons and imprisoned spirits!

Willing sets free: for willing is creating: thus I teach. And you shall learn only for the sake of creating!

And the learning as well you shall only learn from me, the learning-well! He that has ears to hear, let him hear!

17

There stands the boat, — over there it goes, perhaps into the great nothingness.

— But who is willing to go aboard this "perhaps"?

Not one of you is willing to go aboard the boat of death! Why should you be world-weary then?

World-weary! And not once yet have you been earth-removed! Ever lusting for the earth have I found you, ever in love with your own earth-weariness!

Not in vain does your lip hang down: — a little earth-wish still sits upon it!

And in your eye — does not a little cloud of unforgettable bliss still float there?

There are many good inventions on earth, some of them useful, others pleasant: on their account the earth is to be loved.

And so many kinds of well-invented things are there that it is like a woman's breast: useful and pleasant at the same time.

But you world-weary ones! You earth-lazy ones! You should be stroked with switches! With switch strokes your legs should be made lively again.

For: if you are not invalids and worn-out wretches of which the world is weary, then you are sly sluggards and sweet-toothed huggermuggered pleasurecats.

And if you will not run merrily again, then you shall pass away!

To the incurable one should not wish to be a physician: thus Zarathustra teaches: — then you shall pass away!

But it takes more courage to make an end than to make a new verse: all physicians and poets know this. —

18

O my brothers, there are tables which weariness has created and tables which laziness, the rotten-tasting, has created: although they speak alike, they must be heard quite differently. —

See this one languishing here! An inch short of his goal is he, but out of weariness he has lain down defiantly in the dust here: this brave soul!

Now the sun glows on him and the dogs lick his sweat: but he lies here in his defiance and would rather languish:

— languish an inch short of his goal! Verily, you will yet have to drag him by the hair into his heaven, — this hero!

Better yet, let him lie where he has lain and let sleep, the comforter, come to him with cooling, pouring rain:

Let him lie until he wakes up on his own, — until on his own he renounces all weariness and what weariness has instilled in him.

If only, my brothers, you would scare the dogs away from him, the rotten sneaks, and all the swarming vermin: —

— all the swarming vermin of the "cultured," that upon the sweat of every hero — make themselves fat! —

19

I form circles around me and holy boundaries; ever fewer climb with me on ever higher mountains: I build a mountain range out of ever holier mountains. —

But to wheresoever you care to climb with me, O my brothers: see to it that a parasite does not climb with you!

Parasite: that is a creeping, cringing creature that wants to grow fat in your sick, sore corners.

And that is its art, to divine in climbing souls where they are weary: in your sorrow and discontent, in your tender modesty, it builds its disgusting nest.

Where the strong are weak, where the noble are all too gentle, — in there it builds its disgusting nest; the parasite lives where the great have little sore spots.

What is the highest species of all being and the lowest? The parasite is the lowest species; but he that is of the highest species feeds the most parasites.

That soul, namely, which has the longest ladder and can go down the deepest:

how could it not have the most parasites sitting on it? —

— the most extensive soul, which can run and ramble and roam the furthest within itself; the most essential soul, which hurls itself with pleasure into chance: —

— the being soul which plunges into becoming, the having soul which insists upon willing and longing: —

— the self-fleeing soul, which catches up with itself in the widest sphere; the wisest soul, which folly sweet-talks the most: - — the most self-loving soul, in which all things have their current and counter-current and ebb and flow: — O how could the highest soul not have the worst parasites?

20

O my brothers, am I cruel then? But I say: what is falling, we should still push!

Everything today — it is falling, it is falling apart: who would hold it up?

but I — I would still push it!

Do you know the delight which rolls stones into steep depths? — These men of today: just look how they roll into my depths!

A preceding act am I to better players, O my brothers! A precedent! Act on my precedent!

And those you do not teach to fly, teach them — to fall faster! —

21

I love the brave; but it is not enough to wield a broadsword, — one must also know whom to hew!

And often there is more bravery in restraining yourself and passing by:

thereby you preserve yourself for a worthier enemy.

You should only have enemies you may hate, not enemies you may despise:

you must be proud of your enemy: thus I taught once before.

For the worthier enemy, O my friends, you should preserve yourselves:

therefore there is much you must pass by, —

— especially much riff-raff, which noises in your ears about people and peoples.

Keep your eye clear of their For and Against! There is much right, much wrong there: he who looks on flies into a passion.

Viewing thereinto, hewing thereinto — they are one there: therefore go away into the forest and lay your sword to rest!

Go your ways! And let people and peoples go theirs! — dark ways, verily, upon which not even one hope flashes like lightning any longer!

Let the shopkeepers rule there, where all that still glitters is — shopkeeper's gold! It is no longer the time of kings: that which calls itself the people today deserves no kings.

Just look how these peoples themselves now act like the shopkeepers: they glean the least little advantage from every piece of garbage!

They lie in wait for each other, they lie waiting for something from each other, — they call this "good neighborliness." O blessed distant time when a people said to itself: "Over peoples I want to be— master!"

For, my brothers: the best should rule, the best also want to rule! And where the rule is otherwise, there — the best is lacking.

22

If they should — have bread for free, oh my! For what would they cry! Their worktime — that is their true pastime; and they should have it hard!

They are beasts of prey: in their "working" there is still robbing, in their "earning" there is still overreaching! Therefore they should have it hard!

Thus they shall become better beasts of prey, subtler, shrewder, more manlike:

for man is the best beast of prey.

Man has already robbed all the animals of their virtues: that is because of all the animals man has had it the hardest.

Only the birds are above him. And if man learned to fly, oh my! to what height — would his rapacity fly!

23

Thus would I have man and woman: the one fit for war, the other fit for childbirth, but both fit for dancing with head and legs.

And lost be that day to us in which there has not been one bit of dancing!

And false be every truth to us in which there has not been one bit of laughter!

24

Your contracting of marriage: see to it that it is not a bad contract! You contracted too quickly: thus what follows — marriage-breaking!

And better yet marriage-breaking than marriage-bending, marriage-lying!

— Thus spoke a woman to me: "Indeed I broke the marriage, but first the marriage broke — me!"

The badly-paired I always found to be the worst revenge seekers: they make the whole world pay because they can no longer run singly.

That is the reason why I want the honest ones to say to each other: "We love each other: let us see to it that we keep each other beloved! Or shall our promise promise to be a mistake?"

— "Give us a trial period and a little marriage, to see whether we are fit for a big marriage! It is a big thing, always to be two!"

Thus I advise all the honest ones: and what would my love for the Superman be, and for all that is to come, if I advised and spoke otherwise!

Not only to bring something forth, but to bring something up — to that, O my brothers, may the garden of marriage help you!

25

He who has become wise to old sources, behold, at last he will search for wellsprings of the future and new sources. —

O my brothers, it will not be long before new peoples spring up and new wellsprings rush down into new depths.

For the earthquake — it fills in many wells, it makes many languish: it also brings to light inner strengths and secrets.

The earthquake reveals new wellsprings. In the earthquake of old peoples new wellsprings burst forth.

And he who cries out: "Behold, here is a well for many who thirst, one heart for many who yearn, one will for many an instrument": — around him gathers a people, that is: many venturers.

Who can command, who must obey — that is ventured here! Alas, with what long searching and guessing and coming-up-wrong and learning and venturing anew!

Human society: it is a venture, thus I teach, — a long search: it searches, however, for the commander! —

— a venture, O my brothers! And not a covenant! Break, break for me that word of the soft-hearted and half-and-halves!

26

O my brothers! With whom does the greatest danger to all of man's future lie? Is it not with the good and the just? —

— with those who speak and feel in their hearts: "We already know what is good and just, we possess it, too; woe to those who still seek here!"

And whatever harm the wicked may do: the harm the good do is the most harmful harm!

And whatever harm the world-slanderers may do: the harm the good do is the most harmful harm.

O my brothers, there was once one who looked into the hearts of the good and the just and said: "These are the Pharisees." But he was not understood.

The good and the just themselves were not permitted to understand him:

their spirit was imprisoned by their good conscience. The stupidity of the good is unfathomably shrewd.

The truth, however, is this: the good must be Pharisees, — they have no choice!

The good must crucify the one who invents his own virtue! That is the truth!

The second one, however, he who discovered their land, the land, heart, and soil of the good and the just: it was he who asked: "Whom do they hate the most?"

The creator they hate the most: he who breaks tables and old values, the breaker, — they call him lawbreaker.

For the good — they cannot create: they are always the beginning of the end:

—

— they crucify the one who writes new values on new tables, they sacrifice the future to themselves, — they crucify all man's future!

The good — they have always been the beginning of the end. —

27

O my brothers, have you also understood this word? And what I once said about the "last man"? — —

With whom does the greatest danger to all man's future lie? Is it not with the good and the just?

Break, break for me the good and the just! — O my brothers, have you also understood this word?

28

You flee from me? You are terrified? You tremble at this word?

O my brothers, when I bade you break the good and the tables of the good:

only then did I ship man out on his high sea.

And only now does the great terror come to him, the great looking-around, the great sickness, the great nausea, the great seasickness.

False shores and false assurances the good have taught you; you have been born and harbored in the falsehoods of the good. Everything has been thoroughly hooked and crooked by the good.

But he who has discovered the country "Man" has also discovered the country "Man's Future." Now you shall be my seafarers, valiant, patient!

Walk upright betimes, O my brothers, learn to walk upright! The sea rages:

many want to right themselves again on you.

The sea rages: everything is in the sea. Well then! Come on! You old tarhearts!

Fatherland — what of it! There our helm wants to go, where our children's land is! Out there, more raging than the sea, rages our great longing! —

29

"Why so hard!" — the kitchen coal once said to the diamond: "Are we not then close kin?" —

Why so soft? O my brothers, thus I ask you: are you not then — my brothers?

Why so soft, so pliant and compliant? Why so much denial, self-denial, in your hearts? So little destiny in your glances?

And if you would not be destinies and inexorable ones with me: how can you one day — conquer with me?

And if your hardness would not flash and cut and cut to pieces with me:

how can you one day — create with me?

For creators are hard. And blessedness must it seem to you, to press your hand upon millennia as upon wax, —

— blessedness, to write upon the will of millennia as upon bronze, —

harder than bronze, nobler than bronze. Only the noblest is entirely hard.

This new table, O my brothers, I place over you: become hard! —

30

O thou my will! Thou turnaround of all need, my necessity! Preserve me from all small victories!

Thou sending out of my soul which I call fate! Thou In-me! Over-me! Preserve and reserve me for one great fate!

And thy last greatness, my will, reserve it for last, — that thou may be inexorable in thy victory! Alas, who has not been overcome by his victory!

Alas, whose eye would not grow dim in this drunken twilight! Alas, whose foot would not stumble and forget in victory how — to stand!

— That I may one day be ready and ripe at the great noontide: ready and ripe like glowing bronze, lightning-gravid clouds, and swelling milk-udders:

— ready for my self and my most hidden will: a bow on fire for its arrow, an arrow on fire for its star —

— a star, ready and ripe at its noontide, glowing, transfixed, transported by annihilating sun-arrows:

— a sun itself and an inexorable solar will, ready to annihilate in victory!

O will, turnaround of all need, thou my necessity! Preserve me for one great victory!
— —

Thus spake Zarathustra.

The Convalescent

1

One morning, not long after the return to his cave, Zarathustra sprang up from his bed like a madman, cried in a terrible voice, and acted as if someone unwilling to get up still lay on the bed; and so resounded Zarathustra's voice that has animals came to him terrified, and from all the lairs and hiding-places neighboring Zarathustra's cave all the creatures slipped away, — flying, fluttering, creeping, leaping, each according to just the kind of foot or wing it was given. Zarathustra, however, said these words:

Up, abysmal thought, out of my depth! I am your cock and break of day, sleepy worm: up! up! My voice shall cock-a-doodle you awake yet!

Unbind the fetters of your ears: listen! For I want to hear you! up! up! Here is thunder enough to make even the graves sit up and listen!

And wipe the sleep and all that is blind and asinine out of your eyes! Hear me likewise with your eyes; my voice is a cure for those born blind.

And once you are awake, you shall remain eternally awake. It is not my custom to wake great-grandmothers from their sleep in order to bid them — go on sleeping!

You are stirring, stretching, retching? Up! Up! Do not retch — reach me with your speech! Zarathustra summons you, Zarathustra the godless!

I, Zarathustra, the advocate of life, the advocate of suffering, the advocate of the circle — I summon you, my most abysmal thought!

Hail to me! You are coming, — I hear you! My abyss speaks, my lowest depth I have turned up to the light!

Hail to me! Come here! Give me your hand — — ah! Let go! Aah! — —horror, horror, horror — — — woe is me!

2

Hardly had Zarathustra spoken these words, however, when he fell down like a dead man and long remained like a dead man. But when he came to his senses again, he was pale and shaking and remained lying there, desiring neither food nor drink. This condition lasted seven days; his animals, however, did not abandon him day or night, except that the eagle flew off to fetch food. And what he fetched and snatched as plunder he laid upon Zarathustra's bed: so that at last Zarathustra lay amidst yellow and red berries, grapes, rose apples, sweetlyscented herbs, and pine cones. At his feet, however, two lambs were spread out, which the eagle had snatched away with difficulty form their shepherds.

At last, after seven days, Zarathustra rose up from his bed, took a rose apple in his hand, smelled it, and found its odor pleasing. Then his animals thought the time had come to speak with him.

 "O Zarathustra," they said, "seven days now you have lain thus with heavy eyes: will you not get back on your feet again at last?

Step out of your cave: the world awaits you like a garden. The wind plays with strong fragrances willing to go your way; and all the brooks look to run after you.

All things long for you because for seven days you have remained alone, —

step out of your cave! All things are willing to be your physicians!

Perhaps a new perception has come to you, a sour, serious one? Like leavened dough you lay; your soul rose and swelled over all its borders. —"

— "O my animals," replied Zarathustra, "keep chattering thus and let me listen! It refreshes me so to hear you chatter: where there is chatter the world is indeed as a garden to me.

How pleasing it is that there are words and tones: are not words and tones rainbows and seeming bridges between the eternally separated?

To every soul belongs another world; for every soul every other soul is an afterworld.

Precisely between the most similar things semblance lies most beautifully; for the smallest gap is the hardest to bridge.

As for me — how could there be an outside-me? There is no outside! But with all the tones we forget this; how pleasing it is that we forget!

Are things not given names and tones so that man can refresh himself with them? It is a beautiful tomfoolery, speaking; with it man dances over all things.

How pleasing is all speech and all the deceit of tones! With tones our love dances on multi-colored rainbows." —

"O Zarathustra," the animals then said, "to those who think as we do all things dance of themselves: they come and offer their hand and laugh and flee —

and come back.

Everything goes, everything comes back; eternally rolls the wheel of being.

Everything dies, everything blooms again; eternally runs the year of being.

Everything breaks, everything is joined anew; eternally the same house of being builds itself. Everything parts, everything greets each other again; eternally the ring of being remains true to itself.

In every instant begins being; round every 'here' rolls the ball 'there'. The center is everywhere. Curved is the path of eternity." —

— "O you buffoons and hurdy-gurdies," answered Zarathustra and smiled once more;

"How well you know what had to be fulfilled in seven days: —

— and how that monster crawled down my throat and choked me! But I bit the head off and spewed it away from me.

And you, — you have already made a lyre lay out of it? Now, however, I lie here, still weary from this biting and spewing, still ill from my own redemption.

And you watched it all? O my animals, are you also cruel? Did you want to watch my great pain, as men do? For man is the cruelest animal.

At tragedies, bullfights, and crucifixions he has hitherto been happiest on earth; and when he invented hell, behold, that was his heaven on earth.

When the great man cries—: at once the small man comes running; and his tongue hangs out of his mouth lasciviously. But he calls it his "pity."

The small man, especially the poet — how eagerly he accuses life in words!

Hear him, but do not fail to hear the delight that is in all accusation!

These accusers of life: life conquers them with the blink of an eye. "Do you love me?" the impudent one says, "wait a little, I do not have time for you yet."

Man is the cruelest animal towards himself; and with all those who call themselves "sinners" and "cross-bearers" and "penitents," do not fail to hear the sensual delight that is in their lamentations and accusations!

And I myself — would I be man's accuser in this? Alas, my animals, this alone have I learned hitherto, that man's worst is necessary for his best, —

— that all the worst is his best strength and the hardest stone for the highest creator; and that man must become better and badder: —

Not on this cross was I nailed, that I know: man is evil, — but I cried as no one yet has cried:

"Alas, that his worst is so very small! Alas, that his best is so very small!"

The great disgust with man, — this had crawled into my throat and choked me: and what the soothsayer had soothsaid: "All is the same, nothing is worthwhile, knowledge strangles."

A long twilight limped along before me, a dead tired, dead drunk sadness that talked with a yawning mouth.

"Eternally he returns, the man you are weary of, the small man" — thus my sadness yawned and dragged its feet and could not fall asleep.

Man's earth became a hollow to me, her breast sank in, all living things became human mold and bones and decomposed past to me.

My sighing sat on all human graves and could no longer rise; my sighing and inquiring croaked and choked and wore away and wailed away day and night:

— "Alas, man returns eternally! The small man returns eternally!"

Naked had I once seen them both, the greatest man and the smallest man:

all-too-similar to each other, — all-too-human still, even the greatest!

All-too-small, the greatest! — this was my disgust with man! And the eternal return of even the smallest! — this was my disgust with all existence!

Ah, horror! Horror! Horror! — — Thus spake Zarathustra and sighed and shuddered; for he was reminded of his sickness. Then, however, his animals let him speak no further.

"Speak no further, you convalescent!" — thus his animals answered him, "but go out where the world awaits you like a garden.

Go out to the roses and the bees and the flights of doves! But especially to the songbirds: that you may learn singing from them!

Because singing is for convalescents; the healthy can speak. And when the healthy man wants songs, he certainly wants songs different from those of the convalescent."

— "O you buffoons and hurdy-gurdies, do be quiet then!" — replied Zarathustra and smiled at his animals. "How well you know what solace I devised for myself in seven days!

That I had to sing again, — this solace I devised for myself and this convalescence:

and right away you are ready to make a lyre lay out of it?"

— "Speak no further, " his animals answered once again; "better yet, you convalescent, first make ready for yourself a lyre, a new lyre!

For behold, O Zarathustra! New lays require new lyres!

Sing and bubble over, O Zarathustra, heal your soul with new songs: that you may bear your great fate, which has been no man's fate yet.

For your animals know it well, O Zarathustra, who you are and must become: behold, you are the teacher of the eternal return — , that is now your fate!

That you as the first must teach this teaching, — how could this great fate not also be your greatest danger and disease!

Behold, we know what you teach: that all things return eternally, and we ourselves along with them; and that we have already existed countless times, and all things with us.

You teach that there is a great year of becoming, a monster of a great year: it must turn itself over and over again, like an hourglass, so that it can run down and run out again: —

— so that all these years are like themselves in the greatest as well as in the least thing, so that we ourselves in every great year are like ourselves, in the greatest as well as in the least thing.

And if you should want to die now, O Zarathustra: behold, we know too how you would speak to yourself: but your animals beseech you not to die yet!

You would speak and without trembling, breathing, on the contrary, a sigh of bliss: for a great heaviness and uneasiness would be taken from you, you most patient one! —

'Now I die and fade away,' you would say, 'and in an instant I am nothing.

Souls are as mortal as bodies.

But the knot of causes in which I am entangled returns, — it will create me again! I myself belong to the causes of the eternal return.

I come again, with this sun, with this earth, with this eagle, with this serpent — not to a new life or a better life or a similar life:

— I come again eternally to this same and selfsame life, in the greatest as well as in the least thing, to teach again the eternal return of all things, —

— to speak again the word on the great earthly and manly noontide, to proclaim again to man the Superman.

I spake my word, I break on my word: my eternal lot wills it so —, as proclaimer I go under!

The hour has now come for the downgoer to bless himself. Thus — ends Zarathustra's downgoing.'" — —

When the animals had spoken these words, they became silent and waited for Zarathustra to say something to them: but Zarathustra did not hear that they were silent. He lay still, rather, with his eyes closed, like one sleeping, although he did not sleep: for just then he was conferring with his soul. The serpent, however, and the eagle, when they found him thus silent, honored the great stillness around him and prudently withdrew.

On The Great Longing

O my soul, I taught you to say "today" as "one day" and "in days of yore" and to dance your roundelay away over all Here and There and Yonder.

O my soul, I rescued you from all corners, I brushed dust, spiders, and twilight away from you.

O my soul, I washed the petty shame and the shady virtue away from you and persuaded you to stand naked before the eyes of the sun.

With the storm called "spirit" I blew over your surging sea; all the clouds I blew away, I even strangled the strangleress called "sin."

O my soul, I gave you the right to say Nay, like the storm, and Yea, like the open sky says Yea: calm as light you stay and make your way now through negating storms.

O my soul, I gave you back the freedom over the created and the uncreated:

and who knows as you know the sensuality of the future?

O my soul, I taught you the contempt that comes not as worm-eatenness, the great, the loving contempt that loves the most where it despises the most.

O my soul, I taught you to persuade so that even the grounds are swayed:

like the sun which persuades even the sea to its height.

O my soul, I freed you from all obeying, knee-bending, and lord-saying; I even gave you the names "Turnaround In Need" and "Fate."

O my soul, I gave you new names and colorful playthings, I called you "Fate" and "Extent of Extensiveness" and Umbilical Cord Of Time" and "Azure Bell."

O my soul, I gave your soil all wisdom to drink, all new wines and also all immemorially old strong wines of wisdom.

O my soul, every sun I poured forth on you and every night and every silence and every longing: then you shot up like a vine for me.

O my soul, superrich and heavy you stand there now, a vine with swelling udders and crowded brown gold-clusters of grapes: —

— crowded and clouded by your happiness, waiting with plenty and yet modest on account of your waiting.

O my soul, there is now nowhere a soul that would be more loving and encompassing and far-reaching! Where would future and past be closer together than with you?

O my soul, I gave you all and you have left me all empty-handed: Now you say to me, smiling and full of melancholy: "Which of us has to give thanks? —

— should the giver not give thanks that the receiver has received? Is giving not a necessity? Is receiving not — showing mercy?" —

O my soul, I understand the smile of your melancholy: your superrichness itself now stretches out longing hands!

Your fullness looks out over raging seas and searches and waits; the longing of super-fullness looks out from your smiling eye-skies!

And verily, O my soul! Who could see your smile and not melt into tears?

The angels themselves burst into tears at the super-goodness of your smile.

It is your goodness and super-goodness which refuses to wail and weep:

and yet, O my soul, your smile longs for tears and your trembling mouth for sobs.

"Is not all weeping a complaint? And is all complaining not an accusing?"

Thus you talk to yourself and on that account you would rather smile, O my soul, than pour out your sorrow — pour out in trembling tears all your sorrow at your fullness and at all the vine's urgency for the vintager and the vine-knife!

But if you will not weep, will not weep out your purple melancholy, then you will have to sing, O my soul! — Behold, I myself smile, I who prophesy such a thing to you:

— sing, with boisterous song, until all the seas become still, to hearken to your longing, —

— until over still, longing seas the boat glides, the golden wonder around whose gold all good, bad, wondrous things gambol: —

— many creatures great and small also, and all that have light, wondrous feet, so they can run on violet-blue paths, —

— toward the golden wonder, the voluntary ferry-boat and its master: that however, is the vintager, who waits with the adamantine vine-knife, — your great savior, O my soul, the nameless one — for whom only future songs will find names! And verily, already your breath exudes the fragrance of future songs, —

— already you glow and dream, already you drink thirstily at all deep resounding comfort-wells, already your melancholy rests in the bliss of future songs! — —

O my soul, now I have given you all and also my last thing, and you have left me all empty-handed: — that I told you to sing, behold, that was my last thing!

That I told you to sing, speak now, speak: which of us now has to — give thanks? — But better yet: sing to me, sing, O my soul! And let me give thanks! —

Thus spake Zarathustra.

The Other Dance Song

1

Into your eyes I looked lately, O Life: gold I saw glittering in your night-eye, — my heart stood still on account of this delight:

— a golden boat I saw glittering on gloomy waters, a sinking, drinking, rewinking golden seesaw-boat!

At my foot, my dance-mad foot, you cast a glance, a smiling inquiring, melting, seesaw glance:

Twice only you stirred your rattle with your little hands — already my foot seesawed with dance-madness. —

My heels pranced, my toes lent an ear in order to understand you: the dancer, you know, has his ear — in his toes!

I sprang toward you: from my spring you hastily withdrew; and your fleeing, flying hair-tongue darted its tongue in and out at me!

Away from you I sprang and from your serpents: there you stood already, half-turned, your eye full of longing.

With crooked looks — you teach me crooked ways; on crooked ways my foot learns — arch tricks!

I fear you near, I love you far; your fleeing calls me, your seeking stalls me:

— I suffer, but what would I gladly not suffer for you!

You whose coldness kindles, whose hatred seduces, whose flight binds, whose mockery — induces:

— who would not hate you, you great binder, entwiner, seducer, seeker, finder! Who would not love you, you impatient, wind-hastened, guileless childeyed sinner!

Where are you dragging me off to now, you prodigy and problem child?

And now you are fleeing me again, you sweet wildcat and ingrate!

I dance after you, I follow your least little clue. Where are you? Give me your hand! Or just a finger will do!

Here are hollows and thickets: we shall go astray! — Halt! Stand still! Do you not hear owls and bats whistling this way?

You owl! You bat! Are you trying to make a monkey out of me? Where are we? From the dogs you have learned this howling and yelping.

You bare delightfully your little white teeth at me, your wicked eyes leap out at me from beneath a curly little mane.

This is a dance over hill and dale, — would you be my hound or my chamois female?

At my side now! And quickly, you wicked springstress! Up now and over!

— Alas! In springing thereafter I fell headlong!

O see me lying here, pleading for mercy, you haughty lass! Gladly would I go with you — down lovelier paths!

— down paths of love through hushed, varied brush! Or there along the lake: where goldfish swim and dance!

You are weary now? Over there are sheep and sunset skies: is it not nice to sleep when shepherds play their pipes?

You are so very weary? I will carry you there, just let your arms sink! And if you get thirsty, — have I got something, but your mouth would not have it to drink! —

— O this cursed nimble supple serpent and slick witch! Where have you gone? But from your hand on my face I feel two spots and red blotches!

I am truly weary of being your sheepish shepherd all the time! You witch, if until now I have sung for you, now for me you shall — cry!

To the rhythm of my whip you shall cry and dance! Surely I did not forget the whip? — No chance!"

2

Then Life answered me thus and covered her dainty ears the while:

"O Zarathustra! Do not crack your whip so terribly! You know indeed:

noise murders thought, — and just now such tender thoughts come to me.

We are both two true ne'er-do-wells and ne'er-do-ills. Beyond good and evil we found our island and our green meadow — we two alone! Therefore we must indeed suit each other!

And even if we do not love each other thoroughly — , must we then hold a grudge for not being thoroughly loved?

And that I am well-disposed toward you and often too well, that you know:

and the reason is that I am jealous of your wisdom. Ah, that mad old fool of a woman wisdom!

And if your wisdom should ever run away from you, alas! then my love would also run away from you quickly." —

Then Life looked reflectively behind her and around her and softly said: "O Zarathustra, you are not faithful enough to me!

You love me not nearly so much as you say; I know you are thinking of leaving me soon.

There is an old heavy, heavy booming-bell: it booms its way nightly up to your cave: —

— when you hear this bell toll at the midnight hour, then between one and twelve you think of it —

— you think, O Zarathustra, I know it, of leaving me soon!"

"Yes," I answered hesitantly, "but you also know — " And I said something in her ear, right in the midst of her tangled, yellow, silly, shaggy locks.

"You know that, O Zarathustra? No one knows that. —"

And we looked at each other and upon the green meadow over which the cool evening was just coming and we wept together. — Then, however, Life was dearer to me than all my wisdom ever was. —

3

One!

O man! Take heed!

Two!

What words repeat deep midnight's creed?

Three!

"I sleep, I sleep —, Four!

"From deep dream I woke and perceived: —

Five!

"The world is deep, Six!

"And deeper than the day conceived Seven!

"Deep is her woe —, Eight!

"Joy — deeper still than calamity:

Nine!

"Woe bids it: Go!

Ten!

"But all joy wants eternity — , Eleven "— Wants the deep, deep eternity!"

Twelve!

The Seven Seals (Or: The Yea And Amen Lay)

1

If I be a soothsayer and full of that soothsaying spirit which wanders on a high ridge between two seas, —

wanders like a heavy cloud between past and future, — enemy to sultry lowlands and all that is weary and can neither live nor die:

ready for lightning in its dark breast and for the redeeming flash of light, pregnant with lightning bolts which say yea! laugh yea!, ready for soothsaying thunderbolts:

— blessed however is he who is thus pregnant! And verily, he who shall one day kindle the light of the future must hang a long while, like heavy weather on the mountains! —

O how could I not be fervent for eternity and for the bridal ring of rings, —

the ring of return?

Never yet have I found the woman from whom I wanted children, unless it be this woman whom I love: for I love you, O Eternity!

For I love you, Eternity!

2

If ever my wrath broke up graves, moved boundary stones, and rolled old broken tables into steep depths:

if ever my scorn blew away decayed words, and like a broom I came to cross-spiders and as a sweeping wind to old musty burial chambers:

if ever I sat rejoicing where old gods lie buried, world-blessing, world-loving next to the monuments of old world-slanderers: —

— for even churches and gods' graves I love, if only heaven's pure eye looks through their broken roofs; gladly I sit like grass and red poppies on broken churches —

O how could I not be fervent for eternity and for the bridal ring of rings, —

the ring of return?

Never yet have I found the woman from whom I wanted children, unless it be this woman whom I love: for I love you, O Eternity!

For I love you, O Eternity!

3

If ever a breath of creative breath came to me, and of that heavenly necessity which forces even chance events to dance star-dances in the round:

If ever I laughed with the laughter of creative lightning, which the long thunder of the deed follows after rumblingly but obediently:

If ever I played dice with gods at the table of the gods, the earth, so that the earth did quake and break apart and snort up streams of fire:—

— for the earth is a table of the gods, and trembling with creative new words and divine dice-throws: —

O how could I not be fervent for eternity and for the bridal ring of rings, —

the ring of return?

Never yet have I found the woman from whom I wanted children, unless it be this woman whom I love: for I love you, O Eternity!

For I love you, O Eternity!

4

If ever I drank deep from that foaming spice- and mixing bowl in which all things are well-mixed:

if ever my hand poured the furthest with the nearest and fire with spirit and joy with sorrow and the worst with the kindest:

if I myself be a grain of that redeeming salt which makes all things mix well in the mixing bowl: —

— for there is a salt which binds good with evil; and even the most evil thing is worthy of seasoning and of the last foaming-over: —

O how could I not be fervent for eternity and for the bridal ring of rings, —

the ring of return?

Never yet have I found the woman from whom I wanted children, unless it be this woman whom I love: for I love you, O Eternity!

For I love you, O Eternity!

5

If I be fond of the sea and all that is of the nature of the sea, and even most fond when it angrily opposes me:

if that joy in seeking be in me which drives the sails toward the undiscovered, if a seafarer's joy be in my joy:

if ever my rejoicing cried: "The coast has vanished — now the last chain has fallen from me —

— the unbounded roars around me, far out there time and space gleam for me, well them! come one! old heart!" —

O how could I not be fervent for eternity and for the bridal ring of rings, —

the ring of return?

Never yet have I found the woman from whom I wanted children, unless it be this woman whom I love: for I love you, O Eternity!

For I love you, O Eternity!

6

If my virtue be a dancer's virtue, and if often I have leaped with both feet into golden-emerald ecstasy:

if my malice be a laughing malice, at home among rosebeds and lily hedges:

— for in laughter all things evil are together, absolved and resolved as holy, however, by their own bliss: —

and if my alpha and omega be this, that all things heavy shall become light, all bodies dancers, all spirits birds: and verily, this is my alpha and omega! —

O how could I not be fervent for eternity and for the bridal ring of rings, —

the ring of return?

Never yet have I found the woman from whom I wanted children, unless it be this woman whom I love: for I love you, O Eternity!

For I love you, O Eternity!

7

If ever I spread a calm heaven above me and with my own wings flew up to my own heaven:

if I swam playfully in deep light-distances and my freedom's bird-wisdom came: —

— thus, however, speaks bird-wisdom: "Behold, there is no above, no below! Fling yourself all around, out, back, you light one, Sing! speak no more!

— are all words not made for those who are heavy? Do all words not lie for those who are light? Sing! speak no more!" —

O how could I not be fervent for eternity and for the bridal ring of rings, —

the ring of return?

Never yet have I found the woman from whom I wanted children, unless it be this woman whom I love: for I love you, O Eternity!

For I love you, O Eternity!

Fourth and Last Part

Alas, where in the world have greater follies taken place than amongst the pitying ones? And what in the world has caused more suffering than the follies of the pitying ones:

Woe to all lovers who do not yet have a height that is above their pity!

Thus spake the devil to me once: "Even God has his hell: it is his love for man."

And the other day this word I heard him say: "God is dead; God has died of his pity for man."

Thus Spake Zarathustra, Part Two

The Honey Offering

— And again months and years passed over Zarathustra's soul, and he heeded them not; his hair, however, turned white. One day as he sat on a stone in front of his cave and calmly looked out — and one looks out here upon the sea and out across tortuous abysses —, then his animals walked pensively around him and settled themselves at last in front of him.

"O Zarathustra," they said, "perhaps you are looking out for your happiness?"

— "What does happiness matter?" he answered, "I have long ceased to strive for happiness; I strive for my work." — "O Zarathustra," the animals said once more, "you say that like one who has too much of a good thing. Do you not lie in a sky-blue sea of happiness?" — "You buffoons," answered Zarathustra and smiled; "how well you chose your metaphor! But you also know my happiness is heavy and not like a fluid wave: it presses me and refuses to leave me and behaves like molten pitch." —

Then the animals walked pensively around him again and settled themselves once more in front of him. "O Zarathustra," they said, "So is that why you grow ever yellower and darker although your hair looks white and flaxen? But look, you are sitting in your own sticky mess!" — "What is that you say, my animals?"

Zarathustra said and laughed, "verily, I blasphemed when I spoke of pitch. As it is with me, so it is with all fruits that grow ripe. It is the honey in my veins that makes my blood thicker and also my soul stiller." — "Thus will it be, O Zarathustra," answered the animals and pressed themselves up against him; "but do you not want to climb a high mountain today? The air is pure and one sees more of the world today than ever before." — "Yes, my animals," he answered, "you counsel admirably and after my own heart: I shall climb a high mountain today! But make sure honey is at hand there for me, yellow, white, good, icy-cool, golden honeycomb. For know that on high I will make the honey-sacrifice." —

When Zarathustra was on high, however, he sent those animals home that had accompanied him and found that he was alone: — then he laughed wholeheartedly, looked around himself, and spoke thus:

That I spoke of sacrifices and honey-sacrifices was only a trick of speech and, verily, a useful piece of folly. Up here I can surely speak more freely than before hermits' caves and hermits' domestic animals.

What sacrifice! I squander what is given me, I , a squanderer with a thousand hands: how could I ever call that sacrificing?

And when I craved honey I only craved bait and sweet goo and goop which even grumbling bears and strange, sullen, wicked birds lick up with their tongues:

— the best bait, as hunters and fisherman require. For if the world be like a dark forest of beasts and a garden of delight for all wild hunters, then it strikes me even more so as and I prefer it to be an unfathomably rich sea, — a sea full of colorful fish and crabs which even gods might lust after, in which they might want to be fishermen and net-casters: so rich is the world in strange things, great and small!

Especially the human world, the human sea: into that I now cast my golden fishing rod and say: "Open up, you human abyss!

Open up and cast me your fish and glistening crabs! With my best bait I shall entice the strangest human fish today!

— my happiness itself I shall cast out into all places and spaces amidst sunrise, noon, and sunset, to see whether many human fish do not learn to yank and crank on my happiness:

— until biting on my sharp hidden hooks, they must come up to my height, the most motley of abyss-groundlings to the most malicious of all fishers of men.

For this I am at the very bottom and from the very beginning, drawing, drawing in, drawing up, bringing up, a drawer, upbringer, and disciplinarian who once exhorted himself, not for nothing: 'Become who you are!'

Thus men may now come up to me: for I still await the sign that it is time for my descent; not yet do I myself go down, as I must, among men.

That is why I wait here, cunning and mocking on high mountains, not impatient, not patient, as one rather who has also unlearned patience, —

because he no longer 'bears patiently.'

For my fate gives me time: perhaps it has forgotten me? Or does it sit in the shade behind a great stone and catch flies?

And verily, I am much obliged to my fate for not hurrying and harrying me and giving me time for jests and gibes: so that today I have climbed this high mountain to catch fish.

Did a man ever catch fish on high mountains, I wonder? And even if it is folly, what I desire and do up here: better yet this than to become solemn and green and yellow from waiting down below —

— a pompous wrath-snorter from waiting, a holy, howling storm from the mountains, an impatient sort that shouts down into the valleys: 'Listen, or I will lash you with the scourge of God!'

Not that I would hold a grudge against such angry ones: they serve well enough for my laughter! They must be quite impatient, these big clamor-drums which get a chance to speak now or never!

I, however, and my destiny — we do not speak to the Now, we also do not speak to the Never: we have patience and time and overtime for speaking, after all. For one day it must surely come and may not pass by.

What must one day come and may not pass by? Our great Hazar, that is, our great faraway human kingdom, the Zarathustra kingdom of a thousand years — —

How faraway may such a "faraway" be? What is that to me? But as far as that stands, this is no less certain to me — with both feet I stand securely on this ground, —

— on eternal ground, on hard, primeval rock, on this highest, hardest primeval mountain range to which all winds come as to a weather divide, asking Where and Whence? and Whither?

Laugh here, laugh, my hearty, healthy malice! From high mountains cast down your glittering, mocking laughter! Lure for me with your glittering the finest human fish!

And whatever belongs to me in all the seas, my in-and-for-me in all things — fish that out for me, bring that up to me: for that I wait, I, the most malicious of all fishermen.

Out, out, my fish hook! In there, down there, bait of my happiness! Drip down your sweetest dew, my heart's honey! Bite, my fishing hook, all black affliction in the belly!

Out there, out there, my eye! O how many seas around me, what dawning human futures! And above me — what rosy-red stillness! What cloudless silence!

The Cry Of Distress

The next day Zarathustra again sat on the stone in front of his cave, while his animals roamed about in the world outside in order to bring home new food — new honey, too: for Zarathustra had lavishly spent and squandered the old honey down to the last drop. But as he sat there thus, with a stick in his hand, tracing the shadow of his figure upon the earth, reflecting, and verily! not upon himself and his shadow — all at once he was startled and started with fright: for next to his shadow he saw yet another shadow. And as he looked quickly around himself and stood up, behold, there stood next to him the soothsayer, the same one he had once given food and drink at his table, the herald of the great weariness who taught: "All is the same, nothing is worthwhile, the world is without meaning, knowledge strangles." But his face had changed meanwhile; and when Zarathustra looked him in the eye, his heart was startled again: so many bad tidings and ashy-gray bolts of lightning ran across that face.

The soothsayer, who realized what had taken place in Zarathustra's soul, wiped his hand over his face, as if he wanted to wipe it away; Zarathustra did the same, too. And when both of them had silently composed and strengthened themselves thus, they shook hands as a sign that they wanted to recognize each other again.

"Welcome," said Zarathustra, "you soothsayer of the great weariness, not in vain shall you once have been my guest and table mate. Eat and drink today also with me, and forgive a merry old man for sitting at the dinner table with you!" —

"A merry old man?" answered the soothsayer, shaking his head, "but whoever you are or want to be, O Zarathustra, you will not be it up here much longer, —

in a little while your boat shall no longer be sitting high and dry!" "Am I sitting high and dry then?" — asked Zarathustra, laughing. — "The waves around your mountain," answered the soothsayer, "are rising and rising, the waves of great distress and tribulation: and soon they will raise your boat and carry you away."

— Zarathustra was silent at this and marvelled. — "Do you hear nothing yet?"

continued the soothsayer: "is it not rushing and roaring up from the deep?" —

Zarathustra was silent once again and listened: then he heard a long, long cry which the abysses called out and passed back and forth to one another, for none would have it: so evil did it sound.

"You ill herald," Zarathustra said at last, "that is a cry of distress and the cry of a man; it may well come from a black sea. But what is human distress to me!

The last sin which has been reserved for me, — do you know what it is called?"

— "Pity!" answered the soothsayer from an overflowing heart and raised both hands on high — O Zarathustra, I come to seduce you to your last sin!" —

And hardly had these words been spoken when the cry rang out again, and longer and more anxiously than before, no doubt much closer, too. "Do you hear?

Do you hear, O Zarathustra?" cried the soothsayer, "the cry is aimed at you, it calls out to you: come, come, come, it is time, it is high time!" —

Zarathustra was silent at this, confused and convulsed; at last he asked, like one who hesitates with himself: "And who is it that calls to me there?"

"But surely you know," replied the soothsayer furiously, "why do you hide yourself? It is the higher man that cries out for you!"

"The higher man?" cried Zarathustra, seized with horror: what does he want? What does he want? The higher man? What does he want here?" — and his skin was covered with sweat.

The soothsayer, however, offered no answer to Zarathustra's anxiety but listened and listened to the depth. Yet when it remained silent there for a long time, he looked back and saw Zarathustra standing and trembling.

"O Zarathustra," he began in a sad voice, "you do not stand there as one made giddy by his happiness: you had better dance so you do not fall down!

But even if you wanted to dance before me and leap all your side-leaps: still nobody could say to me: 'Look, here dances the last happy man!'

Anyone who searched for him here, at this height, would have come in vain:

caves he would find, possibly, and caves behind caves, hideaways for sly knaves, but no mines of happiness and treasure chambers and new golden lodes of happiness.

Happiness — how could happiness possibly be found with such recluses and solitaries? Must I still seek ultimate happiness on blessed isles and faraway amongst forgotten seas?

But all is the same, nothing is worthwhile, searching does no good, and there are no longer any Blessed Isles!"—

Thus sighed the soothsayer; but with his last sigh Zarathustra became bright and sure again, like one who comes out of a deep gorge into the light. "No!

No! Three times No!" he cried out in a loud voice and stroked his beard — "I know better than that! There are still Blessed Isles! Be silent about that, you sighing sad sack!

Stop splattering about that, you raincloud in the morning! Do I not already stand here wet from your distress and drenched like a dog?

Now I shake myself and run away from you in order to get dry again: you need not be surprised at that! Do I seem discourteous to you? But here is my court.

And as for your higher man: well then! I shall seek him at once in those woods: thence came his cry. Perhaps a wicked beast harasses him there.

He is in my domain: therein he shall not come to harm! And verily, there are many wicked beasts near me."

With these words Zarathustra turned to go. Then the soothsayer said: "O Zarathustra, you are a rogue!

I know it already: you want to get rid of me! You would rather run in the woods and set snares for wicked beasts!

But what good will it do you? — In the evening you will have me again all the same; I will be sitting there in your own cave, patient and heavy like a block of wood — and waiting for you!"

"So be it!" Zarathustra called back as he walked away: "and what is mine in my cave is yours too, my guest!

And if you should find some honey in there, well then! just lick it up, you grumbling bear, and sweeten your soul! For in the evening we both want to be in good spirits, — in good spirits and glad that this day has come to an end! And you yourself shall dance to my songs as my dancing bear.

You do not believe it? You shake your head? Well then! Well then! Old bear!

But I too — am a soothsayer."

Thus spake Zarathustra.

Conversation With The Kings

1

Zarathustra was not yet an hour underway in his mountains and woods when all at once he came upon a strange procession. Right on the path he wanted to go down, along came two kings on foot, adorned with crowns and purple girdles and colorful as flamingoes: they drove a laden ass before them.

"What do these kings want in my kingdom?" Zarathustra said in astonishment to his heart and hid himself quickly behind a bush. But as the kings came up to him, he said in an undertone, like one speaking to himself alone: "Strange!

Strange! What kind of arrangement is this? Two kings I see — and only one ass!"

Then the two kings stopped, smiled, and looked toward the spot where the voice had come from, after which they looked each other in the face. "Such things are also thought amongst ourselves no doubt," said the king on the right, "but one does not speak out about them."

The king on the left, however, shrugged his shoulders and answered: "That may well be a goatherd. Or a hermit who has dwelt too long among rocks and trees. For no society at all also spoils good manners."

"Good manners?" The other king retorted, indignantly and bitterly: "what is it then we are trying to get away from? Is it not 'good manners'? Our 'good society'?

Better, verily, to live among goatherds and hermits than with our gilded, false, over-rouged riffraff, — although they call themselves 'good society', — although they call themselves 'nobility.' But all is false and foul there, first of all the blood, thanks to old bad diseases and worse quack-healers.

The best and dearest to me even today is a healthy peasant, crude, shrewd, stiff-necked, enduring: that is the foremost type today.

The best at present is the peasant; and the peasant type should be master!

But it is the kingdom of the riffraff, — I let nothing fool me. Riffraff, however, that means: mishmash.

Riffraff-mishmash: everything is mixed up with everything else in that, saint and skunk and Junker and Jew and every animal from Noah's ark!

Good manners! All is false and foul with us. No one knows how to show respect any more: precisely that is what we are running away from. They are fulsome, meddlesome dogs, they gild palm leaves.

This loathing chokes me, that even we kings have become fakes, draped and disguised in old yellowed grandfather-splendor, showpieces for the dumbest and the smartest and all those who horse-trade for power today!

We are not the first — and yet must stand for them: of this fraud we finally have become sick and tired.

We have gone out of our way to get away from the rabble, all these crybabies and scribe-blowflies, the shopkeeper stench, the go-getter squirming, the gutter breath —: phooey on living among the rabble, — phooey on standing first among the rabble! Oh, horror! Horror! Horror!

What do we kings matter now!" —

"Your old sickness assails you," the king on the left then said, "nausea assails you, my poor brother. But surely you know that someone is listening to us."

Zarathustra, who had opened wide his eyes and ears at this speech, immediately arose from his hiding place, approached the kings and began:

"He who listens to you, he who gladly listens to you, you kings, he is called Zarathustra.

I am Zarathustra, who once said: 'What do kings matter now!' Forgive me, I was pleased when you said to each other: 'What do we kings matter!'

Here, however, is my kingdom and my domain: what might you possibly be seeking in my kingdom? But perhaps along the way you have found what I am seeking: namely, the higher man."

When the kings heard this, they beat their breasts and said with one voice:

"We are recognized!

With the sword of this word you have hewn through out heart's thickest darkness. You have discovered our distress, for behold! we are on our way to find the higher man —

— the man that is higher than us: although we are kings. We are leading this ass to him. For the highest man should also be the highest master on earth.

There is no harsher misfortune in all human destiny than when the mighty of the earth are not also the first men. Then everything becomes false and distorted and monstrous.

And when they are the very last and more beast than man: then the riffraff rises and rises in price and at last even riffraff-virtue speaks: 'Behold, I alone am virtue!' " —

'What did I just hear?' answered Zarathustra; 'what wisdom from kings! I am thrilled and verily quite filled with the desire to make a rhyme upon it: —

— even if it may be a rhyme not fit for everyone's ears. I have long since forgotten consideration for long ears. Well then! Come on! (But here it happened that the ass also got a word in: he said quite distinctly and with bad intent, Ye-haw.) Once — in the year of our Lord one, no less —

Drunk without wine the Sibyl did confess:

"All's wrong now, woe!

Ruin! Ruin! World's never sunk so low!

Rome's descended to whoredom and whorish stew, Rome's Caesar sunk to brute, God Himself — turned Jew!"

2

In these rhymes of Zarathustra the kings reveled; the king on the right even said: "O Zarathustra, how well we did in setting out to see you!

For your foes showed us your image in their mirror: there you looked with a devil's wry face and sneered: so that we were afraid of you.

But what was the use! Again and again you pierced our ears and hearts with your sayings. So at last we said: what does it matter how he looks!

We must hear him, the one who teaches: 'You shall love peace as a means to new wars, and the short peace more than the long!'

No one ever spoke such warlike words: 'What is good? To be brave is good.

It is the good war that hallows every cause!

O Zarathustra, our fathers' blood stirred in our veins at such words: it was as the speech of spring to old wine-casks.

When the swords flew every which way, like red-flecked snakes, then our fathers knew that life was good; the sun of all peace seemed weak and lukewarm to them; the long peace, however, made for shame.

How they sighed, our fathers, when they saw sparkling bright, dried-up swords on the wall! Like them they thirsted for war. For a sword wants blood to drink and sparkles with desire." ——

— As the kings talked and chattered with such zeal of the happiness of their fathers, Zarathustra was seized by no small desire to mock their zeal: for it was evident that these were very peaceful kings whom he saw before him, men with old and refined faces. But he restrained himself. "Well then!" he said, "Thither the way leads, there lies Zarathustra's cave; and this day shall have a long evening! Now, however, a cry of distress calls me hastily away from you.

It does my cave honor when kings are willing to sit and wait in it: but you will certainly have to wait a long time!

Well then! So what! Where does one today learn better to wait than at court? And all that remains of the virtue of kings, — is it not today called "waiting- ability?"

Thus spake Zarathustra.

The Leech

And Zarathustra walked pensively, farther and deeper through forests and past marshy grounds; but as it happens with everyone who ponders serious matters, he managed to tread unawares upon a man. And behold, all at once a woeful cry and a pair of curses and twenty bad curse words squirted him in the face: so that in his alarm he raised his staff and even struck the downtrodden one. Immediately thereafter, however, he came to his senses; and his heart laughed at the folly he had just committed.

"Forgive me," he said to the downtrodden one, who had risen up furiously and sat back down, "forgive me and hear first of all a parable.

As a wanderer who dreams of distant things stumbles unawares upon a sleeping dog on a lonely street, a dog that lies in the sun:

— as both of them fly up, let fly at each other like deadly enemies, these two who are scared to death: thus it fared with us.

And yet! And yet — how little was lacking for them to be caressing each other instead, this dog and this lonely one! After all, they are both — lonely!"

— "Whoever you may be," said the downtrodden one, still furious, "you also tread too near me with your parable, and not only with your foot!

What, am I a dog then?" — and with that the sitter arose and pulled his naked arm out of the swamp. For at first he had lain stretched out on the ground, concealed and camouflaged like those who lie in wait for swamp game.

"But what are you doing here!" a startled Zarathustra cried out, for he saw a great deal of blood flowing down the naked arm, — "what has happened to you?

Did a bad animal bite you, you unhappy wretch?"

The bleeding man laughed, still angry. "What is it to you?" he said and wanted to move on. "Here I am at home in my domain. Let him who will ask me:

but I will hardly answer a yokel."

"You are mistaken," said Zarathustra with compassion and held him fast, "you are mistaken: here you are not in your domain but in mine, and no one shall come to harm here.

But call me what you will, — I am who I must be. I call myself Zarathustra.

Well then! Thither the way leads to Zarathustra's cave: it is not far, — will you not tend your wounds at my place?

It has gone badly for you in this life, you unhappy wretch: first an animal bit you, and then — a man trampled you!" —

But when the downtrodden one heard the name Zarathustra, he was transformed:

"But what is happening to me! he cried out, "who still matters to me then in this life other than this man, namely Zarathustra, and that one animal that lives on blood, the leech?

On account of the leech I lay here like a fisherman, and my outstretched arm had already been bitten ten times when a still finer leech made a bite for my blood, Zarathustra himself!

O happiness! O miracle! Praised be this day which has allured me into this swamp! Praised be the best, the liveliest cupping glass alive today, praised be the great conscience-leech Zarathustra!" —

Thus spake the downtrodden one; and Zarathustra rejoiced at his words and their fine, reverent manner. "Who are you?" he asked and extended him his hand, "between us much remains to be cleared up and cheered up: but already, it seems to me, a clear, bright day is dawning."

"I am the conscientious one in spirit," the questioned one answered, "and in things of the spirit it is not easy to find one stricter, harder, and harsher than I, save him from whom I learned them, Zarathustra himself.

Better to know nothing than to half-know many things! Better to be a fool on your own account than a wise man in someone else's eyes! I — get down to the ground:

— what does it matter whether it is large or small? Whether it is called swamp or sky? A hand's-breadth of ground is enough for me: provided it is genuine ground and grounding!

— a hand's-breadth of ground: upon that a man can stand. In the true science of conscience there is nothing large and nothing small."

"Then perhaps you are an authority on the leech?" asked Zarathustra; "and you trace the leech down to its ultimate roots, you conscientious one?"

"O Zarathustra, how could I presume to undertake that?

I am a master and authority, however, on the leech's brain: — that is my world!

And it is indeed a world! But forgive me that here my pride speaks, for here I have no equal. That is why I said, 'Here I am at home.'

How long have I traced this one thing, the leech's brain, so that here the slippery truth may no longer slip away from me! Here is my domain!

— on account of this I have thrown everything else away, on account of this everything else has become the same to me; and right beside my knowledge my black ignorance lies down.

My conscience of the spirit demands it thus from me, that I know one thing and nothing else: all the half-in-spirit disgust me, all the hazy, hovering, fanciful ones.

Where my honesty ceases I am blind and also want to be blind. But where I want to know I also want to be honest, namely hard, strict, narrow, cruel, and inexorable.

That you once said, O Zarathustra: 'Spirit is the life which itself cuts into life,' that induced and seduced me to your teaching. And verily, with my own blood I have increased my own knowledge!"

— "As the evidence shows," Zarathustra cut in; for blood was still flowing down the conscientious one's naked arm. The fact was that ten leeches had sunk their teeth into it.

"O you odd fellow, how much this evidence here shows me, namely you yourself! And perhaps I should not pour all of it into your austere ears!

Well then! Thus we part here! But I would be glad to stumble upon you again. Up there the way leads to my cave: this night you shall be my dear guest there!

I would also gladly make amends to your body that Zarathustra stepped on you with his feet: I shall reflect on that. Now, however, a cry of distress calls me hastily away from you."

Thus Spake Zarathustra.

The Sorcerer

1

But when Zarathustra took a turn around a rock, he saw not far below him on the same path a man who threw his limbs about like a raving lunatic and thudded to earth at last and lay flat on his belly.

"Halt!" Zarathustra then said to his heart, "that must surely be the higher man; from him there came that sore cry of distress,— I shall see if I can be of help." But when he ran to the spot where the man lay on the ground, he found a trembling old man with staring eyes; and no matter how hard Zarathustra tried to set him upright and back on his feet again, it was in vain. The unfortunate man did not even seem to notice that anyone was around him: on the contrary, he constantly looked around with pathetic gestures, like one desolated and isolated from all the world. Finally, however, after much trembling, twitching, twisting and turning, he began to yammer thus:

Who warms me, who loves me still?

Give hot hands!

Give heart-braziers!

Laid low, shuddering, Like a half-dead man whose feet someone warms —

Shaken, alas! by unknown fevers, Shivering from sharp, icy-frost arrows, Chased by you, Thought!

Ineffable one! Veiled one! Terrible one!

You hunter behind the clouds!

Struck down by you like a flash of lightning, You scornful eye, that eyes me from the dark:

— thus I lie, Bending myself, contorting myself, tortured By all eternal torment, Thunderstruck By you, cruelest hunter, You unknown-God!

Strike deeper!

Strike yet again!

Puncture, shatter this heart!

Why this torture With dull-toothed arrows?

Why do you look again, Not weary of human agony, With mischief-loving divine-lightning-eyes?

You do not want to kill, Only torture, torture?

Why — torture me, You mischief-loving unknown God? —

Aha! You steal near?

At such a midnight hour What do you want? Speak!

You push me, press me —

Ah! already much too close!

Away! Away!

You hear me breathing, You overhear my heart, You jealous one —

but jealous of what?

Away! Away! Why the ladder?

Do you want to get in, Into my heart, To step into, get into My most secret thoughts?

Shameless one! Unknown one — thief!

What do you mean by stealing?

What do you mean by eavesdropping?

What do you mean by torturing?

You torturer!

You — hangman-God!

Or shall I, like a dog, Roll over for you?

Devoted, enthused-outside-myself, Tailwagging my love to you?

In vain! Stick further, Cruelest thorn! No, No dog — only your game am I, Cruelest hunter!

Your proudest captive, You robber behind the clouds!

Speak at last!

What do you want from me, you waylayer?

You lightning-veiled one! Unknown one! Speak, What do you want, unknown — God?

What? Ransom?

Why do you want ransom?

Demand much — that my pride advises!

And be brief — that my other pride advises!

Aha!

You want — me? Me?

Me — entirely? ...

Aha!

And you torture me, fool that you are, Torture my pride to death?

Give me love — who warms me still?

Who loves me still? — give hot hands, Give heart-braziers, Give me, the loneliest one, Whom ice, alas, sevenfold ice Teaches to yearn for enemies, Even for enemies Give, yes, give over, Cruelest enemy, To me — yourself! ——

Away!

There he himself has flown, My last, only companion, My great enemy, My unknown one, My hangman-God! —

— No! Come back, With all your torture!

To the last of all the lonely ones O come back All the little streams of my tears Run their course to you!

And the final flame of my heart —

It flares up for you!

O come back, My unknown God! My pain! My final—happiness!

2

— But here Zarathustra could restrain himself no longer; he took his staff and began hitting the yammerer with all his might. "Stop it!" he yelled at him with fierce laughter, "stop it, you actor! You counterfeiter! You liar through and through! I know you well!

I will certainly make your legs warm, you wicked sorcerer, I understand well how to heat things up for such as you!"

— "Leave off," said the old man and sprang up from the ground, "do not hit me any more, O Zarathustra! I was only playing a game!

Such things belong to my art; you yourself I wanted to put to the test when I gave you this test performance! And verily, you have seen through me well!

But you too gave me no small test of your own: you are hard, you wise Zarathustra!

You strike hard with your 'truths'; your stick forces from me — this truth!"

— "Do not flatter," answered Zarathustra, still enraged and scowling, "you actor through and through! You are false: why do you talk — of truth?

You peacock of peacocks, you sea of vanity, what did you perform before me, you wicked sorcerer? In whom was I to believe when you yammered in such a manner?"

"The penitent of the spirit," said the old man, him — I played: you yourself once coined this term —

— the poet and sorcerer who turns his spirit against himself in the end, the transformed one who freezes to death on account of his bad science and conscience.

And just confess it: it took you a long time, O Zarathustra, to get past my scam and sham! You believed in my distress when you held my head in both your hands, —

— I heard you yammer, 'We have loved him too little, loved him too little!'

That I deceived you to such a degree, my malice rejoiced inwardly at that."

"You may have deceived subtler ones than I," said Zarathustra harshly. "I am not on the lookout for deceivers, I must be without precaution: thus my lot wills it.

But you — must deceive: to that degree I know you! You must always be double-, triple-, quadruple-, quintuple-dealing! And what you now confessed was not nearly true or false enough for me!

You wicked counterfeiter, how could you do otherwise! Even your sickness would be wearing make-up were you to show yourself to your doctor naked!

Just as even now you 'made-up' your lie before me when you said: 'I was only playing a game! There was seriousness in it, too; you are somewhat of a penitent of the spirit!

I divine you well: you have become the enchanter of all, but you have no lie or ruse left to use against yourself — you are disenchanted with yourself!

You have reaped loathing as your one truth. Not a word of yours is genuine anymore except your mouth: namely, the loathing that clings to your mouth." —

— "But who are you?" the old sorcerer cried here in a defiant voice, "who dares speak to me thus, the greatest man alive today?" — and a green lightning bolt shot from his eye at Zarathustra. But directly thereafter he changed and said sorrowfully:

"O Zarathustra, I am weary of it, my arts are loathsome to me; I am not great, why do I dissimulate? But you know it well — I was seeking greatness!

I wanted to pose as a great man, and persuaded many: but this lie has been too much for me. I am going to pieces over it.

O Zarathustra, everything about me is a lie; but that I am going to pieces —

this, my going to pieces, is no lie!" —

"It does you honor," said Zarathustra gloomily, looking downward with a sidelong glance, "it does you honor that you sought greatness, but it also betrays you. You are not great.

You wicked old sorcerer, this is what is best and most honest in you and what I honor in you, that you grew weary of yourself and expressed it: 'I am not great.'

In this I honor you as a penitent of the spirit: and even if it was only a whiff and a whisk, in that one moment you were — genuine.

But speak up, what do you seek here in my woods and rocks? And when you put yourself in my way, to what test did you want to put me? —

— in what way were you testing me?" —

Thus spake Zarathustra, and his eyes gleamed. The old sorcerer was silent for a while, then he said: "Did I test you? I — only quest.

O Zarathustra, I seek a true, genuine, artless, unambiguous one, a man of all honesty, a vessel of wisdom, a saint of knowledge, a great man!

Do you not know it then, O Zarathustra? I seek Zarathustra."

— And here a long silence ensued between the two; Zarathustra, however, had become so deeply absorbed in thought that he closed his eyes. But then, returning to his interlocutor, he grasped the sorcerer's hand and said, full of politeness and policy:

"Well then! Up there the way leads, there lies Zarathustra's cave. In it you may seek him whom you wish to find.

And ask my animals for advice, my eagle and my serpent: they shall help you seek. My cave is large, however.

I myself, of course — I have never yet seen a great man. Towards what is great the finest eye today is coarse. It is the kingdom of the riffraff.

Many a one have I found indeed that stretched and swelled himself up and the people cried: 'Behold, a great man! But what good are all bellows! In the end the wind comes out.

In the end the frog bursts that has blown itself up too long: then the wind comes out. To prick a swelled-up one in the belly, I call that a fine pastime. Hear that, boys!

This is the day of the riffraff: who even knows what is great, what is small?

Who could have success seeking greatness there? Only a fool: fools succeed.

You seek greatness, you strange fool? Who taught you that? Is today the time for that? O you wicked seeker, why do you seek — to test me?" — —

Thus spake Zarathustra, confident of heart, and went laughingly on his way.

Out Of Service

Not long, however, after Zarathustra had rid himself of the sorcerer, he again saw someone sitting alongside the path he was taking, namely a tall man in black with a pale, haggard face: he vexed him exceedingly. "Woe," he said to his heart, "there sits masked misery, from the species of priests, it seems to me: what do they want in my kingdom?

What! I have hardly escaped that sorcerer: must another necromancer cross my path again, —

— some wizard with his laying on of hands, some dark miracle-worker by the grace of God, an anointed world-slanderer whom the devil may take!

But the devil is never at the place he should be: he always comes too late, that damned dwarf and clubfoot!"

Thus Zarathustra cursed impatiently in his heart and thought how with an averted glance he might slip past the man in black: but behold, it turned out otherwise.

For at just that moment the sitter had already sighted him; and not unlike one who has met with unexpected good fortune, he sprang up and made straight for Zarathustra.

"Whoever you are, you wayfarer," he said, "help one who has lost his way, a seeker, an old man who could easily come to harm here!

This world here is strange and remote to me, I have even heard wild beasts howling; and he who could have offered me shelter is himself no more.

I was in search of the last pious man, a saint and hermit who, alone in his forest, had not yet heard what all the world knows today."

"What does all the world know today?" asked Zarathustra. "Perhaps this, that the old

God is no longer alive, the one in whom all the world once believed?"

"Thou hast said," answered the old man sadly. And I served that old God until his last hours.

But now I am out of service, without a master and yet not free, without a merry hour anymore either, except in remembrances.

Which is why I have climbed in these mountains, to finally have a feast day for myself again, as befits an old pope and church father: for know this, I am the last pope! — a feast day of pious remembrances and divine services.

But now he himself is dead, the most pious man, that saint in the forest who perpetually praised his God with humming and singing.

He himself I found no more when I found his hut, — but there were two wolves within who howled at his death — for all the animals loved him. At that I ran away.

So had I come in vain to these woods and mountains? Then my heart resolved to seek another, the most pious of all those who do not believe in God —, to seek Zarathustra!"

Thus spake the graybeard and peered with a sharp eye at the one who stood before him; Zarathustra, however, seized the hand of the old pope and contemplated it a long while with admiration.

"Behold, you venerable one," he then said, "what a long and handsome hand!

That is the hand of one who has always dispensed blessings. But now it holds fast on him whom you seek, me, Zarathustra.

It is I, the godless Zarathustra, who speaks here: who is more godless than I, that I may rejoice in his teaching?" —

Thus spake Zarathustra and penetrated with his looks the thoughts and hinter-thoughts of the old pope. At last the latter began:

"He who loved and possessed him the most has now also lost him the most —:

— behold, perhaps I myself am now the more godless of us two? But who could rejoice at that!" —

— "You served him to the end?" Zarathustra asked thoughtfully, after a profound silence, "you know how he died? Is it true what they say, that pity choked him, — that he saw how man hung on the cross and could not stand it, that the love of man became his hell and in the end his death?" —

The old pope, however, gave no answer but looked aside shyly and with a painful and gloomy expression.

"Let him go," said Zarathustra after long reflection, in which he still looked the old man straight in the eye.

"Let him go, he is gone. And though it does you honor that you speak only good things of this dead one, you know as well as I do who he was; and that he had strange ways."

"Speaking eye to eyes," said the old pope cheerfully (for he was blind in one eye), in divine matters I am more enlightened than Zarathustra himself — and have the right to be.

My love served him many years, my will followed his will in all things. But a good servant knows everything, and also quite a few things that his master hides from himself.

He was a hidden God, full of secrecy. Verily, even a son he came to have by none other than underhanded means. At the door of his faith stands adultery.

Whoever glorifies him as a God of love does not think highly enough of love itself. Did not this God also want to be judge? But the lover loves beyond reward and recompense.

When he was young, this God out of the Orient, he was harsh and vengeful and built himself a hell for the amusement of his favorites.

In the end, however, he became old and soft and mellow and pitying, more like a grandfather than a father, but most of all like a tottering old grandmother.

There he sat, withered, in his corner by the stove, worrying over his weak legs, world-weary, will-weary, and one day he choked to death on his all-toogreat pity." —

"You old pope," Zarathustra interrupted here, "did you see that with your own two eyes? It could have possibly come off that way: that way and also otherwise.

When gods die, they always die many kinds of death.

But well then! This way or that, this way and that — he is gone! He ran counter to the taste of my eyes and ears, worse I would not say behind his back.

I love all that looks bright and speaks honestly. But he — you know it indeed, you old priest, he had something of your nature about him, of the priestly nature — he was ambiguous.

He was also indistinct. How angry he got with us, this wrath-snorter, for understanding him poorly! But why did he not speak more clearly?

And if the fault lay in our ears, why did he give us ears that heard him poorly? If there was mud in our ears, well then! who put it there?

Too many things he botched, this potter who never finished his apprenticeship.

But that he revenged himself on his earthen and earthly vessels because they turned out badly — that was a sin against good taste.

In piety too there is good taste: it says at last: "Away with such a God! Better to have no God, better to make your own destiny, better to be a fool, better to be a God yourself!"

— "What do I hear!" the old pope said here with pricked-up ears; "O Zarathustra, with such unbelief you are more pious than you know! Some god in you has converted you to your godlessness.

Is it not your piety itself which no longer allows you to believe in a God?

And your overly great honesty will carry you away yet, beyond good and evil!

Behold, what has been reserved for you? You have eyes and hand and mouth predestined for blessing from eternity. One does not bless with the hand alone.

In your presence, although you want to be the godless one, I sense the sacred and pleasant aroma of long blessings: I feel pleased and pained by it.

Let me be your guest, O Zarathustra, for a single night! Nowhere on earth shall I now feel better than with you!" —

"Amen! So be it!" said Zarathustra in great amazement, "up there the way leads, there lies Zarathustra's cave.

Gladly indeed would I see you up there myself, you venerable one, for I love all pious men. But now a cry of distress calls me hastily away from you.

In my domain no one shall come to harm; my cave is a good haven. And I would like best of all to put everyone who is in the doldrums back on firm land and firm legs.

But who could take your melancholy from your shoulders? For that I am too weak. Long, verily, we should have to wait until someone re-awakens your God for you.

For this old God lives no more: he is as dead as a doornail." —

Thus spake Zarathustra.

The Ugliest Man

— And again Zarathustra's feet ran through mountains and forests, and his eyes searched and searched, but he whom they wanted to see was nowhere to be seen, the great crier and sufferer of distress. The entire way, however, he rejoiced in his heart and was thankful. "What good things," he said, "this day has granted me as compensation for having started out badly! What strange partners in conversation I have found!

On their words I shall now chew long as upon good grains; my teeth shall mash and smash them small until they flow like milk into my soul!"- But as the path curved around a rock again, the landscape changed all at once, and Zarathustra entered a kingdom of death. Here black and red cliffs rose up: no grass, no tree, no bird's melody. For it was a valley that all the animals avoided; except that a species of ugly, thick, green snake, when it grew old, came here to die. That is why the shepherds called this valley: Snakes-Death.

Zarathustra, however, was sunk in a black recollection, for to him it seemed as if he had stood in this valley once before. And many weighty things lay heavy on his mind: so that he walked slowly and ever more slowly and at last stood still. But when he opened his eyes he saw, sitting by the path, something shaped like a man, yet hardly like a man, something unspeakable. And all at once a great shame came over Zarathustra at having set eyes on something like that:

blushing up to his white hair, he averted his glance and raised his foot to leave this bad place. But then the dead wasteland became noisy: for from the ground it welled up, gurgling and rattling, as water gurgles and rattles at night in cloggedup waterpipes; until at last it became a human voice and human speech: — it sounded thus:

"Zarathustra! Zarathustra! solve my riddle! Speak! Speak! What is the revenge on the witness?

I entice you back, here is slippery ice! Beware, beware that your pride does not break its legs here!

You think yourself wise, you proud Zarathustra! So solve the riddle then, you hard nutcracker, — the riddle that I am! So speak then: who am I?"

— but when Zarathustra had heard these words, — what do you think happened in his soul at that moment? Pity laid him low; and all at once he sank down, like an oak tree that has long withstood many woodcutters,— heavily, suddenly, to the dismay of even those who wanted to fell it. But in no time he got up from the ground again and his face grew hard.

"I know you well," he said in a bronze-like voice: "You are the murderer of God!

Let me go.

You could not stand him who saw you, — who saw you always and through and through, you ugliest man! You took revenge on this witness!"

Thus spake Zarathustra and wanted to be off; but the unspeakable one seized the end of his garment and began to gurgle and search for words again.

"Stay!" he said at last—

—"Stay! Do not pass by! I have divined which ax felled you to the ground:

hail to you, O Zarathustra, that you stand again!

You have divined, I know it well, how he who slew him feels, — the murderer of God! Stay! Sit down here by me, it will not be in vain.

To whom should I go, if not to you? Stay, sit down! But do not look at me!

Honor thus — my ugliness!

They persecute me: now you are my last refuge. Not with their hatred, not with their bailiffs: — O, at such persecution I would jeer and cheer and take pride in!

Has not all success hitherto been with the well-persecuted? And he who persecutes well easily learns to follow — after all, all he ever does is — come after!

But it is their pity —

— it is their pity from which I flee and flee to you. O Zarathustra, protect me, you, my last refuge, you, the only one who has divined me:

— you have divined how he who slew him feels. Stay! And should you want to go, you impatient one: go not the way by which I came. That way is bad.

Are you angry with me for gibber-jabbering too long already? But know that it is I, the ugliest man, — who also has the largest, heaviest feet. Where I have gone, the way is bad. I tread all paths to death and ruin.

But that you passed me by in silence: that you blushed, I saw it well:

thereby I knew you to be Zarathustra.

Anyone else would have thrown his alms my way, his pity in word and glance. But for that — I am not beggar enough, that you divined —

— for that I am too rich, rich in the great, the terrible, the ugliest, the most unspeakable. Your shame, O Zarathustra, honored me!

With difficulty I escaped the crush of the pity-pushers, — that I might find the only one today who teaches 'Pity is obtrusive' — you, O Zarathustra!

— whether it be the pity of a God or the pity of man: pity goes against modesty.

And not-wanting-to-help can be nobler than that virtue which rushes to help.

Pity, however, this is called virtue itself by all the small people: — they have no respect for great misfortune, for great ugliness, for great failure.

Over them all I look away, as a dog looks away over the backs of swarming herds of sheep. They are small, gray, good-wooled, good-willed people.

As a heron looks away contemptuously over shallow pools, with a laidback head: so I look away over the swarm of gray small waves and wills and souls.

Too long have we given them out to be right, these small people: so that in the end we have given them power as well — now they teach: 'Good is only what small people call good.'

And 'truth' today is what the preacher said who arose himself from them, that odd saint and advocate of the small people who testified of himself: ' I — am the truth.'

For a long time now this immodest one has greatly swelled the small peoples'

heads — he who taught no small error when he taught: 'I — am the truth.'

Was an immodest one ever answered more politely? — You, however, O Zarathustra, passed him by and said: 'No! No! Three times no!'

You warned against his error, you first warned against pity — not to all, not to none, but to you and your kind.

You are ashamed at the shame of the great sufferer; and verily, when you say, 'From pity there comes a heavy cloud this way, take heed, you men!'

— when you teach 'All creators are hard, all great love is above pity': O Zarathustra, how well-schooled you seem to be in weather signs!

You yourself, however — warn yourself as well against your pity! For many are on their way to you, many suffering, doubting, desponding, drowning, freezing ones —

I warn you as well against myself. You have divined my best, my worst riddle, me myself and what I did. I know the ax which fells you.

But he — he had to die: he saw with eyes that saw everything, — he saw man's depths and reasons, all his hidden indignity and ugliness.

His pity knew no shame: he crawled into my filthiest corners. This mostinquisitive, over-obtrusive, over-pitying one had to die.

He saw me always: on such a witness I would have revenge — or not live myself.

The God who saw everything, even man: this God had to die! Man could not stand to have such a witness live."

Thus spake the ugliest man. Zarathustra arose, however, and prepared to take his leave: for he felt frozen down to his innards.

"You unspeakable one," he said, "you have warned me against your way. By way of thanks I shall praise mine to you. Behold, up there lies the cave of Zarathustra.

My cave is large and deep and has many nooks and crannies; the most-hidden one finds his hiding place there.

And close by it there are a hundred by-ways and hideaways for creeping, leaping, and fluttering creatures.

You outcast who has cast himself out, you refuse to live among men and men's pity? Well then, do as I do! Thus you shall also learn from me; only the doer learns.

And speak first and next to my animals! The proudest animal and the wisest animal — they could well be the right counselors for both of us!"

Thus spake Zarathustra and went his way, even more reflectively and slowly than before: for he asked himself many things and hardly knew how to answer himself.

"How poor is man though!" he thought in his heart, "how ugly, how throatrattling, how full of hidden shame!

They tell me that man loves himself: alas, how great this self-love must be!

How much contempt it has going against it!

This one here also loved himself when he despised himself, — a great lover he seems to me, and a great despiser.

None yet have I found who despised himself more profoundly: that too is loftiness. Alas, was he perhaps the higher man whose cry I heard?

I love the great despisers. Man, however, is something that must be overcome."

— —

The Voluntary Beggar

When Zarathustra had left the ugliest man, he was frozen and he felt lonely: for much coldness and loneliness had passed through his mind, so that his limbs also became colder. But as he climbed on and on, up, down, sometimes past green meadows, other times over wild stony beds where an impatient brook had possibly lain down to rest in former days: then suddenly he felt warmer again and heartier in spirit.

"But what has happened to me?" he asked himself, "something warm and living quickens me, it must be in my vicinity.

Already I am less alone; unknown companions and brothers roam around me, their warm breath stirs my soul."

But when he explored around himself and searched for the consolers of his loneliness: behold, they were cows standing next to each other on a knoll; their nearness and odor had warmed his heart. These cows, however, seemed to be eagerly listening to a speaker and paid no heed to the one who approached them.

But as Zarathustra drew quite near them, he distinctly heard a man's voice speaking from out of the midst of the cows; and evidently they had turned their heads all together toward the speaker.

Then Zarathustra sprang forth eagerly and pushed the animals apart, for he feared that someone had suffered injury here, which the cows' pity could hardly remedy. But in this he was mistaken; for behold, there sat a man on the ground, and he seemed to be exhorting the animals to have no fear of him, a peaceable man and preacher-on-the-mount out of whose eyes goodness itself preached.

"What do you seek here?" Zarathustra cried out with wonder.

"What do I seek here?" he answered: "the same thing that you seek, you disturber of the peace! namely, happiness on earth.

That, however, I want to learn from these cows. For, do you know, I have already spent half the morning talking to them and just now they were about to tell me. Why do you disturb them?

Except we turn back and become like cows, we shall not enter the kingdom of heaven. One thing namely we should learn from them: chewing the cud.

And verily, what would it profit a man to gain the whole world and not learn this one thing, chewing the cud! He would not be free of his misery.

— his great misery: but today that is called loathing. Who does not have a heart, mouth, and eyes full of loathing today? Even you! Even you! But just look at these cows!"—

Thus spake the preacher-on-the-mount and then turned his own gaze upon Zarathustra — for until then it had rested lovingly upon the cows —: but now he was transformed. "Who is this with whom I speak?" he cried out in alarm and sprang up from the ground.

"This is the man without loathing, this is Zarathustra himself, the conqueror of the great loathing, this is the eye, this is the mouth, this is the heart of Zarathustra himself."

And while he was speaking thus, he kissed, with overflowing eyes, the hands of him with whom he spoke and acted exactly like one to whom a precious gift and gem has unexpectedly fallen from heaven. The cows, however, watched all this and marvelled.

"Speak not of me, you strange one! Delightful one!" said Zarathustra and restrained his tenderness, "speak first to me of yourself! Are you not the voluntary beggar who once threw great riches away, —

— who was ashamed of his riches and of the rich and fled to the poorest to give them his plenty and his heart? But they did not accept him."

"But they did not accept me," said the voluntary beggar, "you know it indeed. So in the end I went to the animals and to these cows."

"There you learned," Zarathustra interrupted the speaker, "how proper giving is harder than proper receiving, and that good gift-giving is an art and the last, craftiest master-art of kindliness."

"Especially nowadays," answered the voluntary beggar, "today, namely, when everything low has become rebellious and skittish and insolent in its own way: namely in the rabble way.

For the hour has come, you know it indeed, for the big, bad, long, slow slave-and-rabble rebellion: it grows and grows!

Now the lower ranks are enraged by every good action and small giveaway; and the over-rich must be on their guard!

Those today who trickle out in drops, like bulging bottles with all-toosmall necks — such bottles people are fond of breaking the necks of today.

Lascivious greed, bilious envy, grief-stricken vengefulness, rabble pride: all this exploded in my face. It is no longer true that the poor are blessed. The kingdom of heaven, however, is with the cows.

"And why is it not with the rich?" asked Zarathustra temptingly, while he restrained the cows which snorted familiarly upon the peaceable one.

"Why do you tempt me?" he replied. "You know it even better than I. What drove me to the poorest after all? Was it not loathing for our richest?

— for the convicts of riches, who glean their advantage from every piece of trash, with cold eyes, obscene thoughts, for this riff-raff that stinks to high heaven, — for this gilded, falsified rabble, whose fathers were carrion birds or ragpickers or pickpockets, with wives obliging, lustful, forgetful: — all of them not far from being whores, namely —

Rabble above, rabble below! What do 'poor' and 'rich' even mean today? I forgot the difference — so I fled, further, ever further, until I came to these cows."

Thus spake the peaceable one, and even snorted and sweated during his speech: so that the cows marvelled once more. Zarathustra, however, kept looking at him with a smiling face, silently shaking his head as the other talked so harshly.

"You do violence to yourself, you preacher-on-the-mount, when you use such harsh words. Neither your mouth nor your eye was made for such harshness.

Nor, it seems to me, your very stomach either: such anger and hatred and frothing-over makes it queasy. Your stomach requires softer things: you are no butcher.

A planter and root-gatherer rather you seem to me. Perhaps you grind up grain. Surely, however, you are averse to fleshly joys and love honey."

"You have divined me well," replied the voluntary beggar with a relieved heart. "I love honey, I also grind up grain, for I have sought that which tastes lovely and makes for sweet breath.

— also what takes a long time, a day's and mouth's work for gentle dawdlers and idlers. These cows are surely the most proficient at this: they invented for themselves chewing the cud and lying in the sun. They also abstain from all heavy thoughts, which swell the heart."

— "Well then!" said Zarathustra, "you should also see my animals, my eagle and my serpent — of their like there are none on earth today.

Behold, there leads the way to my cave: be its guest this night. And talk to my animals of the happiness of animals, —

— until I come home myself. For now a cry of distress calls me hastily away from you. New honey too you shall find at my place, icy-fresh golden honeycomb:

eat that!

But quickly take leave of your cows now, you strange one! Delightful one!

Even though it may be hard for you. For they are your warmest friends and instructors!"

" — Except for one of whom I am even fonder," answered the voluntary beggar. "You yourself are good and even better than a cow, O Zarathustra!"

"Away, away with you! you wicked flatterer!" Zarathustra cried maliciously, "why do you spoil me with such praise and honey-flattery?"

"Away, away from me!" he cried once more and brandished his stick at the tender beggar: he, however, ran swiftly away.

The Shadow

But no sooner had the voluntary beggar run away than Zarathustra, alone with himself again, heard a new voice behind him: it called out: "Halt! Zarathustra!

So wait then! It is I indeed, O Zarathustra, I, your shadow!" But Zarathustra did not wait, for a sudden annoyance came over him at the great rush and crush in his mountains. "Where has my solitude gone?" he said.

"It is truly becoming too much for me; this mountain range is swarming, my kingdom is no longer of this world, I need new mountains.

My shadow calls me? What does my shadow matter? Let him run after me!

I — shall run away from him."

Thus spake Zarathustra to his heart and ran away. But he who was behind him followed after him: so that presently there were three runners, one after the other, first the voluntary beggar, then Zarathustra, and third and last, his shadow. Not long were they running thus when Zarathustra came to his senses over his folly and with one sudden jerk shook all displeasure and disgust from himself.

"What!" he said, "do not the most ridiculous things always happen to us old hermits and holy men?

Verily, my folly has grown tall in the mountains! Now I hear six old fools'

legs clattering, one after the other!

But does Zarathustra really need to be afraid of a shadow? And after all I think he has longer legs than me."

Thus spake Zarathustra, laughing with his eyes and insides, then stopped and quickly turned around — and behold, he almost threw his follower and shadow to the ground: so closely indeed had this shadow followed at his heels, and so weak was he likewise. For when Zarathustra scrutinized him with his eyes, he was terrified as if by a sudden apparition: so thin, dark, hollow, and deathly-weary did this follower appear.

"Who are you?" asked Zarathustra furiously, "what are you doing here?

And why do you call yourself my shadow? I do not like you."

"Forgive me," answered the shadow, "that it is I; and if I do not please you, well then, O Zarathustra! in that I praise you and your good taste.

I am a wanderer who has already walked a great deal at your heals: always on the way but without a goal, without a home, also: so that truly I am little short of being the Eternal Wandering Jew except that I am not eternal and also not a Jew.

What? Must I always be on the way? Whirled about by every wind, restless, driven onward? O earth, you have grown too round for me!

On every surface I have already sat, like weary dust I have fallen asleep on mirrors and windowpanes: everything takes from me, nothing gives, I grow thin — almost like a shadow.

But after you, O Zarathustra, I have chased and paced the longest, and though I hid myself from you, I was definitely your best shadow: wherever you sat there I sat, too.

With you I haunted the coldest, remotest worlds, like a ghost which freely goes over winter roofs and snow.

With you I strove in everything that is forbidden, worst, remotest: and if anything in me be a virtue, then it is that I had no fear of being forbidden.

With you I shattered whatever my heart revered, I overturned all boundary stones and images, I pursued the most dangerous desires — verily, over every crime I have passed at one time.

With you I unlearned the belief in words and values and great names.

When the devil sheds his skin, does not his name fall off as well? For that is also skin. The devil himself is perhaps — skin.

'Nothing is true, everything is permitted': thus I exhorted myself. With head and heart I plunged myself into the coldest wasters. Alas, how often I stood there naked like a crab after that!

Alas, where have all the good things gone for me, and all shame, and all belief in the good! Alas, where is that innocence I once possessed, the innocence of the good and their noble lies!

Too often, verily, I followed hard on the heels of truth: then she kicked me in the head. Sometimes I meant to lie and behold! only then did I find — the truth.

Too much became clear to me: now it means nothing to me anymore. Nothing that I love lives anymore, — how could I still love myself?

'To live as I please or not to live at all': thus I will it, thus the holiest wills it as well. But alas! how can I even be — pleased?

Do I even have — a goal? A harbor toward which my sail is set?

A fair wind? Alas, only he who knows where he is sailing also knows which wind is good and is his fair wind.

What remains now for me? A heart weary and shameless; a restless will; flutter-wings, a broken backbone.

This quest for my home: O Zarathustra, do you know, this quest has been my inquest; it is eating me up.

'Where is — my home?' I ask and seek and have sought after it, but I have not found it. O eternal everywhere, O eternal nowhere, O eternal — In-vain!"

Thus spake the shadow, and Zarathustra's face grew longer at his words.

"You are my shadow!" he said at last, with sadness.

"Your danger is no small one, you free spirit and wanderer! You have had a bad day: see to it that an even worse evening does not come to you!

To restless ones such as you even prison seems blessed in the end. Have you ever seen how imprisoned criminals sleep? They sleep peacefully, they enjoy their new security.

Beware that in the end a narrow belief does not imprison you, a harsh, stern delusion! For everything narrow and firm induces and seduces you now.

You have lost your goal: alas, how will you while away and smile away this loss? With this loss — you have also lost your way!

You poor rover, roamer, you weary butterfly! Would you like repose and a home tonight? Then go up to my cave!

Over there the way leads to my cave! And now I will quickly run away from you again. Already it is as if a shadow were lying over me.

I want to run alone that it may be bright around me again. For that I must be merry on my legs a long while yet. But this evening with me there will be —

dancing!" — —

Thus spake Zarathustra.

At Noontime

— And Zarathustra ran and ran and found no one anymore and was alone and found himself over and over again and enjoyed and savored his solitude and thought of good things, — for hours. Around the noontime hour, however, when the sun stood directly above Zarathustra's head, he came upon an old crooked and gnarled tree which was embraced by the rich love of a grapevine and hidden from itself: from it hung yellow grapes in abundance, confronting the wanderer.

Then he felt a longing to slake a slight thirst and break off a cluster of grapes; but even as he stretched out his arm to do that, he felt an even greater longing:

namely, to lie down beside the tree at the perfect noon hour and to sleep.

This Zarathustra did; and as soon as he lay on the ground in the stillness and secrecy of the brightly-colored grass, he had already forgotten his slight thirst and fallen asleep. For as Zarathustra's proverb says: One thing is more necessary than another. Only that his eyes remained open: — for they did not grow weary of seeing and praising the tree and the love of the vine. In falling asleep, however, Zarathustra spoke thus to his heart:

"Hush! Hush! Has not the world just now become perfect? But what is happening to me?

As a delicate wind dances, unseen, upon an inlaid sea, light, feather-light:

so — sleep dances upon me.

My eye it closes not, my soul it leaves awake. Light it is, verily! featherlight!

It persuades me, I know not how?, it touches me inwardly with a caressing hand, it forces my hand. Yes, it forces me, so that my soul stretches out: —

— how long and weary she grows, my strange soul! Has a seventh-day evening come to her precisely at noon? Has she already wandered happily among good and ripe things too long?

She stretches herself out long, long — longer! She lies still, my strange soul.

Too many good things has she tasted already; this golden sadness oppresses her, she makes a wry mouth.

— As a ship that comes into its calm cove: — now it leans against the earth, weary from the long voyages and the uncertain seas. Is the earth not truer?

As such a ship rests and nestles itself against the land — then it suffices that a spider spin its thread from the land to it. No stronger ropes are required.

As such a weary ship in the calmest cove: so I too rest near the earth now, true, trusting, waiting, tethered to it with the lightest of threads.

O happiness! O happiness! So, would you sing, O my soul? You lie in the grass. But this is the secret solemn hour when no shepherd plays his flute.

Stay! Hot noontide sleeps upon the meadows. Do not sing! Hush! The world is perfect.

Do not sing, you grass-gosling, O my soul! Do not even whisper! Just look — hush! The old noontide sleeps, he moves his mouth: does he not even now drink a drop of happiness —

— an old brown drop of golden happiness, of golden wine? It skims over him, his happiness laughs. Thus — laughs a god. Hush! —

— 'For happiness, how little indeed suffices for happiness!' Thus I said once and thought myself clever. but it was blasphemy: that I have learned now.

Clever fools speak better.

Precisely the least thing, the slightest, lightest thing, a lizard's rustling, a whiff, a whisk, an eye-glance — little constitutes the nature of the best happiness.

Hush!

— What has happened to me? Listen! Has time perhaps flown away? Am I not falling?

Have I not fallen — listen! into the fountain of eternity?

— What is happening to me? Hush! It pierces me — woe — to the heart?

To the heart! O shatter, shatter, heart, after such happiness, after such piercing!

— What? Has not the world just now become perfect? Round and ripe? O the golden round ring — where does it fly, I wonder? I will run after it! Quickly!

Hush — — "(and here Zarathustra stretched himself and felt that he slept.) "Up," he said to himself, "you sleeper! You noonday sleeper! Well then, come on, old legs! It is time and more than time, many a good stretch of the way still remains for you —

Now you have had a good long rest, how long then? Half an eternity! Well, up now, my old heart! Only after such a sleep, how long may it take you — to wake it off?"

(But then he proceeded to fall asleep again, and his soul spoke against him and defended itself and settled down once again) — "Let me be! Hush! Has not the world just now become perfect? O the golden round ball!" —

"Stand up," said Zarathustra, "you little thief, you lazy day-thief! What!

Still stretching, yawning, sighing, tumbling down into deep fountains?

Who are you though? O my soul!" (and here he was startled, for a sunbeam from heaven fell down upon his face.) "O heaven above me," he said, sighing, and sat upright, "you are looking down at me? You are listening to my strange soul?

When will you drink this drop of dew which has fallen upon all earthly things, — when will you drink this strange soul —

— when, fountain of eternity! you cheerful-frightful noontime-abyss! when will you drink my soul back into yourself?"

Thus spake Zarathustra and arose from his resting place by the tree as if from a strange drunkenness: and behold, the sun still stood straight above his head. But one might rightly gather from this that Zarathustra had not slept long.

The Greeting

It was only late in the afternoon that Zarathustra, after long fruitless searching and wandering around, returned home to his cave. But when he stood opposite it, not more than twenty paces away, what he least expected to happen happened: once again he heard the great cry of distress. And, amazingly! this time it came from his own cave. It was a long, varied, peculiar cry, however, and Zarathustra clearly discerned that it was composed of many voices: heard from afar, though, it might sound like the cry from a single mouth.

Then Zarathustra sprang up towards his cave, and behold! what an eyeful awaited him right after this earful! For they sat all together, those he had passed by during the day: the king on the right and the king on the left, the old sorcerer, the pope, the voluntary beggar, the shadow, the conscientious one in spirit, the sad soothsayer, and the ass; the ugliest man, however, had placed a crown on his head and wound two purple girdles round himself, — for, like all the ugly, he loved to disguise himself and play the dandy. But in the midst of this sad company stood Zarathustra's eagle, ruffled and restless, for he had to answer to too much for which his pride had no answer; the wise serpent hung around his neck, however.

Zarathustra beheld all this with great amazement: then, however, he examined every single one of his guests with genial curiosity, read their souls, and marvelled again. In the meantime the assembled had risen from their seats and waited with reverence for Zarathustra to speak. But Zarathustra spake thus:

"You despairing ones! You strange ones! So I heard your cry of distress? And now, where to seek him whom I sought in vain today: the higher man — :

— in my own cave he sits, the higher man! But why do I marvel at that?

Have I not lured him to myself with honey offerings and cunning bird calls of my happiness?

But methinks you are poor company for each other, you make each other's hearts surly when you sit together, you criers of distress! First there must come one, — one to make you laugh again, a good joyful tomfool, a dancer and wind and wild child, some old buffoon; — what do you think?

But forgive me, you despairing ones, that I speak to you with such petty words, unworthy, verily, of such guests! But you do not guess what makes my heart courageous :—

—you yourselves do, and the sight of you, forgive me! For everyone who looks upon one in despair becomes brave. To encourage one in despair — everyone thinks himself strong enough for that.

To me myself you have given this strength — a good gift, my lofty guests!

An honest-to-goodness guest-gift! Well then, do not be angry now if I offer you something of my own as well.

This is my kingdom here and my dominion: what is mine, however, shall this evening and this night be yours. My animals shall serve you: let my cave be your resting place!

In my house and home no one shall despair, in my preserve I shelter each one from his wild beasts. And that is the first thing I offer you: security!

The second thing, however, is: my little finger. And once you have that, then go ahead, take the whole hand! and the heart with it! Welcome here, welcome, my guests!"

Thus spake Zarathustra and laughed with love and malice. After this greeting his guests bowed once again and were reverentially silent; the king on the right, however, answered him in their name.

"By the way in which, O Zarathustra, you offered us your hand and your greeting, we recognize you as Zarathustra. You humbled yourself before us; you almost offended our reverence —:

— but who could humble himself with such pride as you? We ourselves that raises up, it is refreshment for our eyes and hearts.

To view this alone we would gladly climb mountains higher than this one.

For as curiosity seekers we came, we wanted to see what makes dim eyes bright.

And behold, all our cries of distress are over now. Now our hearts and minds are open and overjoyed. Little is lacking: and our spirits will become highspirited.

Nothing more delightful grows on earth, O Zarathustra, than a lofty, strong will: it is the earth's finest growth. An entire landscape refreshes itself on one such tree.

He who grows up like you, O Zarathustra, I liken to the pine: tall, silent, hard, alone, of the best, most pliant wood, magnificent, —

— in the end, however, reaching out for its domain, with strong green branches, asking strong questions of wind and weather and whatever is at home in high places, — answering more strongly, a commander, a conqueror: O who would not climb high mountains to behold such growth?

Here at your tree, O Zarathustra, the gloomy, the failures also refresh themselves; at the sight of you even the restless become secure and cure their hearts.

And verily, many eyes are turned toward your mountains and tree today; a great longing has arisen and many have learned to ask: who is Zarathustra?

And if ever you dripped your song and your honey into their ears: all the hidden, the lonesome, the twosome said all at once to their hearts: 'Does Zarathustra still live? It no longer pays to live, all is the same, all is in vain: or — we must live with Zarathustra!'

'Why does he not come, he who has announced himself for so long?' thus many ask; 'did solitude swallow him up? Or should we perhaps come to him?'

Now it comes about that solitude itself becomes brittle and breaks apart, like a grave that breaks apart and can no longer hold its dead. Everywhere one sees the resurrected.

Now the waves rise and rise around your mountain, O Zarathustra. And however high your height might be, many must go up to you: your boat shall not be high and dry much longer.

And that we despairing ones came to your cave and already despair no more: it is but a sign and symbol that better ones are on their way to you, —

— for they themselves are on their way to you, the last remnant of God among men, that is: all the men of great longing, great loathing, great disgust, —

— all those who do not want to live unless they learn to hope again — unless they learn from you, O Zarathustra, the great hope!"

Thus spake the king on the right and seized the hand of Zarathustra in order to kiss it; but Zarathustra checked his reverence and stepped back alarmed, as if silently and suddenly fleeing into far distances. After a little while, however, he was already back with his guests, looked at them with bright, searching eyes, and said:

"My guests, you higher men, I will speak plainly and in plain German with you. Not for you have I waited here in these mountains."

("Plainly and in plain German? God help us!" the king on the left said here, in an aside; "you can see he doesn't know our dear Germans, this wise man from the East!"

"But he means 'bluntly and in plain German' — well then! That is not the worst taste nowadays!") "You may truly be higher men all in all," continued Zarathustra, "but for me — you are not high and strong enough.

For me, that is: for the inexorable in me which is silent but will not always be silent. And if you should belong to me, it is surely not as my right arm.

For whoever stands on sickly and frail legs, as you do, wants above all, whether he knows it or hides it from himself: to be spared.

My arms and legs, however, I do not spare; I do not spare my warriors: how could you serve in my war?

With you all my victories would be spoiled. And many of you would fall down if you but heard the loud sound of my drums.

You are not handsome and wellborn enough for me either: I need clean, smooth mirrors for my teaching; on your surface even my own likeness is distorted.

Your shoulders are weighted down by many a burden, many a memory; many a bad dwarf crouches in your corners. There is also hidden rabble in you.

And even though you are high and of a higher kind: much in you is crooked and deformed. There is no blacksmith in the world who could hammer you straight and into shape.

You are only bridges: may higher ones stride across on you! You signify steps: so do not be angry with him who climbs over you to his height!

From your seed a true son and perfect heir may yet grow for me one day:

but that is far off. You yourselves are not those to whom my heritage and name belong.

Not for you do I wait here in these mountains, not with you may I descend for the last time. Only as omens have you come to me, that higher ones are already on the way, —

— not the men of great longing, great loathing, great disgust, and that which you have called the last remnant of God, — No! No! Three times no! For others I wait here in these mountains and will not lift my foot from here without them, — for higher, stronger, more victorious, more joyous ones, ones who are built foursquare in body and soul: laughing lions must come!

Oh, my guests, you oddballs, — have you heard nothing yet of my children?

And that they are on their way to me?

But speak to me of my gardens, of my blessed isles, of my new beautiful kind, — why do you not speak to me of that?

This guest-gift I ask of you from your love, that you speak to me of my children.

With this I am rich, with this I became poor: what did I not give, — what would I not give, to have one thing: these children, this live planting, these life-trees of my will and my highest hope!"

Thus spake Zarathustra and stopped suddenly in his speech: for his longing overcame him and he closed his eyes and mouth at the movement of his heart.

And all his guests were also silent and stood still and dismayed: except that the old soothsayer made signs and gestures with his hands.

The Last Supper

For at this point the soothsayer interrupted the greeting of Zarathustra and his guests: he pressed forward, like one who has no time to lose, grabbed Zarathustra's hand and cried: "But Zarathustra!

One thing is more necessary than another, so you yourself said: well then, one thing is more necessary to me now than anything else.

A word at the right time: did you not invite me to a meal? And here there are many who have come a long way. You do not intend to feed us with speeches, do you?

And, to me, all of you have thought far too much about freezing, drowning, suffocating, and other bodily crises: but nobody has thought about my crisis, namely, dying of hunger —"

(Thus spake the soothsayer; but when Zarathustra's animals heard these words, they ran away in terror. For they saw that whatever they had brought home during the day would not be enough to fill up this one soothsayer.) "With dying of thirst thrown in," the soothsayer went on to say. "And although here I hear water splashing like words of wisdom, that is, copiously and tirelessly: I — want wine!

Not everyone is a born water drinker like Zarathustra. Nor does water do for the weary and the withered: wine is our due, — that alone provides sudden recovery and spur-of-the-moment health!"

On this occasion when the soothsayer longed for wine, it chanced that the king on the left, the quiet one, even got a word in for once. "As for wine," he said, "we have seen to it, I, together with my brother, the king on the right, that we have wine enough, — a whole ass-load. So nothing is lacking but bread."

"Bread?" replied Zarathustra and laughed. "But bread is just what hermits do not have. Man, however, does not live by bread alone, but also by the flesh of good lambs, of which I have two:

— they shall quickly be slaughtered and dressed fragrantly with sage: I love them that way. And there is no lack of roots and fruits either, good enough even for lip-lickers and lip-smackers; in addition, nuts and other riddles for cracking.

Thus we shall have a good meal shortly. But he who wants to eat with us must also be willing to lend a hand, even the kings. For with Zarathustra even a king may be cook."

This proposal appealed to the hearts of all; except that the voluntary beggar objected to the flesh and wine and spices.

"Now just listen to this glutton Zarathustra," he said jokingly: "does one go into caves and high mountains in order to have such meals?

Now I truly understand what he once taught us: 'Praised be the small poverty!"

and why he wants to do away with beggars."

"Be of good cheer," Zarathustra answered him, " as I am. Keep to your custom, you splendid one, grind your grain, drink your water, praise your fare: if only it makes you happy!

I am a law only for my kind, I am not a law for all. But he who belongs to me must be strong of bone as well as light of foot, —

— merry for wars and feasts, no prophet of gloom, no John-a-dreams, ready for the hardest thing as if for his feast, hale and whole.

The best belongs to me and mine; and if it is not given us, then we take it:

the best food, the purest sky, the strongest thoughts, the finest women!" —

Thus spake Zarathustra; the king on the right, however, replied: "Strange!

Have you ever heard such intelligent things out of the mouth of a wise man?

And verily, it is the strangest thing if a wise man, despite all that, is still intelligent and not an ass."

Thus spake the king on the right and marvelled: the ass, however, said with bad intent "Ye-haw" to his speech. But this was the beginning of that long meal which in the history books is called "The Last Supper." At this same event, however, nothing was spoken of other than the higher man.

The Higher Man

1

When I first came to men, I committed the hermit's folly, the great folly: I stood in the marketplace.

And when I talked to all I talked to none. In the evening, however, tightrope walkers were my companions, and corpses; and I myself nearly a corpse.

But with the new morn a new truth came to me: there I learned to say:

"What do I care about marketplace and rabble and rabble-racket and long rabble ears!"

You higher men, learn this from me: in the marketplace no one believes in higher men. And if you want to speak there, well all right! But the rabble blinks:

"We are all equal."

"You higher men," — thus blinks the rabble — "there are no higher men, we are all equal, man is man, before God — we are all equal!"

Before God! — But now this God has died. And before the rabble we do not want to be equal. You higher men, go away from the marketplace!

2

Before God! — But now this God has died. You higher men, this God was your greatest danger.

Only since he has lain in the grave are you risen again. Only now comes the great noontide, only now the higher man becomes — master!

Have you understood this word, O my brothers? You are alarmed: do your hearts become giddy? Does the abyss now yawn before you? Does the hellhound now yelp at you?

Well then! Come on! You higher men! Only now the mountain of man's future is in labor. God has died: now we want, — the Superman to live.

3

The most concerned ask today: "How is man to be preserved?" But Zarathustra is the one and only one to ask: "How is man to be overcome?"

The Superman is dear to my heart, he is my one and only one, — and not man: not the nearest, not the poorest, not the most suffering, not the best. —

O my brothers, what I can love about man is this, that he is a crossing-over and a going-under. And in you too there is much that makes me love and hope.

That you showed contempt, you higher men, that made me hope. For the great despisers are the great venerators.

That you despaired, in that there is much to honor. For you did not learn how to submit, you did not learn petty acts of prudence.

For today the small people have become master: they all preach prudence and deference and diligence and diffidence and submission and the long and-soon of petty virtues.

Whatever is womanish in nature, whatever stems from a slavish nature and especially the rabble-mishmash: that now wants to be the master of all human destiny — O horror! Horror! Horror!

That asks and asks and never grows weary of asking: "How is man to be best, longest, most agreeably preserved? With this — they are the masters of today.

Conquer these masters of today, O my brothers, — these small people: they are the Superman's greatest danger!

Conquer, you higher men, the petty virtues, the petty prudence, the grainof- sand deference, the ants' hodge-podge, the wretched comfort, the "happiness of the greatest number" — !

And rather despair than submit. And verily, I love you for not knowing how to live today, you higher men! So it is you live — best!

4

Have you courage, O my brothers? Are you stout-hearted? Not courage before witnesses, but hermit- and eagle-courage, which no God even watches anymore.

Cold souls, mules, the blind, the intoxicated I do not call stout-hearted. He has heart who knows fear but vanquishes fear; he who sees the abyss, but with pride.

He who sees the abyss, but with eagles' eyes, — he who seizes the abyss with eagles' claws: he has courage. — —

5

"Man is evil" — so said all the wisest ones to console me. Alas, if only it were still true today! For evil is man's best strength.

"Man must become better and badder" — thus I teach. The baddest is necessary for the Superman's best.

It may have been good for that preacher of the small people that he suffered and bore the sins of man. But I take pleasure in great sin as my great consolation.

—

Such a thing, however, is not said for asses' ears. Nor does every word belong in every mouth. These are fine, faraway things: sheeps' hooves should not paw at them!

6

You higher, men do you think I am here to make well what you have made ill?

Or that I wanted to bed you sufferers more comfortably from now on? Or to show new, easier footpaths to you who are unsteady, who have wandered astray, who have climbed astray?

No! No! Three times no! Ever more, ever better ones of your kind shall perish, — for you shall have it ever worse and harder. In this way alone —

— in this way alone man grows tall, to where the lightning strikes and shivers him: high enough for the lightning!

My feeling and longing goes out to the few, the long, the faraway: what is your much, short, small misery to me!

You do not suffer enough yet for me, you have not yet suffered from man.

You would be lying if you said otherwise! None of you suffers what I have suffered.

7

It is not enough for me that the lightning cause no harm any longer. I do not want to divert it: for me it shall learn — to work. —

My wisdom has long since gathered itself like a cloud; it grows stiller and darker. So does any wisdom which shall one day bring forth lightning. —

To these men of today I will not be a light, not be called a light. Them — I will blind: lightning of my wisdom! poke out their eyes!

8

Will nothing beyond your ability: there is a wicked falsehood in those who will beyond their ability.

Especially when they will great things! For they arouse mistrust toward great things, these fine counterfeiters and play-actors: —

— until finally they are false toward themselves, squinty-eyed, whited worm-rot, covered over with strong words, with showpiece virtues, with glittering false works.

Take good care there, you higher men! For nothing is more precious to me and rarer today than honesty.

Is this not the day of the rabble? But the rabble does not know what is large, what is small, what is straight and honest: it is innocently crooked, it lies continually.

9

Have a healthy mistrust today, you higher men, you brave-hearted ones!

You open-hearted ones! And keep your reasons secret! For this is the day of the rabble.

What the rabble once learned to believe without reasons, who could overturn that — with reasons?

And in the marketplace one convinces with gestures. But reasons make the rabble mistrustful.

And if truth triumphed for once, then ask yourself with a healthy mistrust:

"What strong error fought for it?"

Beware of the scholars also! They hate you: for they are unfruitful! They have cold, dried-up eyes; before them every bird lies unplumed.

They plume themselves on the fact that they do not lie: but inability to lie is still a far cry from love of the truth. Beware!

Freedom from fever is still a far cry from insight. Chilled-out spirits I do not believe. He who cannot lie does not know what truth is.

10

If you want to get up high, then use your own legs! Do not let yourselves be carried up, do not set yourselves on foreign backs and heads!

But you are mounted on horseback? You are riding swiftly up to your goal?

All right, my friend! but your lame foot is also on horseback with you!

When you are at your goal, when you leap from your horse: on your very height, you higher man, — you will stumble!

11

You creators, you higher men! One is only pregnant for one's own child.

Let nothing take you in, take you for a ride! Who then is your neighbor? And even if you act "for your neighbor," you certainly do not create for him!

Forget this "for" for me, you creators: your very virtue demands that you have nothing to do with "for" and "to" and "because." You should stop up your ears against these false little words.

This "for your neighbor" is only the virtue of the small people: there it is called "birds of a feather" and "One hand washes the other.": — they have neither the right nor the strength for your self-interest!

In your self-interest, you creators, is the prudence and providence of the pregnant! What no one has yet seen with his eyes, the fruit: this your whole love preserves and protects and nourishes.

Where your whole love is, with your child, there your whole virtue is too!

Your work, your will is your neighbor: do not be taken in be any false values!

12

You creators, you higher men! He who has to give birth is sick; but he who has given birth is unclean. Ask women: they do not give birth for the fun of it.

Pain makes hens and poets cackle.

You creators, much in you is unclean. That is because you have had to be mothers.

A new child: O how much new filth has also come into the world! Go apart!

And he who has given birth should wash his soul clean!

13

Do not be virtuous beyond your powers! And demand nothing from yourselves that goes against probability!

Follow in the footsteps where your father's virtue has already gone! How will you climb high unless your father's will climbs with you?

But he who would be a firstling, see to it that he does not also become a lastling! and where your father's vices are, there you should not mean to imply a saint!

Those whose fathers associated with women and wine and wild swine:

how would it be if they demanded chastity of themselves? It would be folly!

Much, verily, it seems to me, if such a one should be the husband of one or two or three women.

And if he founded monasteries and wrote above the door: "The way to sainthood," I would yet say: Why! It is a new piece of folly.

He founded a refuge and reformatory for himself: much good may it do him!

But I do not believe in it.

Whatever a person brings into solitude grows, including the inner beast.

Thus solitude is inadvisable for many.

Has there ever been anything filthier on earth than the saints of the desert?

Around them not only the devil was loose, — but also the swine.

14

Shy, ashamed, awkward, like a tiger whose leap has failed: thus I often saw you slink aside, you higher men. A throw failed you.

But you dice-throwers, what does it matter? You have not learned to make and mock the game as one must make and mock it. Are we not always sitting at a great game-making and game-mocking table?

And if something great has failed you, are you yourself therefore — a failure?

And if you yourself have failed, is man therefore — a failure? But if man has failed: well then! come on!

15

The higher its kind, the more rarely a thing succeeds. You higher men here, are you not all — failures?

Cheer up, what does it matter! How much is still possible! Learn to laugh at yourselves as one must laugh!

Why even wonder at your failing and half-nailing, you half-broken ones! Is it not pressing and pushing in you — man's future?

Man's farthest, deepest, star-highest, his tremendous strength: is not all this frothing against each other in your pot?

Why wonder that many a pot breaks! Learn to laugh at yourselves as one must laugh! You higher men, O how much is still possible!

And verily, how much has already succeeded! How rich this earth is in small good perfect things, in what has turned out well!

Put small good perfect things around you, you higher men! Their golden ripeness heals the heart. What is perfect teaches hope.

16

What has hitherto been the greatest sin on earth? Was it not the word of him who said: "Woe unto those who laugh here!"

Did he himself find no reasons on earth to laugh? Then he only searched badly. Even a child can find reasons here.

He — did not love enough; otherwise he would have loved us, too, the ones who laugh! But he hated and hooted us; wailing and gnashing of teeth he promised us.

Must one curse right away when one does not love? That — strikes me as bad taste. But thus he did, this absolute one. He came from rabble.

And he himself simply did not love enough: Otherwise he would have been less angry that we did not love him. All great love does not want love: — it wants more.

Avoid all such absolute ones! They are a poor, sick breed, a rabble-breed:

they look poorly upon this life, they give this earth the evil eye.

Avoid all such absolute ones! They have heavy feet and sultry hearts: —

they do not know how to dance. How could the earth possibly be light for such as these!

17

All good things approach their goal crookedly. Like cats they arch their backs, they purr inwardly at their approaching happiness, — all good things laugh.

The stride betrays whether a person already strides on his path: so watch me go! But he who approaches his goal dances.

And, verily, I have not turned into a statue, not yet do I stand here stiff, dull, stony, a pillar; I love running swiftly.

And though there is moor and thick misery on earth: he who has light feet runs away over even the mire and dances as if on cleanly-swept ice.

Lift up your hearts, my brothers, high! higher! And do not forget your legs either! Lift up your legs, too, you good dancers, and better yet: stand on your heads!

18

This crown of the one who laughs, this rose-garland crown: I myself have put on this crown, I myself have pronounced my laughter holy. None other have I found strong enough for it today.

Zarathustra the dancer, Zarathustra the light one, who winks with his wings, ready for flight, winking at all the birds, ready and ripe, a blissful-blithesome one: —

Zarathustra the soothsayer, Zarathustra the soothlaugher, no impatient one, no absolute one, one who loves leaps and side-leaps; I myself have put on this crown!

19

Lift up your hearts, my brothers, high! higher! And do not forget your legs either! Lift up your legs, too, you good dancers, and better yet: stand on your heads!

In happiness too there are heavy animals, there are clodhoppers from the beginning. Strangely they strain themselves, like an elephant straining to stand on its head.

But still it is better to be foolish with happiness than foolish with unhappiness, better to dance like a clod than walk like a cripple. So learn from my wisdom then: even the worst thing has two good reverse sides —

— even the worst thing has good dancing legs: so learn from me yourselves, you higher men, and put yourselves on a proper footing!

So forget for me the sounds of sorrow and all rabble sadness! O how sad even the rabble's clowns seem to me today! But this is the day of the rabble!

20 Be like the wind when it rushes out of its mountain caves: it wants to dance to its own tune, the seas tremble and leap under its footsteps.

That which gives asses wings, which milks lionesses, praised be this good unruly spirit which comes like a stormwind to all present-day and all rabble, —

— foe to all thistle-heads and fiddle-heads and all withered leaves and weeds: praised be this wild, good, free storm-spirit, which dances upon moors and miseries as if upon meadows!

Which hates the rabble-swindbags and all the failed, gloomy brood:

praised be this spirit of all free spirits, the laughing storm which blows dust in the eyes of all black-seeing, abscess-seeking ones!

You higher men, the worst thing about you is: you have all not learned to dance as one must learn to dance — above and beyond yourselves! What does it matter that you have failed!

How much is still possible! So learn to laugh above and beyond yourselves!

Lift up your hearts, you good dancers, high! higher! And do not forget the good laughter either!

This crown of the one who laughs, this rose-garland crown: to you, my brothers, I throw this crown! Laughter I pronounce holy; you higher men, learn — to laugh.

The Song Of Melancholy

1

When Zarathustra gave this speech, he stood near the entrance to his cave; with these last words, however, he slipped away from his guests and fled outside for a little while.

"O pure smells around me," he cried out, "O blissful stillness around me!

But where are my animals? Come here, come here, my eagle and my serpent!

Tell me then, my animals: these higher men all together — perhaps they do not smell so good? O pure smells around me! Only now do I know and feel how I love you, my animals."

— And Zarathustra said once more: "I love you, my animals." The eagle and the serpent, however, nuzzled up and looked up to him when he said these words. Thus they were in a silent threesome together and sniffed and sipped the good air with one another. For the air outside here was better than by the higher men.

2

Hardly had Zarathustra left his cave, however, when the old sorcerer arose, looked cunningly around and said: "He is out!

And already, you higher men — to tickle you with that name of praise and flattery, as he himself does — already my bad spirit of deceit and magic assails me, my melancholy devil, — who is an adversary through and through to this Zarathustra: forgive him! Now he wants to cast a spell before you, it is his hour right now; in vain I struggle with this evil spirit.

To all of you, whatever honors you may grant yourselves with words, whether you call yourselves 'the free spirits' or 'the truthful ones' or 'the penitents of the spirit' or 'the unfettered ones' or 'the ones of great longing'

— to all of you who suffer, as I do, from the great loathing, for whom the old God has died and no new God as yet is lying in cradle and swaddling clothes, —

to all of you my evil spirit and magic spell-devil is well-disposed.

I know you, you higher men, I know him; I also know this fiend whom I love against my will, this Zarathustra: he himself strikes me more often as like a beautiful saint's mask, — like a new, strange masquerade in which my evil spirit, the melancholy devil, takes pleasure: — I love Zarathustra, so it often strikes me, for the sake of my evil spirit. —

But already he assails me and compels me, this spirit of melancholy, this dusk-devil: and verily, you higher men, he desires —

— do but open your eyes! — he desires to come naked, whether male or female I do not know yet: but he comes, he compels me, woe! open your minds!

Day is dying, evening is now coming to all things, even the best things; hear now and see, you higher men, which devil, whether male or female, this spirit of evening-melancholy shall be!"

Thus spake the old sorcerer, looked cunningly around and then seized his harp.

3

In lightlorn air.

When the dew's comfort already Flows down to earth, Lost to view, unheard too —

Then tender footwear wears The comforter dew, like all the comfort-gentle —:

Do you remember then, do you remember, hot heart, How once you thirsted, For heavenly tears and dew drops, Scorched and weary you thirsted, While on yellow grasspaths Malicious evening sun glances Ran around you through black trees, Blinding, sun-glowing glances, gloating?

"The wooer of truth? You?" — so they sneered —

"No! Only a poet!

A beast, cunning, plundering, prowling, That must lie, That must wittingly, willingly lie:

Lusting after booty, Colorfully masked, Himself a mask, Himself booty —

This — the wooer of truth?

No! Only a fool! Only a poet!

Only speaking colorfully, Only screaming colorfully out of fools' masks, Climbing around on lying word-bridges, On colorful rainbows, Between false heaven And false earths, Roving around, hovering around, —

Only a fool! Only a poet!

This — the wooer of truth?

Not still, stiff, smooth, cold, Turned into a picture, A pillar of God, Not placed before temples, A God's doorkeeper:

No! hostile to such statues of truth, More at home in any wilderness than before temples, Full of cats' mischief, Springing through every window, Just like that, into every chance, Sniffing every primeval forest, Sickeningly-longingly sniffing, That you may run in primeval forests Among variegated beasts of prey Sinfully healthy and colorful and beautiful, With lustful lips, Blissfully scornful, blissfully hellish, blissfully bloodthirsty, Running around peeping, prowling, plundering: —

Or like the eagle that looks long, Long, fixedly, into abysses, Into his abysses: — —

O how his looks spiral downward, Down, in, Into ever deeper depths! —

Then, Suddenly, straight sight, Straight flight, Swooping down upon lambs, With ill will towards all lamb souls, Rage-filled ill will towards all that look Sheepish, lamb-eyed, curly-wooled, Gray, with lamb's-sheep's-wellwishing!

Thus Eagle-like, panther-like Are the poets longings, Are your longings beneath a thousand masks, You fool! You poet!

You who have looked at man As God and as sheep —:

Tearing up the God in man As well as the sheep in man, And in tearing, laughing —

This, this is your bliss!

A panther's and eagle's bliss!

A poet's and fool's bliss!" — —

In lightlorn air, When already the crescent moon, Green among crimson reds, And creeping along enviously:

— enemy to the day, With every step secretly Reaping rose-hammocks with a sickle, Till they sink, Nightly down, faintly sinking down: —

Thus I myself sank once Out of my truth-frenzy, Out of my day longings, Weary of the day, sick of the light, — sank downward, eveningward, shadowward:

From one truth Burned and thirsty:

— do you remember yet, do you remember, hot heart, How you thirsted then? —

That I am banished From all truth, Only a fool!

Only a poet!

On Science

Thus sang the sorcerer; and all that were together there went like birds unawares into the net of his cunning and melancholy sensuality. Only the conscientious one in spirit was not caught: he quickly snatched the harp away from the sorcerer and cried: "Air! Let good air in! Let Zarathustra in! You make this cave sultry and poisonous, you wicked old sorcerer!

You seduce, you false one, you subtle one, to unknown wilds and desires.

And woe if such as you speak to and make much ado about the truth!

Woe unto all free spirits that do not beware of such sorcerers! It is all over with their freedom: you lecture and lure them back into prisons, —

— you old melancholy devil, from your lament a bird call sounds, you are like those who with their praise of chastity secretly invite fleshly delights!"

Thus spake the conscientious one; the old sorcerer, however, looked around, enjoyed his victory, and in so doing swallowed the chagrin the conscientious one had caused him. "Be still!" he said in a modest voice, "good songs want to reverberate well; after good songs one should be silent long.

Thus do all these, the higher men. But perhaps you have understood little of my song? In you there is little of the magic spirit."

"You praise me," replied the conscientious one, "by separating me from you, so there! But you others, what do I see? You all still sit there with lustful eyes —:

You free souls, where has your freedom gone? You are almost, methinks, like those who have long watched wicked naked dancing girls: your very souls are dancing!

In you, you higher men, there must be more of what the sorcerer calls his evil spirit of deceit and magic: — we must surely be different.

And verily, we talked and thought enough before Zarathustra came home to his cave, as if I did not know: we are different.

We also seek different things up here, you and I. For I seek more security, therefore I came to Zarathustra. For he is still the sturdiest tower and will —

— today, when everything totters, when all the earth quakes. You, however, when I see the eyes you make, I almost think you seek more insecurity, — more terror, more danger, more earthquakes.

You lust for, thus I almost conceive it, forgive me my conceit, you higher men, —

— you lust for the worst, most dangerous life, that which terrifies me the most, for the life of wild animals, for forests, caves, steep mountains, and blind abysses.

And not those leaders who lead you out of harm's way please you the most, but those who lead you away from all ways, the misleaders. But even if such lusts in you are real, they still seem impossible to me.

For fear — this is man's primary and primordial feeling; fear explains everything, original sin and original virtue. Out of fear grew even my virtue, which is called: science.

The fear namely before a wild animal — this fear has been bred the longest in man, including the animal he hides inside himself and fears: — Zarathustra calls it 'the inner beast.'

Such long ancient fear, at last grown refined, spiritualized, intellectualized — today, methinks, it goes by the name of: science." —

Thus spake the conscientious one; but Zarathustra, who had just returned to his cave and had heard and surmised this last speech, threw a handful of roses at the conscientious one and laughed at his "truths." "What!" he cried, "What did I hear just now? Verily, methinks you are a fool or I myself am one: and your 'truth' I turn lickety-split on its head.

For fear — is the exception with us. Courage, however, and joy and adventure in the uncertain, in the unventured — courage seems to me man's whole prehistory.

The wildest, bravest animals he envied and robbed of all their virtues: only thus did he become — man.

This courage, at last grown refined, spiritualized, intellectualized, this human courage with eagle's wings and serpent's wisdom: today, methinks, it goes by the name of — " "Zarathustra!" all those who sat together cried as one and had a big laugh besides; it arose from them, however, like a heavy cloud. Even the sorcerer laughed and said with wisdom: "Well then! He is gone, my evil spirit!"

"And did I not warn you of him myself when I said he was a cheat, a spirit of falsehood and deceit?

Especially, of course, when he shows himself naked. But what can I do about his mischievous ways! Did I create him and the world?

Well then! Let us make up again and be of good cheer! And although Zarathustra is giving me a dirty look — just look at him! he is angry with me —:

— before the night comes he will learn to love and laud me again, he cannot go long without committing such follies.

He — loves his enemies: of all those I have seen he understands this art the best. But in return he takes revenge — upon his friends!"

Thus spake the old sorcerer, and the higher men applauded him: so that Zarathustra went around and with malice and love shook his friends' hands, —

like one, as it were, who has to make amends and apologize for something to all.

But when he came close by the door to his cave, behold, he lusted once more for the good air outside and for his animals — and he wanted to slip out.

Among Daughters Of The Desert

1

"Do not go away!" said the wanderer then, the one who called himself Zarathustra's shadow, "stay with us, — or else the old gloomy affliction may assail us again.

Already that old sorcerer has treated us with his worst, and just look, there the good pious pope has tears in his eyes and has entirely re-embarked on the sea of melancholy.

These kings here may still put on a brave face before us, I daresay: for of all of us today they have learned that best! But if they had no witnesses, I bet the bad business would also begin again for them —

— the bad business of passing clouds, damp melancholy, overcast skies, stolen suns, howling autumn winds, — the bad business of our howling and distress-crying: stay with us, O Zarathustra! Here there is much hidden misery that wants to speak, much evening, much cloud, much damp air!

You have nourished us with strong manly fare and pithy sayings: do not let the weak womanly spirits assail us again at dessert!

You alone make the air around you strong and clear. Have I ever found on earth such air as with you in your cave?

Many lands have I seen indeed, my nose has learned to examine and appraise many kinds of air: but with you my nostrils taste their greatest delight!

Unless it be, — unless it be —, O forgive me an old recollection! Forgive me an old after-dinner song which I once composed among daughters of the desert:

for with them there was the same good, clear, Oriental air; there I was furthest away from cloudy, clammy, melancholy Old Europe!

At that time I loved a certain kind of Oriental maiden and another blue kingdom of heaven, over which no clouds or thoughts hang.

You would not believe how nicely they sat there when they did not dance, profound but without thoughts, like little secrets, like beribboned riddles, like after-dinner nuts

Many-hued and truly strange, but without clouds: riddles that let themselves be read: for the pleasure of such maidens I then made up an after-dinner psalm."

Thus spake the wanderer and shadow; and before anyone answered him he had already seized the harp of the old sorcerer, crossed his legs, and looked calmly and sagely around him: — with his nostrils, however, he inhaled the air slowly and questioningly, like one who in new lands tastes of new foreign air.

After that he began to sing with a kind of roaring.

2

The desert grows: woe to him who hides deserts!

— Ha! Solemn!

Solemn indeed!

A worthy beginning!

African solemn!

Worthy of a lion Or a moral howling monkey —

— but nothing for you, You dearest lady-loves, At whose feet I For the first time, A European under palm trees, Am allowed to sit. Selah.

Wonderful truly!

Here I sit now, Near the desert, and already So far again from the desert, Even in nothingness still ravaged, Swallowed down, namely, By this smallest of oases—:

— it just opened, yawning, Its lovely mouth, The most fragrant of all little mouths:

Then I fell in, Down, through — in among you, You dearest lady-loves! Selah.

Hail, hail to that whale, If he allowed his guest To have it so well! — do you understand My learned allusion?

Hail to his belly If he had an oasis-belly As lovely as this:

Which I doubt however, — because I come from Europe, Which is more doubt-addicted than any Elderly married woman.

May God make it better!

Amen!

Here I sit now, In this smallest of oases, Like a date, Brown, thoroughly sweet, oozing gold, lusting For a maid's round mouth, But even more for maidenly Icy-cold, snow-white, cutting Incisors: for them, namely, The hearts of all hot dates thirst. Selah.

Similar, all-too-similar To so-called southern fruits I lie here, Sniffed around and played around, By little flying insects, Likewise by still smaller More foolish, more sinful Wishes and whims, —

Encompassed by you, —

You speechless, you ominous Girl-cats, Dudu and Suleika, — ensphinxed, to stuff into one word Many feelings:

(Forgive me God This sin of speech!) — here I sit, sniffing the best air, Edenic air, verily, Bright, light air, golden-striped, As good an air as ever Fell down from the moon —

Was it by chance, Or did it happen through exuberance, As the old poets relate?

But I the doubter doubt it, No doubt because I come From Europe, Which is more doubt-addicted than any Elderly married woman.

May God make it better!

Amen!

Drinking this finest air, With nostrils swollen like goblets Without future, without remembrances, Thus I sit here, you Dearest lady-loves, And look upon the palm tree, How like a dancing girl It bows and kowtows and sways its hips, — one joins along if one watches it long!

Like a dancing girl who, as it would seem to me, Has already stood too long, dangerously long, Always, always on one leg only?

— having forgotten thereon, as it would seem to me, The other leg?

In vain at least I sought the missing Twin-jewel — namely, the other leg —

In the holy neighborhood Of her dearest, daintiest Little pleat- and flutter- and glitter-skirt.

Yes, if you, my fair lady-friends Would believe me completely:

She has lost it!

It is gone!

gone forever!

The other leg!

O too bad about that lovely other leg!

Where — can it possibly be, tarrying and mourning forlornly?

The lonely leg?

In fear perhaps of a Fierce goldilocked Lion-monster?

Or already quite Gnawed off, chewed off —

Pitiful, alas! Alas! Chewed off! Selah.

O weep not, Gentle hearts!

Weep not, you, Date hearts! Milk-breasts!

You little licorice-heart-purses!

Weep no more, Pale Dudu!

Be a man, Suleika! Courage! Courage!

— Or should perhaps Something fortifying, heart-fortifying Be appropriate here?

An anointed saying?

A solemn exhortation? —

Ha! Up, dignity!

Virtuous dignity! European dignity!

Blow, Blow anew, Bellows of virtue!

Ha!

Roar once more, Roar morally!

As a moral lion Roar before the daughters of the desert!

— For virtuous howling, You dearest maidens, Is more than anything else European ardor, European hot-hunger!

And here I stand now, As a European, I can do no other, God help me!

Amen!

The desert grows: woe to him who hides deserts!

The Awakening

1

After the song of the wanderer and shadow, the cave suddenly became full of clamor and laughter: and since all the assembled guests were talking at the same time, and even the ass, with such encouragement, no longer remained silent, a slight antipathy and scorn for his visitors came over Zarathustra: even though he rejoiced at their gladness. For it seemed to him a sign of convalescence.

So he slipped outside and spoke to his animals.

"Where is their distress now?" he said and breathed a sigh of relief himself from his slight disgust, — "with me it seems they have unlearned their distresscrying!

— though unfortunately not yet their crying." And Zarathustra covered his ears, for just then the asses' Ye-haw mingled strangely with the joyful noise of these higher men.

"They are merry," he began again, "and who knows? perhaps at their host's expense; and if they learned to laugh from me, then it is certainly not my laughter that they learned.

But what does it matter! They are old people: they convalesce in their way, they laugh in their way; my ears have surely endured worse and not become surly.

This day is a victory: he yields already, he flees, the spirit of gravity, my old archenemy! How well this day will end, which began so badly and roughly!

And it will end. Already evening is coming: from across the sea he rides here, the good rider! How he sways in his purple saddle, the blessed, homecoming one!

With that the sky looks clear, the world lies deep: O all you oddballs who came to me, it is well worth your while to abide with me!"

Thus spake Zarathustra. And again from the cave came the clamor and laughter of the higher men: then he began once again.

"They are biting, my bait is working, their enemy, the spirit of gravity, is also retreating. Already they are learning to laugh at themselves: do I hear right?

My manly fare is working, my vim- and vigor-aphorisms: and verily, I did not feed them with flatulent vegetables! But with warrior's food, conqueror's food: new appetites I have awakened.

New hopes are in their arms and legs, their hearts are expanding. They are finding new words, soon their spirits will breathe mischief.

Such fare may indeed not be for children, nor for wistful little old and young ladies either. One wins over their innards differently; I am not their physician and teacher.

Loathing is leaving these higher men: well then! — this is my victory. In my kingdom they become secure, all foolish shame runs away, they pour themselves out.

They pour out their hearts, good times return to them, they celebrate and ruminate again, — they become grateful.

This I take to be the best sign. Not long now and they will set up festivals and put up memorials to their old joys.

They are convalescents!" Thus spake Zarathustra joyfully to his heart and gazed out; his animals, however, pressed up against him and honored his happiness and his silence.

2

But suddenly Zarathustra's ear was startled: for the cave, which until then had been full of clamor and laughter, became deathly still all at once; his nose however, smelled a sweetly-smelling dense smoke and incense, as though from burning pine cones.

"What is happening? What are they doing?" he asked himself and stole up to the entrance so he could watch his guests unobserved. But wonder upon wonder!

What was he obliged to see with his own eyes there?

"They have all become pious again, they are praying, they are crazy!" he said, and marvelled beyond measure. And forsooth! all these higher men, the two kings, the retired pope, the wicked sorcerer, the voluntary beggar, the wanderer and shadow, the old soothsayer, the conscientious one in spirit, and the ugliest man: they were all on their knees like children and devout little old ladies and were worshipping the ass. And just then the ugliest man began to gurgle and snortle, as if something inexpressible wanted to come out of him; but when it actually came to be brought forth in words, behold, it was a pious, curious litany in praise of the adored and lightly censed ass. The litany, however, sounded like this:

Amen! And praise and honor and wisdom and glory and strength be to our God, forever and ever!

— The ass, however, cried Ye-haw to that.

He bears our burden, he has assumed the form of a servant, he is patient of heart and never says nay; and he who loves his God chastises him.

— The ass, however, cried Ye-haw to that.

He does not speak: except ever to say yea to the world which he created:

thus he praises his world. His slyness it is, not to speak: thus he is seldom found to be wrong.

— The ass, however, cried Ye-haw to that.

Unshowingly he goes through the world: gray is the body color in which he wraps his virtue. If he has spirit, then he hides it; but everyone believes in his long ears.

— The ass, however, cried Ye-haw to that.

What hidden wisdom is this, to have long ears and say only yea and never nay! Has he not created the world in his own image, namely, as stupid as possible?

— The ass, however, cried Ye-haw to that.

You go straight and crooked ways; you care little about what seems straight or crooked to us men. Beyond good and evil is your kingdom. It is your innocence not to know what innocence is.

— The ass, however, cried Ye-haw to that.

Just look how you turn no one away from you, neither beggars nor kings.

You suffer the little children to come unto you, and when the bad boys entice you, you simply say Ye-haw.

— The ass, however, cried Ye-haw to that.

You love she-asses and fresh figs, you eat anything and everything. A thistle tickles your heart when you feel hungry. Therein lies a God's wisdom.

— The ass, however, cried Ye-haw to that.

The Ass Feast

1

At this point in the litany, however, Zarathustra could no longer control himself; he cried out Ye-haw himself and sprang into the midst of his maddened guests. "But what are you doing here, you dear fellows?" he exclaimed, as he pulled those in prayer up from the ground. "Woe, if someone other than Zarathustra had looked upon you:

Everyone would judge you to be with your new belief either the worst of blasphemers or the silliest of all little old ladies!

And even you, you old pope, how is it in keeping with you yourself to worship an ass as God in this manner here?" —

"O Zarathustra," answered the pope, "forgive me, but in divine matters I am even more enlightened than you. And so it stands to reason.

Better to worship God thus, in this form, than in no form at all! Ponder this saying, my noble friend: you will quickly find that there is wisdom in such a saying.

He who said 'God is a spirit' — he took the greatest step and leap to unbelief yet on earth: such a word is not easily amended again on earth!

My old heart skips and leaps that there is still something on earth to worship.

O Zarathustra, forgive an old pious pope's heart! —"

— "And you," said Zarathustra to the wanderer and shadow, "you call and think yourself a free spirit? And you practice such idolatry and hierolatry here?

Upon my word, you do even worse here than with your bad brown maidens, you bad new believer!"

"Bad enough," answered the wanderer and shadow, "you are right: but what can I do about it! The old God lives again, O Zarathustra, you may say what you will.

It is all the fault of the ugliest man: he has awakened him again. And if he should say that he once killed him: with gods death is always just a prejudice."

— "And you," said Zarathustra, "you wicked old sorcerer, what were you up to? Who in this liberated age could go on believing in you when you believe in such divine asininity?

It was stupidity, what you did; how could you, you clever one, do such a stupid thing?"

"O Zarathustra," answered the clever sorcerer, "you are right, it was a stupid thing, — it has also been hard enough on me."

— "And you too," said Zarathustra to the conscientious one in spirit, "just put your finger up to your nose and think it over! Is there nothing here then that goes against your conscience? Is your spirit not too clean for this praying and this devotees' haze?"

"There is something to this," replied the conscientious one and put his finger up to his nose, "there is something to this spectacle that does even my conscience good.

Perhaps I may not believe in God: certainly, however, it strikes me that God is still most worthy of belief in this form.

God is said to be eternal, according to the testimony of the most pious; he who has that much time takes his time. As slowly and as stupidly as possible:

thereby such a one can still go far in the world.

And he who has too much spirit might very well himself become infatuated with stupidity and folly. Ponder this yourself, O Zarathustra!

You yourself — verily! out of super-abundance and wisdom you too could very well turn into an ass.

Does not the consummate wise man gladly walk the crookedest paths?

Self-evidence teaches this, O Zarathustra, — your self-evidence!"

— "And you at last," said Zarathustra and turned toward the ugliest man, who still lay on the ground, raising up his arm to the ass (for he was giving him wine to drink). "Speak, you unspeakable one, what have you done?

You seem transformed to me, your eye is aglow, the mantle of the sublime covers your ugliness: what have you done?

Is it true what they say, that you awakened him again? And why? Was he not with good reason done in and done away with?

You yourself seem awakened to me: what did you do? Why did you revert?

Why did you become converted? Speak, you unspeakable one!

"O Zarathustra," answered the ugliest man, "you are a knave!

Whether he still lives or lives again or is thoroughly dead, — which of us two knows this best? I ask you.

But one thing I know, — from you yourself I learned it once, O Zarathustra:

he who wants to kill most thoroughly, laughs.

'Not by wrath, but by laughter does one kill' — thus you said once. O Zarathustra, you cryptopath, you annihilator without wrath, you dangerous saint, — you are a knave!"

2

Then it happened, however, that Zarathustra, amazed at such pure and simply knavish answers, sprang back to the door of his cave and, turning toward all his guests, cried out in a strong voice:

"O you jesters all of you, you buffoons! Why do you dissemble and disguise yourselves before me?

How the hearts of each of you squirmed with delight and spite that at last you had once again become like little children, namely, pious, —

— that at last you had done as children do, namely, prayed, folded your hands, and said 'Dear God'!"

But leave this nursery now, my own cave, where all childishness is at home today.

Cool your hot child's horseplay and heart's uproar out here!

To be sure: except ye become as little children, ye shall not enter into that kingdom of heaven. (And Zarathustra pointed upward with his hands.) But we have no desire whatsoever for the kingdom of heaven: we have become men, — so we want the kingdom of the earth."

3

And once again Zarathustra began to speak. "O my new friends," he said —

"you oddballs, you higher men, how well you please me now, —

— since you have become joyful again! You have all truly blossomed: it seems to me that for such flowers as you new feasts are necessary, — a little brave nonsense, some divine service and ass-feast, some old joyful Zarathustra-fool, a bluster-blast of wind that blows your souls bright.

Forget not this night and this ass-feast, you higher men! You invented this by me, I take that to be a good sign — only convalescents invent such things!

And should you celebrate it again, this ass-feast, do it for the love of yourselves, and do it also for the love of me! And in remembrance of me!"

Thus spake Zarathustra.

The Drunken Song

1

Meanwhile, however, one after the other had stepped outside and into the cool, thoughtful night; Zarathustra himself, however, led the ugliest man by the hand, that he might show him his night world and the big round moon and the silvery waterfalls near his cave. There they stood at last silently next to each other, all of them old people, but with comforted brave hearts and amazed at themselves for having it so good on earth; the secrecy of the night, however, came nearer and nearer their hearts. And once again Zarathustra thought to himself:

"O how well they please me now, these higher men!" — but he did not say it aloud, for he honored their happiness and their silence. —

And then happened that which on this long astonishing day was most astonishing: the ugliest man began one more time and for the last time to gurgle and snortle, and when he brought it forth into words, behold, a question popped out of his mouth round and clean, a good deep, clear question which moved the hearts of all who listened to him.

"My friends, all of you," said the ugliest man, "what do you think? For the sake of this day — I am satisfied for the first time to have lived my entire life.

And that I testify to so much is still not enough for me. It is worth while to live on earth: one day, one feast day with Zarathustra has taught me to love the earth.

'Was that — life?' I will say to death. 'Well then! Once more!'

My friends, what do you think? Will you not, as I do, say to death: 'Was that — life? Well then, for Zarathustra's sake! Once more!'" — —

Thus spake the ugliest man; but it was not long before midnight. And what do you think happened then? As soon as the higher men heard his question, they suddenly became aware of their transformation and recuperation and who had given it to them: then they ran up to Zarathustra, thanking, revering, caressing, kissing his hands, each in his own curious manner: so that some laughed, some wept. The old soothsayer, however, danced with delight; and even if he was, as some story-tellers say, full of sweet wine at the time, he was certainly fuller still of sweet life and had renounced all weariness. There are even those who report that the ass danced at that time; not for nothing, namely, had the ugliest man given him wine to drink beforehand. Now that may have been so or else otherwise; and if in truth the ass did not dance that evening, then greater and stranger marvels than the dancing of an ass did take place at that time. In short, as Zarathustra's adage has it: "What does it matter!"

2

But Zarathustra, when this took place with the ugliest man, stood there as if drunk: his glance grew dim, his tongue stammered, his feet staggered. And who could even guess what thoughts passed through Zarathustra's soul then?

Evidently, however, his spirit withdrew and flew on ahead and was in faraway places and, as it were, "on a high mountain ridge," as is written, "between two seas, — between past and future, wandering as a heavy cloud." Gradually, however, while the higher men held him in their arms, he returned to himself somewhat and restrained with his hands the press of reverent and concerned ones; nevertheless, he did not speak. Suddenly, however, he turned his head quickly, for he seemed to hear something: then he put his finger up to his mouth and said:

"Come!"

And immediately it became still and mysterious all around; slowly up from the deep, however, came the sound of a bell. Zarathustra hearkened to it, as did the higher men; but then he put his finger up to his mouth a second time and said again: "Come! Come!

Midnight is approaching!" — and his voice had changed. But still he did not stir from the spot: then it became even more still and mysterious, and everything hearkened, even the ass and Zarathustra's honorary animals, the eagle and the serpent, as well as Zarathustra's cave and the big cool moon and the night itself. Zarathustra, however, put his hand up to his mouth for a third time and said:

"Come! Come! Come! Let us wander now! It is the hour! Let us wander into the night!"

3

You higher men, midnight is approaching: then I will whisper something in your ear, as that old bell whispers it in my ear, —

— as secretly, as horribly, as heartily as that midnight bell which has seen more than any man tells it to me:

— which has already counted your fathers' heart-smart-beats — alas! alas!

how it sighs! how in a dream it laughs! the old deep, deep midnight!

Hush! Hush! Here is many a thing heard that may not be heard by day; now, however, in the cool air, when all your hearts' uproar has also become still, —

— now it speaks, now it is heard, now it steals into nocturnal, overwakeful souls: alas! alas! how it sighs! how in a dream it laughs!

— do you not hear it, how secretly, horribly, heartily it speaks to you, the old deep, deep midnight?

O man, take heed!

4

Woe is me! Where has the time gone? Have I not sunk into deep wells? The world sleeps —

Alas! Alas! The dog howls, the moon shines. Rather would I die, die, than tell you what my midnight heart thinks.

Now I have already died. It is over. Spider, why do you spin around me? Do you want blood? Alas! Alas! The dew is falling, the hour is coming —

— the hour when I shiver and freeze, the hour which asks and asks and asks: "Who has the heart enough for it?

— who shall be lord of the earth? Who will say: 'thus shall you flow, you great and small streams!'"

— the hour draws near: O man, you higher man, take heed! this speech is for fine ears, for thine ears — what words repeat deep midnight's creed?

5

I am borne away, my soul dances. Day's work! Day's work! Who shall be lord of the earth?

The moon is cool, the wind is silent. Alas! Alas! Did you fly high enough yet?

You have been dancing: but a leg is by no means a wing.

You good dancers, now all joy is over: wine has turned to lees, every cup has become brittle, the graves stammer.

You did not fly high enough: now the graves stammer: "Free the dead! Why is night so long? Does not the moon make us drunk?"

You higher men, free the graves, wake up the corpses! Why does the worm still burrow? It draws near, the hour draws near, —

— the bell booms, the heart still rattles, the bore-worm, the heart-worm still burrows. Alas! Alas! The world is deep!

6

Sweet lyre! Sweet lyre! I love your tone, your drunken croaking tone! —

how long, from how far your tone comes to me, from afar, from the ponds of love!

You old bell, you sweet lyre! Every pain has rent your heart, father-pain, fathers' pain, forefathers' pain; your speech has become ripe, —

— ripe like golden autumn and afternoon, like my hermit-heart — now you speak: the world itself has become ripe, the grape turns brown, — now it wants to die, to die of happiness. You higher men, do you not smell it?

A smell is secretly welling up, — a scent and smell of eternity, a rosy-blessed, brown gold-wine-smell of old happiness, — of drunken midnight-death-happiness, which sings: the world is deep, and deeper than the day conceived!

7

Let me be! Let me be! I am too pure for thee. Touch me not! Has not my world just now become perfect?

My skin is too pure for your hands. Let me be, you dumb, doltish, dull day!

Is midnight not brighter?

The purest should be lords of the earth, the least known, the strongest, the midnight souls that are brighter and deeper than any day.

O day, you grope for me? You grope for my happiness? To you I am rich, solitary, a treasure mine, a chamber of gold?

O world, you want me? Do I seem worldly to you? Do I seem spiritual to you? Do I seem godly to you? But day and world, you are too clumsy —

— have cleverer hands, reach for deeper happiness, for deeper unhappiness, reach for some God, do not reach for me:

— my unhappiness, my happiness is deep, you strange day, but yet I am no God, no God's hell: deep is its woe.

8

God's woe is deeper, you strange world! Reach for God's woe, not for me!

What am I? A drunken sweet lyre, —

— a midnight-lyre, a bell-frog that no one understands but which must speak before the deaf, you higher men! For you do not understand me!

Gone! Gone! O youth! O noon! O afternoon! Now evening and night and midnight have come, — the dog howls, the wind:

— is the wind not a dog? It whines, it yelps, it howls, Alas! Alas! how it sighs! how it laughs, how it wheezes and gasps, the midnight!

How prosaically she speaks just now, this drunken poetess! she has overdrunk her drunkenness perhaps? she has become overawake? she ruminates?

— upon her woe she ruminates, in a dream, the old deep midnight, and even more, upon her joy. For joy, though woe is deep: joy is deeper still than calamity.

9

You vine! Why do you praise me? I have cut you after all! I am cruel, you bleed—: what means your praise of my drunken cruelty?

"Whatever has become perfect, everything ripe — wants to die!" so you say.

Blessed, blessed be the vine-dresser's knife! But everything unripe wants to live:

woe!

Woe says: "Go! Away, you woe!" But everything that suffers wants to live, that it may become ripe and full of joy and longing, — longing for the further, the higher, the brighter. "I want heirs," thus says everything that suffers, "I want children, I do not want myself," —

But joy wants neither heirs nor children, — joy wants itself, wants eternity, wants recurrence, wants everything-like-itself eternally.

Woe says: "Break, bleed, heart! Walk, leg! Wing, fly! Get on! Get up! Pain!"

Well then! Come on! O my old heart: Woe bids it: "Go!"

10

You higher men, what think you? Am I a soothsayer? A dreamer? A drunkard?

A dream-interpreter? A midnight-bell?

A drop of dew? A fume and perfume of eternity? Do you not hear it? Do you not smell it? Just now my world has become perfect, midnight is also midday, —

Pain is also a joy, a curse is also a blessing, night is also a sun, — go away or you will learn: a wise man is also a fool.

Have you ever said yes to one joy? O, my friends, then you also said yes to all woe. All things are linked together, threaded together, head-over-heels together, —

— have you ever wanted once twice, have you ever said "You please me, happiness! Hush! Moment!" then you wanted it all back!

— all anew, all eternal, all linked together, threaded together, head-overheels together, O then you so loved the world, —

— you eternal ones, love it eternally and for all time: and to woe as well you say: Go, but come back! For all joy wants — eternity!

11

All joy wants the eternity of all things, wants honey, wants lees, wants drunken midnight, wants graves, wants graves' tear-cheer, wants gilded sunset sky —

— what does joy not want! it is thirstier, heartier, hungrier, more horrible, more stealthy than all woe, it wants itself, it bites into itself, the will of the ring strives within it, —

— it wants love, it wants hate, it is overrich, bestows, throws away, begs that someone take it, thanks the taker, it would dearly love to be hated, —

— so rich is joy that it thirsts for woe, for hell, for shame, for the lame, for the world, — for this world, O you know it for sure!

You higher men, for you it longs, joy, the unruly, happy one — for your woe, you failures! All eternal joy longs for the failures.

For all joy wants itself, therefore it also wants calamity! O happiness, O pain! O break, heart! You higher men, do learn this, joy wants eternity, — joy wants the eternity of all things, wants the deep, deep eternity!

12

Have you learned my song now? Have you guessed what it means? Well then! Come on! You higher men, then sing me now my roundelay!

Sing me yourselves now the song whose name is "Once more," whose sense is "Unto all eternity!" — sing, you higher men, Zarathustra's roundelay!

O man! Take heed!

What words repeat deep midnight's creed?

"I sleep, I sleep —, "From deep dream I woke and perceived: —

"The world is deep, "And deeper than the day conceived.

"Deep is her woe—, "Joy — deeper still than calamity:

"Woe bids it: Go!

"But all joy wants eternity —, "— Wants the deep, deep eternity!"

The Sign

The morning after this night, however, Zarathustra sprang up from his bed, girded his loins, and came out of his cave, glowing and strong, like a morning sun that comes out of dark mountains.

"You great star," he said, as he had said once before, "you deep eye of happiness, what would all your happiness be if you had not those for whom you shine?

And if they remained in their chambers while you were already awake and coming and dispensing and distributing: how angry your proud shame would be over that!

Well then! They still sleep, these higher men, while I am awake: these are not my proper companions! Not for them do I wait here in my mountains.

To my work I want to get, to my day: but they do not get what the signs of my morning are, my step — is no wake-up call for them.

They still sleep in my cave, their dream still drinks on my drunken songs.

But the ear that is all ears for me, — the obedient ear is lacking in their limbs."

— This Zarathustra had said to his heart as the sun arose: then he looked up inquiringly, for he heard the sharp cry of his eagle above him. "Well then!" he shouted on high, "thus is it pleasing and fitting to me. My animals are awake, for I am awake. My eagle is awake and like me honors the sun. With eagles' talons he grasps for the new light. You are my proper animals; I love you.

But I still lack my proper men!" —

Thus spake Zarathustra; but then it happened that he suddenly heard himself swarmed around and fluttered around, as if by a myriad of birds, — the whirring of so many wings, however, and the crowding around his head was so great that he closed his eyes. And verily, like a cloud it fell upon him, like a cloud of arrows showering itself upon a new foe. But behold, here it was a cloud of love, and upon a new friend.

"What is happening to me?" thought Zarathustra in his astonished heart and sat down slowly on the large stone which lay next to the exit to his cave.

But as he reached around him and above him and below him with his hands and warded off the tender birds, behold, then something even stranger happened to him: for hereby he reached unawares into a thick warm clump of hair; at the same time, however, a roar rang out before him, — a gentle, long lion's roar.

"The sign is at hand," said Zarathustra, and he had a change of heart. And in truth, when it grew clear before him, a yellow, powerful animal lay there at his feet and nestled its head on his knee and would not leave him for love, behaving like a dog that has found his master again. The doves, however, were no less zealous with their love than the lion; and whenever a dove flitted across the lion's nose, the lion shook his head and marveled and laughed about it.

To all this Zarathustra said but a word: "My children are near, my children" —, then he became quite mute. His heart, however, was loosed, and tears dropped down from his eyes and fell upon his hands. And he heeded nothing anymore and sat there motionless, without defending himself against the animals anymore either. Then the doves flew here and there and perched on his shoulder and caressed his white hair and did not grow weary of tenderness and rejoicing. The strong lion, however, continually licked the tears which fell down upon Zarathustra's hands and roared and growled shyly. Thus these animals carried on.

All this lasted a long time, or a short time: for, properly speaking, there is no time on earth for such things —. Meanwhile, however, the higher men in Zarathustra's cave had awakened and arranged themselves in a train in order to go and meet Zarathustra and bid him good morning: for they had found when they awoke that already he no longer tarried among them. But when they reached the door of the cave and the sound of their footsteps had run on ahead of them, then the lion was mightily startled, turned suddenly away from Zarathustra and sprang toward the cave, roaring wildly: the higher men, however, when they heard him roar, all cried out, as if with one voice, fled back, and vanished in a trice.

Zarathustra himself, however, dazed and estranged, arose from his seat, stood there amazed, questioned his heart, deliberated and was alone. "What did I hear, though?" he said at last slowly. "What just happened to me?"

And then the recollection came to him and at one glance he grasped all that had taken place between yesterday and today. "Here is indeed the stone," he said and stroked his beard, "upon which I sat yesterday morning; and here the soothsayer came to me, and here I first heard the cry of distress.

O you higher men, yes, it was of your distress that this soothsayer soothsaid to me yesterday morning, to your distress he wanted to induce and seduce me: 'O Zarathustra,' he said to me, 'I come to seduce you to your last sin.'

"To my last sin?" cried Zarathustra and laughed angrily at his own words:

"but what has been reserved for me as my last sin?"

— And once again Zarathustra sank into himself and sat down on the large stone and pondered. Suddenly he sprang up, —

"Pity! Pity for the higher man!" he cried out, and his countenance turned to bronze. "Well then! That — has had its time!

My suffering and my pity — what does that matter!

Do I strive for happiness? I strive for my work!

Well then! The lion has come, my children are near, Zarathustra has become ripe, my hour is come: —

This is my morning, my day is begun: up now, up, you great noontide!" — —

Thus spake Zarathustra and left his cave, glowing and strong, like a morning sun that comes out of dark mountains.

The Anti-Christ

1.

—Let us look each other in the face. We are Hyperboreans—we know well enough how remote our place is. "Neither by land nor by water will you find the road to the Hyperboreans": even Pindar,[1] in his day, knew that much about us.

Beyond the North, beyond the ice, beyond death— our life, our happiness.... We have discovered that happiness; we know the way; we got our knowledge of it from thousands of years in the labyrinth. Who else has found it?—The man of today?—"I don't know either the way out or the way in; I am whatever doesn't know either the way out or the way in"—so sighs the man of today.... This is the sort of modernity that made us ill,—we sickened on lazy peace, cowardly compromise, the whole virtuous dirtiness of the modern Yea and Nay. This tolerance and largeur of the heart that "forgives" everything because it "understands" everything is a sirocco to us. Rather live amid the ice than among modern virtues and other such south-winds!... We were brave enough; we spared neither ourselves nor others; but we were a long time finding out where to direct our courage. We grew dismal; they called us fatalists. Our fate—it was the fulness, the tension, the storing up of powers. We thirsted for the lightnings and great deeds; we kept as far as possible from the happiness of the weakling, from "resignation"... There was thunder in our air; nature, as we embodied it, became

overcast— for we had not yet found the way. The formula of our happiness: a Yea, a Nay, a straight line, a goal....

[1] Cf. the tenth Pythian ode. See also the fourth book of Herodotus. The Hyperboreans were a mythical people beyond the Rhipaean mountains, in the far North. They enjoyed unbroken happiness and perpetual youth.

2.

What is good?—Whatever augments the feeling of power, the will to power, power itself, in man.

What is evil?—Whatever springs from weakness.

What is happiness?—The feeling that power increases—that resistance is overcome.

Not contentment, but more power; not peace at any price, but war; not virtue, but efficiency (virtue in the Renaissance sense, virtu, virtue free of moral acid).

The weak and the botched shall perish: first principle of our charity. And one should help them to it.

What is more harmful than any vice?—Practical sympathy for the botched and the weak—Christianity....

3.

The problem that I set here is not what shall replace mankind in the order of living creatures (—man is an end—): but what type of man must be bred, must be willed, as being the most valuable, the most worthy of life, the most secure guarantee of the future.

This more valuable type has appeared often enough in the past: but always as a happy accident, as an exception, never as deliberately willed. Very often it has been precisely the most feared; hitherto it has been almost the terror of terrors;—and out of that terror the contrary type has been willed, cultivated and attained: the domestic animal, the herd animal, the sick brute-man—the Christian....

4.

Mankind surely does not represent an evolution toward a better or stronger

or higher level, as progress is now understood. This "progress" is merely a modern idea, which is to say, a false idea. The European of today, in his essential worth, falls far below the European of the Renaissance; the process of evolution does not necessarily mean elevation, enhancement, strengthening.

True enough, it succeeds in isolated and individual cases in various parts of the earth and under the most widely different cultures, and in these cases a higher type certainly manifests itself; something which, compared to mankind in the mass, appears as a sort of superman. Such happy strokes of high success have always been possible, and will remain possible, perhaps, for all time to come. Even whole races, tribes and nations may occasionally represent such lucky accidents.

5.

We should not deck out and embellish Christianity: it has waged a war to the death against this higher type of man, it has put all the deepest instincts of this type under its ban, it has developed its concept of evil, of the Evil One himself, out of these instincts— the strong man as the typical reprobate, the "outcast among men." Christianity has taken the part of all the weak, the low, the botched; it has made an ideal out of antagonism to all the self-preservative instincts of sound life; it has corrupted even the faculties of those natures that are intellectually most vigorous, by representing the highest intellectual values as sinful, as misleading, as full of temptation. The most lamentable example: the corruption of Pascal, who believed that his intellect had been destroyed by original sin, whereas it was actually destroyed by Christianity!—

6.

It is a painful and tragic spectacle that rises before me: I have drawn back the curtain from the rottenness of man. This word, in my mouth, is at least free from one suspicion: that it involves a moral accusation against humanity. It is used—and I wish to emphasize the fact again—without any moral significance:

and this is so far true that the rottenness I speak of is most apparent to me precisely in those quarters where there has been most aspiration, hitherto, toward "virtue" and "godliness." As you probably surmise, I understand rottenness in the sense of décadence: my argument is that all the values on which mankind now fixes its highest aspirations are décadence-values.

I call an animal, a species, an individual corrupt, when it loses its instincts, when it chooses, when it prefers, what is injurious to it. A history of the "higher feelings," the "ideals of humanity"—and it is possible that I'll have to write it— would almost explain why man is so degenerate. Life itself appears to me as an instinct for growth, for survival, for the accumulation of forces, for power: whenever the will to power fails there is disaster. My contention is that all the highest values of humanity have been emptied of this will—that the values of décadence, of nihilism, now prevail under the holiest names.

7.

Christianity is called the religion of pity.—Pity stands in opposition to all the tonic passions that augment the energy of the feeling of aliveness: it is a depressant. A man loses power when he pities. Through pity that drain upon strength which suffering works is multiplied a thousandfold. Suffering is made contagious by pity; under certain circumstances it may lead to a total sacrifice of life and living energy—a loss out of all proportion to the magnitude of the cause (—the case of the death of the Nazarene). This is the first view of it; there is, however, a still more important one. If one measures the effects of pity by the gravity of the reactions it sets up, its character as a menace to life appears in a much clearer light. Pity thwarts the whole law of evolution, which is the law of natural selection. It preserves whatever is ripe for destruction; it fights on the side of those disinherited and condemned by life; by maintaining life in so many of the botched of all kinds, it gives life itself a gloomy and dubious aspect.

Mankind has ventured to call pity a virtue (—in every superior moral system it appears as a weakness—); going still further, it has been called the virtue, the source and
. foundation of all other virtues—but let us always bear in mind that this was from the standpoint of a philosophy that was nihilistic, and upon whose shield the denial of life was inscribed. Schopenhauer was right in this: that by means of pity life is denied, and made worthy of denial—pity is the technic of nihilism. Let me repeat: this depressing and contagious instinct stands against all those instincts which work for the preservation and enhancement of life: in the rôle of protector of the miserable, it is a prime agent in the promotion of décadence—pity persuades to extinction.... Of course, one doesn't say "extinction": one says "the other world," or "God," or "the true life," or Nirvana, salvation, blessedness.... This innocent rhetoric, from the realm of religious-ethical balderdash, appears a good deal less innocent when one reflects upon the tendency that it conceals beneath sublime words: the tendency to destroy life.

Schopenhauer was hostile to life: that is why pity appeared to him as a virtue....

Aristotle, as every one knows, saw in pity a sickly and dangerous state of mind,

the remedy for which was an occasional purgative: he regarded tragedy as that purgative. The instinct of life should prompt us to seek some means of puncturing any such pathological and dangerous accumulation of pity as that appearing in Schopenhauer's case (and also, alack, in that of our whole literary décadence, from St. Petersburg to

Paris, from Tolstoi to Wagner), that it may burst and be discharged.... Nothing is more unhealthy, amid all our unhealthy modernism, than Christian pity. To be the doctors here, to be unmerciful here, to wield the knife here—all this is our business, all this is our sort of humanity, by this sign we are philosophers, we Hyperboreans!—

8.

It is necessary to say just whom we regard as our antagonists: theologians and all who have any theological blood in their veins—this is our whole philosophy.... One must have faced that menace at close hand, better still, one must have had experience of it directly and almost succumbed to it, to realize that it is not to be taken lightly (—the alleged free-thinking of our naturalists and physiologists seems to me to be a joke— they have no passion about such things; they have not suffered—). This poisoning goes a great deal further than most people think: I find the arrogant habit of the theologian among all who regard themselves as "idealists"—among all who, by virtue of a higher point of departure, claim a right to rise above reality, and to look upon it with suspicion.... The idealist, like the ecclesiastic, carries all sorts of lofty concepts in his hand (—and not only in his hand!); he launches them with benevolent contempt against "understanding," "the senses," "honor," "good living," "science"; he sees such things as beneath him, as pernicious and seductive forces, on which "the soul" soars as a pure thing-in-itself—as if humility, chastity, poverty, in a word, holiness, had not already done much more damage to life than all imaginable horrors and vices.... The pure soul is a pure lie.... So long as the priest, that professional denier, calumniator and poisoner of life, is accepted as a higher variety of man, there can be no answer to the question, What is truth? Truth has already been stood on its head when the obvious attorney of mere emptiness is mistaken for its representative....

9.

Upon this theological instinct I make war: I find the tracks of it everywhere.

Whoever has theological blood in his veins is shifty and dishonourable in all things. The pathetic thing that grows out of this condition is called faith: in other words, closing one's eyes upon one's self once for all, to avoid suffering the sight of incurable falsehood. People erect a concept of morality, of virtue, of holiness upon this false view of all things; they ground good conscience upon faulty vision; they argue that no other sort of vision has value any more, once they have made theirs sacrosanct with the names of "God," "salvation" and "eternity." I unearth this theological instinct in all directions: it is the most widespread and the most subterranean form of falsehood to be found on earth.

Whatever a theologian regards as true must be false: there you have almost a criterion of truth. His profound instinct of self-preservation stands against truth ever coming into honour in any way, or even getting stated. Wherever the influence of theologians is felt there is a transvaluation of values, and the concepts "true" and "false" are forced to change places: whatever is most damaging to life is there called "true," and whatever exalts it, intensifies it, approves it, justifies it and makes it triumphant is there called "false."... When theologians, working through the "consciences" of princes (or of peoples—), stretch out their hands for power, there is never any doubt as to the fundamental issue: the will to make an end, the nihilistic will exerts that power....

10.

Among Germans I am immediately understood when I say that theological blood is the ruin of philosophy. The Protestant pastor is the grandfather of German philosophy; Protestantism itself is its peccatum originale. Definition of Protestantism: hemiplegic paralysis of Christianity— and of reason.... One need only utter the words "Tübingen School" to get an understanding of what German philosophy is at bottom—a very artful form of theology.... The Suabians are the best liars in Germany; they lie innocently.... Why all the rejoicing over the appearance of Kant that went through the learned world of Germany, three-fourths of which is made up of the sons of preachers and teachers— why the German conviction still echoing, that with Kant came a change for the better?

The theological instinct of German scholars made them see clearly just what had become possible again.... A backstairs leading to the old ideal stood open; the concept of the "true world," the concept of morality as the essence of the world (—the two most vicious errors that ever existed!), were once more, thanks to a subtle and wily scepticism, if not actually demonstrable, then at least no longer refutable.... Reason, the prerogative of reason, does not go so far.... Out of reality there had been made "appearance"; an absolutely false world, that of being, had been turned into reality.... The success of Kant is merely a theological success; he was, like Luther and Leibnitz, but one more impediment to German integrity, already far from steady.—

11.

A word now against Kant as a moralist. A virtue must be our invention; it must spring out of our personal need and defence. In every other case it is a source of danger. That which does not belong to our life menaces it; a virtue which has its roots in mere respect for the concept of "virtue," as Kant would have it, is pernicious. "Virtue," "duty," "good for its own sake," goodness grounded upon impersonality or a notion of universal validity—these are all chimeras, and in them one finds only an expression of the decay, the last collapse of life, the Chinese spirit of Königsberg. Quite the contrary is demanded by the most profound laws of self-preservation and of growth: to wit, that every man find his own virtue, his own categorical imperative. A nation goes to pieces when it confounds its duty with the general concept of duty. Nothing works a more complete and penetrating disaster than every "impersonal" duty, every sacrifice before the Moloch of abstraction.—To think that no one has thought of Kant's categorical imperative as dangerous to life!... The theological instinct alone took it under protection!—An action prompted by the life-instinct proves that it is a right action by the amount of pleasure that goes with it: and yet that Nihilist, with his bowels of Christian dogmatism, regarded pleasure as an objection....

What destroys a man more quickly than to work, think and feel without inner necessity, without any deep personal desire, without pleasure—as a mere automaton of duty? That is the recipe for décadence, and no less for idiocy....

Kant became an idiot.—And such a man was the contemporary of Goethe! This calamitous spinner of cobwebs passed for the German philosopher—still passes today!... I forbid myself to say what I think of the Germans.... Didn't Kant see in the French Revolution the transformation of the state from the inorganic form to the organic? Didn't he ask himself if there was a single event that could be explained save on the assumption of a moral faculty in man, so that on the basis of it, "the tendency of mankind toward the good" could be explained, once and for all time? Kant's answer: "That is revolution." Instinct at fault in everything and anything, instinct as a revolt against nature, German décadence as a philosophy— that is Kant!—

12.

I put aside a few sceptics, the types of decency in the history of philosophy:

the rest haven't the slightest conception of intellectual integrity. They behave like women, all these great enthusiasts and prodigies—they regard "beautiful feelings" as arguments, the "heaving breast" as the bellows of divine inspiration, conviction as the criterion of truth. In the end, with "German" innocence, Kant tried to give a scientific flavour to this form of corruption, this dearth of intellectual conscience, by calling it "practical reason." He deliberately invented a variety of reasons for use on occasions when it was desirable not to trouble with reason—that is, when morality, when the sublime command "thou shalt," was heard. When one recalls the fact that, among all peoples, the philosopher is no more than a development from the old type of priest, this inheritance from the priest, this fraud upon self, ceases to be remarkable. When a man feels that he has a divine mission, say to lift up, to save or to liberate mankind— when a man feels the divine spark in his heart and believes that he is the mouthpiece of supernatural imperatives—when such a mission inflames him, it is only natural that he should stand beyond all merely reasonable standards of judgment. He feels that he is himself sanctified by this mission, that he is himself a type of a higher order!... What has a priest to do with philosophy! He stands far above it!

—And hitherto the priest has ruled!—He has determined the meaning of "true" and "not true"!...

13.

Let us not underestimate this fact: that we ourselves, we free spirits, are already a "transvaluation of all values," a visualized declaration of war and victory against all the old concepts of "true" and "not true." The most valuable intuitions are the last to be attained; the most valuable of all are those which determine methods. All the methods, all the principles of the scientific spirit of today, were the targets for thousands of years of the most profound contempt; if a man inclined to them he was excluded from the society of "decent" people—he passed as "an enemy of God," as a scoffer at the truth, as one "possessed." As a man of science, he belonged to the Chandala[2]. ... We have had the whole pathetic stupidity of mankind against us—their every notion of what the truth ought to be, of what the service of the truth ought to be—their every "thou shalt" was launched against us.... Our objectives, our methods, our quiet, cautious, distrustful manner—all appeared to them as absolutely discreditable and contemptible.—Looking back, one may almost ask one's self with reason if it was not actually an aesthetic sense that kept men blind so long: what they demanded of the truth was picturesque effectiveness, and of the learned a strong appeal to their senses. It was our modesty that stood out longest against their taste.... How well they guessed that, these turkey-cocks of God!

[2] The lowest of the Hindu castes.

14.

We have unlearned something. We have become more modest in every way.

We no longer derive man from the "spirit," from the "godhead"; we have dropped him back among the beasts. We regard him as the strongest of the beasts because he is the craftiest; one of the results thereof is his intellectuality. On the other hand, we guard ourselves against a conceit which would assert itself even here: that man is the great second thought in the process of organic evolution. He is, in truth, anything but the crown of creation: beside him stand many other animals, all at similar stages of development.... And even when we say that we say a bit too much, for man, relatively speaking, is the most botched of all the animals and the sickliest, and he has wandered the most dangerously from his instincts—though for all that, to be sure, he remains the most interesting!—As regards the lower animals, it was Descartes who first had the really admirable daring to describe them as machina; the whole of our physiology is directed toward proving the truth of this doctrine. Moreover, it is illogical to set man apart, as Descartes did: what we know of man today is limited precisely by the extent to which we have regarded him, too, as a machine. Formerly we accorded to man, as his inheritance from some higher order of beings, what was called "free will"; now we have taken even this will from him, for the term no longer describes anything that we can understand. The old word "will" now connotes only a sort of result, an individual reaction, that follows inevitably upon a series of partly discordant and partly harmonious stimuli—the will no longer "acts," or "moves."... Formerly it was thought that man's consciousness, his "spirit," offered evidence of his high origin, his divinity. That he might be perfected, he was advised, tortoise-like, to draw his senses in, to have no traffic with earthly things, to shuffle off his mortal coil—then only the important part of him, the "pure spirit," would remain. Here again we have thought out the thing better: to us consciousness, or "the spirit," appears as a symptom of a relative imperfection of the organism, as an experiment, a groping, a misunderstanding, as an affliction which uses up nervous force unnecessarily—we deny that anything can be done perfectly so long as it is done consciously. The "pure spirit" is a piece of pure stupidity: take away the nervous system and the senses, the so-called "mortal shell," and the rest is miscalculation—that is all!...

15.

Under Christianity neither morality nor religion has any point of contact with actuality. It offers purely imaginary causes ("God," "soul," "ego," "spirit," "free will"—or even "unfree"), and purely imaginary effects ("sin," "salvation," "grace," "punishment," "forgiveness of sins"). Intercourse between imaginary beings

("God,"

"spirits,"

"souls");

an

imaginary

natural

history

(anthropocentric; a total denial of the concept of natural causes); an imaginary psychology (misunderstandings of self, misinterpretations of agreeable or disagreeable general feelings—for example, of the states of the nervus sympathicus with the help of the sign-language of religio-ethical balderdash—, "repentance," "pangs of conscience," "temptation by the devil," "the presence of God"); an imaginary teleology (the "kingdom of God," "the last judgment," "eternal life").—This purely fictitious world, greatly to its disadvantage, is to be differentiated from the world of dreams; the latter at least reflects reality, whereas the former falsifies it, cheapens it and denies it. Once the concept of "nature" had been opposed to the concept of "God," the word "natural" necessarily took on the meaning of "abominable"—the whole of that fictitious world has its sources in hatred of the natural (—the real!—), and is no more than evidence of a profound uneasiness in the presence of reality.... This explains everything. Who alone has any reason for living his way out of reality? The man who suffers under it. But to suffer from reality one must be a botched reality....

The preponderance of pains over pleasures is the cause of this fictitious morality and religion: but such a preponderance also supplies the formula for décadence....

16.

A criticism of the Christian concept of God leads inevitably to the same conclusion.—A nation that still believes in itself holds fast to its own god. In him it does honour to the conditions which enable it to survive, to its virtues—it projects its joy in itself, its feeling of power, into a being to whom one may offer thanks. He who is rich will give of his riches; a proud people need a god to whom they can make sacrifices.... Religion, within these limits, is a form of gratitude. A man is grateful for his own existence: to that end he needs a god.—

Such a god must be able to work both benefits and injuries; he must be able to play either friend or foe—he is wondered at for the good he does as well as for the evil he does. But the castration, against all nature, of such a god, making him a god of goodness alone, would be contrary to human inclination. Mankind has just as much need for an evil god as for a good god; it doesn't have to thank mere tolerance and humanitarianism for its own existence.... What would be the value of a god who knew nothing of anger, revenge, envy, scorn, cunning, violence? who had perhaps never experienced the rapturous ardeurs of victory and of destruction? No one would understand such a god: why should any one want him?—True enough, when a nation is on the downward path, when it feels its belief in its own future, its hope of freedom slipping from it, when it begins to see submission as a first necessity and the virtues of submission as measures of self-preservation, then it must overhaul its god. He then becomes a hypocrite, timorous and demure; he counsels "peace of soul," hate-no-more, leniency, "love" of friend and foe. He moralizes endlessly; he creeps into every private virtue; he becomes the god of every man; he becomes a private citizen, a cosmopolitan.... Formerly he represented a people, the strength of a people, everything aggressive and thirsty for power in the soul of a people; now he is simply the good god.... The truth is that there is no other alternative for gods: either they are the will to power—in which case they are national gods— or incapacity for power—in which case they have to be good....

17.

Wherever the will to power begins to decline, in whatever form, there is always an accompanying decline physiologically, a décadence. The divinity of this décadence, shorn of its masculine virtues and passions, is converted perforce into a god of the physiologically degraded, of the weak. Of course, they do not call themselves the weak; they call themselves "the good."... No hint is needed to indicate the moments in history at which the dualistic fiction of a good and an evil god first became possible. The same instinct which prompts the inferior to reduce their own god to "goodness-in-itself" also prompts them to eliminate all good qualities from the god of their superiors; they make revenge on their masters by making a devil of the latter's god.—The good god, and the devil like him—both are abortions of décadence.—How can we be so tolerant of the naïveté of Christian theologians as to join in their doctrine that the evolution of the concept of god from "the god of Israel," the god of a people, to the Christian god, the essence of all goodness, is to be described as progress?—But even Renan does this. As if Renan had a right to be naïve! The contrary actually stares one in the face. When everything necessary to ascending life; when all that is strong, courageous, masterful and proud has been eliminated from the concept of a god; when he has sunk step by step to the level of a staff for the weary, a sheet-anchor for the drowning; when he becomes the poor man's god, the sinner's god, the invalid's god par excellence, and the attribute of "saviour" or "redeemer" remains as the one essential attribute of divinity—just what is the significance of such a metamorphosis? what does such a reduction of the godhead imply?—To be sure, the "kingdom of God" has thus grown larger. Formerly he had only his own people, his "chosen" people. But since then he has gone wandering, like his people themselves, into foreign parts; he has given up settling down quietly anywhere; finally he has come to feel at home everywhere, and is the great cosmopolitan—until now he has the "great majority" on his side, and half the earth. But this god of the "great majority," this democrat among gods, has not become a proud heathen god: on the contrary, he remains a Jew, he remains a god in a corner, a god of all the dark nooks and crevices, of all the noisesome quarters of the world!... His earthly kingdom, now as always, is a kingdom of the underworld, a souterrain kingdom, a ghetto kingdom.... And he himself is so pale, so weak, so décadent.... Even the palest of the pale are able to master him —messieurs the metaphysicians, those albinos of the intellect. They spun their webs around him for so long that finally he was hypnotized, and began to spin himself, and became another metaphysician. Thereafter he resumed once more his old business of spinning the world out of his inmost being sub specie Spinozae; thereafter he became ever thinner and paler—became the "ideal," became "pure spirit," became "the absolute," became "the thing-in-itself."... The collapse of a god: he became a "thing-in-itself."

18.

The Christian concept of a god—the god as the patron of the sick, the god as a spinner of cobwebs, the god as a spirit—is one of the most corrupt concepts that has ever been set up in the world: it probably touches low-water mark in the ebbing evolution of the god-type. God degenerated into the contradiction of life.

Instead of being its transfiguration and eternal Yea! In him war is declared on life, on nature, on the will to live! God becomes the formula for every slander upon the "here and now," and for every lie about the "beyond"! In him nothingness is deified, and the will to nothingness is made holy!...

19.

The fact that the strong races of northern Europe did not repudiate this Christian god does little credit to their gift for religion—and not much more to their taste. They ought to have been able to make an end of such a moribund and worn-out product of the décadence. A curse lies upon them because they were not equal to it; they made illness, decrepitude and contradiction a part of their instincts—and since then they have not managed to create any more gods. Two thousand years have come and gone—and not a single new god! Instead, there still exists, and as if by some intrinsic right,—as if he were the ultimatum and maximum of the power to create gods, of the creator spiritus in mankind—this pitiful god of Christian monotono-theism! This hybrid image of decay, conjured up out of emptiness, contradiction and vain imagining, in which all the instincts of décadence, all the cowardices and wearinesses of the soul find their sanction!

20.

In my condemnation of Christianity I surely hope I do no injustice to a related religion with an even larger number of believers: I allude to Buddhism.

Both are to be reckoned among the nihilistic religions—they are both décadence religions—but they are separated from each other in a very remarkable way. For the fact that he is able to compare them at all the critic of Christianity is indebted to the scholars of India.—Buddhism is a hundred times as realistic as Christianity—it is part of its living heritage that it is able to face problems objectively and coolly; it is the product of long centuries of philosophical speculation. The concept, "god," was already disposed of before it appeared.

Buddhism is the only genuinely positive religion to be encountered in history, and this applies even to its epistemology (which is a strict phenomenalism). It does not speak of a "struggle with sin," but, yielding to reality, of the "struggle with suffering." Sharply differentiating itself from Christianity, it puts the self-deception that lies in moral concepts behind it; it is, in my phrase, beyond good and evil.—The two physiological facts upon which it grounds itself and upon which it bestows its chief attention are: first, an excessive sensitiveness to sensation, which manifests itself as a refined susceptibility to pain, and secondly, an extraordinary spirituality, a too protracted concern with concepts and logical procedures, under the influence of which the instinct of personality has yielded to a notion of the "impersonal." (—Both of these states will be familiar to a few of my readers, the objectivists, by experience, as they are to me). These physiological states produced a depression, and Buddha tried to combat it by hygienic measures. Against it he prescribed a life in the open, a life of travel; moderation in eating and a careful selection of foods; caution in the use of intoxicants; the same caution in arousing any of the passions that foster a bilious habit and heat the blood; finally, no worry, either on one's own account or on account of others. He encourages ideas that make for either quiet contentment or good cheer—he finds means to combat ideas of other sorts. He understands good, the state of goodness, as something which promotes health. Prayer is not included, and neither is asceticism. There is no categorical imperative nor any disciplines, even within the walls of a monastery (—it is always possible to leave —). These things would have been simply means of increasing the excessive sensitiveness above mentioned. For the same reason he does not advocate any conflict with unbelievers; his teaching is antagonistic to nothing so much as to revenge, aversion, ressentiment (—"enmity never brings an end to enmity": the moving refrain of all Buddhism....) And in all this he was right, for it is precisely these passions which, in view of his main regiminal purpose, are unhealthful. The mental fatigue that he observes, already plainly displayed in too much "objectivity" (that is, in the individual's loss of interest in himself, in loss of balance and of "egoism"), he combats by strong efforts to lead even the spiritual interests back to the ego. In Buddha's teaching egoism is a duty. The "one thing needful," the question "how can you be delivered from suffering," regulates and determines the whole spiritual diet. (—Perhaps one will here recall that Athenian who also declared war upon pure "scientificality," to wit, Socrates, who also elevated egoism to the estate of a morality).

21.

The things necessary to Buddhism are a very mild climate, customs of great gentleness and liberality, and no militarism; moreover, it must get its start among the higher and better educated classes. Cheerfulness, quiet and the absence of desire are the chief desiderata, and they are attained. Buddhism is not a religion in which perfection is merely an object of aspiration: perfection is actually normal.—

Under Christianity the instincts of the subjugated and the oppressed come to the fore: it is only those who are at the bottom who seek their salvation in it.

Here the prevailing pastime, the favourite remedy for boredom is the discussion of sin, self-criticism, the inquisition of conscience; here the emotion produced by power (called "God") is pumped up (by prayer); here the highest good is regarded as unattainable, as a gift, as "grace." Here, too, open dealing is lacking; concealment and the darkened room are Christian. Here body is despised and hygiene is denounced as sensual; the church even ranges itself against cleanliness (—the first Christian order after the banishment of the Moors closed the public baths, of which there were 270 in Cordova alone). Christian, too, is a certain cruelty toward one's self and toward others; hatred of unbelievers; the will to persecute. Sombre and disquieting ideas are in the foreground; the most esteemed states of mind, bearing the most respectable names, are epileptoid; the diet is so regulated as to engender morbid symptoms and over-stimulate the nerves. Christian, again, is all deadly enmity to the rulers of the earth, to the "aristocratic"—along with a sort of secret rivalry with them (—one resigns one's "body" to them; one wants only one's "soul"...). And Christian is all hatred of the intellect, of pride, of courage, of freedom, of intellectual libertinage; Christian is all hatred of the senses, of joy in the senses, of joy in general....

22.

When Christianity departed from its native soil, that of the lowest orders, the underworld of the ancient world, and began seeking power among barbarian peoples, it no longer had to deal with exhausted men, but with men still inwardly savage and capable of self-torture—in brief, strong men, but bungled men. Here, unlike in the case of the Buddhists, the cause of discontent with self, suffering through self, is not merely a general sensitiveness and susceptibility to pain, but, on the contrary, an inordinate thirst for inflicting pain on others, a tendency to obtain subjective satisfaction in hostile deeds and ideas. Christianity had to embrace barbaric concepts and valuations in order to obtain mastery over barbarians: of such sort, for example, are the sacrifices of the first-born, the drinking of blood as a sacrament, the disdain of the intellect and of culture; torture in all its forms, whether bodily or not; the whole pomp of the cult.

Buddhism is a religion for peoples in a further state of development, for races that have become kind, gentle and over-spiritualized (—Europe is not yet ripe for it—): it is a summons that takes them back to peace and cheerfulness, to a careful rationing of the spirit, to a certain hardening of the body. Christianity aims at mastering beasts of prey; its modus operandi is to make them ill—to make feeble is the Christian recipe for taming, for "civilizing." Buddhism is a religion for the closing, over-wearied stages of civilization. Christianity appears before civilization has so much as begun—under certain circumstances it lays the very foundations thereof.

23.

Buddhism, I repeat, is a hundred times more austere, more honest, more objective. It no longer has to justify its pains, its susceptibility to suffering, by interpreting these things in terms of sin—it simply says, as it simply thinks, "I suffer." To the barbarian, however, suffering in itself is scarcely understandable: what he needs, first of all, is an explanation as to why he suffers. (His mere instinct prompts him to deny his suffering altogether, or to endure it in silence.) Here the word "devil" was a blessing: man had to have an omnipotent and terrible enemy—there was no need to be ashamed of suffering at the hands of such an enemy.—

At the bottom of Christianity there are several subtleties that belong to the Orient. In the first place, it knows that it is of very little consequence whether a thing be true or not, so long as it is believed to be true. Truth and faith: here we have two wholly distinct worlds of ideas, almost two diametrically opposite worlds—the road to the one and the road to the other lie miles apart. To understand that fact thoroughly—this is almost enough, in the Orient, to make one a sage. The Brahmins knew it, Plato knew it, every student of the esoteric knows it. When, for example, a man gets any pleasure out of the notion that he has been saved from sin, it is not necessary for him to be actually sinful, but merely to feel sinful. But when faith is thus exalted above everything else, it necessarily follows that reason, knowledge and patient inquiry have to be discredited: the road to the truth becomes a forbidden road.—Hope, in its stronger forms, is a great deal more powerful stimulans to life than any sort of realized joy can ever be. Man must be sustained in suffering by a hope so high that no conflict with actuality can dash it—so high, indeed, that no fulfilment can satisfy it: a hope reaching out beyond this world. (Precisely because of this power that hope has of making the suffering hold out, the Greeks regarded it as the evil of evils, as the most malign of evils; it remained behind at the source of all evil.)[3]—In order that love may be possible, God must become a person; in order that the lower instincts may take a hand in the matter God must be young.

To satisfy the ardor of the woman a beautiful saint must appear on the scene, and to satisfy that of the men there must be a virgin. These things are necessary if Christianity is to assume lordship over a soil on which some aphrodisiacal or Adonis cult has already established a notion as to what a cult ought to be. To insist upon chastity greatly strengthens the vehemence and subjectivity of the religious instinct—it makes the cult warmer, more enthusiastic, more soulful.—

Love is the state in which man sees things most decidedly as they are not. The force of illusion reaches its highest here, and so does the capacity for sweetening, for transfiguring. When a man is in love he endures more than at any other time; he submits to anything. The problem was to devise a religion which would allow one to love: by this means the worst that life has to offer is overcome—it is scarcely even noticed.—So much for the three Christian virtues:

faith, hope and charity: I call them the three Christian ingenuities.—Buddhism is in too late a stage of development, too full of positivism, to be shrewd in any such way.—

[3] That is, in Pandora's box.

24.

Here I barely touch upon the problem of the origin of Christianity. The first thing necessary to its solution is this: that Christianity is to be understood only by examining the soil from which it sprung—it is not a reaction against Jewish instincts; it is their inevitable product; it is simply one more step in the awe-inspiring logic of the Jews. In the words of the Saviour, "salvation is of the Jews." [4]—The second thing to remember is this: that the psychological type of the Galilean is still to be recognized, but it was only in its most degenerate form (which is at once maimed and overladen with foreign features) that it could serve in the manner in which it has been used: as a type of the Saviour of mankind.—

[4] John iv, 22.

The Jews are the most remarkable people in the history of the world, for when they were confronted with the question, to be or not to be, they chose, with perfectly unearthly deliberation, to be at any price: this price involved a radical falsification of all nature, of all naturalness, of all reality, of the whole inner world, as well as of the outer. They put themselves against all those conditions under which, hitherto, a people had been able to live, or had even been permitted to live; out of themselves they evolved an idea which stood in direct opposition to natural conditions—one by one they distorted religion, civilization, morality, history and psychology until each became a contradiction of its natural significance. We meet with the same phenomenon later on, in an incalculably exaggerated form, but only as a copy: the Christian church, put beside the "people of God," shows a complete lack of any claim to originality. Precisely for this reason the Jews are the most fateful people in the history of the world: their influence has so falsified the reasoning of mankind in this matter that today the Christian can cherish anti-Semitism without realizing that it is no more than the final consequence of Judaism.

In my "Genealogy of Morals" I give the first psychological explanation of the concepts underlying those two antithetical things, a noble morality and a ressentiment morality, the second of which is a mere product of the denial of the former. The Judaeo-Christian moral system belongs to the second division, and in every detail. In order to be able to say Nay to everything representing an ascending evolution of life—that is, to well-being, to power, to beauty, to self-approval—the instincts of ressentiment, here become downright genius, had to invent an other world in which the acceptance of life appeared as the most evil and abominable thing imaginable. Psychologically, the Jews are a people gifted with the very strongest vitality, so much so that when they found themselves facing impossible conditions of life they chose voluntarily, and with a profound talent for self-preservation, the side of all those instincts which make for décadence— not as if mastered by them, but as if detecting in them a power by which "the world" could be defied. The Jews are the very opposite of décadents: they have simply been forced into appearing in that guise, and with a degree of skill approaching the non plus ultra of histrionic genius they have managed to put themselves at the head of all décadent movements (—for example, the Christianity of Paul—), and so make of them something stronger than any party frankly saying Yes to life. To the sort of men who reach out for power under Judaism and Christianity,—that is to say, to the priestly class— décadence is no more than a means to an end. Men of this sort have a vital interest in making mankind sick, and in confusing the values of "good" and "bad," "true" and "false" in a manner that is not only dangerous to life, but also slanders it.

25.

The history of Israel is invaluable as a typical history of an attempt to denaturize all natural values: I point to five facts which bear this out. Originally, and above all in the time of the monarchy, Israel maintained the right attitude of things, which is to say, the natural attitude. Its Jahveh was an expression of its consciousness of power, its joy in itself, its hopes for itself: to him the Jews looked for victory and salvation and through him they expected nature to give them whatever was necessary to their existence— above all, rain. Jahveh is the god of Israel, and consequently the god of justice: this is the logic of every race that has power in its hands and a good conscience in the use of it. In the religious ceremonial of the Jews both aspects of this self-approval stand revealed. The nation is grateful for the high destiny that has enabled it to obtain dominion; it is grateful for the benign procession of the seasons, and for the good fortune attending its herds and its crops.—This view of things remained an ideal for a long while, even after it had been robbed of validity by tragic blows: anarchy within and the Assyrian without. But the people still retained, as a projection of their highest yearnings, that vision of a king who was at once a gallant warrior and an upright judge—a vision best visualized in the typical prophet (i. e. , critic and satirist of the moment), Isaiah.— But every hope remained unfulfilled. The old god no longer could do what he used to do. He ought to have been abandoned. But what actually happened? Simply this: the conception of him was changed—the conception of him was denaturized; this was the price that had to be paid for keeping him.—Jahveh, the god of "justice"—he is in accord with Israel no more, he no longer vizualizes the national egoism; he is now a god only conditionally.... The public notion of this god now becomes merely a weapon in the hands of clerical agitators, who interpret all happiness as a reward and all unhappiness as a punishment for obedience or disobedience to him, for "sin": that most fraudulent of all imaginable interpretations, whereby a "moral order of the world" is set up, and the fundamental concepts, "cause" and "effect," are stood on their heads. Once natural causation has been swept out of the world by doctrines of reward and punishment some sort of un-natural causation becomes necessary: and all other varieties of the denial of nature follow it. A god who demands—in place of a god who helps, who gives counsel, who is at bottom merely a name for every happy inspiration of courage and self-reliance....

Morality is no longer a reflection of the conditions which make for the sound life and development of the people; it is no longer the primary life-instinct; instead it has become abstract and in opposition to life—a fundamental perversion of the fancy, an "evil eye" on all things. What is Jewish, what is Christian morality?

Chance robbed of its innocence; unhappiness polluted with the idea of "sin"; well-being represented as a danger, as a "temptation"; a physiological disorder produced by the canker worm of conscience....

26.

The concept of god falsified; the concept of morality falsified;—but even here Jewish priest-craft did not stop. The whole history of Israel ceased to be of any value: out with it!—These priests accomplished that miracle of falsification of which a great part of the Bible is the documentary evidence; with a degree of contempt unparalleled, and in the face of all tradition and all historical reality, they translated the past of their people into religious terms, which is to say, they converted it into an idiotic mechanism of salvation, whereby all offences against Jahveh were punished and all devotion to him was rewarded. We would regard this act of historical falsification as something far more shameful if familiarity with the ecclesiastical interpretation of history for thousands of years had not blunted our inclinations for uprightness in historicis. And the philosophers support the church: the lie about a "moral order of the world" runs through the whole of philosophy, even the newest. What is the meaning of a "moral order of the world"? That there is a thing called the will of God which, once and for all time, determines what man ought to do and what he ought not to do; that the worth of a people, or of an individual thereof, is to be measured by the extent to which they or he obey this will of God; that the destinies of a people or of an individual are controlled by this will of God, which rewards or punishes according to the degree of obedience manifested.—In place of all that pitiable lie reality has this to say: the priest, a parasitical variety of man who can exist only at the cost of every sound view of life, takes the name of God in vain: he calls that state of human society in which he himself determines the value of all things "the kingdom of God"; he calls the means whereby that state of affairs is attained "the will of God"; with cold-blooded cynicism he estimates all peoples, all ages and all individuals by the extent of their subservience or opposition to the power of the priestly order. One observes him at work: under the hand of the Jewish priesthood the great age of Israel became an age of decline; the Exile, with its long series of misfortunes, was transformed into a punishment for that great age—during which priests had not yet come into existence. Out of the powerful and wholly free heroes of Israel's history they fashioned, according to their changing needs, either wretched bigots and hypocrites or men entirely "godless." They reduced every great event to the idiotic formula: "obedient or disobedient to God."—They went a step further: the "will of God" (in other words some means necessary for preserving the power of the priests) had to be determined—and to this end they had to have a "revelation." In plain English, a gigantic literary fraud had to be perpetrated, and "holy scriptures" had to be concocted—and so, with the utmost hierarchical pomp, and days of penance and much lamentation over the long days of "sin" now ended, they were duly published. The "will of God," it appears, had long stood like a rock; the trouble was that mankind had neglected the "holy scriptures".... But the "will of God" had already been revealed to Moses.... What happened? Simply this: the priest had formulated, once and for all time and with the strictest meticulousness, what tithes were to be paid to him, from the largest to the smallest (—not forgetting the most appetizing cuts of meat, for the priest is a great consumer of beefsteaks); in brief, he let it be known just what he wanted, what "the will of God" was.... From this time forward things were so arranged that the priest became indispensable everywhere; at all the great natural events of life, at birth, at marriage, in sickness, at death, not to say at the "sacrifice" (that is, at meal-times), the holy parasite put in his appearance, and proceeded to denaturize it— in his own phrase, to "sanctify" it.... For this should be noted: that every natural habit, every natural institution (the state, the administration of justice, marriage, the care of the sick and of the poor), everything demanded by the life-instinct, in short, everything that has any value in itself, is reduced to absolute worthlessness and even made the reverse of valuable by the parasitism of priests (or, if you chose, by the "moral order of the world"). The fact requires a sanction—a power to grant values becomes necessary, and the only way it can create such values is by denying nature.... The priest depreciates and desecrates nature: it is only at this price that he can exist at all.—Disobedience to God, which actually means to the priest, to "the law," now gets the name of "sin"; the means prescribed for "reconciliation with God" are, of course, precisely the means which bring one most effectively under the thumb of the priest; he alone can "save"....

Psychologically considered, "sins" are indispensable to every society organized on an ecclesiastical basis; they are the only reliable weapons of power; the priest lives upon sins; it is necessary to him that there be "sinning".... Prime axiom:

"God forgiveth him that repenteth"—in plain English, him that submitteth to the priest.

27.

Christianity sprang from a soil so corrupt that on it everything natural, every natural value, every reality was opposed by the deepest instincts of the ruling class—it grew up as a sort of war to the death upon reality, and as such it has never been surpassed. The "holy people," who had adopted priestly values and priestly names for all things, and who, with a terrible logical consistency, had rejected everything of the earth as "unholy," "worldly," "sinful"—this people put its instinct into a final formula that was logical to the point of self-annihilation: as Christianity it actually denied even the last form of reality, the "holy people," the "chosen people," Jewish reality itself. The phenomenon is of the first order of importance: the small insurrectionary movement which took the name of Jesus of Nazareth is simply the Jewish instinct redivivus—in other words, it is the priestly instinct come to such a pass that it can no longer endure the priest as a fact; it is the discovery of a state of existence even more fantastic than any before it, of a vision of life even more unreal than that necessary to an ecclesiastical organization. Christianity actually denies the church....

I am unable to determine what was the target of the insurrection said to have been led (whether rightly or wrongly) by Jesus, if it was not the Jewish church—"church" being here used in exactly the same sense that the word has today. It was an insurrection against the "good and just," against the "prophets of Israel," against the whole hierarchy of society— not against corruption, but against caste, privilege, order, formalism. It was unbelief in "superior men," a Nay flung at everything that priests and theologians stood for. But the hierarchy that was called into question, if only for an instant, by this movement was the structure of piles which, above everything, was necessary to the safety of the Jewish people in the midst of the "waters"—it represented their last possibility of survival; it was the final residuum of their independent political existence; an attack upon it was an attack upon the most profound national instinct, the most powerful national will to live, that has ever appeared on earth. This saintly anarchist, who aroused the people of the abyss, the outcasts and "sinners," the Chandala of Judaism, to rise in revolt against the established order of things— and in language which, if the Gospels are to be credited, would get him sent to Siberia today—this man was certainly a political criminal, at least in so far as it was possible to be one in so absurdly unpolitical a community. This is what brought him to the cross: the proof thereof is to be found in the inscription that was put upon the cross. He died for his own sins—there is not the slightest ground for believing, no matter how often it is asserted, that he died for the sins of others.—

28.

As to whether he himself was conscious of this contradiction—whether, in fact, this was the only contradiction he was cognizant of—that is quite another question. Here, for the first time, I touch upon the problem of the psychology of the Saviour.—I confess, to begin with, that there are very few books which offer me harder reading than the Gospels. My difficulties are quite different from those which enabled the learned curiosity of the German mind to achieve one of its most unforgettable triumphs. It is a long while since I, like all other young scholars, enjoyed with all the sapient laboriousness of a fastidious philologist the work of the incomparable Strauss. [5] At that time I was twenty years old: now I am too serious for that sort of thing. What do I care for the contradictions of "tradition"? How can any one call pious legends "traditions"? The histories of saints present the most dubious variety of literature in existence; to examine them by the scientific method, in the entire absence of corroborative documents, seems to me to condemn the whole inquiry from the start—it is simply learned idling....

[5] David Friedrich Strauss (1808-74), author of "Das Leben Jesu" (1835-6), a very famous work in its day. Nietzsche here refers to it.

29.

What concerns me is the psychological type of the Saviour. This type might be depicted in the Gospels, in however mutilated a form and however much overladen with extraneous characters—that is, in spite of the Gospels; just as the figure of Francis of Assisi shows itself in his legends in spite of his legends. It is not a question of mere truthful evidence as to what he did, what he said and how he actually died; the question is, whether his type is still conceivable, whether it has been handed down to us.—All the attempts that I know of to read the history of a "soul" in the Gospels seem to me to reveal only a lamentable psychological levity. M. Renan, that mountebank in psychologicus, has contributed the two most unseemly notions to this business of explaining the type of Jesus: the notion of the genius and that of the hero ("héros"). But if there is anything essentially unevangelical, it is surely the concept of the hero. What the Gospels make instinctive is precisely the reverse of all heroic struggle, of all taste for conflict: the very incapacity for resistance is here converted into something moral: ("resist not evil!"—the most profound sentence in the Gospels, perhaps the true key to them), to wit, the blessedness of peace, of gentleness, the inability to be an enemy. What is the meaning of "glad tidings"?—The true life, the life eternal has been found—it is not merely promised, it is here, it is in you; it is the life that lies in love free from all retreats and exclusions, from all keeping of distances.

Every one is the child of God—Jesus claims nothing for himself alone—as the child of God each man is the equal of every other man.... Imagine making Jesus a hero!— And what a tremendous misunderstanding appears in the word "genius"! Our whole conception of the "spiritual," the whole conception of our civilization, could have had no meaning in the world that Jesus lived in. In the strict sense of the physiologist, a quite different word ought to be used here....

We all know that there is a morbid sensibility of the tactile nerves which causes those suffering from it to recoil from every touch, and from every effort to grasp a solid object. Brought to its logical conclusion, such a physiological habitus becomes an instinctive hatred of all reality, a flight into the "intangible," into the "incomprehensible"; a distaste for all formulae, for all conceptions of time and space, for everything established— customs, institutions, the church—; a feeling of being at home in a world in which no sort of reality survives, a merely "inner" world, a "true" world, an "eternal" world.... "The Kingdom of God is within you"....

30.

The instinctive hatred of reality: the consequence of an extreme susceptibility to pain and irritation—so great that merely to be "touched" becomes unendurable, for every sensation is too profound.

The instinctive exclusion of all aversion, all hostility, all bounds and distances in feeling: the consequence of an extreme susceptibility to pain and irritation—so great that it senses all resistance, all compulsion to resistance, as unbearable anguish (—that is to say, as harmful, as prohibited by the instinct of self-preservation), and regards blessedness (joy) as possible only when it is no longer necessary to offer resistance to anybody or anything, however evil or dangerous—love, as the only, as the ultimate possibility of life....

These are the two physiological realities upon and out of which the doctrine of salvation has sprung. I call them a sublime super-development of hedonism upon a thoroughly unsalubrious soil. What stands most closely related to them, though with a large admixture of Greek vitality and nerve-force, is epicureanism, the theory of salvation of paganism. Epicurus was a typical décadent: I was the first to recognize him.—The fear of pain, even of infinitely slight pain—the end of this can be nothing save a religion of love....

31.

I have already given my answer to the problem. The prerequisite to it is the assumption that the type of the Saviour has reached us only in a greatly distorted form. This distortion is very probable: there are many reasons why a type of that sort should not be handed down in a pure form, complete and free of additions.

The milieu in which this strange figure moved must have left marks upon him, and more must have been imprinted by the history, the destiny, of the early Christian communities; the latter indeed, must have embellished the type retrospectively with characters which can be understood only as serving the purposes of war and of propaganda. That strange and sickly world into which the Gospels lead us—a world apparently out of a Russian novel, in which the scum of society, nervous maladies and "childish" idiocy keep a tryst—must, in any case, have coarsened the type: the first disciples, in particular, must have been forced to translate an existence visible only in symbols and incomprehensibilities into their own crudity, in order to understand it at all—in their sight the type could take on reality only after it had been recast in a familiar mould.... The prophet, the messiah, the future judge, the teacher of morals, the worker of wonders, John the Baptist—all these merely presented chances to misunderstand it.... Finally, let us not underrate the proprium of all great, and especially all sectarian veneration: it tends to erase from the venerated objects all its original traits and idiosyncrasies, often so painfully strange— it does not even see them. It is greatly to be regretted that no Dostoyevsky lived in the neighbourhood of this most interesting décadent—I mean some one who would have felt the poignant charm of such a compound of the sublime, the morbid and the childish. In the last analysis, the type, as a type of the décadence, may actually have been peculiarly complex and contradictory: such a possibility is not to be lost sight of.

Nevertheless, the probabilities seem to be against it, for in that case tradition would have been particularly accurate and objective, whereas we have reasons for assuming the contrary. Meanwhile, there is a contradiction between the peaceful preacher of the mount, the sea-shore and the fields, who appears like a new Buddha on a soil very unlike India's, and the aggressive fanatic, the mortal enemy of theologians and ecclesiastics, who stands glorified by Renan's malice as "le grand maître en ironie." I myself haven't any doubt that the greater part of this venom (and no less of esprit) got itself into the concept of the Master only as a result of the excited nature of Christian propaganda: we all know the unscrupulousness of sectarians when they set out to turn their leader into an apologia for themselves. When the early Christians had need of an adroit, contentious, pugnacious and maliciously subtle theologian to tackle other theologians, they created a "god" that met that need, just as they put into his mouth without hesitation certain ideas that were necessary to them but that were utterly at odds with the Gospels—"the second coming," "the last judgment," all sorts of expectations and promises, current at the time.—

32.

I can only repeat that I set myself against all efforts to intrude the fanatic into the figure of the Saviour: the very word impérieux, used by Renan, is alone enough to annul the type. What the "glad tidings" tell us is simply that there are no more contradictions; the kingdom of heaven belongs to children; the faith that is voiced here is no more an embattled faith—it is at hand, it has been from the beginning, it is a sort of recrudescent childishness of the spirit. The physiologists, at all events, are familiar with such a delayed and incomplete puberty in the living organism, the result of degeneration. A faith of this sort is not furious, it does not denounce, it does not defend itself: it does not come with "the sword"—it does not realize how it will one day set man against man. It does not manifest itself either by miracles, or by rewards and promises, or by "scriptures": it is itself, first and last, its own miracle, its own reward, its own promise, its own "kingdom of God." This faith does not formulate itself—it simply lives, and so guards itself against formulae. To be sure, the accident of environment, of educational background gives prominence to concepts of a certain sort: in primitive Christianity one finds only concepts of a Judaeo-Semitic character (—that of eating and drinking at the last supper belongs to this category—an idea which, like everything else Jewish, has been badly mauled by the church). But let us be careful not to see in all this anything more than symbolical language, semantics[6] an opportunity to speak in parables. It is only on the theory that no work is to be taken literally that this anti-realist is able to speak at all. Set down among Hindus he would have made use of the concepts of Sankhya, [7] and among Chinese he would have employed those of Lao-tse[8]— and in neither case would it have made any difference to him.—With a little freedom in the use of words, one might actually call Jesus a "free spirit" [9]—he cares nothing for what is established: the word killeth,[10] whatever is established killeth. The idea of "life" as an experience, as he alone conceives it, stands opposed to his mind to every sort of word, formula, law, belief and dogma. He speaks only of inner things: "life" or "truth" or "light" is his word for the innermost—in his sight everything else, the whole of reality, all nature, even language, has significance only as sign, as allegory.—Here it is of paramount importance to be led into no error by the temptations lying in Christian, or rather ecclesiastical prejudices: such a symbolism par excellence stands outside all religion, all notions of worship, all history, all natural science, all worldly experience, all knowledge, all politics, all psychology, all books, all art—his "wisdom" is precisely a pure ignorance[11] of all such things. He has never heard of culture; he doesn't have to make war on it—he doesn't even deny it.... The same thing may be said of the state, of the whole bourgeoise social order, of labour, of war—he has no ground for denying "the world," for he knows nothing of the ecclesiastical concept of "the world".... Denial is precisely the thing that is impossible to him.—In the same way he lacks argumentative capacity, and has no belief that an article of faith, a "truth," may be established by proofs (— his proofs are inner "lights," subjective sensations of happiness and self-approval, simple "proofs of power"—). Such a doctrine cannot contradict: it doesn't know that other doctrines exist, or can exist, and is wholly incapable of imagining anything opposed to it.... If anything of the sort is ever encountered, it laments the "blindness" with sincere sympathy—for it alone has "light"—but it does not offer objections....

[6] The word Semiotik is in the text, but it is probable that Semantik is what Nietzsche had in mind.

[7] One of the six great systems of Hindu philosophy.

[8] The reputed founder of Taoism.

[9] Nietzsche's name for one accepting his own philosophy.

[10] That is, the strict letter of the law—the chief target of Jesus's early preaching.

[11] A reference to the "pure ignorance" (reine Thorheit) of Parsifal.

33.

In the whole psychology of the "Gospels" the concepts of guilt and punishment are lacking, and so is that of reward. "Sin," which means anything that puts a distance between God and man, is abolished— this is precisely the "glad tidings." Eternal bliss is not merely promised, nor is it bound up with conditions: it is conceived as the only reality—what remains consists merely of signs useful in speaking of it.

The results of such a point of view project themselves into a new way of life, the special evangelical way of life. It is not a "belief" that marks off the Christian; he is distinguished by a different mode of action; he acts differently.

He offers no resistance, either by word or in his heart, to those who stand against him. He draws no distinction between strangers and countrymen, Jews and Gentiles ("neighbour," of course, means fellow-believer, Jew). He is angry with no one, and he despises no one. He neither appeals to the courts of justice nor heeds their mandates ("Swear not at all"). [12] He never under any circumstances divorces his wife, even when he has proofs of her infidelity.—And under all of this is one principle; all of it arises from one instinct.—

[12] Matthew v, 34.

The life of the Saviour was simply a carrying out of this way of life—and so was his death.... He no longer needed any formula or ritual in his relations with God— not even prayer. He had rejected the whole of the Jewish doctrine of repentance and atonement; he knew that it was only by a way of life that one could feel one's self "divine," "blessed," "evangelical," a "child of God." Not by "repentance," not by "prayer and forgiveness" is the way to God: only the Gospel way leads to God— it is itself "God!"—What the Gospels abolished was the Judaism in the concepts of "sin," "forgiveness of sin," "faith," "salvation through faith"—the whole ecclesiastical dogma of the Jews was denied by the "glad tidings."

The deep instinct which prompts the Christian how to live so that he will feel that he is "in heaven" and is "immortal," despite many reasons for feeling that he is not "in heaven": this is the only psychological reality in "salvation."—

A new way of life, not a new faith....

34.

If I understand anything at all about this great symbolist, it is this: that he regarded only subjective realities as realities, as "truths"—that he saw everything else, everything natural, temporal, spatial and historical, merely as signs, as materials for parables. The concept of "the Son of God" does not connote a concrete person in history, an isolated and definite individual, but an "eternal" fact, a psychological symbol set free from the concept of time. The same thing is true, and in the highest sense, of the God of this typical symbolist, of the "kingdom of God," and of the "sonship of God." Nothing could be more un-Christian than the crude ecclesiastical notions of God as a person, of a "kingdom of God" that is to come, of a "kingdom of heaven" beyond, and of a "son of God" as the second person of the Trinity. All this—if I may be forgiven the phrase—is like thrusting one's fist into the eye (and what an eye!) of the Gospels: a disrespect for symbols amounting to world-historical cynicism.... But it is nevertheless obvious enough what is meant by the symbols "Father" and "Son"—not, of course, to every one—: the word "Son" expresses entrance into the feeling that there is a general transformation of all things (beatitude), and "Father" expresses that feeling itself—the sensation of eternity and of perfection.

—I am ashamed to remind you of what the church has made of this symbolism: has it not set an Amphitryon story[13] at the threshold of the Christian "faith"?

And a dogma of "immaculate conception" for good measure?... And thereby it has robbed conception of its immaculateness—

[13] Amphitryon was the son of Alcaeus, King of Tiryns. His wife was Alcmene.

During his absence she was visited by Zeus, and bore Heracles.

The "kingdom of heaven" is a state of the heart—not something to come "beyond the world" or "after death." The whole idea of natural death is absent from the Gospels: death is not a bridge, not a passing; it is absent because it belongs to a quite different, a merely apparent world, useful only as a symbol.

The "hour of death" is not a Christian idea—"hours," time, the physical life and its crises have no existence for the bearer of "glad tidings."... The "kingdom of God" is not something that men wait for: it had no yesterday and no day after tomorrow, it is not going to come at a "millennium"—it is an experience of the heart, it is everywhere and it is nowhere....

35.

This "bearer of glad tidings" died as he lived and taught— not to "save mankind," but to show mankind how to live. It was a way of life that he bequeathed to man: his demeanour before the judges, before the officers, before his accusers—his demeanour on the cross. He does not resist; he does not defend his rights; he makes no effort to ward off the most extreme penalty—more, he invites it.... And he prays, suffers and loves with those, in those, who do him evil.... Not to defend one's self, not to show anger, not to lay blames.... On the contrary, to submit even to the Evil One—to love him....

36.

—We free spirits—we are the first to have the necessary prerequisite to understanding what nineteen centuries have misunderstood—that instinct and passion for integrity which makes war upon the "holy lie" even more than upon all other lies.... Mankind was unspeakably far from our benevolent and cautious neutrality, from that discipline of the spirit which alone makes possible the solution of such strange and subtle things: what men always sought, with shameless egoism, was their own advantage therein; they created the church out of denial of the Gospels....

Whoever sought for signs of an ironical divinity's hand in the great drama of existence would find no small indication thereof in the stupendous question-mark that is called Christianity. That mankind should be on its knees before the very antithesis of what was the origin, the meaning and the law of the Gospels— that in the concept of the "church" the very things should be pronounced holy that the "bearer of glad tidings" regards as beneath him and behind him—it would be impossible to surpass this as a grand example of world-historical irony —

37.

—Our age is proud of its historical sense: how, then, could it delude itself into believing that the crude fable of the wonder-worker and Saviour constituted the beginnings of Christianity—and that everything spiritual and symbolical in it only came later? Quite to the contrary, the whole history of Christianity—from the death on the cross onward—is the history of a progressively clumsier misunderstanding of an original symbolism. With every extension of Christianity among larger and ruder masses, even less capable of grasping the principles that gave birth to it, the need arose to make it more and more vulgar and barbarous—it absorbed the teachings and rites of all the subterranean cults of the imperium Romanum, and the absurdities engendered by all sorts of sickly reasoning. It was the fate of Christianity that its faith had to become as sickly, as low and as vulgar as the needs were sickly, low and vulgar to which it had to administer. A sickly barbarism finally lifts itself to power as the church—the church, that incarnation of deadly hostility to all honesty, to all loftiness of soul, to all discipline of the spirit, to all spontaneous and kindly humanity.— Christian values— noble values: it is only we, we free spirits, who have re-established this greatest of all antitheses in values!...

38.

—I cannot, at this place, avoid a sigh. There are days when I am visited by a feeling blacker than the blackest melancholy— contempt of man. Let me leave no doubt as to what I despise, whom I despise: it is the man of today, the man with whom I am unhappily contemporaneous. The man of today—I am suffocated by his foul breath!... Toward the past, like all who understand, I am full of tolerance, which is to say, generous self-control: with gloomy caution I pass through whole millenniums of this madhouse of a world, call it "Christianity," "Christian faith" or the "Christian church," as you will—I take care not to hold mankind responsible for its lunacies. But my feeling changes and breaks out irresistibly the moment I enter modern times, our times. Our age knows better.... What was formerly merely sickly now becomes indecent—it is indecent to be a Christian today. And here my disgust begins. —I look about me: not a word survives of what was once called "truth"; we can no longer bear to hear a priest pronounce the word. Even a man who makes the most modest pretensions to integrity must know that a theologian, a priest, a pope of today not only errs when he speaks, but actually lies—and that he no longer escapes blame for his lie through "innocence" or "ignorance." The priest knows, as every one knows, that there is no longer any "God," or any "sinner," or any "Saviour"— that "free will" and the "moral order of the world" are lies—: serious reflection, the profound self-conquest of the spirit, allow no man to pretend that he does not know it.... All the ideas of the church are now recognized for what they are—as the worst counterfeits in existence, invented to debase nature and all natural values; the priest himself is seen as he actually is—as the most dangerous form of parasite, as the venomous spider of creation.... We know, our conscience now knows—just what the real value of all those sinister inventions of priest and church has been and what ends they have served, with their debasement of humanity to a state of self-pollution, the very sight of which excites loathing,— the concepts "the other world," "the last judgment," "the immortality of the soul," the "soul" itself: they are all merely so many instruments of torture, systems of cruelty, whereby the priest becomes master and remains master....

Every one knows this, but nevertheless things remain as before. What has become of the last trace of decent feeling, of self-respect, when our statesmen, otherwise an unconventional class of men and thoroughly anti-Christian in their acts, now call themselves Christians and go to the communion-table?... A prince at the head of his armies, magnificent as the expression of the egoism and arrogance of his people—and yet acknowledging, without any shame, that he is a Christian!... Whom, then, does Christianity deny? what does it call "the world"?

To be a soldier, to be a judge, to be a patriot; to defend one's self; to be careful of one's honour; to desire one's own advantage; to be proud ... every act of everyday, every instinct, every valuation that shows itself in a deed, is now anti-Christian: what a monster of falsehood the modern man must be to call himself nevertheless, and without shame, a Christian!—

39.

—I shall go back a bit, and tell you the authentic history of Christianity.—

The very word "Christianity" is a misunderstanding—at bottom there was only one Christian, and he died on the cross. The "Gospels" died on the cross. What, from that moment onward, was called the "Gospels" was the very reverse of what he had lived: "bad tidings," a Dysangelium. [14] It is an error amounting to nonsensicality to see in "faith," and particularly in faith in salvation through Christ, the distinguishing mark of the Christian: only the Christian way of life, the life lived by him who died on the cross, is Christian.... To this day such a life is still possible, and for certain men even necessary: genuine, primitive Christianity will remain possible in all ages.... Not faith, but acts; above all, an avoidance of acts, a different state of being.... States of consciousness, faith of a sort, the acceptance, for example, of anything as true—as every psychologist knows, the value of these things is perfectly indifferent and fifth-rate compared to that of the instincts: strictly speaking, the whole concept of intellectual causality is false. To reduce being a Christian, the state of Christianity, to an acceptance of truth, to a mere phenomenon of consciousness, is to formulate the negation of Christianity. In fact, there are no Christians. The "Christian"—he who for two thousand years has passed as a Christian—is simply a psychological self-delusion. Closely examined, it appears that, despite all his "faith," he has been ruled only by his instincts—and what instincts!—In all ages—for example, in the case of Luther—"faith" has been no more than a cloak, a pretense, a curtain behind which the instincts have played their game—a shrewd blindness to the domination of certain of the instincts.... I have already called "faith" the specially Christian form of shrewdness—people always talk of their "faith" and act according to their instincts.... In the world of ideas of the Christian there is nothing that so much as touches reality: on the contrary, one recognizes an instinctive hatred of reality as the motive power, the only motive power at the bottom of Christianity. What follows therefrom? That even here, in psychologicis, there is a radical error, which is to say one conditioning fundamentals, which is to say, one in substance. Take away one idea and put a genuine reality in its place—and the whole of Christianity crumbles to nothingness!—Viewed calmly, this strangest of all phenomena, a religion not only depending on errors, but inventive and ingenious only in devising injurious errors, poisonous to life and to the heart—this remains a spectacle for the gods— for those gods who are also philosophers, and whom I have encountered, for example, in the celebrated dialogues at Naxos. At the moment when their disgust leaves them (—and us!) they will be thankful for the spectacle afforded by the Christians: perhaps because of this curious exhibition alone the wretched little planet called the earth deserves a glance from omnipotence, a show of divine interest.... Therefore, let us not underestimate the Christians: the Christian, false to the point of innocence, is far above the ape—in its application to the Christians a well-known theory of descent becomes a mere piece of politeness....

[14] So in the text. One of Nietzsche's numerous coinages, obviously suggested by Evangelium, the German for gospel.

40.

—The fate of the Gospels was decided by death—it hung on the "cross."...

It was only death, that unexpected and shameful death; it was only the cross, which was usually reserved for the canaille only—it was only this appalling paradox which brought the disciples face to face with the real riddle: "Who was it? what was it?"—The feeling of dismay, of profound affront and injury; the suspicion that such a death might involve a refutation of their cause; the terrible question, "Why just in this way?"—this state of mind is only too easy to understand. Here everything must be accounted for as necessary; everything must have a meaning, a reason, the highest sort of reason; the love of a disciple excludes all chance. Only then did the chasm of doubt yawn: "Who put him to death? who was his natural enemy?"—this question flashed like a lightning-stroke. Answer: dominant Judaism, its ruling class. From that moment, one found one's self in revolt against the established order, and began to understand Jesus as in revolt against the established order. Until then this militant, this nay-saying, nay-doing element in his character had been lacking; what is more, he had appeared to present its opposite. Obviously, the little community had not understood what was precisely the most important thing of all: the example offered by this way of dying, the freedom from and superiority to every feeling of ressentiment—a plain indication of how little he was understood at all!

All that Jesus could hope to accomplish by his death, in itself, was to offer the strongest possible proof, or example, of his teachings in the most public manner....

But his disciples were very far from forgiving his death—though to have done so would have accorded with the Gospels in the highest degree; and neither were they prepared to offer themselves, with gentle and serene calmness of heart, for a similar death....

On the contrary, it was precisely the most unevangelical of feelings, revenge, that now possessed them. It seemed impossible that the cause should perish with his death: "recompense" and "judgment" became necessary (—yet what could be less evangelical than "recompense," "punishment," and "sitting in judgment"!). Once more the popular belief in the coming of a messiah appeared in the foreground; attention was rivetted upon an historical moment: the "kingdom of God" is to come, with judgment upon his enemies....

But in all this there was a wholesale misunderstanding: imagine the "kingdom of God" as a last act, as a mere promise! The Gospels had been, in fact, the incarnation, the fulfilment, the realization of this "kingdom of God." It was only now that all the familiar contempt for and bitterness against Pharisees and theologians began to appear in the character of the Master—he was thereby turned into a Pharisee and theologian himself! On the other hand, the savage veneration of these completely unbalanced souls could no longer endure the Gospel doctrine, taught by Jesus, of the equal right of all men to be children of God: their revenge took the form of elevating Jesus in an extravagant fashion, and thus separating him from themselves: just as, in earlier times, the Jews, to revenge themselves upon their enemies, separated themselves from their God, and placed him on a great height.

The One God and the Only Son of God: both were products of ressentiment....

41.

—And from that time onward an absurd problem offered itself: "how could God allow it!" To which the deranged reason of the little community formulated an answer that was terrifying in its absurdity: God gave his son as a sacrifice for the forgiveness of sins. At once there was an end of the gospels! Sacrifice for sin, and in its most obnoxious and barbarous form: sacrifice of the innocent for the sins of the guilty! What appalling paganism!—Jesus himself had done away with the very concept of "guilt," he denied that there was any gulf fixed between God and man; he lived this unity between God and man, and that was precisely his "glad tidings".... And not as a mere privilege!—From this time forward the type of the Saviour was corrupted, bit by bit, by the doctrine of judgment and of the second coming, the doctrine of death as a sacrifice, the doctrine of the resurrection, by means of which the entire concept of "blessedness," the whole and only reality of the gospels, is juggled away—in favour of a state of existence after death!...

St. Paul, with that rabbinical impudence which shows itself in all his doings, gave a logical quality to that conception, that indecent conception, in this way: "If Christ did not rise from the dead, then all our faith is in vain!"—

And at once there sprang from the Gospels the most contemptible of all unfulfillable promises, the shameless doctrine of personal immortality.... Paul even preached it as a reward....

42.

One now begins to see just what it was that came to an end with the death on the cross: a new and thoroughly original effort to found a Buddhistic peace movement, and so establish happiness on earth—real, not merely promised. For this remains—as I have already pointed out—the essential difference between the two religions of décadence: Buddhism promises nothing, but actually fulfils; Christianity promises everything, but fulfils nothing.—Hard upon the heels of the "glad tidings" came the worst imaginable: those of Paul. In Paul is incarnated the very opposite of the "bearer of glad tidings"; he represents the genius for hatred, the vision of hatred, the relentless logic of hatred. What, indeed, has not this dysangelist sacrificed to hatred! Above all, the Saviour: he nailed him to his own cross. The life, the example, the teaching, the death of Christ, the meaning and the law of the whole gospels—nothing was left of all this after that counterfeiter in hatred had reduced it to his uses. Surely not reality; surely not historical truth!... Once more the priestly instinct of the Jew perpetrated the same old master crime against history—he simply struck out the yesterday and the day before yesterday of Christianity, and invented his own history of Christian beginnings. Going further, he treated the history of Israel to another falsification, so that it became a mere prologue to his achievement: all the prophets, it now appeared, had referred to his "Saviour.".... Later on the church even falsified the history of man in order to make it a prologue to Christianity.... The figure of the Saviour, his teaching, his way of life, his death, the meaning of his death, even the consequences of his death—nothing remained untouched, nothing remained in even remote contact with reality. Paul simply shifted the centre of gravity of that whole life to a place behind this existence—in the lie of the "risen" Jesus. At bottom, he had no use for the life of the Saviour—what he needed was the death on the cross, and something more. To see anything honest in such a man as Paul, whose home was at the centre of the Stoical enlightenment, when he converts an hallucination into a proof of the resurrection of the Saviour, or even to believe his tale that he suffered from this hallucination himself—this would be a genuine niaiserie in a psychologist. Paul willed the end; therefore he also willed the means.... What he himself didn't believe was swallowed readily enough by the idiots among whom he spread his teaching.—What he wanted was power; in Paul the priest once more reached out for power—he had use only for such concepts, teachings and symbols as served the purpose of tyrannizing over the masses and organizing mobs. What was the only part of Christianity that Mohammed borrowed later on? Paul's invention, his device for establishing priestly tyranny and organizing the mob: the belief in the immortality of the soul — that is to say, the doctrine of "judgment" ....

43.

When the centre of gravity of life is placed, not in life itself, but in "the beyond"—in nothingness—then one has taken away its centre of gravity altogether. The vast lie of personal immortality destroys all reason, all natural instinct—henceforth, everything in the instincts that is beneficial, that fosters life and that safeguards the future is a cause of suspicion. So to live that life no longer has any meaning: this is now the "meaning" of life.... Why be public-spirited? Why take any pride in descent and forefathers? Why labour together, trust one another, or concern one's self about the common welfare, and try to serve it?... Merely so many "temptations," so many strayings from the "straight path."—"One thing only is necessary".... That every man, because he has an "immortal soul," is as good as every other man; that in an infinite universe of things the "salvation" of every individual may lay claim to eternal importance; that insignificant bigots and the three-fourths insane may assume that the laws of nature are constantly suspended in their behalf—it is impossible to lavish too much contempt upon such a magnification of every sort of selfishness to infinity, to insolence. And yet Christianity has to thank precisely this miserable flattery of personal vanity for its triumph—it was thus that it lured all the botched, the dissatisfied, the fallen upon evil days, the whole refuse and off-scouring of humanity to its side. The "salvation of the soul"—in plain English: "the world revolves around me."... The poisonous doctrine, "equal rights for all," has been propagated as a Christian principle: out of the secret nooks and crannies of bad instinct Christianity has waged a deadly war upon all feelings of reverence and distance between man and man, which is to say, upon the first prerequisite to every step upward, to every development of civilization—out of the ressentiment of the masses it has forged its chief weapons against us, against everything noble, joyous and high-spirited on earth, against our happiness on earth.... To allow "immortality" to every Peter and Paul was the greatest, the most vicious outrage upon noble humanity ever perpetrated.— And let us not underestimate the fatal influence that Christianity has had, even upon politics! Nowadays no one has courage any more for special rights, for the right of dominion, for feelings of honourable pride in himself and his equals—for the pathos of distance.... Our politics is sick with this lack of courage!—The aristocratic attitude of mind has been undermined by the lie of the equality of souls; and if belief in the "privileges of the majority" makes and will continue to make revolutions—it is Christianity, let us not doubt, and Christian valuations, which convert every revolution into a carnival of blood and crime! Christianity is a revolt of all creatures that creep on the ground against everything that is lofty: the gospel of the "lowly" lowers....

44.

—The gospels are invaluable as evidence of the corruption that was already persistent within the primitive community. That which Paul, with the cynical logic of a rabbi, later developed to a conclusion was at bottom merely a process of decay that had begun with the death of the Saviour.—These gospels cannot be read too carefully; difficulties lurk behind every word. I confess—I hope it will not be held against me— that it is precisely for this reason that they offer first-rate joy to a psychologist—as the opposite of all merely naïve corruption, as refinement par excellence, as an artistic triumph in psychological corruption.

The gospels, in fact, stand alone. The Bible as a whole is not to be compared to them.

Here we are among Jews: this is the first thing to be borne in mind if we are not to lose the thread of the matter. This positive genius for conjuring up a delusion of personal "holiness" unmatched anywhere else, either in books or by men; this elevation of fraud in word and attitude to the level of an art—all this is not an accident due to the chance talents of an individual, or to any violation of nature. The thing responsible is race. The whole of Judaism appears in Christianity as the art of concocting holy lies, and there, after many centuries of earnest Jewish training and hard practice of Jewish technic, the business comes to the stage of mastery. The Christian, that ultima ratio of lying, is the Jew all over again—he is threefold the Jew.... The underlying will to make use only of such concepts, symbols and attitudes as fit into priestly practice, the instinctive repudiation of every other mode of thought, and every other method of estimating values and utilities—this is not only tradition, it is inheritance: only as an inheritance is it able to operate with the force of nature. The whole of mankind, even the best minds of the best ages (with one exception, perhaps hardly human—), have permitted themselves to be deceived. The gospels have been read as a book of innocence ... surely no small indication of the high skill with which the trick has been done.—Of course, if we could actually see these astounding bigots and bogus saints, even if only for an instant, the farce would come to an end,—and it is precisely because I cannot read a word of theirs without seeing their attitudinizing that I have made an end of them.... I simply cannot endure the way they have of rolling up their eyes.—For the majority, happily enough, books are mere literature.—Let us not be led astray: they say "judge not," and yet they condemn to hell whoever stands in their way. In letting God sit in judgment they judge themselves; in glorifying God they glorify themselves; in demanding that every one show the virtues which they themselves happen to be capable of—still more, which they must have in order to remain on top—they assume the grand air of men struggling for virtue, of men engaging in a war that virtue may prevail. "We live, we die, we sacrifice ourselves for the good" (—"the truth," "the light," "the kingdom of God"): in point of fact, they simply do what they cannot help doing. Forced, like hypocrites, to be sneaky, to hide in corners, to slink along in the shadows, they convert their necessity into a duty: it is on grounds of duty that they account for their lives of humility, and that humility becomes merely one more proof of their piety.... Ah, that humble, chaste, charitable brand of fraud! "Virtue itself shall bear witness for us."... One may read the gospels as books of moral seduction: these petty folks fasten themselves to morality—they know the uses of morality!

Morality is the best of all devices for leading mankind by the nose!—The fact is that the conscious conceit of the chosen here disguises itself as modesty: it is in this way that they, the "community," the "good and just," range themselves, once and for always, on one side, the side of "the truth"—and the rest of mankind, "the world," on the other.... In that we observe the most fatal sort of megalomania that the earth has ever seen: little abortions of bigots and liars began to claim exclusive rights in the concepts of "God," "the truth," "the light," "the spirit," "love," "wisdom" and "life," as if these things were synonyms of themselves and thereby they sought to fence themselves off from the "world"; little super-Jews, ripe for some sort of madhouse, turned values upside down in order to meet their notions, just as if the Christian were the meaning, the salt, the standard and even the last judgment of all the rest.... The whole disaster was only made possible by the fact that there already existed in the world a similar megalomania, allied to this one in race, to wit, the Jewish: once a chasm began to yawn between Jews and Judaeo-Christians, the latter had no choice but to employ the self-preservative measures that the Jewish instinct had devised, even against the Jews themselves, whereas the Jews had employed them only against non-Jews. The Christian is simply a Jew of the "reformed" confession.—

45.

—I offer a few examples of the sort of thing these petty people have got into their heads—what they have put into the mouth of the Master: the unalloyed creed of "beautiful souls."—

"And whosoever shall not receive you, nor hear you, when ye depart thence, shake off the dust under your feet for a testimony against them. Verily I say unto you, it shall be more tolerable for Sodom and Gomorrha in the day of judgment, than for that city" (Mark vi, 11)—How evangelical!...

"And whosoever shall offend one of these little ones that believe in me, it is better for him that a millstone were hanged about his neck, and he were cast into the sea" (Mark ix, 42).—How evangelical!...

"And if thine eye offend thee, pluck it out: it is better for thee to enter into the kingdom of God with one eye, than having two eyes to be cast into hell fire; Where the worm dieth not, and the fire is not quenched." (Mark ix, 47.[15])—It is not exactly the eye that is meant....

[15] To which, without mentioning it, Nietzsche adds verse 48.

"Verily I say unto you, That there be some of them that stand here, which shall not taste of death, till they have seen the kingdom of God come with power." (Mark ix, 1.)—Well lied, lion! [16]. ...

[16] A paraphrase of Demetrius' "Well roar'd, Lion!" in act v, scene 1 of "A Midsummer Night's Dream." The lion, of course, is the familiar Christian symbol for Mark.

"Whosoever will come after me, let him deny himself, and take up his cross, and follow me. For..." (Note of a psychologist. Christian morality is refuted by its fors: its reasons are against it,—this makes it Christian.) Mark viii, 34.—

"Judge not, that ye be not judged. With what measure ye mete, it shall be measured to you again." (Matthew vii, 1. [17])—What a notion of justice, of a "just" judge!...

[17] Nietzsche also quotes part of verse 2.

"For if ye love them which love you, what reward have ye? do not even the publicans the same? And if ye salute your brethren only, what do ye more than others? do not even the publicans so?" (Matthew v, 46. [18])—Principle of "Christian love": it insists upon being well paid in the end....

[18] The quotation also includes verse 47.

"But if ye forgive not men their trespasses, neither will your Father forgive your trespasses." (Matthew vi, 15.)—Very compromising for the said "father."...

"But seek ye first the kingdom of God, and his righteousness; and all these things shall be added unto you." (Matthew vi, 33.)—All these things: namely, food, clothing, all the necessities of life. An error, to put it mildly.... A bit before this God appears as a tailor, at least in certain cases....

"Rejoice ye in that day, and leap for joy: for, behold, your reward is great in heaven: for in the like manner did their fathers unto the prophets." (Luke vi, 23.) — Impudent rabble! It compares itself to the prophets....

"Know ye not that ye are the temple of God, and that the spirit of God dwelleth in you? If any man defile the temple of God, him shall God destroy; for the temple of God is holy, which temple ye are." (Paul, 1 Corinthians iii, 16. [19])

—For that sort of thing one cannot have enough contempt....

[19] And 17.

"Do ye not know that the saints shall judge the world? and if the world shall be judged by you, are ye unworthy to judge the smallest matters?" (Paul, 1 Corinthians vi, 2.)—Unfortunately, not merely the speech of a lunatic.... This frightful impostor then proceeds: "Know ye not that we shall judge angels? how much more things that pertain to this life?"...

"Hath not God made foolish the wisdom of this world? For after that in the wisdom of God the world by wisdom knew not God, it pleased God by the foolishness of preaching to save them that believe.... Not many wise men after the flesh, not men mighty, not many noble are called: But God hath chosen the foolish things of the world to confound the wise; and God hath chosen the weak things of the world to confound the things which are mighty; And base things of the world, and things which are despised, hath God chosen, yea, and things which are not, to bring to nought things that are: That no flesh should glory in his presence." (Paul, 1 Corinthians i, 20ff.[20])—In order to understand this passage, a first-rate example of the psychology underlying every Chandala-morality, one should read the first part of my "Genealogy of Morals": there, for the first time, the antagonism between a noble morality and a morality born of ressentiment and impotent vengefulness is exhibited. Paul was the greatest of all apostles of revenge....

[20] Verses 20, 21, 26, 27, 28, 29.

46.

— What follows, then? That one had better put on gloves before reading the New Testament. The presence of so much filth makes it very advisable. One would as little choose "early Christians" for companions as Polish Jews: not that one need seek out an objection to them.... Neither has a pleasant smell.—I have searched the New Testament in vain for a single sympathetic touch; nothing is there that is free, kindly, open-hearted or upright. In it humanity does not even make the first step upward—the instinct for cleanliness is lacking.... Only evil instincts are there, and there is not even the courage of these evil instincts. It is all cowardice; it is all a shutting of the eyes, a self-deception. Every other book becomes clean, once one has read the New Testament: for example, immediately after reading Paul I took up with delight that most charming and wanton of scoffers, Petronius, of whom one may say what Domenico Boccaccio wrote of Cæsar Borgia to the Duke of Parma: "è tutto festo"—immortally healthy, immortally cheerful and sound.... These petty bigots make a capital miscalculation. They attack, but everything they attack is thereby distinguished.

Whoever is attacked by an "early Christian" is surely not befouled.... On the contrary, it is an honour to have an "early Christian" as an opponent. One cannot read the New Testament without acquired admiration for whatever it abuses— not to speak of the "wisdom of this world," which an impudent wind-bag tries to dispose of "by the foolishness of preaching."... Even the scribes and pharisees are benefitted by such opposition: they must certainly have been worth something to have been hated in such an indecent manner. Hypocrisy—as if this were a charge that the "early Christians" dared to make!—After all, they were the privileged, and that was enough: the hatred of the Chandala needed no other excuse. The "early Christian"—and also, I fear, the "last Christian," whom I may perhaps live to see—is a rebel against all privilege by profound instinct—he lives and makes war for ever for "equal rights."... Strictly speaking, he has no alternative. When a man proposes to represent, in his own person, the "chosen of God"—or to be a "temple of God," or a "judge of the angels"—then every other criterion, whether based upon honesty, upon intellect, upon manliness and pride, or upon beauty and freedom of the heart, becomes simply "worldly"— evil in itself.... Moral: every word that comes from the lips of an "early Christian" is a lie, and his every act is instinctively dishonest—all his values, all his aims are noxious, but whoever he hates, whatever he hates, has real value.... The Christian, and particularly the Christian priest, is thus a criterion of values.

—Must I add that, in the whole New Testament, there appears but a solitary figure worthy of honour? Pilate, the Roman viceroy. To regard a Jewish imbroglio seriously—that was quite beyond him. One Jew more or less—what did it matter?... The noble scorn of a Roman, before whom the word "truth" was shamelessly mishandled, enriched the New Testament with the only saying that has any value—and that is at once its criticism and its destruction: "What is truth?..."

47.

—The thing that sets us apart is not that we are unable to find God, either in history, or in nature, or behind nature—but that we regard what has been honoured as God, not as "divine," but as pitiable, as absurd, as injurious; not as a mere error, but as a crime against life.... We deny that God is God.... If any one were to show us this Christian God, we'd be still less inclined to believe in him.

—In a formula: deus, qualem Paulus creavit, dei negatio.—Such a religion as Christianity, which does not touch reality at a single point and which goes to pieces the moment reality asserts its rights at any point, must be inevitably the deadly enemy of the "wisdom of this world," which is to say, of science—and it will give the name of good to whatever means serve to poison, calumniate and cry down all intellectual discipline, all lucidity and strictness in matters of intellectual conscience, and all noble coolness and freedom of the mind. "Faith," as an imperative, vetoes science— in praxi, lying at any price.... Paul well knew that lying—that "faith"—was necessary; later on the church borrowed the fact from Paul.—The God that Paul invented for himself, a God who "reduced to absurdity" "the wisdom of this world" (especially the two great enemies of superstition, philology and medicine), is in truth only an indication of Paul's resolute determination to accomplish that very thing himself: to give one's own will the name of God, thora—that is essentially Jewish. Paul wants to dispose of the "wisdom of this world": his enemies are the good philologians and physicians of the Alexandrine school—on them he makes his war. As a matter of fact no man can be a philologian or a physician without being also Antichrist.

That is to say, as a philologian a man sees behind the "holy books," and as a physician he sees behind the physiological degeneration of the typical Christian.

The physician says "incurable"; the philologian says "fraud."...

48.

—Has any one ever clearly understood the celebrated story at the beginning of the Bible—of God's mortal terror of science?... No one, in fact, has understood it. This priest-book par excellence opens, as is fitting, with the great inner difficulty of the priest: he faces only one great danger; ergo, "God" faces only one great danger.—

The old God, wholly "spirit," wholly the high-priest, wholly perfect, is promenading his garden: he is bored and trying to kill time. Against boredom even gods struggle in vain. [21] What does he do? He creates man—man is entertaining.... But then he notices that man is also bored. God's pity for the only form of distress that invades all paradises knows no bounds: so he forthwith creates other animals. God's first mistake: to man these other animals were not entertaining—he sought dominion over them; he did not want to be an "animal" himself.—So God created woman. In the act he brought boredom to an end— and also many other things! Woman was the second mistake of God.—"Woman, at bottom, is a serpent, Heva"—every priest knows that; "from woman comes every evil in the world"—every priest knows that, too. Ergo, she is also to blame for science.... It was through woman that man learned to taste of the tree of knowledge.—What happened? The old God was seized by mortal terror. Man himself had been his greatest blunder; he had created a rival to himself; science makes men godlike—it is all up with priests and gods when man becomes scientific!— Moral: science is the forbidden per se; it alone is forbidden. Science is the first of sins, the germ of all sins, the original sin. This is all there is of morality. —"Thou shall not know":—the rest follows from that.—God's mortal terror, however, did not hinder him from being shrewd. How is one to protect one's self against science? For a long while this was the capital problem.

Answer: Out of paradise with man! Happiness, leisure, foster thought—and all thoughts are bad thoughts!—Man must not think.—And so the priest invents distress, death, the mortal dangers of childbirth, all sorts of misery, old age, decrepitude, above all, sickness—nothing but devices for making war on science! The troubles of man don't allow him to think.... Nevertheless—how terrible!—, the edifice of knowledge begins to tower aloft, invading heaven, shadowing the gods—what is to be done?—

The old God invents war; he separates the peoples; he makes men destroy one another (—the priests have always had need of war....). War—among other things, a great disturber of science!—Incredible! Knowledge, deliverance from the priests, prospers in spite of war.—So the old God comes to his final resolution: "Man has become scientific— there is no help for it: he must be drowned! "... [21] A paraphrase of Schiller's "Against stupidity even gods struggle in vain."

49.

—I have been understood. At the opening of the Bible there is the whole psychology of the priest.—The priest knows of only one great danger: that is science—the sound comprehension of cause and effect. But science flourishes, on the whole, only under favourable conditions—a man must have time, he must have an overflowing intellect, in order to "know."... "Therefore, man must be made unhappy,"—this has been, in all ages, the logic of the priest.—It is easy to see just what, by this logic, was the first thing to come into the world:—"sin."...

The concept of guilt and punishment, the whole "moral order of the world," was set up against science— against the deliverance of man from priests.... Man must not look outward; he must look inward. He must not look at things shrewdly and cautiously, to learn about them; he must not look at all; he must suffer.... And he must suffer so much that he is always in need of the priest.—Away with physicians! What is needed is a Saviour. —The concept of guilt and punishment, including the doctrines of "grace," of "salvation," of "forgiveness"— lies through and through, and absolutely without psychological reality—were devised to destroy man's sense of causality: they are an attack upon the concept of cause and effect!—And not an attack with the fist, with the knife, with honesty in hate and love! On the contrary, one inspired by the most cowardly, the most crafty, the most ignoble of instincts! An attack of priests! An attack of parasites! The vampirism of pale, subterranean leeches!... When the natural consequences of an act are no longer "natural," but are regarded as produced by the ghostly creations of superstition—by "God," by "spirits," by "souls"—and reckoned as merely "moral" consequences, as rewards, as punishments, as hints, as lessons, then the whole ground-work of knowledge is destroyed— then the greatest of crimes against humanity has been perpetrated.—I repeat that sin, man's self-desecration par excellence, was invented in order to make science, culture, and every elevation and ennobling of man impossible; the priest rules through the invention of sin.—

50.

—In this place I can't permit myself to omit a psychology of "belief," of the "believer," for the special benefit of "believers." If there remain any today who do not yet know how indecent it is to be "believing"— or how much a sign of décadence, of a broken will to live—then they will know it well enough tomorrow. My voice reaches even the deaf.—It appears, unless I have been incorrectly informed, that there prevails among Christians a sort of criterion of truth that is called "proof by power." "Faith makes blessed: therefore it is true."—It might be objected right here that blessedness is not demonstrated, it is merely promised: it hangs upon "faith" as a condition—one shall be blessed because one believes.... But what of the thing that the priest promises to the believer, the wholly transcendental "beyond"—how is that to be demonstrated?

—The "proof by power," thus assumed, is actually no more at bottom than a belief that the effects which faith promises will not fail to appear. In a formula: "I believe that faith makes for blessedness— therefore, it is true."... But this is as far as we may go. This "therefore" would be absurdum itself as a criterion of truth.—But let us admit, for the sake of politeness, that blessedness by faith may be demonstrated (— not merely hoped for, and not merely promised by the suspicious lips of a priest): even so, could blessedness—in a technical term, pleasure—ever be a proof of truth? So little is this true that it is almost a proof against truth when sensations of pleasure influence the answer to the question "What is true?" or, at all events, it is enough to make that "truth" highly suspicious. The proof by "pleasure" is a proof of "pleasure"—nothing more; why in the world should it be assumed that true judgments give more pleasure than false ones, and that, in conformity to some pre-established harmony, they necessarily bring agreeable feelings in their train?—The experience of all disciplined and profound minds teaches the contrary. Man has had to fight for every atom of the truth, and has had to pay for it almost everything that the heart, that human love, that human trust cling to. Greatness of soul is needed for this business: the service of truth is the hardest of all services.—What, then, is the meaning of integrity in things intellectual? It means that a man must be severe with his own heart, that he must scorn "beautiful feelings," and that he makes every Yea and Nay a matter of conscience!—Faith makes blessed: therefore, it lies....

51.

The fact that faith, under certain circumstances, may work for blessedness, but that this blessedness produced by an idée fixe by no means makes the idea itself true, and the fact that faith actually moves no mountains, but instead raises them up where there were none before: all this is made sufficiently clear by a walk through a lunatic asylum. Not, of course, to a priest: for his instincts prompt him to the lie that sickness is not sickness and lunatic asylums not lunatic asylums. Christianity finds sickness necessary, just as the Greek spirit had need of a superabundance of health—the actual ulterior purpose of the whole system of salvation of the church is to make people ill. And the church itself—doesn't it set up a Catholic lunatic asylum as the ultimate ideal?—The whole earth as a madhouse?—The sort of religious man that the church wants is a typical décadent; the moment at which a religious crisis dominates a people is always marked by epidemics of nervous disorder; the "inner world" of the religious man is so much like the "inner world" of the overstrung and exhausted that it is difficult to distinguish between them; the "highest" states of mind, held up before mankind by Christianity as of supreme worth, are actually epileptoid in form—the church has granted the name of holy only to lunatics or to gigantic frauds in majorem dei honorem.... Once I ventured to designate the whole Christian system of training[22] in penance and salvation (now best studied in England) as a method of producing a folie circulaire upon a soil already prepared for it, which is to say, a soil thoroughly unhealthy. Not every one may be a Christian: one is not "converted" to Christianity—one must first be sick enough for it.... We others, who have the courage for health and likewise for contempt, —we may well despise a religion that teaches misunderstanding of the body! that refuses to rid itself of the superstition about the soul! that makes a "virtue" of insufficient nourishment! that combats health as a sort of enemy, devil, temptation! that persuades itself that it is possible to carry about a "perfect soul" in a cadaver of a body, and that, to this end, had to devise for itself a new concept of "perfection," a pale, sickly, idiotically ecstatic state of existence, so-called "holiness"—a holiness that is itself merely a series of symptoms of an impoverished, enervated and incurably disordered body!... The Christian movement, as a European movement, was from the start no more than a general uprising of all sorts of outcast and refuse elements (—who now, under cover of Christianity, aspire to power). It does not represent the decay of a race; it represents, on the contrary, a conglomeration of décadence products from all directions, crowding together and seeking one another out. It was not, as has been thought, the corruption of antiquity, of noble antiquity, which made Christianity possible; one cannot too sharply challenge the learned imbecility which today maintains that theory. At the time when the sick and rotten Chandala classes in the whole imperium were Christianized, the contrary type, the nobility, reached its finest and ripest development. The majority became master; democracy, with its Christian instincts, triumphed.... Christianity was not "national," it was not based on race—it appealed to all the varieties of men disinherited by life, it had its allies everywhere. Christianity has the rancour of the sick at its very core—the instinct against the healthy, against health.

Everything that is well-constituted, proud, gallant and, above all, beautiful gives offence to its ears and eyes. Again I remind you of Paul's priceless saying: "And God hath chosen the weak things of the world, the foolish things of the world, the base things of the world, and things which are despised" :[23] this was the formula; in hoc signo the décadence triumphed.— God on the cross—is man always to miss the frightful inner significance of this symbol?—Everything that suffers, everything that hangs on the cross, is divine.... We all hang on the cross, consequently we are divine.... We alone are divine.... Christianity was thus a victory: a nobler attitude of mind was destroyed by it—Christianity remains to this day the greatest misfortune of humanity.—

[22] The word training is in English in the text.

[23] 1 Corinthians i, 27, 28.

52.

Christianity also stands in opposition to all intellectual well-being,—sick reasoning is the only sort that it can use as Christian reasoning; it takes the side of everything that is idiotic; it pronounces a curse upon "intellect," upon the superbia of the healthy intellect. Since sickness is inherent in Christianity, it follows that the typically Christian state of "faith" must be a form of sickness too, and that all straight, straightforward and scientific paths to knowledge must be banned by the church as forbidden ways. Doubt is thus a sin from the start....

The complete lack of psychological cleanliness in the priest—revealed by a glance at him—is a phenomenon resulting from décadence,—one may observe in hysterical women and in rachitic children how regularly the falsification of instincts, delight in lying for the mere sake of lying, and incapacity for looking straight and walking straight are symptoms of décadence. "Faith" means the will to avoid knowing what is true. The pietist, the priest of either sex, is a fraud because he is sick: his instinct demands that the truth shall never be allowed its rights on any point. "Whatever makes for illness is good; whatever issues from abundance, from superabundance, from power, is evil": so argues the believer.

The impulse to lie—it is by this that I recognize every foreordained theologian.

—Another characteristic of the theologian is his unfitness for philology. What I here mean by philology is, in a general sense, the art of reading with profit—the capacity for absorbing facts without interpreting them falsely, and without losing caution, patience and subtlety in the effort to understand them. Philology as ephexis[24] in interpretation: whether one be dealing with books, with newspaper reports, with the most fateful events or with weather statistics—not to mention the "salvation of the soul."... The way in which a theologian, whether in Berlin or in Rome, is ready to explain, say, a "passage of Scripture," or an experience, or a victory by the national army, by turning upon it the high illumination of the Psalms of David, is always so daring that it is enough to make a philologian run up a wall. But what shall he do when pietists and other such cows from Suabia[25] use the "finger of God" to convert their miserably commonplace and huggermugger existence into a miracle of "grace," a "providence" and an "experience of salvation"? The most modest exercise of the intellect, not to say of decency, should certainly be enough to convince these interpreters of the perfect childishness and unworthiness of such a misuse of the divine digital dexterity. However small our piety, if we ever encountered a god who always cured us of a cold in the head at just the right time, or got us into our carriage at the very instant heavy rain began to fall, he would seem so absurd a god that he'd have to be abolished even if he existed. God as a domestic servant, as a letter carrier, as an almanac-man—at bottom, he is a mere name for the stupidest sort of chance.... "Divine Providence," which every third man in "educated Germany" still believes in, is so strong an argument against God that it would be impossible to think of a stronger. And in any case it is an argument against Germans!...

[24] That is, to say, scepticism. Among the Greeks scepticism was also occasionally called ephecticism.

[25] A reference to the University of Tübingen and its famous school of Biblical criticism. The leader of this school was F. C. Baur, and one of the men greatly influenced by it was Nietzsche's pet abomination, David F. Strauss, himself a Suabian.

Vide § 10 and § 28.

53.

—It is so little true that martyrs offer any support to the truth of a cause that I am inclined to deny that any martyr has ever had anything to do with the truth at all. In the very tone in which a martyr flings what he fancies to be true at the head of the world there appears so low a grade of intellectual honesty and such insensibility to the problem of "truth," that it is never necessary to refute him.

Truth is not something that one man has and another man has not: at best, only peasants, or peasant-apostles like Luther, can think of truth in any such way. One may rest assured that the greater the degree of a man's intellectual conscience the greater will be his modesty, his discretion, on this point. To know in five cases, and to refuse, with delicacy, to know anything further.... "Truth," as the word is understood by every prophet, every sectarian, every free-thinker, every Socialist and every churchman, is simply a complete proof that not even a beginning has been made in the intellectual discipline and self-control that are necessary to the unearthing of even the smallest truth.—The deaths of the martyrs, it may be said in passing, have been misfortunes of history: they have misled.... The conclusion that all idiots, women and plebeians come to, that there must be something in a cause for which any one goes to his death (or which, as under primitive Christianity, sets off epidemics of death-seeking)—this conclusion has been an unspeakable drag upon the testing of facts, upon the whole spirit of inquiry and investigation. The martyrs have damaged the truth....

Even to this day the crude fact of persecution is enough to give an honourable name to the most empty sort of sectarianism.—But why? Is the worth of a cause altered by the fact that some one had laid down his life for it?—An error that becomes honourable is simply an error that has acquired one seductive charm the more: do you suppose, Messrs. Theologians, that we shall give you the chance to be martyred for your lies?— One best disposes of a cause by respectfully putting it on ice—that is also the best way to dispose of theologians.... This was precisely the world-historical stupidity of all the persecutors: that they gave the appearance of honour to the cause they opposed—that they made it a present of the fascination of martyrdom.... Women are still on their knees before an error because they have been told that some one died on the cross for it. Is the cross, then, an argument? —But about all these things there is one, and one only, who has said what has been needed for thousands of years— Zarathustra.

They made signs in blood along the way that they went, and their folly taught them that the truth is proved by blood.

But blood is the worst of all testimonies to the truth; blood poisoneth even the purest teaching and turneth it into madness and hatred in the heart.

And when one goeth through fire for his teaching—what doth that prove? Verily, it is more when one's teaching cometh out of one's own burning! [26]

[26] The quotations are from "Also sprach Zarathustra" ii, 24: "Of Priests."

54.

Do not let yourself be deceived: great intellects are sceptical. Zarathustra is a sceptic. The strength, the freedom which proceed from intellectual power, from a superabundance of intellectual power, manifest themselves as scepticism. Men of fixed convictions do not count when it comes to determining what is fundamental in values and lack of values. Men of convictions are prisoners.

They do not see far enough, they do not see what is below them: whereas a man who would talk to any purpose about value and non-value must be able to see five hundred convictions beneath him—and behind him.... A mind that aspires to great things, and that wills the means thereto, is necessarily sceptical. Freedom from any sort of conviction belongs to strength, and to an independent point of view.... That grand passion which is at once the foundation and the power of a sceptic's existence, and is both more enlightened and more despotic than he is himself, drafts the whole of his intellect into its service; it makes him unscrupulous; it gives him courage to employ unholy means; under certain circumstances it does not begrudge him even convictions. Conviction as a means: one may achieve a good deal by means of a conviction. A grand passion makes use of and uses up convictions; it does not yield to them—it knows itself to be sovereign.—On the contrary, the need of faith, of something unconditioned by yea or nay, of Carlylism, if I may be allowed the word, is a need of weakness.

The man of faith, the "believer" of any sort, is necessarily a dependent man— such a man cannot posit himself as a goal, nor can he find goals within himself.

The "believer" does not belong to himself; he can only be a means to an end; he must be used up; he needs some one to use him up. His instinct gives the highest honours to an ethic of self-effacement; he is prompted to embrace it by everything: his prudence, his experience, his vanity. Every sort of faith is in itself an evidence of self-effacement, of self-estrangement.... When one reflects how necessary it is to the great majority that there be regulations to restrain them from without and hold them fast, and to what extent control, or, in a higher sense, slavery, is the one and only condition which makes for the well-being of the weak-willed man, and especially woman, then one at once understands conviction and "faith." To the man with convictions they are his backbone. To avoid seeing many things, to be impartial about nothing, to be a party man through and through, to estimate all values strictly and infallibly—these are conditions necessary to the existence of such a man. But by the same token they are antagonists of the truthful man—of the truth.... The believer is not free to answer the question, "true" or "not true," according to the dictates of his own conscience: integrity on this point would work his instant downfall. The pathological limitations of his vision turn the man of convictions into a fanatic— Savonarola, Luther, Rousseau, Robespierre, Saint-Simon—these types stand in opposition to the strong, emancipated spirit. But the grandiose attitudes of these sick intellects, these intellectual epileptics, are of influence upon the great masses—fanatics are picturesque, and mankind prefers observing poses to listening to reasons....

55.

—One step further in the psychology of conviction, of "faith." It is now a good while since I first proposed for consideration the question whether convictions are not even more dangerous enemies to truth than lies. ("Human, All-Too-Human," I, aphorism 483.)[27] This time I desire to put the question definitely: is there any actual difference between a lie and a conviction?—All the world believes that there is; but what is not believed by all the world!—Every conviction has its history, its primitive forms, its stage of tentativeness and error: it becomes a conviction only after having been, for a long time, not one, and then, for an even longer time, hardly one. What if falsehood be also one of these embryonic forms of conviction?—Sometimes all that is needed is a change in persons: what was a lie in the father becomes a conviction in the son.—I call it lying to refuse to see what one sees, or to refuse to see it as it is: whether the lie be uttered before witnesses or not before witnesses is of no consequence. The most common sort of lie is that by which a man deceives himself: the deception of others is a relatively rare offence.—Now, this will not to see what one sees, this will not to see it as it is, is almost the first requisite for all who belong to a party of whatever sort: the party man becomes inevitably a liar. For example, the German historians are convinced that Rome was synonymous with despotism and that the Germanic peoples brought the spirit of liberty into the world: what is the difference between this conviction and a lie? Is it to be wondered at that all partisans, including the German historians, instinctively roll the fine phrases of morality upon their tongues—that morality almost owes its very survival to the fact that the party man of every sort has need of it every moment?—"This is our conviction: we publish it to the whole world; we live and die for it—let us respect all who have convictions!"—I have actually heard such sentiments from the mouths of anti-Semites. On the contrary, gentlemen! An anti-Semite surely does not become more respectable because he lies on principle.... The priests, who have more finesse in such matters, and who well understand the objection that lies against the notion of a conviction, which is to say, of a falsehood that becomes a matter of principle because it serves a purpose, have borrowed from the Jews the shrewd device of sneaking in the concepts, "God," "the will of God" and "the revelation of God" at this place. Kant, too, with his categorical imperative, was on the same road: this was his practical reason. [28] There are questions regarding the truth or untruth of which it is not for man to decide; all the capital questions, all the capital problems of valuation, are beyond human reason.... To know the limits of reason— that alone is genuine philosophy.... Why did God make a revelation to man? Would God have done anything superfluous?

Man could not find out for himself what was good and what was evil, so God taught him His will.... Moral: the priest does not lie—the question, "true" or

"untrue," has nothing to do with such things as the priest discusses; it is impossible to lie about these things. In order to lie here it would be necessary to know what is true. But this is more than man can know; therefore, the priest is simply the mouthpiece of God.—Such a priestly syllogism is by no means merely Jewish and Christian; the right to lie and the shrewd dodge of "revelation" belong to the general priestly type—to the priest of the décadence as well as to the priest of pagan times (—Pagans are all those who say yes to life, and to whom "God" is a word signifying acquiescence in all things).—The "law," the "will of God," the "holy book," and "inspiration"—all these things are merely words for the conditions under which the priest comes to power and with which he maintains his power,—these concepts are to be found at the bottom of all priestly organizations, and of all priestly or priestly-philosophical schemes of governments. The "holy lie"—common alike to Confucius, to the Code of Manu, to Mohammed and to the Christian church—is not even wanting in Plato. "Truth is here": this means, no matter where it is heard, the priest lies....

[27] The aphorism, which is headed "The Enemies of Truth," makes the direct statement: "Convictions are more dangerous enemies of truth than lies."

[28] A reference, of course, to Kant's "Kritik der praktischen Vernunft" (Critique of Practical Reason).

56.

—In the last analysis it comes to this: what is the end of lying? The fact that, in Christianity, "holy" ends are not visible is my objection to the means it employs. Only bad ends appear: the poisoning, the calumniation, the denial of life, the despising of the body, the degradation and self-contamination of man by the concept of sin— therefore, its means are also bad.—I have a contrary feeling when I read the Code of Manu, an incomparably more intellectual and superior work, which it would be a sin against the intelligence to so much as name in the same breath with the Bible. It is easy to see why: there is a genuine philosophy behind it, in it, not merely an evil-smelling mess of Jewish rabbinism and superstition,—it gives even the most fastidious psychologist something to sink his teeth into. And, not to forget what is most important, it differs fundamentally from every kind of Bible: by means of it the nobles, the philosophers and the warriors keep the whip-hand over the majority; it is full of noble valuations, it shows a feeling of perfection, an acceptance of life, and triumphant feeling toward self and life—the sun shines upon the whole book.—All the things on which Christianity vents its fathomless vulgarity—for example, procreation, women and marriage—are here handled earnestly, with reverence and with love and confidence. How can any one really put into the hands of children and ladies a book which contains such vile things as this: "to avoid fornication, let every man have his own wife, and let every woman have her own husband; ... it is better to marry than to burn"? [29] And is it possible to be a Christian so long as the origin of man is Christianized, which is to say, befouled, by the doctrine of the immaculata conceptio?... I know of no book in which so many delicate and kindly things are said of women as in the Code of Manu; these old grey-beards and saints have a way of being gallant to women that it would be impossible, perhaps, to surpass. "The mouth of a woman," it says in one place, "the breasts of a maiden, the prayer of a child and the smoke of sacrifice are always pure." In another place: "there is nothing purer than the light of the sun, the shadow cast by a cow, air, water, fire and the breath of a maiden." Finally, in still another place—perhaps this is also a holy lie—: "all the orifices of the body above the navel are pure, and all below are impure. Only in the maiden is the whole body pure."

[29] 1 Corinthians vii, 2, 9.

57.

One catches the unholiness of Christian means in flagranti by the simple process of putting the ends sought by Christianity beside the ends sought by the Code of Manu—by putting these enormously antithetical ends under a strong light. The critic of Christianity cannot evade the necessity of making Christianity contemptible.—A book of laws such as the Code of Manu has the same origin as every other good law-book: it epitomizes the experience, the sagacity and the ethical experimentation of long centuries; it brings things to a conclusion; it no longer creates. The prerequisite to a codification of this sort is recognition of the fact that the means which establish the authority of a slowly and painfully attained truth are fundamentally different from those which one would make use of to prove it. A law-book never recites the utility, the grounds, the casuistical antecedents of a law: for if it did so it would lose the imperative tone, the "thou shall," on which obedience is based. The problem lies exactly here.—At a certain point in the evolution of a people, the class within it of the greatest insight, which is to say, the greatest hindsight and foresight, declares that the series of experiences determining how all shall live—or can live—has come to an end. The object now is to reap as rich and as complete a harvest as possible from the days of experiment and hard experience. In consequence, the thing that is to be avoided above everything is further experimentation—the continuation of the state in which values are fluent, and are tested, chosen and criticized ad infinitum. Against this a double wall is set up: on the one hand, revelation, which is the assumption that the reasons lying behind the laws are not of human origin, that they were not sought out and found by a slow process and after many errors, but that they are of divine ancestry, and came into being complete, perfect, without a history, as a free gift, a miracle...; and on the other hand, tradition, which is the assumption that the law has stood unchanged from time immemorial, and that it is impious and a crime against one's forefathers to bring it into question. The authority of the law is thus grounded on the thesis: God gave it, and the fathers lived it.—The higher motive of such procedure lies in the design to distract consciousness, step by step, from its concern with notions of right living (that is to say, those that have been proved to be right by wide and carefully considered experience), so that instinct attains to a perfect automatism —a primary necessity to every sort of mastery, to every sort of perfection in the art of life. To draw up such a law-book as Manu's means to lay before a people the possibility of future mastery, of attainable perfection—it permits them to aspire to the highest reaches of the art of life. To that end the thing must be made unconscious: that is the aim of every holy lie.—The order of castes, the highest, the dominating law, is merely the ratification of an order of nature, of a natural law of the first rank, over which no arbitrary fiat, no "modern idea," can exert any influence. In every healthy society there are three physiological types, gravitating toward differentiation but mutually conditioning one another, and each of these has its own hygiene, its own sphere of work, its own special mastery and feeling of perfection. It is not Manu but nature that sets off in one class those who are chiefly intellectual, in another those who are marked by muscular strength and temperament, and in a third those who are distinguished in neither one way or the other, but show only mediocrity—the last-named represents the great majority, and the first two the select. The superior caste—I call it the fewest—has, as the most perfect, the privileges of the few: it stands for happiness, for beauty, for everything good upon earth. Only the most intellectual of men have any right to beauty, to the beautiful; only in them can goodness escape being weakness. Pulchrum est paucorum hominum:[30] goodness is a privilege. Nothing could be more unbecoming to them than uncouth manners or a pessimistic look, or an eye that sees ugliness—or indignation against the general aspect of things. Indignation is the privilege of the Chandala; so is pessimism. "The world is perfect"—so prompts the instinct of the intellectual, the instinct of the man who says yes to life. "Imperfection, whatever is inferior to us, distance, the pathos of distance, even the Chandala themselves are parts of this perfection." The most intelligent men, like the strongest, find their happiness where others would find only disaster: in the labyrinth, in being hard with themselves and with others, in effort; their delight is in self-mastery; in them asceticism becomes second nature, a necessity, an instinct. They regard a difficult task as a privilege; it is to them a recreation to play with burdens that would crush all others.... Knowledge—a form of asceticism.—They are the most honourable kind of men: but that does not prevent them being the most cheerful and most amiable. They rule, not because they want to, but because they are; they are not at liberty to play second.—The second caste: to this belong the guardians of the law, the keepers of order and security, the more noble warriors, above all, the king as the highest form of warrior, judge and preserver of the law.

The second in rank constitute the executive arm of the intellectuals, the next to them in rank, taking from them all that is rough in the business of ruling—their followers, their right hand, their most apt disciples.—In all this, I repeat, there is nothing arbitrary, nothing "made up"; whatever is to the contrary is made up— by it nature is brought to shame.... The order of castes, the order of rank, simply formulates the supreme law of life itself; the separation of the three types is necessary to the maintenance of society, and to the evolution of higher types, and the highest types—the inequality of rights is essential to the existence of any rights at all.—A right is a privilege. Every one enjoys the privileges that accord with his state of existence. Let us not underestimate the privileges of the mediocre. Life is always harder as one mounts the heights—the cold increases, responsibility increases. A high civilization is a pyramid: it can stand only on a broad base; its primary prerequisite is a strong and soundly consolidated mediocrity. The handicrafts, commerce, agriculture, science, the greater part of art, in brief, the whole range of occupational activities, are compatible only with mediocre ability and aspiration; such callings would be out of place for exceptional men; the instincts which belong to them stand as much opposed to aristocracy as to anarchism. The fact that a man is publicly useful, that he is a wheel, a function, is evidence of a natural predisposition; it is not society, but the only sort of happiness that the majority are capable of, that makes them intelligent machines. To the mediocre mediocrity is a form of happiness; they have a natural instinct for mastering one thing, for specialization. It would be altogether unworthy of a profound intellect to see anything objectionable in mediocrity in itself. It is, in fact, the first prerequisite to the appearance of the exceptional: it is a necessary condition to a high degree of civilization. When the exceptional man handles the mediocre man with more delicate fingers than he applies to himself or to his equals, this is not merely kindness of heart—it is simply his duty.... Whom do I hate most heartily among the rabbles of today?

The rabble of Socialists, the apostles to the Chandala, who undermine the workingman's instincts, his pleasure, his feeling of contentment with his petty existence—who make him envious and teach him revenge.... Wrong never lies in unequal rights; it lies in the assertion of "equal" rights.... What is bad? But I have already answered: all that proceeds from weakness, from envy, from revenge.—The anarchist and the Christian have the same ancestry....

[30] Few men are noble.

58.

In point of fact, the end for which one lies makes a great difference: whether one preserves thereby or destroys. There is a perfect likeness between Christian and anarchist: their object, their instinct, points only toward destruction. One need only turn to history for a proof of this: there it appears with appalling distinctness. We have just studied a code of religious legislation whose object it was to convert the conditions which cause life to flourish into an "eternal" social organization,—Christianity found its mission in putting an end to such an organization, because life flourished under it. There the benefits that reason had produced during long ages of experiment and insecurity were applied to the most remote uses, and an effort was made to bring in a harvest that should be as large, as rich and as complete as possible; here, on the contrary, the harvest is blighted overnight.... That which stood there aere perennis, the imperium Romanum, the most magnificent form of organization under difficult conditions that has ever been achieved, and compared to which everything before it and after it appears as patchwork, bungling, dilletantism—those holy anarchists made it a matter of "piety" to destroy "the world," which is to say, the imperium Romanum, so that in the end not a stone stood upon another—and even Germans and other such louts were able to become its masters.... The Christian and the anarchist: both are décadents; both are incapable of any act that is not disintegrating, poisonous, degenerating, blood-sucking; both have an instinct of mortal hatred of everything that stands up, and is great, and has durability, and promises life a future.... Christianity was the vampire of the imperium Romanum, —overnight it destroyed the vast achievement of the Romans: the conquest of the soil for a great culture that could await its time. Can it be that this fact is not yet understood? The imperium Romanum that we know, and that the history of the Roman provinces teaches us to know better and better,—this most admirable of all works of art in the grand manner was merely the beginning, and the structure to follow was not to prove its worth for thousands of years. To this day, nothing on a like scale sub specie aeterni has been brought into being, or even dreamed of!—This organization was strong enough to withstand bad emperors: the accident of personality has nothing to do with such things—the first principle of all genuinely great architecture. But it was not strong enough to stand up against the corruptest of all forms of corruption—against Christians.... These stealthy worms, which under the cover of night, mist and duplicity, crept upon every individual, sucking him dry of all earnest interest in real things, of all instinct for reality—this cowardly, effeminate and sugar-coated gang gradually alienated all "souls," step by step, from that colossal edifice, turning against it all the meritorious, manly and noble natures that had found in the cause of Rome their own cause, their own serious purpose, their own pride. The sneakishness of hypocrisy, the secrecy of the conventicle, concepts as black as hell, such as the sacrifice of the innocent, the unio mystica in the drinking of blood, above all, the slowly rekindled fire of revenge, of Chandala revenge—all that sort of thing became master of Rome: the same kind of religion which, in a pre-existent form, Epicurus had combatted. One has but to read Lucretius to know what Epicurus made war upon— not paganism, but "Christianity," which is to say, the corruption of souls by means of the concepts of guilt, punishment and immortality.—He combatted the subterranean cults, the whole of latent Christianity—to deny immortality was already a form of genuine salvation.— Epicurus had triumphed, and every respectable intellect in Rome was Epicurean — when Paul appeared ... Paul, the Chandala hatred of Rome, of "the world," in the flesh and inspired by genius—the Jew, the eternal Jew par excellence....

What he saw was how, with the aid of the small sectarian Christian movement that stood apart from Judaism, a "world conflagration" might be kindled; how, with the symbol of "God on the cross," all secret seditions, all the fruits of anarchistic intrigues in the empire, might be amalgamated into one immense power. "Salvation is of the Jews."—Christianity is the formula for exceeding and summing up the subterranean cults of all varieties, that of Osiris, that of the Great Mother, that of Mithras, for instance: in his discernment of this fact the genius of Paul showed itself. His instinct was here so sure that, with reckless violence to the truth, he put the ideas which lent fascination to every sort of Chandala religion into the mouth of the "Saviour" as his own inventions, and not only into the mouth—he made out of him something that even a priest of Mithras could understand.... This was his revelation at Damascus: he grasped the fact that he needed the belief in immortality in order to rob "the world" of

its value, that the concept of "hell" would master Rome—that the notion of a "beyond"
is the death of life.... Nihilist and Christian: they rhyme in German, and they do more
than rhyme....

59.

The whole labour of the ancient world gone for naught: I have no word to describe the
feelings that such an enormity arouses in me.—And, considering the fact that its labour
was merely preparatory, that with adamantine self- consciousness it laid only the
foundations for a work to go on for thousands of years, the whole meaning of antiquity
disappears!... To what end the Greeks? to what end the Romans?—All the prerequisites
to a learned culture, all the methods of science, were already there; man had already
perfected the great and incomparable art of reading profitably—that first necessity to
the tradition of culture, the unity of the sciences; the natural sciences, in alliance with
mathematics and mechanics, were on the right road,— the sense of fact, the last and
more valuable of all the senses, had its schools, and its traditions were already centuries
old! Is all this properly understood? Every essential to the beginning of the work was
ready:—and the most essential, it cannot be said too often, are methods, and also the
most difficult to develop, and the longest opposed by habit and laziness. What we have
today reconquered, with unspeakable self-discipline, for ourselves—for certain bad
instincts, certain Christian instincts, still lurk in our bodies—that is to say, the keen
eye for reality, the cautious hand, patience and seriousness in the smallest things, the
whole integrity of knowledge—all these things were already there, and had been there
for two thousand years! More, there was also a refined and excellent tact and taste! Not
as mere brain-drilling! Not as "German" culture, with its loutish manners! But as body,
as bearing, as instinct—in short, as reality.... All gone for naught! Overnight it became
merely a memory!—The Greeks! The Romans!

Instinctive nobility, taste, methodical inquiry, genius for organization and
administration, faith in and the will to secure the future of man, a great yes to everything
entering into the imperium Romanum and palpable to all the senses, a grand style that
was beyond mere art, but had become reality, truth, life....—All overwhelmed in a
night, but not by a convulsion of nature! Not trampled to death by Teutons and others
of heavy hoof! But brought to shame by crafty, sneaking, invisible, anæmic vampires!
Not conquered,—only sucked dry!...

Hidden vengefulness, petty envy, became master! Everything wretched, intrinsically
ailing, and invaded by bad feelings, the whole ghetto-world of the soul, was at once on
top!—One needs but read any of the Christian agitators, for example, St. Augustine,
in order to realize, in order to smell, what filthy fellows came to the top. It would be
an error, however, to assume that there was any lack of understanding in the leaders
of the Christian movement:—ah, but they were clever, clever to the point of holiness,
these fathers of the church! What they lacked was something quite different. Nature
neglected—perhaps forgot—to give them even the most modest endowment of
respectable, of upright, of cleanly instincts.... Between ourselves, they are not even
men.... If Islam despises Christianity, it has a thousandfold right to do so: Islam at least
assumes that it is dealing with men....

60.

Christianity destroyed for us the whole harvest of ancient civilization, and later it also destroyed for us the whole harvest of Mohammedan civilization. The wonderful culture of the Moors in Spain, which was fundamentally nearer to us and appealed more to our senses and tastes than that of Rome and Greece, was trampled down (—I do not say by what sort of feet—) Why? Because it had to thank noble and manly instincts for its origin—because it said yes to life, even to the rare and refined luxuriousness of Moorish life!... The crusaders later made war on something before which it would have been more fitting for them to have grovelled in the dust—a civilization beside which even that of our nineteenth century seems very poor and very "senile."—What they wanted, of course, was booty: the orient was rich.... Let us put aside our prejudices! The crusades were a higher form of piracy, nothing more! The German nobility, which is fundamentally a Viking nobility, was in its element there: the church knew only too well how the German nobility was to be won....

The German noble, always the "Swiss guard" of the church, always in the service of every bad instinct of the church— but well paid.... Consider the fact that it is precisely the aid of German swords and German blood and valour that has enabled the church to carry through its war to the death upon everything noble on earth! At this point a host of painful questions suggest themselves. The German nobility stands outside the history of the higher civilization: the reason is obvious....

Christianity, alcohol—the two great means of corruption.... Intrinsically there should be no more choice between Islam and Christianity than there is between an Arab and a Jew. The decision is already reached; nobody remains at liberty to choose here. Either a man is a Chandala or he is not.... "War to the knife with Rome! Peace and friendship with Islam!": this was the feeling, this was the act, of that great free spirit, that genius among German emperors, Frederick II. What!

must a German first be a genius, a free spirit, before he can feel decently? I can't make out how a German could ever feel Christian....

61.

Here it becomes necessary to call up a memory that must be a hundred times more painful to Germans. The Germans have destroyed for Europe the last great harvest of civilization that Europe was ever to reap—the Renaissance. Is it understood at last, will it ever be understood, what the Renaissance was? The transvaluation of Christian values,—an attempt with all available means, all instincts and all the resources of genius to bring about a triumph of the opposite values, the more noble values.... This has been the one great war of the past; there has never been a more critical question than that of the Renaissance—it is my question too—; there has never been a form of attack more fundamental, more direct, or more violently delivered by a whole front upon the center of the enemy! To attack at the critical place, at the very seat of Christianity, and there enthrone the more noble values—that is to say, to insinuate them into the instincts, into the most fundamental needs and appetites of those sitting there.... I see before me the possibility of a perfectly heavenly enchantment and spectacle: —it seems to me to scintillate with all the vibrations of a fine and delicate beauty, and within it there is an art so divine, so infernally divine, that one might search in vain for thousands of years for another such possibility; I see a spectacle so rich in significance and at the same time so wonderfully full of paradox that it should arouse all the gods on Olympus to immortal laughter

— Cæsar Borgia as pope! ... Am I understood?... Well then, that would have been the sort of triumph that I alone am longing for today—: by it Christianity would have been swept away!—What happened? A German monk, Luther, came to Rome. This monk, with all the vengeful instincts of an unsuccessful priest in him, raised a rebellion against the Renaissance in Rome.... Instead of grasping, with profound thanksgiving, the miracle that had taken place: the conquest of Christianity at its capital—instead of this, his hatred was stimulated by the spectacle. A religious man thinks only of himself.— Luther saw only the depravity of the papacy at the very moment when the opposite was becoming apparent: the old corruption, the peccatum originale, Christianity itself, no longer occupied the papal chair! Instead there was life! Instead there was the triumph of life! Instead there was a great yea to all lofty, beautiful and daring things!... And Luther restored the church: he attacked it.... The Renaissance—an event without meaning, a great futility!—Ah, these Germans, what they have not cost us! Futility— that has always been the work of the Germans.—The Reformation; Leibnitz; Kant and so-called German philosophy; the war of "liberation"; the empire—every time a futile substitute for something that once existed, for something irrecoverable.... These Germans, I confess, are my enemies: I despise all their uncleanliness in concept and valuation, their cowardice before every honest yea and nay. For nearly a thousand years they have tangled and confused everything their fingers have touched; they have on their conscience all the half-way measures, all the three-eighths-way measures, that Europe is sick of,—they also have on their conscience the uncleanest variety of Christianity that exists, and the most incurable and indestructible—

Protestantism.... If mankind never manages to get rid of Christianity the Germans will be to blame....

62.

—With this I come to a conclusion and pronounce my judgment. I condemn

Christianity; I bring against the Christian church the most terrible of all the accusations that an accuser has ever had in his mouth. It is, to me, the greatest of all imaginable corruptions; it seeks to work the ultimate corruption, the worst possible corruption. The Christian church has left nothing untouched by its depravity; it has turned every value into worthlessness, and every truth into a lie, and every integrity into baseness of soul. Let any one dare to speak to me of its "humanitarian" blessings! Its deepest necessities range it against any effort to abolish distress; it lives by distress; it creates distress to make itself immortal....

For example, the worm of sin: it was the church that first enriched mankind with this misery!—The "equality of souls before God"—this fraud, this pretext for the rancunes of all the base-minded—this explosive concept, ending in revolution, the modern idea, and the notion of overthrowing the whole social order—this is Christian dynamite.... The "humanitarian" blessings of Christianity forsooth! To breed out of humanitas a self-contradiction, an art of self-pollution, a will to lie at any price, an aversion and contempt for all good and honest instincts! All this, to me, is the "humanitarianism" of Christianity!—Parasitism as the only practice of the church; with its anæmic and "holy" ideals, sucking all the blood, all the love, all the hope out of life; the beyond as the will to deny all reality; the cross as the distinguishing mark of the most subterranean conspiracy ever heard of,— against health, beauty, well-being, intellect, kindness of soul— against life itself....

This eternal accusation against Christianity I shall write upon all walls, wherever walls are to be found—I have letters that even the blind will be able to see.... I call Christianity the one great curse, the one great intrinsic depravity, the one great instinct of revenge, for which no means are venomous enough, or secret, subterranean and small enough,—I call it the one immortal blemish upon the human race....

And mankind reckons time from the dies nefastus when this fatality befell —from the first day of Christianity!— Why not rather from its last? — From today? —The transvaluation of all values!...

THE RELIGIOUS MOOD

45. The human soul and its limits, the range of man's inner experiences hitherto attained, the heights, depths, and distances of these experiences, the entire history of the soul UP TO THE PRESENT TIME, and its still unexhausted possibilities: this is the preordained hunting-domain for a born psychologist and lover of a "big hunt". But how often must he say despairingly to himself: "A single individual! alas, only a single individual! and this great forest, this virgin forest!" So he would like to have some hundreds of hunting assistants, and fine trained hounds, that he could send into the history of the human soul, to drive HIS game together. In vain: again and again he experiences, profoundly and bitterly, how difficult it is to find assistants and dogs for all the things that directly excite his curiosity. The evil of sending scholars into new and dangerous hunting-domains, where courage, sagacity, and subtlety in every sense are required, is that they are no longer serviceable just when the "BIG hunt," and also the great danger commences,—it is precisely then that they lose their keen eye and nose. In order, for instance, to divine and determine what sort of history the problem of KNOWLEDGE AND CONSCIENCE has hitherto had in the souls of homines religiosi, a person would perhaps himself have to possess as profound, as bruised, as immense an experience as the intellectual conscience of Pascal; and then he would still require that wide-spread heaven of clear, wicked spirituality, which, from above, would be able to oversee, arrange, and effectively formulize this mass of dangerous and painful experiences.—But who could do me this service! And who would have time to wait for such servants!— they evidently appear too rarely, they are so improbable at all times!

Eventually one must do everything ONESELF in order to know something; which means that one has MUCH to do!

—But a curiosity like mine is once for all the most agreeable of vices—pardon me!

I mean to say that the love of truth has its reward in heaven, and already upon earth.

46. Faith, such as early Christianity desired, and not infrequently achieved in the midst of a skeptical and southernly free-spirited world, which had centuries of struggle between philosophical schools behind it and in it, counting besides the education in tolerance which the Imperium Romanum gave—this faith is NOT that sincere, austere slave-faith by which perhaps a Luther or a Cromwell, or some other northern barbarian of the spirit remained attached to his God and Christianity, it is much rather the faith of Pascal, which resembles in a terrible manner a continuous suicide of reason—a tough, long-lived, worm-like reason, which is not to be slain at once and with a single blow. The Christian faith from the beginning, is sacrifice the sacrifice of all freedom, all pride, all self-confidence of spirit, it is at the same time subjection, self-derision, and self-mutilation. There is cruelty and religious Phoenicianism in this faith, which is adapted to a tender, many-sided, and very fastidious conscience, it takes for granted that the subjection of the spirit is indescribably PAINFUL, that all the past and all the habits of such a spirit resist the absurdissimum, in the form of which "faith" comes to it. Modern men, with their obtuseness as regards all Christian nomenclature, have

no longer the sense for the terribly superlative conception which was implied to an antique taste by the paradox of the formula,

"God on the Cross". Hitherto there had never and nowhere been such boldness in inversion, nor anything at once so dreadful, questioning, and questionable as this formula: it promised a transvaluation of all ancient values—It was the Orient, the PROFOUND Orient, it was the Oriental slave who thus took revenge on Rome and its noble, light-minded toleration, on the Roman "Catholicism" of non-faith, and it was always not the faith, but the freedom from the faith, the half-stoical and smiling indifference to the seriousness of the faith, which made the slaves indignant at their masters and revolt against them. "Enlightenment" causes revolt, for the slave desires the unconditioned, he understands nothing but the tyrannous, even in morals, he loves as he hates, without NUANCE, to the very depths, to the point of pain, to the point of sickness—his many HIDDEN sufferings make him revolt against the noble taste which seems to DENY suffering. The skepticism with regard to suffering, fundamentally only an attitude of aristocratic morality, was not the least of the causes, also, of the last great slave-insurrection which began with the French Revolution.

47. Wherever the religious neurosis has appeared on the earth so far, we find it connected with three dangerous prescriptions as to regimen: solitude, fasting, and sexual abstinence—but without its being possible to determine with certainty which is cause and which is effect, or IF any relation at all of cause and effect exists there. This latter doubt is justified by the fact that one of the most regular symptoms among savage as well as among civilized peoples is the most sudden and excessive sensuality, which then with equal suddenness transforms into penitential paroxysms, world-renunciation, and will-renunciation, both symptoms perhaps explainable as disguised epilepsy? But nowhere is it MORE obligatory to put aside explanations around no other type has there grown such a mass of absurdity and superstition, no other type seems to have been more interesting to men and even to philosophers— perhaps it is time to become just a little indifferent here, to learn caution, or, better still, to look AWAY, TO GO AWAY—Yet in the background of the most recent philosophy, that of Schopenhauer, we find almost as the problem in itself, this terrible note of interrogation of the religious crisis and awakening. How is the negation of will POSSIBLE? how is the saint possible?—that seems to have been the very question with which Schopenhauer made a start and became a philosopher. And thus it was a genuine Schopenhauerian consequence, that his most convinced adherent (perhaps also his last, as far as Germany is concerned), namely, Richard Wagner, should bring his own life-work to an end just here, and should finally put that terrible and eternal type upon the stage as Kundry, type vecu, and as it loved and lived, at the very time that the mad-doctors in almost all European countries had an opportunity to study the type close at hand, wherever the religious neurosis—or as I call it, "the religious mood"—made its latest epidemical outbreak and display as the "Salvation Army"—If it be a question, however, as to what has been so extremely interesting to men of all sorts in all ages, and even to philosophers, in the whole phenomenon of the saint, it is undoubtedly the appearance of the miraculous therein—namely, the immediate SUCCESSION OF OPPOSITES, of states of the soul regarded as morally antithetical: it was believed here to be self-evident that a "bad man" was all at once turned into a "saint," a good man. The hitherto existing psychology was wrecked at this point, is it

not possible it may have happened principally because psychology had placed itself under the dominion of morals, because it BELIEVED in oppositions of moral values, and saw, read, and INTERPRETED these oppositions into the text and facts of the case? What? "Miracle" only an error of interpretation? A lack of philology?

48. It seems that the Latin races are far more deeply attached to their Catholicism than we Northerners are to Christianity generally, and that consequently unbelief in Catholic countries means something quite different from what it does among Protestants— namely, a sort of revolt against the spirit of the race, while with us it is rather a return to the spirit (or non-spirit) of the race.

We Northerners undoubtedly derive our origin from barbarous races, even as regards our talents for religion—we have POOR talents for it. One may make an exception in the case of the Celts, who have theretofore furnished also the best soil for Christian infection in the North: the Christian ideal blossomed forth in France as much as ever the pale sun of the north would allow it. How strangely pious for our taste are still these later French skeptics, whenever there is any Celtic blood in their origin! How Catholic, how un-German does Auguste Comte's Sociology seem to us, with the Roman logic of its instincts! How Jesuitical, that amiable and shrewd cicerone of Port Royal, Sainte-Beuve, in spite of all his hostility to Jesuits! And even Ernest Renan: how inaccessible to us Northerners does the language of such a Renan appear, in whom every instant the merest touch of religious thrill throws his refined voluptuous and comfortably couching soul off its balance! Let us repeat after him these fine sentences—and what wickedness and haughtiness is immediately aroused by way of answer in our probably less beautiful but harder souls, that is to say, in our more German souls!—"DISONS DONC HARDIMENT QUE LA RELIGION EST UN PRODUIT DE L'HOMME NORMAL, QUE L'HOMME EST LE PLUS DANS LE VRAI QUANT IL EST LE PLUS RELIGIEUX ET LE PLUS ASSURE D'UNE DESTINEE INFINIE.... C'EST QUAND IL EST BON QU'IL VEUT QUE LA VIRTU CORRESPONDE A UN ORDER ETERNAL, C'EST QUAND IL CONTEMPLE LES CHOSES D'UNE MANIERE DESINTERESSEE QU'IL TROUVE LA MORT REVOLTANTE ET ABSURDE. COMMENT NE PAS SUPPOSER QUE C'EST DANS CES MOMENTS-LA, QUE L'HOMME VOIT LE MIEUX?"...

These sentences are so extremely ANTIPODAL to my ears and habits of thought, that in my first impulse of rage on finding them, I wrote on the margin, "LA NIAISERIE RELIGIEUSE PAR EXCELLENCE!"—until in my later rage I even took a fancy to them, these sentences with their truth absolutely inverted! It is so nice and such a distinction to have one's own antipodes!

49. That which is so astonishing in the religious life of the ancient Greeks is the irrestrainable stream of GRATITUDE which it pours forth—it is a very superior kind of man who takes SUCH an attitude towards nature and life.—

Later on, when the populace got the upper hand in Greece, FEAR became rampant also in religion; and Christianity was preparing itself.

50. The passion for God: there are churlish, honest-hearted, and importunate kinds of it, like that of Luther—the whole of Protestantism lacks the southern DELICATEZZA.

There is an Oriental exaltation of the mind in it, like that of an undeservedly favoured or elevated slave, as in the case of St. Augustine, for instance, who lacks in an offensive manner, all nobility in bearing and desires.

There is a feminine tenderness and sensuality in it, which modestly and unconsciously longs for a UNIO MYSTICA ET PHYSICA, as in the case of Madame de Guyon. In many cases it appears, curiously enough, as the disguise of a girl's or youth's puberty; here and there even as the hysteria of an old maid, also as her last ambition. The Church has frequently canonized the woman in such a case.

51. The mightiest men have hitherto always bowed reverently before the saint, as the enigma of self-subjugation and utter voluntary privation—why did they thus bow? They divined in him—and as it were behind the questionableness of his frail and wretched appearance—the superior force which wished to test itself by such a subjugation; the strength of will, in which they recognized their own strength and love of power, and knew how to honour it: they honoured something in themselves when they honoured the saint. In addition to this, the contemplation of the saint suggested to them a suspicion: such an enormity of self-negation and anti-naturalness will not have been coveted for nothing—they have said, inquiringly. There is perhaps a reason for it, some very great danger, about which the ascetic might wish to be more accurately informed through his secret interlocutors and visitors? In a word, the mighty ones of the world learned to have a new fear before him, they divined a new power, a strange, still unconquered enemy:—it was the "Will to Power" which obliged them to halt before the saint. They had to question him.

52. In the Jewish "Old Testament," the book of divine justice, there are men, things, and sayings on such an immense scale, that Greek and Indian literature has nothing to compare with it. One stands with fear and reverence before those stupendous remains of what man was formerly, and one has sad thoughts about old Asia and its little out-pushed peninsula Europe, which would like, by all means, to figure before Asia as the "Progress of Mankind." To be sure, he who is himself only a slender, tame house-animal, and knows only the wants of a house-animal (like our cultured people of today, including the Christians of "cultured" Christianity), need neither be amazed nor even sad amid those ruins—the taste for the Old Testament is a touchstone with respect to "great" and "small": perhaps he will find that the New Testament, the book of grace, still appeals more to his heart (there is much of the odour of the genuine, tender, stupid beadsman and petty soul in it). To have bound up this New Testament (a kind of ROCOCO of taste in every respect) along with the Old Testament into one book, as the "Bible," as "The Book in Itself," is perhaps the greatest audacity and "sin against the Spirit" which literary Europe has upon its conscience.

53. Why Atheism nowadays? "The father" in God is thoroughly refuted; equally so "the judge," "the rewarder." Also his "free will": he does not hear— and even if he did, he would not know how to help. The worst is that he seems incapable of communicating himself clearly; is he uncertain?—This is what I have made out (by questioning and listening at a variety of conversations) to be the cause of the decline of European theism; it appears to me that though the religious instinct is in vigorous growth,—it rejects the theistic satisfaction with profound distrust.

54. What does all modern philosophy mainly do? Since Descartes—and indeed more in defiance of him than on the basis of his procedure—an ATTENTAT has been made on the part of all philosophers on the old conception of the soul, under the guise of a criticism of the subject and predicate conception —that is to say, an ATTENTAT on the fundamental presupposition of Christian doctrine. Modern philosophy, as epistemological skepticism, is secretly or openly ANTI-CHRISTIAN, although (for keener ears, be it said) by no means anti-religious. Formerly, in effect, one believed in "the soul" as one believed in grammar and the grammatical subject: one said, "I" is the condition, "think" is the predicate and is conditioned—to think is an activity for which one MUST suppose a subject as cause. The attempt was then made, with marvelous tenacity and subtlety, to see if one could not get out of this net,—to see if the opposite was not perhaps true: "think" the condition, and "I" the conditioned; "I," therefore, only a synthesis which has been MADE by thinking itself. KANT really wished to prove that, starting from the subject, the subject could not be proved—nor the object either: the possibility of an APPARENT EXISTENCE of the subject, and therefore of "the soul," may not always have been strange to him,—the thought which once had an immense power on earth as the Vedanta philosophy.

55. There is a great ladder of religious cruelty, with many rounds; but three of these are the most important. Once on a time men sacrificed human beings to their God, and perhaps just those they loved the best—to this category belong the firstling sacrifices of all primitive religions, and also the sacrifice of the Emperor Tiberius in the Mithra-Grotto on the Island of Capri, that most terrible of all Roman anachronisms. Then, during the moral epoch of mankind, they sacrificed to their God the strongest instincts they possessed, their "nature"; THIS festal joy shines in the cruel glances of ascetics and "anti-natural" fanatics.

Finally, what still remained to be sacrificed? Was it not necessary in the end for men to sacrifice everything comforting, holy, healing, all hope, all faith in hidden harmonies, in future blessedness and justice? Was it not necessary to sacrifice God himself, and out of cruelty to themselves to worship stone, stupidity, gravity, fate, nothingness? To sacrifice God for nothingness—this paradoxical mystery of the ultimate cruelty has been reserved for the rising generation; we all know something thereof already.

56. Whoever, like myself, prompted by some enigmatical desire, has long endeavoured to go to the bottom of the question of pessimism and free it from the half-Christian, half-German narrowness and stupidity in which it has finally presented itself to this century, namely, in the form of Schopenhauer's philosophy; whoever, with an Asiatic and super-Asiatic eye, has actually looked inside, and into the most world-renouncing of all possible modes of thought— beyond good and evil, and no longer like Buddha and Schopenhauer, under the dominion and delusion of morality,—whoever has done this, has perhaps just thereby, without really desiring it, opened his eyes to behold the opposite ideal: the ideal of the most world-approving, exuberant, and vivacious man, who has not only learnt to compromise and arrange with that which was and is, but wishes to have it again AS IT WAS AND IS, for all eternity, insatiably calling out da capo, not only to himself, but to the whole piece and play; and not only the play, but actually to him who requires the play—and makes it necessary; because he always requires himself anew—and makes himself necessary.—

What? And this would not be—circulus vitiosus deus?

57. The distance, and as it were the space around man, grows with the strength of his intellectual vision and insight: his world becomes profounder; new stars, new enigmas, and notions are ever coming into view. Perhaps everything on which the intellectual eye has exercised its acuteness and profundity has just been an occasion for its exercise, something of a game, something for children and childish minds. Perhaps the most solemn conceptions that have caused the most fighting and suffering, the conceptions "God" and "sin," will one day seem to us of no more importance than a child's plaything or a child's pain seems to an old man;—and perhaps another plaything and another pain will then be necessary once more for "the old man"—always childish enough, an eternal child!

58. Has it been observed to what extent outward idleness, or semi-idleness, is necessary to a real religious life (alike for its favourite microscopic labour of self-examination, and for its soft placidity called "prayer," the state of perpetual readiness for the "coming of God"), I mean the idleness with a good conscience, the idleness of olden times and of blood, to which the aristocratic sentiment that work is DISHONOURING—that it vulgarizes body and soul—is not quite unfamiliar? And that consequently the modern, noisy, time-engrossing, conceited, foolishly proud laboriousness educates and prepares for "unbelief" more than anything else? Among these, for instance, who are at present living apart from religion in Germany, I find "free-thinkers" of diversified species and origin, but above all a majority of those in whom laboriousness from generation to generation has dissolved the religious instincts; so that they no longer know what purpose religions serve, and only note their existence in the world with a kind of dull astonishment. They feel themselves already fully occupied, these good people, be it by their business or by their pleasures, not to mention the "Fatherland," and the newspapers, and their "family duties"; it seems that they have no time whatever left for religion; and above all, it is not obvious to them whether it is a question of a new business or a new pleasure—for it is impossible, they say to themselves, that people should go to church merely to spoil their tempers. They are by no means enemies of religious customs; should certain circumstances, State affairs perhaps, require their participation in such customs, they do what is required, as so many things are done—with a patient and unassuming seriousness, and without much curiosity or discomfort;—they live too much apart and outside to feel even the necessity for a FOR or AGAINST in such matters. Among those indifferent persons may be reckoned nowadays the majority of German Protestants of the middle classes, especially in the great laborious centres of trade and commerce; also the majority of laborious scholars, and the entire University personnel (with the exception of the theologians, whose existence and possibility there always gives psychologists new and more subtle puzzles to solve). On the part of pious, or merely church-going people, there is seldom any idea of HOW MUCH good-will, one might say arbitrary will, is now necessary for a German scholar to take the problem of religion seriously; his whole profession (and as I have said, his whole workmanlike laboriousness, to which he is compelled by his modern conscience) inclines him to a lofty and almost charitable serenity as regards religion, with which is occasionally mingled a slight disdain for the "uncleanliness" of spirit which he takes for granted wherever any one still professes to belong to the Church. It is only with the help of history (NOT through his own personal experience,

therefore) that the scholar succeeds in bringing himself to a respectful seriousness, and to a certain timid deference in presence of religions; but even when his sentiments have reached the stage of gratitude towards them, he has not personally advanced one step nearer to that which still maintains itself as Church or as piety; perhaps even the contrary. The practical indifference to religious matters in the midst of which he has been born and brought up, usually sublimates itself in his case into circumspection and cleanliness, which shuns contact with religious men and things; and it may be just the depth of his tolerance and humanity which prompts him to avoid the delicate trouble which tolerance itself brings with it.—Every age has its own divine type of naivete, for the discovery of which other ages may envy it: and how much naivete— adorable, childlike, and boundlessly foolish naivete is involved in this belief of the scholar in his superiority, in the good conscience of his tolerance, in the unsuspecting, simple certainty with which his instinct treats the religious man as a lower and less valuable type, beyond, before, and ABOVE which he himself has developed—he, the little arrogant dwarf and mob-man, the sedulously alert, head-and-hand drudge of "ideas," of "modern ideas"!

59. Whoever has seen deeply into the world has doubtless divined what wisdom there is in the fact that men are superficial. It is their preservative instinct which teaches them to be flighty, lightsome, and false. Here and there one finds a passionate and exaggerated adoration of "pure forms" in philosophers as well as in artists: it is not to be doubted that whoever has NEED of the cult of the superficial to that extent, has at one time or another made an unlucky dive BENEATH it. Perhaps there is even an order of rank with respect to those burnt children, the born artists who find the enjoyment of life only in trying to FALSIFY its image (as if taking wearisome revenge on it), one might guess to what degree life has disgusted them, by the extent to which they wish to see its image falsified, attenuated, ultrified, and deified,—one might reckon the homines religiosi among the artists, as their HIGHEST rank. It is the profound, suspicious fear of an incurable pessimism which compels whole centuries to fasten their teeth into a religious interpretation of existence: the fear of the instinct which divines that truth might be attained TOO soon, before man has become strong enough, hard enough, artist enough.... Piety, the "Life in God," regarded in this light, would appear as the most elaborate and ultimate product of the FEAR of truth, as artist-adoration and artist-intoxication in presence of the most logical of all falsifications, as the will to the inversion of truth, to untruth at any price. Perhaps there has hitherto been no more effective means of beautifying man than piety, by means of it man can become so artful, so superficial, so iridescent, and so good, that his appearance no longer offends.

60. To love mankind FOR GOD'S SAKE—this has so far been the noblest and remotest sentiment to which mankind has attained. That love to mankind, without any redeeming intention in the background, is only an ADDITIONAL folly and brutishness, that the inclination to this love has first to get its proportion, its delicacy, its gram of salt and sprinkling of ambergris from a higher inclination—whoever first perceived and "experienced" this, however his tongue may have stammered as it attempted to express such a delicate matter, let him for all time be holy and respected, as the man who has so far flown highest and gone astray in the finest fashion!

61. The philosopher, as WE free spirits understand him—as the man of the greatest

responsibility, who has the conscience for the general development of mankind,—will use religion for his disciplining and educating work, just as he will use the contemporary political and economic conditions. The selecting and disciplining influence—destructive, as well as creative and fashioning—which can be exercised by means of religion is manifold and varied, according to the sort of people placed under its spell and protection. For those who are strong and independent, destined and trained to command, in whom the judgment and skill of a ruling race is incorporated, religion is an additional means for overcoming resistance in the exercise of authority—as a bond which binds rulers and subjects in common, betraying and surrendering to the former the conscience of the latter, their inmost heart, which would fain escape obedience. And in the case of the unique natures of noble origin, if by virtue of superior spirituality they should incline to a more retired and contemplative life, reserving to themselves only the more refined forms of government (over chosen disciples or members of an order), religion itself may be used as a means for obtaining peace from the noise and trouble of managing GROSSER affairs, and for securing immunity from the UNAVOIDABLE filth of all political agitation. The Brahmins, for instance, understood this fact. With the help of a religious organization, they secured to themselves the power of nominating kings for the people, while their sentiments prompted them to keep apart and outside, as men with a higher and super-regal mission. At the same time religion gives inducement and opportunity to some of the subjects to qualify themselves for future ruling and commanding the slowly ascending ranks and classes, in which, through fortunate marriage customs, volitional power and delight in self-control are on the increase. To them religion offers sufficient incentives and temptations to aspire to higher intellectuality, and to experience the sentiments of authoritative self-control, of silence, and of solitude. Asceticism and Puritanism are almost indispensable means of educating and ennobling a race which seeks to rise above its hereditary baseness and work itself upwards to future supremacy. And finally, to ordinary men, to the majority of the people, who exist for service and general utility, and are only so far entitled to exist, religion gives invaluable contentedness with their lot and condition, peace of heart, ennoblement of obedience, additional social happiness and sympathy, with something of transfiguration and embellishment, something of justification of all the commonplaceness, all the meanness, all the semi-animal poverty of their souls. Religion, together with the religious significance of life, sheds sunshine over such perpetually harassed men, and makes even their own aspect endurable to them, it operates upon them as the Epicurean philosophy usually operates upon sufferers of a higher order, in a refreshing and refining manner, almost TURNING suffering TO ACCOUNT, and in the end even hallowing and vindicating it. There is perhaps nothing so admirable in Christianity and Buddhism as their art of teaching even the lowest to elevate themselves by piety to a seemingly higher order of things, and thereby to retain their satisfaction with the actual world in which they find it difficult enough to live—this very difficulty being necessary.

62. To be sure—to make also the bad counter-reckoning against such religions, and to bring to light their secret dangers—the cost is always excessive and terrible when religions do NOT operate as an educational and disciplinary medium in the hands of the philosopher, but rule voluntarily and PARAMOUNTLY, when they wish to be the final end, and not a means along with other means. Among men, as among all other animals, there is a surplus of defective, diseased, degenerating, infirm, and necessarily

suffering individuals; the successful cases, among men also, are always the exception; and in view of the fact that man is THE ANIMAL NOT YET PROPERLY ADAPTED TO HIS ENVIRONMENT, the rare exception. But worse still. The higher the type a man represents, the greater is the improbability that he will SUCCEED; the accidental, the law of irrationality in the general constitution of mankind, manifests itself most terribly in its destructive effect on the higher orders of men, the conditions of whose lives are delicate, diverse, and difficult to determine.

What, then, is the attitude of the two greatest religions above-mentioned to the SURPLUS of failures in life? They endeavour to preserve and keep alive whatever can be preserved; in fact, as the religions FOR SUFFERERS, they take the part of these upon principle; they are always in favour of those who suffer from life as from a disease, and they would fain treat every other experience of life as false and impossible. However highly we may esteem this indulgent and preservative care (inasmuch as in applying to others, it has applied, and applies also to the highest and usually the most suffering type of man), the hitherto PARAMOUNT religions—to give a general appreciation of them—are among the principal causes which have kept the type of "man" upon a lower level—they have preserved too much THAT WHICH SHOULD HAVE PERISHED. One has to thank them for invaluable services; and who is sufficiently rich in gratitude not to feel poor at the contemplation of all that the "spiritual men" of Christianity have done for Europe hitherto! But when they had given comfort to the sufferers, courage to the oppressed and despairing, a staff and support to the helpless, and when they had allured from society into convents and spiritual penitentiaries the broken-hearted and distracted: what else had they to do in order to work systematically in that fashion, and with a good conscience, for the preservation of all the sick and suffering, which means, in deed and in truth, to work for the DETERIORATION OF THE EUROPEAN RACE? To REVERSE all estimates of value—THAT is what they had to do! And to shatter the strong, to spoil great hopes, to cast suspicion on the delight in beauty, to break down everything autonomous, manly, conquering, and imperious—all instincts which are natural to the highest and most successful type of "man"—into uncertainty, distress of conscience, and self-destruction; forsooth, to invert all love of the earthly and of supremacy over the earth, into hatred of the earth and earthly things—THAT is the task the Church imposed on itself, and was obliged to impose, until, according to its standard of value, "unworldliness," "unsensuousness," and "higher man" fused into one sentiment. If one could observe the strangely painful, equally coarse and refined comedy of European Christianity with the derisive and impartial eye of an Epicurean god, I should think one would never cease marvelling and laughing; does it not actually seem that some single will has ruled over Europe for eighteen centuries in order to make a SUBLIME ABORTION of man? He, however, who, with opposite requirements (no longer Epicurean) and with some divine hammer in his hand, could approach this almost voluntary degeneration and stunting of mankind, as exemplified in the European Christian (Pascal, for instance), would he not have to cry aloud with rage, pity, and horror: "Oh, you bunglers, presumptuous pitiful bunglers, what have you done! Was that a work for your hands? How you have hacked and botched my finest stone! What have you presumed to do!"—I should say that Christianity has hitherto been the most portentous of presumptions. Men, not great enough, nor hard enough, to be entitled as artists to take part in fashioning MAN; men, not sufficiently strong and far-sighted to ALLOW, with sublime self-constraint, the obvious law of the thousandfold failures and perishings to prevail; men, not sufficiently noble to see the radically different grades of rank and intervals of rank that separate man from man:—SUCH men, with their "equality before God," have hitherto swayed the destiny of Europe; until at last a dwarfed, almost ludicrous species has been produced, a gregarious animal, something obliging, sickly, mediocre, the European of the present day.

European Nihilism

I. A PLAN.

1. Nihilism is at our door: whence comes this most gruesome of all guests to us?—To begin with, it is a mistake to point to "social evils," "physiological degeneration," or even to corruption as a cause of Nihilism. This is the most straightforward and most sympathetic age that ever was. Evil, whether spiritual, physical, or intellectual, is, in itself, quite unable to introduce Nihilism, i.e., the absolute repudiation of worth, purpose, desirability. These evils allow of yet other and quite different explanations. But there is one very definite explanation of the phenomena: Nihilism harbours in the heart of Christian morals.

2. The downfall of Christianity,—through its morality (which is insuperable), which finally turns against the Christian God Himself (the sense of truth, highly developed through Christianity, ultimately revolts against the falsehood and fictitiousness of all Christian interpretations of the world and its history. The recoil-stroke of "God is Truth" in the fanatical Belief, is: "All is false." Buddhism of action....).

3. Doubt in morality is the decisive factor. The downfall of the moral interpretation of the universe, which loses its raison d'être once it has tried to take flight to a Beyond, meets its end in Nihilism. "Nothing has any purpose" (the inconsistency of one explanation of the world, to which men have devoted untold energy,—gives rise to the suspicion that all explanations may perhaps be false). The Buddhistic feature: a yearning for nonentity (Indian Buddhism has no fundamentally moral development at the back of it; that is why Nihilism in its case means only morality not overcome; existence is regarded as a punishment and conceived as an error; error is thus held to be punishment—a moral valuation). Philosophical attempts to overcome the "moral God" (Hegel, Pantheism). The vanquishing of popular ideals: the wizard, the saint, the bard. Antagonism of "true" and "beautiful" and "good."

4. Against "purposelessness" on the one hand, against moral valuations on the other: how far has all science and philosophy been cultivated heretofore under the influence of moral judgments? And have we not got the additional factor—the enmity of science, into the bargain? Or the prejudice against science? Criticism of Spinoza. Christian valuations everywhere present as remnants in socialistic and positivistic systems. A criticism of Christian morality is altogether lacking.

5. The Nihilistic consequences of present natural science (along with its attempts to escape into a Beyond). Out of its practice there finally arises a certain self-annihilation, an antagonistic attitude towards itself—a sort of anti-scientificality. Since Copernicus man has been rolling away from the centre towards x.

6. The Nihilistic consequences of the political and politico-economical way of thinking, where all principles at length become tainted with the atmosphere of the platform: the breath of mediocrity, insignificance, dishonesty, etc. Nationalism. Anarchy, etc. Punishment. Everywhere the deliverer is missing, either as a class or as a single man— the justifier.

7. Nihilistic consequences of history and of the "practical historian," i.e., the romanticist. The attitude of art is quite unoriginal in modern life. Its gloominess. Goethe's so-called Olympian State.

8. Art and the preparation of Nihilism. Romanticism (the conclusion of Wagner's Ring of the Nibelung).

I.

NIHILISM.

1. NIHILISM AS AN OUTCOME OF THE VALUATIONS AND INTERPRETATIONS OF EXISTENCE WHICH HAVE PREVAILED HERETOFORE.

2.

What does Nihilism mean?—That the highest values are losing their value. There is no bourne. There is no answer to the question: "to what purpose?"

3.

Thorough Nihilism is the conviction that life is absurd, in the light of the highest values already discovered; it also includes the view that we have not the smallest right to assume the existence of transcendental objects or things in themselves, which would be either divine or morality incarnate.

This view is a result of fully developed "truthfulness": therefore a consequence of the belief in morality.

4.

What advantages did the Christian hypothesis of morality offer?

(1) It bestowed an intrinsic value upon men, which contrasted with their apparent insignificance and subordination to chance in the eternal flux of becoming and perishing.

(2) It served the purpose of God's advocates, inasmuch as it granted the world a certain perfection despite its sorrow and evil—it also granted the world that proverbial "freedom": evil seemed full of meaning.

(3) It assumed that man could have a knowledge of absolute values, and thus granted him adequate perception for the most important things.

(4) It prevented man from despising himself as man, from turning against life, and from being driven to despair by knowledge: it was a self-preservative measure.

In short: Morality was the great antidote against practical and theoretical Nihilism.

5.

But among the forces reared by morality, there was truthfulness: this in the end turns against morality, exposes the teleology of the latter, its interestedness, and now the recognition of this lie so long incorporated, from which we despaired of ever freeing ourselves, acts just like a stimulus. We perceive certain needs in ourselves, implanted during the long dynasty of the moral interpretation of life, which now seem to us to be needs of untruth: on the other hand, those very needs represent the highest values owing to which we are able to endure life. We have ceased from attaching any worth to what we know, and we dare not attach any more worth to that with which we would fain deceive ourselves—from this antagonism there results a process of dissolution.

6.

This is the antinomy: In so far as we believe in morality, we condemn existence.

7.

The highest values in the service of which man ought to live, more particularly when they oppressed and constrained him most—these social values, owing to their tone-strengthening tendencies, were built over men's heads as though they were the will of God or "reality," or the actual world, or even a hope of a world to come. Now that the lowly origin of these values has become known, the whole universe seems to have been transvalued and to have lost its significance—but this is only an intermediate stage.

8.

The consequence of Nihilism (disbelief in all values) as a result of a moral valuation:—We have grown to dislike egotism (even though we have realised the impossibility of altruism);—we have grown to dislike what is most necessary (although we have recognised the impossibility of a liberum arbitrium and of an "intelligible freedom"[1]). We perceive that we do not reach the spheres in which we have set our values—at the same time those other spheres in which we live have not thereby gained one iota in value. On the contrary, we are tired, because we have lost the main incentive to live. "All in vain hitherto!"

9.

"Pessimism as a preparatory state to Nihilism."

10.

A. Pessimism viewed as strength—in what respect? In the energy of its logic, as anarchy, Nihilism, and analysis.

B. Pessimism regarded as collapse—in what sense? In the sense of its being a softening influence, a sort of cosmopolitan befingering, a "tout comprendre," and historical spirit.

Critical tension: extremes make their appearance and become dominant.

11.

The logic of Pessimism leads finally to Nihilism: what is the force at work?—The notion that there are no values, and no purpose: the recognition of the part that moral valuations have played in all other lofty values.

 Result: moral valuations are condemnations, negations; morality is the abdication of the will to live....

[1] This is a Kantian term. Kant recognised two kinds of Freedom—the practical and the transcendental kind. The first belongs to the phenomenal, the second to the intelligible world.—TRANSLATOR'S NOTE.

12.

THE COLLAPSE OF COSMOPOLITAN VALUES.

A.

Nihilism will have to manifest itself as a psychological condition, first when we have sought in all that has happened a purpose which is not there: so that the seeker will ultimately lose courage. Nihilism is therefore the coming into consciousness of the long waste of strength, the pain of "futility," uncertainty, the lack of an opportunity to recover in some way, or to attain to a state of peace concerning anything—shame in one's own presence, as if one had cheated oneself too long.... The purpose above-mentioned might have been achieved: in the form of a "realisation" of a most high canon of morality in all worldly phenomena, the moral order of the universe; or in the form of the increase of love and harmony in the traffic of humanity; or in the nearer approach to a general condition of happiness; or even in the march towards general nonentity—any sort of goal always constitutes a purpose. The common factor to all these appearances is that something will be attained, through the process itself: and now we perceive that Becoming has been aiming at nothing, and has achieved nothing. Hence the disillusionment in regard to a so-called purpose in existence, as a cause of Nihilism; whether this be in respect of a very definite purpose, or generalised into the recognition that all the hypotheses are false which have hitherto been offered as to the object of life, and which relate to the whole of "Evolution" (man no longer an assistant in, let alone the culmination of, the evolutionary process).

Nihilism will manifest itself as a psychological condition, in the second place, when man has fixed a totality, a systematisation, even an organisation in and behind all phenomena, so that the soul thirsting for respect and admiration will wallow in the general idea of a highest ruling and administrative power (if it be the soul of a logician, the sequence of consequences and perfect reasoning will suffice to conciliate everything). A kind of unity, some form of "monism":' and as a result of this belief man becomes obsessed by a feeling of profound relativity and dependence in the presence of an All which is infinitely superior to him, a sort of divinity. "The general good exacts the surrender of the individual ..." but lo, there is no such general good! At bottom, man loses the belief in his own worth when no infinitely precious entity manifests itself through him—that is to say, he conceived such an All, in order to be able to believe in his own worth.

Nihilism, as a psychological condition, has yet a third and last form. Admitting these two points of view: that no purpose can be assigned to Becoming, and that no great entity rules behind all Becoming, in which the individual may completely lose himself as in an element of superior value; there still remains the subterfuge which would consist in condemning this whole world of Becoming as an illusion, and in discovering a world which would lie beyond it, and would be a real world. The moment, however, that man perceives that this world has been devised only for the purpose of meeting certain psychological needs, and that he has no right whatsoever to it, the final form of Nihilism comes into being, which comprises a denial of a metaphysical world, and which forbids itself all belief in a real world. From this standpoint, the reality of Becoming is the only reality that is admitted: all bypaths to back-worlds and false godheads are abandoned—but this world is no longer endured, although no one wishes to disown it.

What has actually happened? The feeling of worthlessness was realised when it was understood that neither the notion of "Purpose" nor that of "Unity" nor that of "Truth" could be made to interpret the general character of existence. Nothing is achieved or obtained thereby; the unity which intervenes in the multiplicity of events is entirely lacking: the character of existence is not "true," it is false; there is certainly no longer any reason to believe in a real world. In short, the categories, "Purpose," "Unity," "Being," by means of which we had lent some worth to life, we have once more divorced from it—and the world now appears worthless to us....

B.

Admitting that we have recognised the impossibility of interpreting world by means of these three categories, and that from this standpoint the world begins to be worthless to us; we must ask ourselves whence we derived our belief in these three categories. Let us see if it is possible to refuse to believe in them. If we can deprive them of their value, the proof that they cannot be applied to the world, is no longer a sufficient reason for depriving that world of its value.

Result: The belief in the categories of reason[2] is the cause of Nihilism—we have measured the worth of the world according to categories which can only be applied to a purely fictitious world.

Conclusion: All values with which we have tried, hitherto, to lend the world some worth, from our point of view, and with which we have therefore deprived it of all worth (once these values have been shown to be inapplicable)—all these values, are, psychologically, the results of certain views of utility, established for the purpose of maintaining and increasing the dominion of certain communities: but falsely projected into the nature of things. It is always man's exaggerated ingenuousness to regard himself as the sense and measure of all things.

[2] This probably refers to Kant's celebrated table of twelve categories. The four classes, quantity, quality, relation, and modality, are each provided with three categories.— TRANSLATOR'S NOTE.

13.

Nihilism represents an intermediary pathological condition (the vast generalisation, the conclusion that there is no purpose in anything, is pathological): whether it be that the productive forces are not yet strong enough—or that decadence still hesitates and has not yet discovered its expedients.

The conditions of this hypothesis:—That there is no truth; that there is no absolute state of affairs—no "thing-in-itself." This alone is Nihilism, and of the most extreme kind. It finds that the value of things consists precisely in the fact that these values are not real and never have been real, but that they are only a symptom of strength on the part of the valuer, a simplification serving the purposes of existence.

14.

Values and their modification are related to the growth of power of the valuer.

The measure of disbelief and of the "freedom of spirit" which is tolerated, viewed as an expression of the growth of power.

"Nihilism" viewed as the ideal of the highest spiritual power, of the over-rich life, partly destructive, partly ironical.

15.

What is belief? How is a belief born? All belief assumes that something is true.

The extremest form of Nihilism would mean that all belief—all assumption of truth— is false: because no real world is at hand. It were therefore: only an appearance seen in perspective, whose origin must be found in us (seeing that we are constantly in need of a narrower, a shortened, and simplified world).

This should be realised, that the extent to which we can, in our heart of hearts, acknowledge appearance, and the necessity of falsehood, without going to rack and ruin, is the measure of strength.

In this respect, Nihilism, in that it is the negation of a real world and of Being, might be a divine view of the world.

16.

If we are disillusioned, we have not become so in regard to life, but owing to the fact that our eyes have been opened to all kinds of "desiderata." With mocking anger we survey that which is called "Ideal": we despise ourselves only because we are unable at every moment of our lives to quell that absurd emotion which is called "Idealism." This pampering by means of ideals is stronger than the anger of the disillusioned one.

17.

To what extent does Schopenhauerian Nihilism continue to be the result of the same ideal as that which gave rise to Christian Theism? The amount of certainty concerning the most exalted desiderata, the highest values and the greatest degree of perfection, was so great, that the philosophers started out from it as if it had been an a priori and absolute fact: "God" at the head, as the given quantity—Truth. "To become like God," "to be absorbed into the Divine Being"—these were for centuries the most ingenuous and most convincing desiderata (but that which convinces is not necessarily true on that account: it is nothing more nor less than convincing. An observation for donkeys).

The granting of a personal-reality to this accretion of ideals has been unlearned: people have become atheistic. But has the ideal actually been abandoned? The latest metaphysicians, as a matter of fact, still seek their true "reality" in it—the "thing-in-itself" beside which everything else is merely appearance. Their dogma is, that because our world of appearance is so obviously not the expression of that ideal, it therefore cannot be "true"—and at bottom does not even lead back to that metaphysical world as cause. The unconditioned, in so far as it stands for that highest degree of perfection, cannot possibly be the reason of all the conditioned. Schopenhauer, who desired it otherwise, was obliged to imagine this metaphysical basis as the antithesis to the ideal, as "an evil, blind will": thus it could be "that which appears," that which manifests itself in the world of appearance. But even so, he did not give up that ideal absolute—he circumvented it....

(Kant seems to have needed the hypothesis of "intelligible freedom,"[3] in order to relieve the ens perfectum of the responsibility of having contrived this world as it is, in short, in order to explain evil: scandalous logic for a philosopher!).

[3] See Note on p. 11.

18.

The most general sign of modern times: in his own estimation, man has lost an infinite amount of dignity. For a long time he was the centre and tragic hero of life in general; then he endeavoured to demonstrate at least his relationship to the most essential and in itself most valuable side of life—as all metaphysicians do, who wish to hold fast to the dignity of man, in their belief that moral values are cardinal values. He who has let God go, clings all the more strongly to the belief in morality.

19.

Every purely moral valuation (as, for instance, the Buddhistic) terminates in Nihilism: Europe must expect the same thing! It is supposed that one can get along with a morality bereft of a religious background; but in this direction the road to Nihilism is opened. There is nothing in religion which compels us to regard ourselves as valuing creatures.

20.

The question which Nihilism puts, namely, "to what purpose?" is the outcome of a habit, hitherto, to regard the purpose as something fixed, given and exacted from outside—that is to say, by some supernatural authority. Once the belief in this has been unlearned, the force of an old habit leads to the search after another authority, which would know how to speak unconditionally, and could point to goals and missions. The authority of the conscience now takes the first place (the more morality is emancipated from theology, the more imperative does it become) as a compensation for the personal authority. Or the authority of reason. Or the gregarious instinct (the herd). Or history with its immanent spirit, which has its goal in itself, and to which one can abandon oneself. One would like to evade the will, as also the willing of a goal and the risk of setting oneself a goal. One would like to get rid of the responsibility (Fatalism would be accepted). Finally: Happiness and with a dash of humbug, the happiness of the greatest number.

It is said:—

(1) A definite goal is quite unnecessary.

(2) Such a goal cannot possibly be foreseen. Precisely now, when will in its fullest strength were necessary, it is in the weakest and most pusillanimous condition. Absolute mistrust concerning the organising power of the will.

21.

The perfect Nihilist.—The Nihilist's eye idealises in an ugly sense, and is inconstant to what it remembers: it allows its recollections to go astray and to fade, it does not protect them from that cadaverous coloration with which weakness dyes all that is distant and past. And what it does not do for itself it fails to do for the whole of mankind as well—that is to say, it allows it to drop.

22.

Nihilism. It may be two things:—

A. Nihilism as a sign of enhanced spiritual strength: active Nihilism.

B. Nihilism as a sign of the collapse and decline of spiritual strength: passive Nihilism.

23.

Nihilism, a normal condition.

It may be a sign of strength; spiritual vigour may have increased to such an extent that the goals toward which man has marched hitherto (the "convictions," articles of faith) are no longer suited to it (for a faith generally expresses the exigencies of the conditions of existence, a submission to the authority of an order of things which conduces to the prosperity, the growth and power of a living creature ...); on the other hand, a sign of insufficient strength, to fix a goal, a "wherefore," and a faith for itself.

It reaches its maximum of relative strength, as a powerful destructive force, in the form of active Nihilism.

Its opposite would be weary Nihilism, which no longer attacks: its most renowned form being Buddhism: as passive Nihilism, a sign of weakness: spiritual strength may be fatigued, exhausted, so that the goals and values which have prevailed hitherto are no longer suited to it and are no longer believed in—so that the synthesis of values and goals (upon which every strong culture stands) decomposes, and the different values contend with one another: Disintegration, then everything which is relieving, which heals, becalms, or stupefies, steps into the foreground under the cover of various disguises, either religious, moral, political or æsthetic, etc.

24.

Nihilism is not only a meditating over the "in vain!"—not only the belief that everything deserves to perish; but one actually puts one's shoulder to the plough; one destroys. This, if you will, is illogical; but the Nihilist does not believe in the necessity of being logical.... It is the condition of strong minds and wills; and to these it is impossible to be satisfied with the negation of judgment: the negation by deeds proceeds from their nature. Annihilation by the reasoning faculty seconds annihilation by the hand.

25.

Concerning the genesis of the Nihilist. The courage of all one really knows comes but late in life. It is only quite recently that I have acknowledged to myself that heretofore I have been a Nihilist from top to toe. The energy and thoroughness with which I marched forward as a Nihilist deceived me concerning this fundamental principle. When one is progressing towards a goal it seems impossible that "aimlessness per se" should be one's fundamental article of faith.

26.

The Pessimism of strong natures. The "wherefore" after a terrible struggle, even after victory. That something may exist which is a hundred times more important than the question, whether we feel well or unwell, is the fundamental instinct of all strong natures—and consequently too, whether the others feel well or unwell. In short, that we have a purpose, for which we would not even hesitate to sacrifice men, run all risks, and bend our backs to the worst: this is the great passion.

2. FURTHER CAUSES OF NIHILISM.

27.

The causes of Nihilism: (1) The higher species is lacking, i.e., the species whose inexhaustible fruitfulness and power would uphold our belief in Man (think only of what is owed to Napoleon—almost all the higher hopes of this century).

(2) The inferior species ("herd," "ass," "society") is forgetting modesty, and inflates its needs into cosmic and metaphysical values. In this way all life is vulgarised: for inasmuch as the mass of mankind rules, it tyrannises over the exceptions, so that these lose their belief in themselves and become Nihilists.

All attempts to conceive of a new species come to nothing ("romanticism," the artist, the philosopher; against Carlyle's attempt to lend them the highest moral values).

The result is that higher types are resisted.

The downfall and insecurity of all higher types. The struggle against genius ("popular poetry," etc.). Sympathy with the lowly and the suffering as a standard for the elevation of the soul.

The philosopher is lacking, the interpreter of deeds, and not alone he who poetises them.

28.

Imperfect Nihilism—its forms: we are now surrounded by them.

All attempts made to escape Nihilism, which do not consist in transvaluing the values that have prevailed hitherto, only make the matter worse; they complicate the problem.

29.

The varieties of self-stupefaction. In one's heart of hearts, not to know, whither? Emptiness. The attempt to rise superior to it all by means of emotional intoxication: emotional intoxication in the form of music, in the form of cruelty in the tragic joy over the ruin of the noblest, and in the form of blind, gushing enthusiasm over individual men or distinct periods (in the form of hatred, etc.). The attempt to work blindly, like a scientific instrument; to keep an eye on the many small joys, like an investigator, for instance (modesty towards oneself); the mysticism of the voluptuous joy of eternal emptiness; art "for art's sake" ("le fait"), "immaculate investigation," in the form of narcotics against the disgust of oneself; any kind of incessant work, any kind of small foolish fanaticism; the medley of all means, illness as the result of general profligacy (dissipation kills pleasure).

(1) As a result, feeble will-power.

(2) Excessive pride and the humiliation of petty weakness felt as a contrast.

30.

The time is coming when we shall have to pay for having been Christians for two thousand years: we are losing the equilibrium which enables us to live—for a long while we shall not know in what direction we are travelling. We are hurling ourselves headlong into the opposite valuations, with that degree of energy which could only have been engendered in man by an overvaluation of himself.

Now, everything is false from the root, words and nothing but words, confused, feeble, or over-strained.

(a) There is a seeking after a sort of earthly solution of the problem of life, but in the same sense as that of the final triumph of truth, love, justice (socialism: "equality of persons").

(b) There is also an attempt to hold fast to the moral ideal (with altruism, self-sacrifice, and the denial of the will, in the front rank).

(c) There is even an attempt to hold fast to a "Beyond": were it only as an antilogical x; but it is forthwith interpreted in such a way that a kind of metaphysical solace, after the old style, may be derived from it.

(d) There is an attempt to read the phenomena of life in such a way as to arrive at the divine guidance of old, with its powers of rewarding, punishing, educating, and of generally conducing to a something better in the order of things.

(e) People once more believe in good and evil; so that the victory of the good and the annihilation of the evil is regarded as a duty (this is English, and is typical of that blockhead, John Stuart Mill).

(f) The contempt felt for "naturalness," for the desires and for the ego: the attempt to regard even the highest intellectuality of art as a result of an impersonal and disinterested attitude.

(g) The Church is still allowed to meddle in all the essential occurrences and incidents in the life of the individual, with a view to consecrating it and giving it a loftier meaning: we still have the "Christian State" and the "Christian marriage."

31.

There have been more thoughtful and more destructively thoughtful[4] times than ours: times like those in which Buddha appeared, for instance, in which the people themselves, after centuries of sectarian quarrels, had sunk so deeply into the abyss of philosophical dogmas, as, from time to time, European people have done in regard to the fine points of religious dogma. "Literature" and the press would be the last things to seduce one to any high opinion of the spirit of our times: the millions of Spiritists, and a Christianity with gymnastic exercises of that ghastly ugliness which is characteristic of all English inventions, throw more light on the subject.

European Pessimism is still in its infancy—a fact which argues against it: it has not yet attained to that prodigious and yearning fixity of sight to which it attained in India once upon a time, and in which nonentity is reflected; there is still too much of the "ready-made," and not enough of the "evolved" in its constitution, too much learned and poetic Pessimism; I mean that a good deal of it has been discovered, invented, and "created," but not caused.

[4] zerdachtere.

32.

Criticism of the Pessimism which has prevailed hitherto. The want of the eudæmonological standpoint, as a last abbreviation of the question: what is the purpose of it all? The reduction of gloom.

Our Pessimism: the world has not the value which we believed it to have,—our faith itself has so increased our instinct for research that we are compelled to say this to-day. In the first place, it seems of less value: at first it is felt to be of less value,—only in this sense are we pessimists,—that is to say, with the will to acknowledge this transvaluation without reserve, and no longer, as heretofore, to deceive ourselves and chant the old old story.

It is precisely in this way that we find the pathos which urges us to seek for new values. In short: the world might have far more value than we thought—we must get behind the naïveté of our ideals, for it is possible that, in our conscious effort to give it the highest interpretation, we have not bestowed even a moderately just value upon it.

What has been deified? The valuing instinct inside the community (that which enabled it to survive).

What has been calumniated? That which has tended to separate higher men from their inferiors, the instincts which cleave gulfs and build barriers.

33.

Causes effecting the rise of Pessimism:—

(1) The most powerful instincts and those which promised most for the future have hitherto been calumniated, so that life has a curse upon it.

(2) The growing bravery and the more daring mistrust on the part of man have led him to discover the fact that these instincts cannot be cut adrift from life, and thus he turns to embrace life.

(3) Only the most mediocre, who are not conscious of this conflict, prosper; the higher species fail, and as an example of degeneration tend to dispose all hearts against them—on the other hand, there is some indignation caused by the mediocre positing themselves as the end and meaning of all things. No one can any longer reply to the question: "Why?"

(4) Belittlement, susceptibility to pain, unrest, haste, and confusion are steadily increasing—the materialisation of all these tendencies, which is called "civilisation," becomes every day more simple, with the result that, in the face of the monstrous machine, the individual despairs and surrenders.

34.

Modern Pessimism is an expression of the uselessness only of the modern world, not of the world and existence as such.

35.

The "preponderance of pain over pleasure" or the reverse (Hedonism); both of these doctrines are already signposts to Nihilism....

For here, in both cases, no other final purpose is sought than the phenomenon pleasure or pain.

But only a man who no longer dares to posit a will, a purpose, and a final goal can speak in this way—according to every healthy type of man, the worth of life is certainly not measured by the standard of these secondary things. And a preponderance of pain would be possible and, in spite of it, a mighty will, a saying of yea to life, and a holding of this preponderance for necessary.

"Life is not worth living"; "Resignation"; "what is the good of tears?"—this is a feeble and sentimental attitude of mind. "Un monstre gai vaut mieux qu'un sentimental ennuyeux."

36.

The philosophie Nihilist is convinced that all phenomena are without sense and are in vain, and that there ought to be no such thing as Being without sense and in vain. But whence comes this "There ought not to be?"—whence this "sense" and this standard? At bottom the Nihilist supposes that the sight of such a desolate, useless Being is unsatisfying to the philosopher, and fills him with desolation and despair. This aspect of the case is opposed to our subtle sensibilities as a philosopher. It leads to the absurd conclusion that the character of existence must perforce afford pleasure to the philosopher if it is to have any right to subsist.

Now it is easy to understand that happiness and unhappiness, within the phenomena of this world, can only serve the purpose of means: the question yet remaining to be answered is, whether it will ever be possible for us to perceive the "object" and "purpose" of life—whether the problem of purposelessness or the reverse is not quite beyond our ken.

37.

The development of Nihilism out of Pessimism. The denaturalisation of Values. Scholasticism of values. The values isolated, idealistic, instead of ruling and leading action, turn against it and condemn it.

Opposites introduced in the place of natural gradations and ranks. Hatred of the order of rank. Opposites are compatible with a plebeian age, because they are more easy to grasp.

The rejected world is opposed to an artificially constructed "true and valuable" one. At last we discover out of what material the "true" world was built; all that remains, now, is the rejected world, and to the account of our reasons for rejecting it we place our greatest disillusionment.

At this point Nihilism is reached; the directing values have been retained—nothing more!

This gives rise to the problem of strength and weakness:—

(1) The weak fall to pieces upon it;

(2) The strong destroy what does not fall to pieces of its own accord;

(3) The strongest overcome the directing values.

The whole condition of affairs produces the tragic age.

3. THE NIHILISTIC MOVEMENT AS AN EXPRESSION OF DECADENCE.

38.

Just lately an accidental and in every way inappropriate term has been very much misused: everywhere people are speaking of "Pessimism," and there is a fight around the question (to which some replies must be forthcoming): which is right—Pessimism or Optimism?

People have not yet seen what is so terribly-obvious—namely, that Pessimism is not a problem but a symptom,—that the term ought to be replaced by "Nihilism,"—that the question, "to be or not to be," is itself an illness, a sign of degeneracy, an idiosyncrasy.

The Nihilistic movement is only an expression of physiological decadence.

39.

To be understood:—That every kind of decline and tendency to sickness has incessantly been at work in helping to create general evaluations: that in those valuations which now dominate, decadence has even begun to preponderate, that we have not only to combat the conditions which present misery and degeneration have brought into being; but that all decadence, previous to that of our own times, has been transmitted and has therefore remained an active force amongst us. A universal departure of this kind, on the part of man, from his fundamental instincts, such universal decadence of the valuing judgment, is the note of interrogation par excellence, the real riddle, which the animal "man" sets to all philosophers.

40.

The notion "decadence":—Decay, decline, and waste, are, per se, in no way open to objection;they are the natural consequences of life and vital growth. The phenomenon of decadence is just as necessary to life as advance or progress is: we are not in a position which enables us to suppress it. On the contrary, reason would have it retain its rights.

It is disgraceful on the part of socialist-theorists to argue that circumstances and social combinations could be devised which would put an end to all vice, illness, crime, prostitution, and poverty.... But that is tantamount to condemning Life ... a society is not at liberty to remain young. And even in its prime it must bring forth ordure and decaying matter. The more energetically and daringly it advances, the richer will it be in failures and in deformities, and the nearer it will be to its fall. Age is not deferred by means of institutions. Nor is illness. Nor is vice.

41.

Fundamental aspect of the nature of decadence: what has heretofore been regarded as its causes are its effects.

In this way, the whole perspective of the problems of morality is altered.

All the struggle of morals against vice, luxury, crime, and even against illness, seems a naïveté, a superfluous effort: there is no such thing as "improvement" (a word against repentance).

Decadence itself is not a thing that can be withstood: it is absolutely necessary and is proper to all ages and all peoples. That which must be withstood, and by all means in our power, is the spreading of the contagion among the sound parts of the organism.

Is that done? The very reverse is done. It is precisely on this account that one makes a stand on behalf of humanity.

How do the highest values created hitherto stand in relation to this fundamental question in biology? Philosophy, religion, morality, art, etc.

(The remedy: militarism, for instance, from Napoleon onwards, who regarded civilisation as his natural enemy.)

42.

All those things which heretofore have been regarded as the causes of degeneration, are really its effects.

But those things also which have been regarded as the remedies of degeneration are only palliatives of certain effects thereof: the "cured" are types of the degenerate.

The results of decadence: vice—viciousness; illness—sickliness; crime—criminality; celibacy—sterility; hysteria—the weakness of the will; alcoholism; pessimism, anarchy; debauchery (also of the spirit). The calumniators, underminers, sceptics, and destroyers.

43.

Concerning the notion "decadence." (1) Scepticism is a result of decadence: just as spiritual debauchery is.

 (2) Moral corruption is a result of decadence (the weakness of the will and the need of strong stimulants).

(3) Remedies, whether psychological or moral, do not alter the march of decadence, they do not arrest anything; physiologically they do not count.

A peep into the enormous futility of these pretentious "reactions"; they are forms of anæsthetising oneself against certain fatal symptoms resulting from the prevailing condition of things; they do not eradicate the morbid element; they are often heroic attempts to cancel the decadent man, to allow only a minimum of his deleterious influence to survive.

(4) Nihilism is not a cause, but only the rationale of decadence.

(5) The "good" and the "bad" are no more than two types of decadence: they come together in all its fundamental phenomena.

(6) The social problem is a result of decadence.

(7) Illnesses, more particularly those attacking the nerves and the head, are signs that the defensive strength of strong nature is lacking; a proof of this is that irritability which causes pleasure and pain to be regarded as problems of the first order.

44.

The most common types of decadence: (1) In the belief that they are remedies, cures are chosen which only precipitate exhaustion;—this is the case with Christianity (to point to the most egregious example of mistaken instinct);—this is also the case with "progress."

(2) The power of resisting stimuli is on the wane—chance rules supreme: events are inflated and drawn out until they appear monstrous ... a suppression of the "personality," a disintegration of the will; in this regard we may mention a whole class of morality, the altruistic, that which is incessantly preaching pity, and whose most essential feature

is the weakness of the personality, so that it rings in unison, and, like an over-sensitive string, does not cease from vibrating ... extreme irritability....

(3) Cause and effect are confounded: decadence is not understood as physiological, and its results are taken to be the causes of the general indisposition:—this applies to all religious morality.

(4) A state of affairs is desired in which suffering shall cease; life is actually considered the cause of all ills—unconscious and insensitive states (sleep and syncope) are held in incomparably higher esteem than the conscious states; hence a method of life.

45.

Concerning the hygiene of the "weak." All that is done in weakness ends in failure. Moral: do nothing. The worst of it is, that precisely the strength required in order to stop action, and to cease from reacting, is most seriously diseased under the influence of weakness: that one never reacts more promptly or more blindly than when one should not react at all.

The strength of a character is shown by the ability to delay and postpone reaction: a certain ἀδιαφορία is just as proper to it, as involuntariness in recoiling, suddenness and lack of restraint in "action," are proper to weakness. The will is weak: and the recipe for preventing foolish acts would be: to have a strong will and to do nothing—contradiction. A sort of self-destruction, the instinct of self-preservation is compromised.... The weak man injures himself.... That is the decadent type.

As a matter of fact, we meet with a vast amount of thought concerning the means wherewith impassibility may be induced. To this extent, the instincts are on the right scent; for to do nothing is more useful than to do something....

All the practices of private orders, of solitary philosophers, and of fakirs, are suggested by a correct consideration of the fact, that a certain kind of man is most useful to himself when he hinders his own action as much as possible.

Relieving measures: absolute obedience, mechanical activity, total isolation from men and things that might exact immediate decisions and actions.

46.

Weakness of Will: this is a fable that can lead astray. For there is no will, consequently neither a strong nor a weak one. The multiplicity and disintegration of the instincts, the want of system in their relationship, constitute what is known as a "weak will"; their co-ordination, under the government of one individual among them, results in a "strong will"—in the first case vacillation and a lack of equilibrium is noticeable: in the second, precision and definite direction.

47.

That which is inherited is not illness, but a predisposition to illness: a lack of the powers of resistance against injurious external influences, etc. etc, broken powers of resistance; expressed morally: resignation and humility in the presence of the enemy.

I have often wondered whether it would not be possible to class all the highest values of the philosophies, moralities, and religions which have been devised hitherto, with the values of the feeble, the insane and the neurasthenic in a milder form, they present the same evils.

The value of all morbid conditions consists in the fact that they magnify certain normal phenomena which are difficult to discern in normal conditions....

Health and illness are not essentially different, as the ancient doctors believed and as a few practitioners still believe to-day. They cannot be imagined as two distinct principles or entities which fight for the living organism and make it their battlefield. That is nonsense and mere idle gossip, which no longer holds water. As a matter of fact, there is only a difference of degree between these two living conditions: exaggeration, want of proportion, want of harmony among the normal phenomena, constitute the morbid state (Claude Bernard).

Just as "evil" may be regarded as exaggeration, discord, and want of proportion, so can "good" be regarded as a sort of protective diet against the danger of exaggeration, discord, and want of proportion.

Hereditary weakness as a dominant feeling: the cause of the prevailing values.

N.B.—Weakness is in demand—why?... mostly because people cannot be anything else than weak.

Weakening considered a duty: The weakening of the desires, of the feelings of pleasure and of pain, of the will to power, of the will to pride, to property and to more property; weakening in the form of humility; weakening in the form of a belief; weakening in the form of repugnance and shame in the presence of all that is natural—in the form of a denial of life, in the form of illness and chronic feebleness; weakening in the form of a refusal to take revenge, to offer resistance, to become an enemy, and to show anger.

Blunders in the treatment: there is no attempt at combating weakness by means of any fortifying system; but by a sort of justification consisting of moralising; i.e., by means of interpretation.

Two totally different conditions are confused: for instance, the repose of strength, which is essentially abstinence from reaction (the prototype of the gods whom nothing moves), and the peace of exhaustion, rigidity to the point of anæsthesia. All these philosophic and ascetic modes of procedure aspire to the second state, but actually pretend to attain to the first ... for they ascribe to the condition they have reached the attributes that would be in keeping only with a divine state.

48.

The most dangerous misunderstanding.—There is one concept which apparently allows of no confusion or ambiguity, and that is the concept exhaustion. Exhaustion may be acquired or inherited—in any case it alters the aspect and value of things.

Unlike him who involuntarily gives of the superabundance which he both feels and represents, to the things about him, and who sees them fuller, mightier, and more pregnant with promises,—who, in fact, can bestow,—the exhausted one belittles and disfigures everything he sees—he impoverishes its worth: he is detrimental....

No mistake seems possible in this matter: and yet history discloses the terrible fact, that the exhausted have always been confounded with those with the most abundant resources, and the latter with the most detrimental.

The pauper in vitality, the feeble one, impoverishes even life: the wealthy man, in vital powers, enriches it. The first is the parasite of the second: the second is a bestower of his abundance. How is confusion possible?

When he who was exhausted came forth with the bearing of a very active and energetic man (when degeneration implied a certain excess of spiritual and nervous discharge), he was mistaken for the wealthy man. He inspired terror. The cult of the madman is also always the cult of him who is rich in vitality, and who is a powerful man. The fanatic, the one possessed, the religious epileptic, all eccentric creatures have been regarded as the highest types of power: as divine.

This kind of strength which inspires terror seemed to be, above all, divine: this was the starting-point of authority; here wisdom was interpreted, hearkened to, and sought. Out of this there was developed, everywhere almost, a will to "deify," i.e., to a typical degeneration of spirit, body, and nerves: an attempt to discover the road to this higher form of being. To make oneself ill or mad, to provoke the symptoms of serious disorder—was called getting stronger, becoming more superhuman, more terrible and more wise. People thought they would thus attain to such wealth of power, that they would be able to dispense it. Wheresoever there have been prayers, some one has been sought who had something to give away.

What led astray, here, was the experience of intoxication. This increases the feeling of power to the highest degree, therefore, to the mind of the ingenuous, it is power. On the highest altar of power the most intoxicated man must stand, the ecstatic. (There are two causes of intoxication: superabundant life, and a condition of morbid nutrition of the brain.)

49.

Acquired, not inherited exhaustion: (1) inadequate nourishment, often the result of ignorance concerning diet, as, for instance, in the case of scholars; (2) erotic precocity: the damnation more especially of the youth of France—Parisian youths, above all, who are already dirtied and ruined when they step out of their lycées into the world, and who cannot break the chains of despicable tendencies; ironical and scornful towards themselves—galley-slaves despite all their refinement (moreover, in the majority of cases, already a symptom of racial and family decadence, as all hypersensitiveness is; and examples of the infection of environment: to be influenced by one's environment is also a sign of decadence); (3) alcoholism, not the instinct but the habit, foolish imitation, the cowardly or vain adaptation to a ruling fashion. What a blessing a Jew is among Germans! See the obtuseness, the flaxen head, the blue eye, and the lack of intellect in the face, the language, and the bearing; the lazy habit of stretching the limbs, and the need of repose among Germans—a need which is not the result of overwork, but of the disgusting excitation and over-excitation caused by alcohol.

50.

A theory of exhaustion.—Vice, the insane (also artists), the criminals, the anarchists—these are not the oppressed classes, but the outcasts of the community of all classes hitherto.

Seeing that all our classes are permeated by these elements, we have grasped the fact that modern society is not a "society" or a "body," but a diseased agglomeration of Chandala,—a society which no longer has the strength even to excrete.

To what extent living together for centuries has very much deepened sickliness:

modern virtuee }

 modern intellect } as forms of disease.

 modern science }

51.

The state of corruption.—The interrelation of all forms of corruption should be understood, and the Christian form (Pascal as the type), as also the socialistic and communistic (a result of the Christian), should not be overlooked (from the standpoint of natural science, the highest conception of society according to socialists, is the lowest in the order of rank among societies); the "Beyond" —corruption: as though outside the real world of Becoming there were a world of Being.

Here there must be no compromise, but selection, annihilation, and war—the Christian Nihilistic standard of value must be withdrawn from all things and attacked beneath every disguise ... for instance, from modern sociology, music, and Pessimism (all forms of the Christian ideal of values).

Either one thing or the other is true—that is to say, tending to elevate the type man....

The priest, the shepherd of souls, should be looked upon as a form of life which must be suppressed. All education, hitherto, has been helpless, adrift, without ballast, and afflicted with the contradiction of values.

Either one thing or the other is true—that is to say, tending to elevate the type man....

The priest, the shepherd of souls, should be looked upon as a form of life which must be suppressed. All education, hitherto, has been helpless, adrift, without ballast, and afflicted with the contradiction of values.

52.

If Nature have no pity on the degenerate, it is not therefore immoral: the growth of physiological and moral evils in the human race, is rather the result of morbid and unnatural morality. The sensitiveness of the majority of men is both morbid and unnatural.

Why is it that mankind is corrupt in a moral and physiological respect? The body degenerates if one organ is unsound. The right of altruism cannot be traced to physiology, neither can the right to help and to the equality of fate: these are all premiums for degenerates and failures.

There can be no solidarity in a society containing unfruitful, unproductive, and destructive members, who, by the bye, are bound to have offspring even more degenerate than they are themselves.

53.

Decadence exercises a profound and perfectly unconscious influence, even over the ideals of science: all our sociology is a proof of this proposition, and it has yet to be reproached with the fact that it has only the experience of society in the process of decay, and inevitably takes its own decaying instincts as the basis of sociological judgment.

The declining vitality of modern Europe formulates its social ideals in its decaying instincts: and these ideals are all so like those of old and effete races, that they might be mistaken for one another.

The gregarious instinct, then,—now a sovereign power,—is something totally different from the instinct of an aristocratic society: and the value of the sum depends upon the value of the units constituting it.... The whole of our sociology knows no other instinct than that of the herd, i.e., of a multitude of mere ciphers—of which every cipher has "equal rights," and where it is a virtue to be——naught....

The valuation with which the various forms of society are judged to-day is absolutely the same with that which assigns a higher place to peace than to war: but this principle is contrary to the teaching of biology, and is itself a mere outcome of decadent life. Life is a result of war, society is a means to war.... Mr. Herbert Spencer was a decadent in biology, as also in morality (he regarded the triumph of altruism as a desideratum!!!).

54.

After thousands of years of error and confusion, it is my good fortune to have rediscovered the road which leads to a Yea and to a Nay.

I teach people to say Nay in the face of all that makes for weakness and exhaustion.

I teach people to say Yea in the face of all that makes for strength, that preserves strength, and justifies the feeling of strength.

Up to the present, neither the one nor the other has been taught; but rather virtue, disinterestedness, pity, and even the negation of life. All these are values proceeding from exhausted people.

After having pondered over the physiology of exhaustion for some time, I was led to the question: to what extent the judgments of exhausted people had percolated into the world of values.

The result at which I arrived was as startling as it could possibly be—even for one like myself who was already at home in many a strange world: I found that all prevailing values—that is to say, all those which had gained ascendancy over humanity, or at least over its tamer portions, could be traced back to the judgment of exhausted people.

Under the cover of the holiest names, I found the most destructive tendencies; people had actually given the name "God" to all that renders weak, teaches weakness, and infects with weakness.... I found that the "good man" was a form of self-affirmation on the part of decadence.

That virtue which Schopenhauer still proclaimed as superior to all, and as the most fundamental of all virtues; even that same pity I recognised as more dangerous than any vice. Deliberately to thwart the law of selection among species, and their natural means of purging their stock of degenerate members—this, up to my time, had been the greatest of all virtues....

One should do honour to the fatality which says to the feeble: "perish!"

The opposing of this fatality, the botching of mankind and the allowing of it to putrefy, was given the name "God" One shall not take the name of the Lord one's God in vain....

The race is corrupted—not by its vices, but by its ignorance: it is corrupted because it has not recognised exhaustion as exhaustion: physiological misunderstandings are the cause of all evil.

Virtue is our greatest misunderstanding.

Problem: how were the exhausted able to make the laws of values? In other words, how did they who are the last, come to power?... How did the instincts of the animal man ever get to stand on their heads?...

4. THE CRISIS: NIHILISM AND THE IDEA OF RECURRENCE.

55.

Extreme positions are not relieved by more moderate ones, but by extreme opposite positions. And thus the belief in the utter immorality of nature, and in the absence of all purpose and sense, are psychologically necessary attitudes when the belief in God and in an essentially moral order of things is no longer tenable.

Nihilism now appears, not because the sorrows of existence are greater than they were formerly, but because, in a general way, people have grown suspicious of the "meaning" which might be given to evil and even to existence. One interpretation has been overthrown: but since it was held to be the interpretation, it seems as though there were no meaning in existence at all, as though everything were in vain.

***

It yet remains to be shown that this "in vain!" is the character of present Nihilism. The mistrust of our former valuations has increased to such an extent that it has led to the question: "are not all 'values' merely allurements prolonging the duration of the comedy, without, however, bringing the unravelling any closer?" The "long period of time" which has culminated in an "in vain," without either goal or purpose, is the most paralysing of thoughts, more particularly when one sees that one is duped without, however, being able to resist being duped.

***

Let us imagine this thought in its worst form: existence, as it is, without either a purpose or a goal, but inevitably recurring, without an end in nonentity: "Eternal Recurrence."

This is the extremest form of Nihilism: nothing (purposelessness) eternal!

European form of Buddhism: the energy of knowledge and of strength drives us to such a belief. It is the most scientific of all hypotheses. We deny final purposes. If existence had a final purpose it would have reached it.

***

It should be understood that what is being aimed at, here, is a contradiction of Pantheism: for "everything perfect, divine, eternal," also leads to the belief in Eternal Recurrence. Question: has this pantheistic and affirmative attitude to all things also been made possible by morality? At bottom only the moral God has been overcome. Is there any sense in imagining a God "beyond good and evil"? Would Pantheism in this sense be possible? Do we withdraw the idea of purpose from the process, and affirm the process notwithstanding? This were so if, within that process, something were attained every moment—and always the same thing. Spinoza won an affirmative position of this sort, in the sense that every moment, according to him, has a logical necessity: and he triumphed by means of his fundamentally logical instinct over a like conformation of the world.

***

But his case is exceptional. If every fundamental trait of character, which lies beneath every act, and which finds expression in every act, were recognised by the individual as his fundamental trait of character, this individual would be driven to regard every moment of his existence in general, triumphantly as good. It would simply be necessary for that fundamental trait of character to be felt in oneself as something good, valuable, and pleasurable.

***

Now, in the case of those men and classes of men who were treated with violence and oppressed by their fellows, morality saved life from despair and from the leap into nonentity:. for impotence in relation to mankind and not in relation to Nature is what generates the most desperate bitterness towards existence. Morality treated the powerful, the violent, and the "masters" in general, as enemies against whom the common man must be protected—that is to say, emboldened, strengthened. Morality has therefore always taught the most profound hatred and contempt of the fundamental trait of character of all rulers—i.e., their Will to Power. To suppress, to deny, and to decompose this morality, would mean to regard this most thoroughly detested instinct with the reverse of the old feeling and valuation. If the sufferer and the oppressed man were to lose his belief in his right to contemn the Will to Power, his position would be desperate. This would be so if the trait above-mentioned were essential to life, in which case it would follow that even that will to morality was only a cloak to this "Will to Power," as are also even that hatred and contempt. The oppressed man would then perceive that he stands on the same platform with the oppressor, and that he has no individual privilege, nor any higher rank than the latter.

***

On the contrary! There is nothing on earth which can have any value, if it have not a modicum of power—granted, of course, that life itself is the Will to Power. Morality protected the botched and bungled against Nihilism, in that it gave every one of them infinite worth, metaphysical worth, and classed them altogether in one order which did not correspond with that of worldly power and order of rank: it taught submission, humility, etc. Admitting that the belief in this morality be destroyed, the botched and the bungled would no longer have any comfort, and would perish.

This perishing seems like self-annihilation, like an instinctive selection of that which must be destroyed. The symptoms of this self-destruction of the botched and the bungled: self-vivisection, poisoning, intoxication, romanticism, and, above all, the instinctive constraint to acts whereby the powerful are made into mortal enemies (training, so to speak, one's own hangmen), the will to destruction as the will of a still deeper instinct—of the instinct of self-destruction, of the Will to Nonentity.

***

Nihilism is a sign that the botched and bungled in order to be destroyed, that, having been deprived of morality, they no longer have any reason to "resign themselves," that they take up their stand on the territory of the opposite principle, and will also exercise power themselves, by compelling the powerful to become their hangmen. This is the European form of Buddhism, that active negation, after all existence has lost its meaning.

***

It must not be supposed that "poverty" has grown more acute, on the contrary! "God, morality, resignation" were remedies in the very deepest stages of misery: active Nihilism made its appearance in circumstances which were relatively much more favourable. The fact, alone, that morality is regarded as overcome, presupposes a certain degree of intellectual culture; while this very culture, for its part, bears evidence to a certain relative well-being. A certain intellectual fatigue, brought on by the long struggle concerning philosophical opinions, and carried to hopeless scepticism against philosophy, shows moreover that the level of these Nihilists is by no means a low one. Only think of the conditions in which Buddha appeared! The teaching of the eternal recurrence would have learned principles to go upon (just as Buddha's teaching, for instance, had the notion of causality, etc.).

***

What do we mean to-day by the words "botched and bungled"? In the first place, they are used physiologically and not politically. The unhealthiest kind of man all over Europe (in all classes) is the soil out of which Nihilism grows: this species of man will regard eternal recurrence as damnation—once he is bitten by the thought, he can no longer recoil before any action. He would not extirpate passively, but would cause everything to be extirpated which is meaningless and without a goal to this extent; although it is only a spasm, or sort of blind rage in the presence of the fact that everything has existed again and again for an eternity—even this period of Nihilism and destruction. The value of such a crisis is that it purifies, that it unites similar elements, and makes them mutually destructive, that it assigns common duties to men of opposite persuasions, and brings the weaker and more uncertain among them to the light, thus taking the first step towards a new order of rank among forces from the standpoint of health: recognising commanders as commanders, subordinates as subordinates. Naturally irrespective of all the present forms of society.

***

What class of men will prove they are strongest in this new order of things? The most moderate—they who do not require any extreme forms of belief, they who not only admit of, but actually like, a certain modicum of chance and nonsense; they who can think of man with a very moderate view of his value, without becoming weak and small on that account; the most rich in health, who are able to withstand a maximum amount of sorrow, and who are therefore not so very much afraid of sorrow—men who are certain of their power, and who represent with conscious pride the state of strength to which man has attained.

***

How could such a man think of Eternal Recurrence?

56.

The Periods of European Nihilism.

The Period of Obscurity: all kinds of groping measures devised to preserve old institutions and not to arrest the progress of new ones.

The Period of Light: men see that old and new are fundamental contraries; that the old values are born of descending life, and that the new ones are born of ascending life— that all old ideals are unfriendly to life (born of decadence and determining it, however much they may be decked out in the Sunday finery of morality). We understand the old, but are far from being sufficiently strong for the new.

The Periods of the Three Great Passions: contempt, pity, destruction.

The Periods of Catastrophes: the rise of a teaching which will sift mankind ... which drives the weak to some decision and the strong also.

II.

CONCERNING THE HISTORY OF EUROPEAN NIHILISM.

(A) MODERN GLOOMINESS.

57.

My friends, we had a hard time as youths; we even suffered from youth itself as though it were a serious disease. This is owing to the age in which we were born—an age of enormous internal decay and disintegration which, with all its weakness and even with the best of its strength, is opposed to the spirit of youth. Disintegration—that is to say, uncertainty—is peculiar to this age: nothing stands on solid ground or on a sound faith. People live for the morrow, because the day-after-to-morrow is doubtful. All our road is slippery and dangerous, while the ice which still bears us has grown unconscionably thin: we all feel the mild and gruesome breath of the thaw-wind—soon, where we are walking, no one will any longer be able to stand!

58.

If this is not an age of decay and of diminishing vitality, it is at least one of indiscriminate and arbitrary experimentalising—and it is probable that out of an excess of abortive experiments there has grown this general impression, as of decay: and perhaps decay itself.

59.

Concerning the history of modern gloominess.

The state-nomads (officials, etc.): "homeless"—.

The break-up of the family.

The "good man" as a symptom of exhaustion.

Justice as Will to Power (Rearing).

Lewdness and neurosis.

Black music: whither has real music gone?

The anarchist.

Contempt of man, loathing.

Most profound distinction: whether hunger or satiety is creative? The first creates the Ideals of Romanticism.

Northern unnaturalness.

The need of Alcohol: the "need" of the working classes.

Philosophical Nihilism.

60.

The slow advance and rise of the middle and lower classes (including the lower kind of spirit and body), which was already well under way before the French Revolution, and would have made the same progress forward without the latter,—in short, then, the preponderance of the herd over all herdsmen and bell-wethers,—brings in its train:—

(1) Gloominess of spirit (the juxtaposition of a stoical and a frivolous appearance of happiness, peculiar to noble cultures, is on the decline; much suffering is allowed to be seen and heard which formerly was borne in concealment);

(2) Moral hypocrisy (a way of distinguishing oneself through morality, but by means of the values of the herd: pity, solicitude, moderation; and not by means of those virtues which are recognised and honoured outside the herd's sphere of power);

(3) A really large amount of sympathy with both pain and joy (a feeling of pleasure resulting from being herded together, which is peculiar to all gregarious animals— "public spirit," "patriotism," everything, in fact, which is apart from the individual).

61.

Our age, with its indiscriminate endeavours to mitigate distress, to honour it, and to wage war in advance with unpleasant possibilities, is an age of the poor. Our "rich people"—they are the poorest! The real purpose of all wealth has been forgotten.

62.

Criticism of modern man:—"the good man," but corrupted and misled by bad institutions (tyrants and priests);—reason elevated to a position of authority;—history is regarded as the surmounting of errors;—the future is regarded as progress;—the Christian state ("God of the armies");—Christian sexual intercourse (as marriage);— the realm of "justice" (the cult of "mankind");—"freedom."

The romantic attitudes of the modern man;—the noble man (Byron, Victor Hugo, George Sand);—taking the part of the oppressed and the bungled and the botched: motto for historians and romancers;—the Stoics of duty;—disinterestedness regarded as art and as knowledge;—altruism as the most mendacious form of egoism (utilitarianism), the most sentimental form of egoism.

All this savours of the eighteenth century. But it had other qualities which were not inherited, namely, a certain insouciance, cheerfulness, elegance, spiritual clearness. The spiritual tempo has altered; the pleasure which was begotten by spiritual refinement and clearness has given room to the pleasure of colour, harmony, mass, reality, etc. etc. Sensuality in spiritual things. In short, it is the eighteenth century of Rousseau.

63.

Taken all in all, a considerable amount of humanity has been attained by our men of to-day. That we feel this is in itself a proof of the fact that we have become so sensitive in regard to small cases of distress, that we somewhat unjustly overlook what has been achieved.

Here we must make allowances for the fact that a great deal of decadence is rife, and that, through such eyes, our world must appear bad and wretched. But these eyes have always seen in the same way, in all ages.

(1) A certain hypersensitiveness, even in morality.

(2) The quantum of bitterness and gloominess, which pessimism bears with it in its judgments—both together have helped to bring about the preponderance of the other and opposite point of view, that things are not well with our morality.

The fact of credit, of the commerce of the world, and the means of traffic—are expressions of an extraordinarily mild trustfulness in men.... To that may also be added—

(3) The deliverance of science from moral and religious prejudices: a very good sign, though for the most part misunderstood.

In my own way, I am attempting a justification of history.

64.

The second appearance of Buddhism.—Its precursory signs: the increase of pity. Spiritual exhaustion. The reduction of all problems to the question of pleasure and pain. The glory of war which calls forth a counter-stroke. Just as the sharp demarcation of nations generates a counter-movement in the form of the most hearty "Fraternity." The fact that it is impossible for religion to carry on its work any longer with dogma and fables.

The catastrophe of Nihilism will put an end to all this Buddhistic culture.

65.

That which is most sorely afflicted to-day is the instinct and will of tradition: all institutions which owe their origin to this instinct, are opposed to the tastes of the age.... At bottom, nothing is thought or done which is not calculated to tear up this spirit of tradition by the roots. Tradition is looked upon as a fatality; it is studied and acknowledged (in the form of "heredity"), but people will not have anything to do with it. The extension of one will over long periods of time, the selection of conditions and valuations which make it possible to dispose of centuries in advance—this, precisely, is what is most utterly anti-modern. From which it follows, that disorganising principles give our age its specific character.

66.

"Be simple"—a demand which, when made to us complicated and incomprehensible triers of the heart and reins, is a simple absurdity.... Be natural: but even if we are unnatural—what then?

67.

The means employed in former times in order to arrive at similarly constituted and lasting types, throughout long generations: entailed property and the respect of parents (the origin of the faith in gods and heroes as ancestors).

Now, the subdivision of property belongs to the opposite tendency. The centralisation of an enormous number of, different interests in one soul: which, to that end, must be very strong and mutable.

68.

Why does everything become mummery.—The modern man is lacking in unfailing instinct (instinct being understood here to mean that which is the outcome of a long period of activity in the same occupation on the part of one family of men); the incapability of producing anything perfect, is simply the result of this lack of instinct: one individual alone cannot make up for the schooling his ancestors should have transmitted to him.

What a morality or book of law creates: that deep instinct which renders automatism and perfection possible in life and in work.

But now we have reached the opposite point; yes, we wanted to reach it—the most extreme consciousness, through introspection on the part of man and of history: and thus we are practically most distant from perfection in Being, doing, and willing: our desires—even our will to knowledge—shows how prodigiously decadent we are. We are striving after the very reverse of what strong races and strong natures will have— understanding is an end....

That Science is possible in the way in which it is practised to-day, proves that all elementary instincts, the instincts which ward off danger and protect life, are no longer active. We no longer save, we are merely spending the capital of our forefathers, even in the way in which we pursue knowledge.

69.

Nihilistic trait.

(a) In the natural sciences ("purposelessness"), causality, mechanism, "conformity to law," an interval, a remnant.

(b) Likewise in politics: the individual lacks the belief in his own right, innocence; falsehood rules supreme, as also the worship of the moment.

(d) Likewise in political economy: the abolition of slavery: the lack of a redeeming class, and of one who justifies—the rise of anarchy. "Education"?

(d) Likewise in history: fatalism, Darwinism; the last attempts at reconciling reason and Godliness fail. Sentimentality in regard to the past: biographies can no longer be endured! (Phenomenalism even here: character regarded as a mask; there are no facts.)

(e) Likewise in Art: romanticism and its counter-stroke (repugnance towards romantic ideals and lies). The latter, morally, as a sense of greatest truthfulness, but pessimistic. Pure "artists" (indifference as to the "subject"). (The psychology of the father-confessor and puritanical psychology—two forms of psychological romanticism: but also their counter-stroke, the attempt to maintain a purely artistic attitude towards "men"—but even in this respect no one dares to make the opposite valuation.)

70.

Against the teaching of the influence of environment and external causes: the power coming from inside is infinitely superior; much that appears like influence acting from without is merely the subjection of environment to this inner power.

 Precisely the same environment may be used and interpreted in opposite ways: there are no facts. A genius is not explained by such theories concerning origins.

71.

"Modernity" regarded in the light of nutrition and digestion.

Sensitiveness is infinitely more acute (beneath moral vestments: the increase of pity), the abundance of different impressions is greater than ever. The cosmopolitanism of articles of diet, of literature, newspapers, forms, tastes, and even landscapes. The speed of this affluence is prestissimo; impressions are wiped out, and people instinctively guard against assimilating anything or against taking anything seriously and "digesting" it; the result is a weakening of the powers of digestion. There begin a sort of adaptation to this accumulation of impressions. Man unlearns the art of doing, and all he does is to react to stimuli coming from his environment. He spends his strength, partly in the process of assimilation, partly in defending himself, and again partly in responding to stimuli. Profound enfeeblement of spontaneity:—the historian, the critic, the analyst, the interpreter, the observer, the collector, the reader,—all reactive talents,—all science!

Artificial modification of one's own nature in order to make it resemble a "mirror"; one is interested, but only epidermally: this is systematic coolness, equilibrium, a steady low temperature, just beneath the thin surface on which warmth, movement, "storm," and undulations play.

Opposition of external mobility to a certain dead heaviness and fatigue.

72.

Where must our modern world be classed—under exhaustion or under increasing strength? Its multiformity and lack of repose are brought about by the highest form of consciousness.

73.

Overwork, curiosity and sympathy—our modern vices.

74.

A contribution to the characterisation of "Modernity."—Exaggerated development of intermediate forms; the decay of types; the break-up of tradition, schools; the predominance of the instincts (philosophically prepared: the unconscious has the greater value) after the appearance of the enfeeblement of will power and of the will to an end and to the means thereto.

75.

A capable artisan or scholar cuts a good figure if he have his pride in his art, and looks pleasantly and contentedly upon life. On the other hand, there is no sight more wretched than that of a cobbler or a schoolmaster who, with the air of a martyr, gives one to understand that he was really born for something better. There is nothing better than what is good! and that is: to have a certain kind of capacity and to use it. This is virtù in the Italian style of the Renaissance.

Nowadays, when the state has a nonsensically oversized belly, in all fields and branches of work there are "representatives" over and above the real workman: for instance, in addition to the scholars, there are the journalists; in addition to the suffering masses, there is a crowd of jabbering and bragging ne'er-do-wells who "represent" that suffering—not to speak of the professional politicians who, though quite satisfied with their lot, stand up in Parliament and, with strong lungs, "represent" grievances. Our modern life is extremely expensive, thanks to the host of middlemen that infest it; whereas in the city of antiquity, and in many a city of Spain and Italy to-day, where there is an echo of the ancient spirit, the man himself comes forward and will have nothing to do with a representative or an intermediary in the modern style—except perhaps to kick him hence!

76.

The pre-eminence of the merchant and the middleman, even in the most intellectual spheres: the journalist, the "representative," the historian (as an intermediary between the past and the present), the exotic and cosmopolitan, the middleman between natural science and philosophy, the semi-theologians.

77.

The men I have regarded with the most loathing, heretofore, are the parasites of intellect: they are to be found everywhere, already, in our modern Europe, and as a matter of fact their conscience is as light as it possibly can be. They may be a little turbid, and savour somewhat of Pessimism, but in the main they are voracious, dirty, dirtying, stealthy, insinuating, light-fingered gentry, scabby—and as innocent as all small sinners and microbes are. They live at the expense of those who have intellect and who distribute it liberally: they know that it is peculiar to the rich mind to live in a disinterested fashion, without taking too much petty thought for the morrow, and to distribute its wealth prodigally. For intellect is a bad domestic economist, and pays no heed whatever to the fact that everything lives on it and devours it.

78.

MODERN MUMMERY

The motleyness of modern men and its charm Essentially a mask and a sign of boredom.

The journalist.

The political man (in the "national swindle").

Mummery in the arts:—

The lack of honesty in preparing and schooling oneself for them (Fromentin);

 The Romanticists (their lack of philosophy and science and their excess in literature);

The novelists (Walter Scott, but also the monsters of the Nibelung, with their inordinately nervous music);

The lyricists.

"Scientifically."

Virtuosos (Jews).

The popular ideals are overcome, but not yet in the presence of the people:

The saint, the sage, the prophet.

79.

The want of discipline in the modern spirit concealed beneath all kinds of moral finery.—The show-words are: Toleration (for the "incapacity of saying yes or no"); la largeur de sympathie (= a third of indifference, a third of curiosity, and a third of morbid susceptibility); "objectivity" (the lack of personality and of will, and the inability to "love"); "freedom" in regard to the rule (Romanticism); "truth" as opposed to falsehood and lying (Naturalism); the "scientific spirit" (the "human document": or, in plain English, the serial story which means "addition"—instead of "composition"); "passion" in the place of disorder and intemperance; "depth" in the place of confusion and the pell-mell of symbols.

80.

Concerning the criticism of big words.—I am full of mistrust and malice towards what is called "ideal": this is my Pessimism, that I have recognised to what extent "sublime sentiments" are a source of evil—that is to say, a belittling and depreciating of man.

Every time "progress" is expected to result from an ideal, disappointment invariably follows; the triumph of an ideal has always been a retrograde movement.

Christianity, revolution, the abolition of slavery, equal rights, philanthropy, love of peace, justice, truth: all these big words are only valuable in a struggle, as banners: not as realities, but as show-words, for something quite different (yea, even quite opposed to what they mean!).

81.

The kind of man is known who has fallen in love with the sentence "tout comprendre à est tout pardonner" It is the weak and, above all, the disillusioned: if there is something to pardon in everything, there is also something to contemn! It is the philosophy of disappointment, which here swathes itself so humanly in pity, and gazes out so sweetly.

They are Romanticists, whose faith has gone to pot: now they at least wish to look on and see how everything vanishes and fades. They call it l'art pour l'art, "objectivity," etc.

82.

The main symptoms of Pessimism:—Dinners at Magny's; Russian Pessimism (Tolstoy, Dostoiewsky); æsthetic Pessimism, l'art pour l'art, "description" (the romantic and the anti-romantic Pessimism); Pessimism in the theory of knowledge (Schopenhauer: phenomenalism); anarchical Pessimism; the "religion of pity," Buddhistic preparation; the Pessimism of culture (exoticness, cosmopolitanism); moral Pessimism, myself.

83.

"Without the Christian Faith" said Pascal, "you would yourselves be like nature and history, un monstre et un chaos." We fulfilled this prophecy: once the weak and optimistic eighteenth century had embellished and rationalised man.

Schopenhauer and Pascal.—I none essential point, Schopenhauer is the first who takes up Pascal's movement again: un monstre et un chaos, consequently something that must be negatived ... history, nature, and man himself!

"Our inability to know the truth is the result of our corruption, of our moral decay" says Pascal. And Schopenhauer says essentially the same. "The more profound the corruption of reason is, the more necessary is the doctrine of salvation"—or, putting it into Schopenhauerian phraseology, negation.

84.

Schopenhauer as an epigone (state of affairs before the Revolution):—Pity, sensuality, art, weakness of will, Catholicism of the most intellectual desires—that is, at bottom, the good old eighteenth century.

Schopenhauer's fundamental misunderstanding of the will (just as though passion, instinct, and desire were the essential factors of will) is typical: the depreciation of the will to the extent of mistaking it altogether. Likewise the hatred of willing: the attempt at seeing something superior—yea, even superiority itself, and that which really matters, in non-willing, in the "subject-being without aim or intention." Great symptom of fatigue or of the weakness of will: for this, in reality, is what treats the passions as master, and directs them as to the way and to the measure....

85.

The undignified attempt has been made to regard Wagner and Schopenhauer as types of the mentally unsound: an infinitely more essential understanding of the matter would have been gained if the exact decadent type which each of them represents had been scientifically and accurately defined.

86.

In my opinion, Henrik Ibsen has become very German. With all his robust idealism and "Will to Truth," he never dared to ring himself free from moral-illusionism which says "freedom," and will not admit, even to itself, what freedom is: the second stage in the metamorphosis of the "Will to Power" in him who lacks it. In the first stage, one demands justice at the hands of those who have power. In the second, one speaks of "freedom," that is to say, one wishes to "shake oneself free" from those who have power. In the third stage, one speaks of "equal rights"—that is to say, so long as one is not a predominant personality one wishes to prevent one's competitors from growing in power.

87.

The Decline of Protestantism: theoretically and historically understood as a half-measure. Undeniable predominance of Catholicism to-day: Protestant feeling is so dead that the strongest anti-Protestant movements (Wagner's Parsifal, for instance) are no longer regarded as such. The whole of the more elevated intellectuality in France is Catholic in instinct; Bismarck recognised that there was no longer any such thing as Protestantism.

88.

Protestantism, that spiritually unclean and tiresome form of decadence, in which Christianity has known how to survive in the mediocre North, is something incomplete and complexly valuable for knowledge, in so far as it was able to bring experiences of different kinds and origins into the same heads.

89.

What has the German spirit not made out of Christianity! And, to refer to Protestantism again, how much beer is there not still in Protestant Christianity! Can a crasser, more indolent, and more lounging form of Christian belief be imagined, than that of the average German Protestant?... It is indeed a very humble Christianity. I call it the Homœopathy of Christianity! I am reminded that, to-day, there also exists a less humble sort of Protestantism; it is taught by royal chaplains and anti-Semitic speculators: but nobody has ever maintained that any "spirit" "hovers" over these waters. It is merely a less respectable form of Christian faith, not by any means a more comprehensible one.

90.

Progress.—Let us be on our guard lest we deceive ourselves! Time flies forward apace,—we would fain believe that everything flies forward with it,—that evolution is an advancing development.... That is the appearance of things which deceives the most circumspect. But the nineteenth century shows no advance whatever on the sixteenth: and the German spirit of 1888 is an example of a backward movement when compared with that of 1788.... Mankind does not advance, it does not even exist. The aspect of the whole is much more like that of a huge experimenting workshop where some things in all ages succeed, while an incalculable number of things fail; where all order, logic, co-ordination, and responsibility is lacking. How dare we blink the fact that the rise of Christianity is a decadent movement?—that the German Reformation was a recrudescence of Christian barbarism?—that the Revolution destroyed the instinct for an organisation of society on a large scale?... Man is not an example of progress as compared with animals: the tender son of culture is an abortion compared with the Arab or the Corsican; the Chinaman is a more successful type—that is to say, richer in sustaining power than the European.

(B) THE LAST CENTURIES.

91.

Gloominess and pessimistic influence necessarily follow in the wake of enlightenment. Towards 1770 a falling-off in cheerfulness was already noticeable; women, with that very feminine instinct which always defends virtue, believed that immorality was the cause of it. Galiani hit the bull's eye: he quotes Voltaire's verse:

"Un monstre gai vaut mieux

 Qu'un sentimental ennuyeux."

 If now I maintain that I am ahead, by a century or two of enlightenment, of Voltaire and Galiani—who was much more profound, how deeply must I have sunk into gloominess! This is also true, and betimes I somewhat reluctantly manifested some caution in regard to the German and Christian narrowness and inconsistency of Schopenhauerian or, worse still, Leopardian Pessimism, and sought the most characteristic form (Asia). But, in order to endure that extreme Pessimism (which here and there peeps out of my Birth of Tragedy), to live alone "without God or morality," I was compelled to invent a counter-prop for myself. Perhaps I know best why man is the only animal that laughs: he alone surfers so excruciatingly that he was compelled to invent laughter. The unhappiest and most melancholy animal is, as might have been expected, the most cheerful.

92.

In regard to German culture, I have always had a feeling as of decline. The fact that I learned to know a declining form of culture has often made me unfair towards the whole phenomenon of European culture. The Germans always follow at some distance behind: they always go to the root of things, for instance:—

Dependance upon foreigners; Kant—Rousseau, the sensualists, Hume, Swedenborg.

Schopenhauer—the Indians and Romanticism, Voltaire.

Wagner—the French cult of the ugly and of grand opera, Paris, and the flight into primitive barbarism (the marriage of brother and sister).

The law of the laggard (the provinces go to Paris, Germany goes to France).

How is it that precisely Germans discovered the Greek (the more an instinct is developed, the more it is tempted to run for once into its opposite).

Music is the last breath of every culture.

93.

Renaissance and Reformation.—What does the Renaissance prove? That the reign of the "individual" can be only a short one. The output is too great; there is not even the possibility of husbanding or of capitalising forces, and exhaustion sets in step by step. These are times when everything is squandered, when even the strength itself with which one collects, capitalises, and heaps riches upon riches, is squandered. Even the opponents of such movements are driven to preposterous extremes in the dissipation of their strength: and they too are very soon exhausted, used up, and completely sapped.

In the Reformation we are face to face with a wild and plebeian counterpart of the Italian Renaissance, generated by similar impulses, except that the former, in the backward and still vulgar North, had to assume a religious form—there the concept of a higher life had not yet been divorced from that of a religious one.

Even the Reformation was a movement for individual liberty; "every one his own priest" is really no more than a formula for libertinage. As a matter of fact, the words "Evangelical freedom" would have sufficed—and all instincts which had reasons for remaining concealed broke out like wild hounds, the most brutal needs suddenly acquired the courage to show themselves, everything seemed justified ... men refused to specify the kind of freedom they had aimed at, they preferred to shut their eyes. But the fact that their eyes were closed and that their lips were moistened with gushing orations, did not prevent their hands from being ready to snatch at whatever there was to snatch at, that the belly became the god of the "free gospel," and that all lusts of revenge and of hatred were indulged with insatiable fury.

This lasted for a while: then exhaustion supervened, just as it had done in Southern Europe; and again here, it was a low form of exhaustion, a sort of general ruere in servitium.... Then the disreputable century of Germany dawned.

94.

Chivalry—the position won by power: its gradual break-up (and partial transference to broader and more bourgeois spheres). In the case of Larochefoucauld we find a knowledge of the actual impulses of a noble temperament—together with the gloomy Christian estimate of these impulses.

The protraction of Christianity through the French Revolution. The seducer is Rousseau; he once again liberates woman, who thenceforward is always represented as ever more interesting—suffering. Then come the slaves and Mrs. Beecher-Stowe. Then the poor and the workmen. Then the vicious and the sick—all this is drawn into the foreground (even for the purpose of disposing people in favour of the genius, it has been customary for five hundred years to press him forward as the great sufferer!). Then comes the cursing of all voluptuousness (Baudelaire and Schopenhauer), the most decided conviction that the lust of power is the greatest vice; absolute certainty that morality and disinterestedness are identical things; that the "happiness of all" is a goal worth striving after (i.e., Christ's Kingdom of Heaven). We are on the best road to it: the Kingdom of Heaven of the poor in spirit has begun.—Intermediate stages: the bourgeois (as a result of the nouveau riche) and the workman (as a result of the machine).

Greek and French culture of the time of Louis XIV. compared. A decided belief in oneself. A leisure-class which makes things hard for itself and exercises a great deal of self-control. The power of form, the will to form oneself. "Happiness" acknowledged as a purpose. Much strength and energy behind all formality of manners. Pleasure at the sight of a life that is seemingly so easy. The Greeks seemed like children to the French.

95.

The Three Centuries.

Their different kinds of sensitiveness may perhaps be best expressed as follows:—

Aristocracy: Descartes, the reign of reason, evidence showing the sovereignty of the will.

Feminism: Rousseau, the reign of feeling, evidence showing the sovereignty of the senses; all lies.

Animalism: Schopenhauer, the reign of passion, evidence showing the sovereignty of animality, more honest, but gloomy.

The seventeenth century is aristocratic, all for order, haughty towards everything animal, severe in regard to the heart, "austere," and even free from sentiment, "non-German," averse to all that is burlesque and natural, generalising and maintaining an attitude of sovereignty towards the past for it believes in itself. At bottom it partakes very much of the beast of prey, and practises asceticism in order to remain master. It is the century of strength of will, as also that of strong passion.

The eighteenth century is dominated by woman, it is gushing, spiritual, and flat; but with intellect at the service of aspirations and of the heart, it is a libertine in the pleasures of intellect, undermining all authorities; emotionally intoxicated, cheerful, clear, humane, and sociable, false to itself and at bottom very rascally....

The nineteenth century is more animal, more subterranean, hateful, realistic, plebeian, and on that very account "better," "more honest," more submissive to "reality" of what kind soever, and truer; but weak of will, sad, obscurely exacting and fatalistic. It has no feeling of timidity or reverence, either in the presence of "reason" or the "heart"; thoroughly convinced of the dominion of the desires (Schopenhauer said "Will," but nothing is more characteristic of his philosophy than that it entirely lacks all actual willing). Even morality is reduced to an instinct ("Pity").

Auguste Comte is the continuation of the eighteenth century (the dominion of the heart over the head, sensuality in the theory of knowledge, altruistic exaltation).

The fact that science has become as sovereign as it is to-day, proves how the nineteenth century has emancipated itself from the dominion of ideals. A certain absence of "needs" and wishes makes our scientific curiosity and rigour possible—this is our kind of virtue.

Romanticism is the counterstroke of the eighteenth century; a sort of accumulated longing for its grand style of exaltation (as a matter of fact, largely mingled with mummery and self-deception: the desire was to represent strong nature and strong passion).

The nineteenth century instinctively goes in search of theories by means of which it may feel its fatalistic, submission to the empire of facts justified. Hegel's success against sentimentality and romantic idealism was already a sign of its fatalistic trend of thought, in its belief that superior reason belongs to the triumphant side, and in its justification of the actual "state" (in the place of "humanity," etc.).—Schopenhauer: we are something foolish, and at the best self-suppressive. The success of determinism, the genealogical derivation of obligations which were formerly held to be absolute, the teaching of environment and adaptation, the reduction of will to a process of reflex movement, the denial of the will as a "working cause"; finally—a real process of re-christening: so little will is observed that the word itself becomes available for another purpose. Further theories: the teaching of objectivity, "will-less" contemplation, as the only road to truth, as also to beauty (also the belief in "genius," in order to have the right to be submissive); mechanism, the determinable rigidity of the mechanical process; so-called "Naturalism," the elimination of the choosing, directing, interpreting subject, on principle.

Kant, with his "practical reason," with his moral fanaticism, is quite eighteenth century style; still completely outside the historical movement, without any notion whatsoever of the reality of his time, for instance, revolution; he is not affected by Greek philosophy; he is a phantasist of the notion of duty, a sensualist with a hidden leaning to dogmatic pampering.

The return to Kant in our century means a return to the eighteenth century, people desire to create themselves a right to the old ideas and to the old exaltation—hence a theory of knowledge which "describes limits," that is to say, which admits of the option of fixing a Beyond to the domain of reason.

Hegel's way of thinking is not so very far removed from that of Goethe: see the latter on the subject of Spinoza, for instance. The will to deify the All and Life, in order to find both peace and happiness in contemplating them: Hegel looks for reason everywhere—in the presence of reason man may be submissive and resigned. In Goethe we find a kind of fatalism which is almost joyous and confiding, which neither revolts nor weakens, which strives to make a totality out of itself, in the belief that only in totality does everything seem good and justified, and find itself resolved.

96.

The period of rationalism—followed by a period of sentimentality. To what extent does Schopenhauer come under "sentimentality"? (Hegel under intellectuality?)

97.

The seventeenth century suffers from humanity as from a host of contradictions ("l'amas de contradictions" that we are); it endeavours to discover man, to co-ordinate him, to excavate him: whereas the eighteenth century tries to forget what is known of man's nature, in order to adapt him to its Utopia. "Superficial, soft, humane"—gushes over "humanity."

The seventeenth century tries to banish all traces of the individual in order that the artist's work may resemble life as much as possible. The eighteenth century strives to create interest in the author by means of the work. The seventeenth century seeks art in art, a piece of culture; the eighteenth uses art in its propaganda for political and social reforms.

"Utopia," the "ideal man," the deification of Nature, the vanity of making one's own personality the centre of interest, subordination to the propaganda of social ideas, charlatanism—all this we derive from the eighteenth century.

The style of the seventeenth century: propre exact et libre.

The strong individual who is self-sufficient, or who appeals ardently to God—and that obtrusiveness and indiscretion of modern authors—these things are opposites. "Showing-oneself-off"—what a contrast to the Scholars of Port-Royal!

 Alfieri had a sense for the grand style.

The hate of the burlesque (that which lacks dignity), the lack of a sense of Nature belongs to the seventeenth century.

98.

Against Rousseau.—Alas! man is no longer sufficiently evil; Rousseau's opponents, who say that "man is a beast of prey," are unfortunately wrong. Not the corruption of man, but the softening and moralising of him is the curse. In the sphere which Rousseau attacked most violently, the relatively strongest and most successful type of man was still to be found (the type which still possessed the great passions intact: Will to Power, Will to Pleasure, the Will and Ability to Command). The man of the eighteenth century must be compared with the man of the Renaissance (also with the man of the seventeenth century in France) if the matter is to be understood at all: Rousseau is a symptom of self-contempt and of inflamed vanity—both signs that the dominating will is lacking: he moralises and seeks the cause of his own misery after the style of a revengeful man in the ruling classes.

99.

Voltaire—Rousseau.—A state of nature is terrible; man is a beast of prey: our civilisation is an extraordinary triumph over this beast of prey in nature—this was Voltaires conclusion. He was conscious of the mildness, the refinements, the intellectual joys of the civilised state; he despised obtuseness, even in the form of virtue, and the lack of delicacy even in ascetics and monks.

The moral depravity of man seemed to pre-occupy Rousseau; the words "unjust," "cruel," are the best possible for the purpose of exciting the instincts of the oppressed, who otherwise find themselves under the ban of the vetitum and of disgrace; so that their conscience is opposed to their indulging any insurrectional desires. These emancipators seek one thing above all: to give their party the great accents and attitudes of higher Nature.

100.

Rousseau; the rule founded on sentiment; Nature as the source of justice; man perfects himself in proportion as he approaches Nature (according to Voltaire, in proportion as he leaves Nature behind). The very same periods seem to the one to demonstrate the progress of humanity and, to the other, the increase of injustice and inequality.

Voltaire, who still understood umanità in the sense of the Renaissance, as also virtù (as "higher culture"), fights for the cause of the "honnêtes gens" "la bonne compagnie" taste, science, arts, and even for the cause of progress and civilisation.

The flare-up occurred towards 1760: On the one hand the citizen of Geneva, on the other le seigneur de Ferney. It is only from that moment and henceforward that Voltaire was the man of his age, the philosopher, the representative of Toleration and of Disbelief (theretofore he had been merely un bel esprit). His envy and hatred of Rousseau's success forced him upwards.

"Pour 'la canaille' un dieu rémunérateur et vengeur"—Voltaire.

The criticism of both standpoints in regard to the value of civilisation. To Voltaire nothing seems finer than the social invention: there is no higher goal than to uphold and perfect it. L'honnêteté consists precisely in respecting social usage; virtue in a certain obedience towards various necessary "prejudices" which favour the maintenance of society. Missionary of Culture, aristocrat, representative of the triumphant and ruling classes and their values. But Rousseau remained a plebeian, even as hommes de lettres, this was preposterous; his shameless contempt for everything that was not himself.

The morbid feature in Rousseau is the one which happens to have been most admired and imitated. (Lord Byron resembled him somewhat, he too screwed himself up to sublime attitudes and to revengeful rage—a sign of vulgarity; later on, when Venice restored his equilibrium, he understood what alleviates most and does the most good ... l'insouciance.)

In spite of his antecedents, Rousseau is proud of himself; but he is incensed if he is reminded of his origin....

In Rousseau there was undoubtedly some brain trouble; in Voltaire—rare health and lightsomeness. The revengefulness of the sick; his periods of insanity as also those of his contempt of man, and of his mistrust.

Rousseau's defence of Providence (against Voltaire's Pessimism): he had need of God in order to be able to curse society and civilisation; everything must be good per se, because God had created it; man alone has corrupted man. The "good man" as a man of Nature was pure fantasy; but with the dogma of God's authorship he became something probable and even not devoid of foundation.

Romanticism à la Rousseau: passion ("the sovereign right of passion"); "naturalness"; the fascination of madness (foolishness reckoned as greatness); the senseless vanity of the weak; the revengefulness of the masses elevated to the position of justice ("in politics, for one hundred years, the leader has always been this invalid").

101.

Kant: makes the scepticism of Englishmen, in regard to the theory of knowledge, possible for Germans.

(1) By enlisting in its cause the interest of the German's religious and moral needs: just as the new academicians used scepticism for the same reasons, as a preparation for Platonism (vide Augustine); just as Pascal even used moral scepticism in order to provoke (to justify) the need of belief;

(2) By complicating and entangling it with scholastic flourishes in view of making it more acceptable to the German's scientific taste in form (for Locke and Hume, alone, were too illuminating, too clear—that is to say, judged according to the German valuing instinct, "too superficial").

Kant: a poor psychologist and mediocre judge of human nature, made hopeless mistakes in regard to great historical values (the French Revolution); a moral fanatic à la Rousseau; with a subterranean current of Christian values; a thorough dogmatist, but bored to extinction by this tendency, to the extent of wishing to tyrannise over it, but quickly tired, even of 'scepticism; and not yet affected by any cosmopolitan thought or antique beauty ... a dawdler and a go-between, not at all original (like Leibnitz, something between mechanism and spiritualism; like Goethe, something between the taste of the eighteenth century and that of the "historical sense" [which is essentially a sense of exoticism]; like German music, between French and Italian music; like Charles the Great, who mediated and built bridges between the Roman Empire and Nationalism—a dawdler par excellence).

102.

In what respect have the Christian centuries with their Pessimism been stronger centuries than the eighteenth—and how do they correspond with the tragic age of the Greeks?

The nineteenth century versus the eighteenth. How was it an heir?—how was it a step backwards from the latter? (more lacking in "spirit" and in taste)—how did it show an advance on the latter? (more gloomy, more realistic, stronger).

103.

How can we explain the fact that we feel something in common with the Campagna romana? And the high mountain chain?

Chateaubriand in a letter to M. de Fontanes in 1803 writes his first impression of the Campagna romana.

The President de Brosses says of the Campagna romana: "Il fallait que Romulus fût ivre quand il songea à bâtir une ville dans un terrain aussi laid."

Even Delacroix would have nothing to do with Rome, it frightened him. He loved Venice, just as Shakespeare, Byron, and Georges Sand did. Théophile Gautier's and Richard Wagner's dislike of Rome must not be forgotten.

Lamartine has the language for Sorrento and Posilippo.

Victor Hugo raves about Spain, "parce que aucune autre nation n'a moins emprunté à l'antiquité, parce qu'elle n'a subi aucune influence classique."

104.

The two great attempts that were made to overcome the eighteenth century:

Napoleon, in that he called man, the soldier, and the great struggle for power, to life again, and conceived Europe as a political power.

Goethe, in that he imagined a European culture which would consist of the whole heritage of what humanity had attained to up to his time.

German culture in this century inspires mistrust—the music of the period lacks that complete element which liberates and binds as well, to wit—Goethe.

The pre-eminence of music in the romanticists of 1830 and 1840. Delacroix. Ingres—a passionate musician (admired Gluck, Haydn, Beethoven, Mozart), said to his pupils in Rome: "Si je pouvais vous rendre tous musiciens, vous y gagneriez comme peintres"— likewise Horace Vernet, who was particularly fond of Don Juan (as Mendelssohn assures us, 1831); Stendhal, too, who says of himself: "Combien de lieues ne ferais-je pas à pied, et à combien de jours de prison ne me soumetterais-je pas pour entendre Don Juan ou le Matrimonio segreto; et je ne sais pour quelle autre chose je ferais cet effort." He was then fifty-six years old.

The borrowed forms, for instance: Brahms as a typical "Epigone," likewise Mendelssohn's cultured Protestantism (a former "soul" is turned into poetry posthumously ...)

—the moral and poetical substitutions in Wagner, who used one art as a stop-gap to make up for what another lacked.

—the "historical sense," inspiration derived from poems, sagas.

—that characteristic transformation of which G. Flaubert is the most striking example among Frenchmen, and Richard Wagner the most striking example among Germans, shows how the romantic belief in love and the future changes into a longing for nonentity in 1830-50.

106.

How is it that German music reaches its culminating point in the age of German romanticism? How is it that German music lacks Goethe? On the other hand, how much Schiller, or more exactly, how much "Thekla"[5] is there not in Beethoven!

Schumann has Eichendorff, Uhland, Heine, Hoffman, Tieck, in him. Richard Wagner has Freischütz, Hoffmann, Grimm, the romantic Saga, the mystic Catholicism of instinct, symbolism, "the free-spiritedness of passion" (Rousseau's intention). The Flying Dutchman savours of France, where le ténébreux (1830) was the type of the seducer.

The cult of music, the revolutionary romanticism of form. Wagner synthesises German and French romanticism.

[5] Thekla is the sentimental heroine in Schiller's Wallenstein.—TRANSLATOR'S NOTE.

107.

From the point of view only of his value to Germany and to German culture, Richard Wagner is still a great problem, perhaps a German misfortune: in any case, however, a fatality. But what does it matter? Is he not very much more than a German event? It also seems to me that to no country on earth is he less related than to Germany; nothing was prepared there for his advent; his whole type is simply strange amongst Germans; there he stands in their midst, wonderful, misunderstood, incomprehensible. But people carefully avoid acknowledging this: they are too kind, too square-headed—too German for that. "Credo quia absurdus est": thus did the German spirit wish it to be, in this case too—hence it is content meanwhile to believe everything Richard Wagner wanted to have believed about himself. In all ages the spirit of Germany has been deficient in subtlety and divining powers concerning psychological matters. Now that it happens to be under the high pressure of patriotic nonsense and self-adoration, it is visibly growing thicker and coarser: how could it therefore be equal to the problem of Wagner!

108.

The Germans are not yet anything, but they are becoming something; that is why they have not yet any culture;—that is why they cannot yet have any culture!—They are not yet anything: that means they are all kinds of things. They are becoming something: that means that they will one day cease from being all kinds of things. The latter is at bottom only a wish, scarcely a hope yet. Fortunately it is a wish with which one can live, a question of will, of work, of discipline, a question of training, as also of resentment, of longing, of privation, of discomfort,—yea, even of bitterness,—in short, we Germans will get something out of ourselves, something that has not yet been wanted of us—we want something more!

That this "German, as he is not as yet"—has a right to something better than the present German "culture"; that all who wish to become something better, must wax angry when they perceive a sort of contentment, an impudent "setting-oneself-at-ease," or "a process of self-censing," in this quarter: that is my second principle, in regard to which my opinions have not yet changed.

(C) SIGNS OF INCREASING STRENGTH.

109.

First Principle: everything that characterises modern men savours of decay: but side by side with the prevailing sickness there are signs of a strength and powerfulness of soul which are still untried. The same causes which tend to promote the belittling of men, also force the stronger and rarer individuals upwards to greatness.

110.

General survey: the ambiguous character of our modern world—precisely the same symptoms might at the same time be indicative of either decline or strength. And the signs of strength and of emancipation dearly bought, might in view of traditional (or hereditary) appreciations concerned with the feelings, be misunderstood as indications of weakness. In short, feeling, as a means of fixing valuations, is not on a level with the times.

Generalised: Every valuation is always backward; it is merely the expression of the conditions which favoured survival and growth in a much earlier age: it struggles against new conditions of existence out of which it did not arise, and which it therefore necessarily misunderstands: it hinders, and excites suspicion against, all that is new.

111.

The problem of the nineteenth century.—To discover whether its strong and weak side belong to each other. Whether they have been cut from one and the same piece. Whether the variety of its ideals and their contradictions are conditioned by a higher purpose: whether they are something higher.—For it might be the prerequisite of greatness, that growth should take place amid such violent tension. Dissatisfaction, Nihilism, might be a good sign.

112.

General survey.—As a matter of fact, all abundant growth involves a concomitant process of crumbling to bits and decay: suffering and the symptoms of decline belong to ages of enormous progress; every fruitful and powerful movement of mankind has always brought about a concurrent Nihilistic movement. Under certain circumstances, the appearance of the extremest form of Pessimism and actual Nihilism might be the sign of a process of incisive and most essential growth, and of mankind's transit into completely new conditions of existence. This is what I have understood.

113.

A.

Starting out with a thoroughly courageous appreciation of our men of to-day:—we must not allow ourselves to be deceived by appearance: this mankind is much less effective, but it gives quite different pledges of lasting strength, its tempo is slower, but the rhythm itself is richer. Healthiness is increasing, the real conditions of a healthy body are on the point of being known, and will gradually be created, "asceticism" is regarded with irony. The fear of extremes, a certain confidence in the "right way," no raving: a periodical self-habituation to narrower values (such as "mother-land," "science," etc.).

This whole picture, however, would still be ambiguous: it might be a movement either of increase or decline in Life.

B.

The belief in "progress"—in lower spheres of intelligence, appears as increasing life: but this is self-deception;

in higher spheres of intelligence it is a sign of declining life.

Description of the symptoms.

The unity of the aspect: uncertainty in regard to the standard of valuation.

Fear of a general "in vain."

Nihilism.

114.

As a matter of fact, we are no longer so urgently in need of an antidote against the first Nihilism: Life is no longer so uncertain, accidental, and senseless in modern Europe. All such tremendous exaggeration of the value of men, of the value of evil, etc., are not so necessary now; we can endure a considerable diminution of this value, we may grant a great deal of nonsense and accident: the power man has acquired now allows of a lowering of the means of discipline, of which the strongest was the moral interpretation of the universe. The hypothesis "God" is much too extreme.

115.

If anything shows that our humanisation is a genuine sign of progress, it is the fact that we no longer require excessive contraries, that we no longer require contraries at all....

We may love the senses; for we have spiritualised them in every way and made them artistic;

We have a right to all things which hitherto have been most calumniated.

116.

The reversal of the order of rank.—Those pious counterfeiters—the priests—are becoming Chandala in our midst:—they occupy the position of the charlatan, of the quack, of the counterfeiter, of the sorcerer: we regard them as corrupters of the will, as the great slanderers and vindictive enemies of Life, and as the rebels among the bungled and the botched. We have made our middle class out of our servant-caste—the Sudra—that is to say, our people or the body which wields the political power.

On the other hand, the Chandala of former times is paramount: the blasphemers, the immoralists, the independents of all kinds, the artists, the Jews, the minstrels—and, at bottom, all disreputable classes are in the van.

We have elevated ourselves to honourable thoughts,—even more, we determine what honour is on earth,—"nobility." ... All of us to-day are advocates of life.—We Immoralists are to-day the strongest power: the other great powers are in need of us ... we re-create the world in our own image.

We have transferred the label "Chandala" to the priests, the backworldsmen, and to the deformed Christian society which has become associated with these people, together with creatures of like origin, the pessimists, Nihilists, romanticists of pity, criminals, and men of vicious habits—the whole sphere in which the idea of "God" is that of Saviour....

We are proud of being no longer obliged to be liars, slanderers, and detractors of Life....

117.

The advance of the nineteenth century upon the eighteenth (at bottom we good Europeans are carrying on a war against the eighteenth century):

(1) "The return to Nature" is getting to be understood, ever more definitely, in a way which is quite the reverse of that in which Rousseau used the phrase—away from idylls and operas!

(2) Ever more decided, more anti-idealistic, more objective, more fearless, more industrious, more temperate, more suspicious of sudden changes, anti-revolutionary;

(3) The question of bodily health is being pressed ever more decidedly in front of the health of "the soul": the latter is regarded as a condition brought about by the former, and bodily health is believed to be, at least, the prerequisite to spiritual health.

118.

If anything at all has been achieved, it is a more innocent attitude towards the senses, a happier, more favourable demeanour in regard to sensuality, resembling rather the position taken up by Goethe; a prouder feeling has also been developed in knowledge, and the "reine Thor"[6] meets with little faith.

[6] This is a reference to Wagner's Parsifal. The character as is well known, is written

to represent a son of heart's affliction, and a child of wisdom—humble, guileless, loving, pure, and a fool.—TRANSLATOR'S NOTE.

119.

We "objective people."—It is not "pity" that opens up the way for us to all that is most remote and most strange in life and culture; but our accessibility and ingenuousness, which precisely does not "pity," but rather takes pleasure in hundreds of things which formerly caused pain (which in former days either outraged or moved us, or in the presence of which we were either hostile or indifferent). Pain in all its various phases is now interesting to us: on that account we are certainly not the more pitiful, even though the sight of pain may shake us to our foundations and move us to tears: and we are absolutely not inclined to be more helpful in view thereof.

In this deliberate desire to look on at all pain and error, we have grown stronger and more powerful than in the eighteenth century; it is a proof of our increase of strength (we have drawn closer to the seventeenth and sixteenth centuries). But it is a profound mistake to regard our "romanticism" as a proof of our "beautified souls." We want stronger sensations than all coarser ages and classes have wanted. (This fact must not be confounded with the needs of neurotics and decadents; in their case, of course, there is a craving for pepper —even for cruelty.)

We are all seeking conditions which are emancipated from the bourgeois, and to a greater degree from the priestly, notion of morality (every book which savours at all of priestdom and theology gives us the impression of pitiful niaiserie and mental indigence). "Good company," in fact, finds everything insipid which is not forbidden and considered compromising in bourgeois circles; and the case is the same with books, music, politics, and opinions on women.

120.

The simplification of man in the nineteenth century (The eighteenth century was that of elegance, subtlety, and generous feeling).—Not "return to nature"; for no natural humanity has ever existed yet. Scholastic, unnatural, and antinatural values are the rule and the beginning; man only reaches Nature after a long struggle—he never turns his "back" to her.... To be natural means, to dare to be as immoral as Nature is.

We are coarser, more direct, richer in irony towards generous feelings, even when we are beneath them.

Our haute volée, the society consisting of our rich and leisured men, is more natural: people hunt each other, the love of the sexes is a kind of sport in which marriage is both a charm and an obstacle; people entertain each other and live for the sake of pleasure; bodily advantages stand in the first rank, and curiosity and daring are the rule.

Our attitude towards knowledge is more natural; we are innocent in our absolute spiritual debauchery, we hate pathetic and hieratic manners, we delight in that which is most strictly prohibited, we should scarcely recognise any interest in knowledge if we were bored in acquiring it.

Our attitude to morality is also more natural. Principles have become a laughing-stock; no one dares to speak of his "duty," unless in irony. But a helpful, benevolent disposition is highly valued. (Morality is located in instinct and the rest is despised. Besides this there are few points of honour.)

Our attitude to politics is more natural: we see problems of power, of the quantum of power, against another quantum. We do not believe in a right that does not proceed from a power which is able to uphold it. We regard all rights as conquests.

Our valuation of great men and things is more natural: we regard passion as a privilege; we can conceive of nothing great which does not involve a great crime; all greatness is associated in our minds with a certain standing-beyond-the-pale in morality.

Our attitude to Nature is more natural: we no longer love her for her "innocence," her "reason," her "beauty," we have made her beautifully devilish and "foolish." But instead of despising her on that account, since then we have felt more closely related to her and more familiar in her presence. She does not aspire to virtue: we therefore respect her.

Our attitude towards Art is more natural: we do not exact beautiful, empty lies, etc., from her; brutal positivism reigns supreme, and it ascertains things with perfect calm.

In short: there are signs showing that the European of the nineteenth century is less ashamed of his instincts; he has gone a long way towards acknowledging his unconditional naturalness and immorality, without bitterness: on the contrary, he is strong enough to endure this point of view alone.

To some ears this will sound as though corruption had made strides: and certain it is that man has not drawn nearer to the "Nature" which Rousseau speaks about, but has gone one step farther in the civilisation before which Rousseau stood in horror. We have grown stronger, we have drawn nearer to the seventeenth century, more particularly to the taste which reigned towards its close (Dancourt, Le Sage, Renard).

121.

Culture versus Civilisation.—The culminating stages of culture and civilisation lie apart: one must not be led astray as regards the fundamental antagonism existing between culture and civilisation. From the moral standpoint, great periods in the history of culture have always been periods of corruption; while on the other hand, those periods in which man was deliberately and compulsorily tamed ("civilisation") have always been periods of intolerance towards the most intellectual and most audacious natures. Civilisation desires something different from what culture strives after: their aims may perhaps be opposed....

122.

What I warn people against: confounding the instincts of decadence with those of humanity;

Confounding the dissolving means of civilisation and those which necessarily promote decadence, with culture;

Confounding debauchery, and the principle, "laisser aller," with the Will to Power (the latter is the exact reverse of the former).

123.

The unsolved problems which I set anew: the problem of civilisation, the struggle between Rousseau and Voltaire about the year 1760. Man becomes deeper, more mistrustful, more "immoral," stronger, more self-confident—and therefore "more natural"; that is "progress." In this way, by a process of division of labour, the more evil strata and the milder and tamer strata of society get separated: so that the general facts are not visible at first sight.... It is a sign of strength, and of the self-control and fascination of the strong, that these stronger strata possess the arts in order to make their greater powers for evil felt as something "higher" As soon as there is "progress" there is a transvaluation of the strengthened factors into the "good."

124.

Man must have the courage of his natural instincts restored to him.—

The poor opinion he has of himself must be destroyed (not in the sense of the individual, but in the sense of the natural man ...)—

The contradictions in things must be eradicated, after it has been well understood that we were responsible for them—

Social idiosyncrasies must be stamped out of existence (guilt, punishment, justice, honesty, freedom, love, etc. etc.)—

An advance towards "naturalness": in all political questions, even in the relations between parties, even in merchants', workmen's, or contractors' parties, only questions of power come into play:— "what one can do" is the first question, what one ought to do is only a secondary consideration.

125.

Socialism—or the tyranny of the meanest and the most brainless,—that is to say, the superficial, the envious, and the mummers, brought to its zenith,—is, as a matter, of fact, the logical conclusion of "modern ideas" and their latent anarchy: but in the genial atmosphere of democratic well-being the capacity for forming resolutions or even for coming to an end at all, is paralysed. Men follow—but no longer their reason. That is why socialism is on the whole a hopelessly bitter affair: and there is nothing more amusing than to observe the discord between the poisonous and desperate faces of present-day socialists—and what wretched and nonsensical feelings does not their style reveal to us!—and the childish lamblike happiness of their hopes and desires. Nevertheless, in many places in Europe, there may be violent hand-to-hand struggles and irruptions on their account: the coming century is likely to be convulsed in more than one spot, and the Paris Commune, which finds defenders and advocates even in Germany, will seem to have been but a slight indigestion compared with what is to come. Be this as it may, there will always be too many people of property for socialism ever to signify anything more than an attack of illness: and these people of property are like one man with one faith, "one must possess something in order to be some one." This, however, is the oldest and most wholesome of all instincts; I should add: "one must desire more than one has in order to become more." For this is the teaching which life itself preaches to all living things: the morality of Development. To have and to wish to have more, in a word, Growth—that is life itself. In the teaching of socialism "a will to the denial of life" is but poorly concealed: botched men and races they must be who have devised a teaching of this sort. In fact, I even wish a few experiments might be made to show that in a socialistic society, life denies itself, and itself cuts away its own roots. The earth is big enough and man is still unexhausted enough for a practical lesson of this sort and demonstratio ad absurdum—even if it were accomplished only by a vast expenditure of lives—to seem worth while to me. Still, Socialism, like a restless mole beneath the foundations of a society wallowing in stupidity, will be able to achieve something useful and salutary: it delays "Peace on Earth" and the whole process of character-softening of the democratic herding animal; it forces the European to have an extra supply of intellect,—that is to say, craft and caution, and prevents his entirely abandoning the manly and warlike qualities,—it also saves Europe awhile from the marasmus femininus which is threatening it.

126.

The most favourable obstacles and remedies of modernity:

(1) Compulsory military service with real wars in which all joking is laid aside.

(2) National thick-headedness (which simplifies and concentrates).

(3) Improved nutrition (meat).

(4) Increasing cleanliness and wholesomeness in the home.

(5) The predominance of physiology over theology, morality, economics, and politics.

(6) Military discipline in the exaction and the practice of one's "duty" (it is no longer customary to praise).

127.

I am delighted at the military development of Europe, also at the inner anarchical conditions: the period of quietude and "Chinadom" which Galiani prophesied for this century is now over. Personal and manly capacity, bodily capacity recovers its value, valuations are becoming more physical, nutrition consists ever more and more of flesh. Fine men have once more become possible. Bloodless sneaks (with mandarins at their head, as Comte imagined them) are now a matter of the past. The savage in every one of us is acknowledged, even the wild animal. Precisely on that account, philosophers will have a better chance. —Kant is a scarecrow!

128.

I have not yet seen any reasons to feel discouraged. He who acquires and preserves a strong will, together with a broad mind, has a more favourable chance now than ever he had. For the plasticity of man has become exceedingly great in democratic Europe:

men who learn easily, who readily adapt themselves, are the rule: the gregarious animal of a high order of intelligence is prepared. He who would command finds those who must obey: I have Napoleon and Bismarck in mind, for instance. The struggle against strong and unintelligent wills, which forms the surest obstacle in one's way, is really insignificant Who would not be able to knock down these "objective" gentlemen with weak wills, such as Ranke and Renan!

129.

Spiritual enlightenment is an unfailing means of making men uncertain, weak of will, and needful of succour and support; in short, of developing the herding instincts in them. That is why all great artist-rulers, hitherto (Confucius in China, the Roman Empire, Napoleon, Popedom—at a time when they had the courage of their worldliness and frankly pursued power) in whom the ruling instincts, that had prevailed until their time, culminated, also made use of the spiritual enlightenment—or at least allowed it to be supreme (after the style of the Popes of the Renaissance). The self-deception of the masses on this point, in every democracy for instance, is of the greatest possible value: all that makes men smaller and more amenable is pursued under the title "progress."

130.

The highest equity and mildness as a condition of weakness (the New Testament and the early Christian community—manifesting itself in the form of utter foolishness in the Englishmen, Darwin and Wallace). Your equity, ye higher men, drives you to universal suffrage, etc.; your "humanity" urges you to be milder towards crime and stupidity. In the end you will thus help stupidity and harmlessness to conquer.

Outwardly: Ages of terrible wars, insurrections, explosions. Inwardly: ever more and more weakness among men; events take the form of excitants. The Parisian as the type of the European extreme.

Consequences: (1) Savages (at first, of course, in conformity with the culture that has reigned hitherto); (2) Sovereign individuals (where powerful barbarous masses and emancipation from all that has been, are crossed). The age of greatest stupidity, brutality, and wretchedness in the masses, and in the highest individuals.

131.

An incalculable number of higher individuals now perish: but he who escapes their fate is as strong as the devil. In this respect we are reminded of the conditions which prevailed in the Renaissance.

132.

How are Good Europeans such as ourselves distinguished from the patriots? In the first place, we are atheists and immoralists, but we take care to support the religions and the morality which we associate with the gregarious instinct: for by means of them, an order of men is, so to speak, being prepared, which must at some time or other fall into our hands, which must actually crave for our hands.

Beyond Good and Evil,—certainly; but we insist upon the unconditional and strict preservation of herd-morality.

We reserve ourselves the right to several kinds of philosophy which it is necessary to learn: under certain circumstances, the pessimistic kind as a hammer; a European Buddhism might perhaps be indispensable.

We should probably support the development and the maturation of democratic tendencies; for it conduces to weakness of will: in "Socialism" we recognise a thorn which prevents smug ease.

Attitude towards the people.. Our prejudices; we pay attention to the results of cross-breeding.

Detached, well-to-do, strong: irony concerning the "press" and its culture. Our care: that scientific men should not become journalists. We mistrust any form of culture that tolerates news-paper reading or writing.

We make our accidental positions (as Goethe and Stendhal did), our experiences, a foreground, and we lay stress upon them, so that we may deceive concerning our backgrounds. We ourselves wait and avoid putting our heart into them. They serve us as refuges, such as a wanderer might require and use—but we avoid feeling at home in them. We are ahead of our fellows in that we have had a disciplina voluntatis. All strength is directed to the development of the will, an art which allows us to wear masks, an art of understanding beyond the passions (also "super-European" thought at times).

This is our preparation before becoming the law-givers of the future and the lords of the earth; if not we, at least our children. Caution where marriage is concerned.

133.

The twentieth century.—The Abbé Galiani says somewhere: "La prévoyance est la cause des guerres actuelles de l'Europe. Si l'on voulait se donner la peine de ne rien prévoir, tout le monde serait tranquille, et je ne crois pas qu'on serait plus malheureux parce qu'on ne ferait pas la guerre." As I in no way share the unwarlike views of my deceased friend Galiani, I have no fear whatever of saying something beforehand with the view of conjuring in some way the cause of wars.

A condition of excessive consciousness, after the worst of earthquakes: with new questions.

134.

It is the time of the great noon, of the most appalling enlightenment: my particular kind of Pessimism: the great starting-point.

(1) Fundamental contradiction between civilisation and the elevation of man.

(2) Moral valuations regarded as a history of lies and the art of calumny in the service of the Will to Power (of the will of the herd, which rises against stronger men).

(3) The conditions which determine every elevation in culture (the facilitation of a selection being made at the cost of a crowd) are the conditions of all growth.

(4). The multiformity of the world as a question of strength, which sees all things in the perspective of their growth. The moral Christian values to be regarded as the insurrection and mendacity of slaves (in comparison with the aristocratic values of the ancient world).